NETSCAPE VIRTUOSO

2ND EDITION

Elissa Keeler
Robert Miller

MIS: PRESS

A Subsidiary of
Henry Holt and Co., Inc.

First Edition—1996

Printed in the United States of America.

Library of Congress Cataloging-in-Publication Data

Keeler, Elissa.
   Netscape Virtuoso / by Elissa Keeler and Robert Miller. --2nd ed.
       p.   cm.
   ISBN 1-55828-495-8
   1. Netscape.   2. World Wide Web (Information retrieval system)
I. Miller, Robert (Robert William) II. Title.
TK5105.883.N48K44   1996
005.7'1369--dc20   96-25893
                                                        CIP

Trademarks

Throughout this book, trademarked names are used. Rather than put a trademark symbol after every occurrence of a trademarked name, we used the names in an editorial fashion only, and to the benefit of the trademark owner, with no intention of infringement of the trademark. Where such designations appear in this book, they have been printed with initial caps.

Associate Publisher: Paul Farrell
Executive Editor: Cary Sullivan
Editor: Debra Williams Cauley
Copy Edit Manager: Shari Chappell
Copy Editor: Annette Sroka Devlin
Technical Editor: Scott Dare
Production Editor: Anthony Washington

FOREWORD

When people first find out that we write books together, they're not interested in what kind of books we write. Instead, they want to know how we've managed to produce two books and still stay married (to each other). The answer is simple—a clear-cut division of labor. As a veteran telecommunications engineer, software developer and university lecturer, Robert's in charge of determining which technological content is important and finding a way to make it comprehensible to a lay audience. The explanation of technical topics such as stateless protocols, MIME types and dual-key encryption spring primarily from his strong desire to demystify computers and networks in the mind of the general public.

As writer and project manager, my job is to turn Robert's animated, intense verbal descriptions into organized, coherent prose. Since I'm not an engineer, it's also my job to ask hundreds of questions and make him explain the material over and over in different ways until we find the descriptions that make the most sense to other non-engineers. Together, we hope that we've achieved the right balance of technical information and reader-friendly descriptions to create a book that's both engaging and informative.

—Elissa Keeler Miller

ACKNOWLEDGMENTS

This book couldn't exist without the efforts of several dedicated and talented people. Scott Dare provided on-the-mark technical commentary as well as boundless optimism. Annette Sroka Devlin's meticulous and patient attention to the copy ensured that it's coherent and clear. The book looks as great as it does because of Anthony Washington's fabulous design and production skills. Shari Chappell made sure that the copy and production process ran like clockwork. And, as always, our editor Debra Williams Cauley was a paragon of composure, organization, and uncommon sensibility during an often-hectic development cycle.

We must also thank the faculty and staff of the University of Houston's College of Education and the Houston Consortium of Urban Professional Development and Technology Schools, without whose resources and support this project would not have been possible.

Finally, we're grateful to our friends and family who have remained supportive despite the fact that we can't be reached by telephone anymore; our lines are always tied up because we're surfing the Web.

CONTENTS

Part Two: Helper Applications, Plug-Ins, and Java

Chapter 8: MIME Types, Helper Applications, and Plug-Ins 145

Chapter 9: Helper Applications for Windows 163

Part Three: Using Other Internet Services

Part Six: Emerging Technologies and Trends on the Web

INTRODUCTION

WHAT THIS BOOK IS ABOUT

The World Wide Web is the fastest growing Internet service ever, and at this time, more than 80% of all people accessing the Web are using the tremendously popular Netscape Navigator browser software, with good reason. The Netscape interface is both elegant and easy to use—so much so, in fact, that many people just master the basic browsing functions and never learn about how the browser actually works or explore its powerful though somewhat more esoteric capabilities. *Netscape Virtuoso* takes you past basic rote-level operations to provide you with complete knowledge of how and why the software works the way it does so that you understand what's actually going on when you're engaging in the most talked-about activity of the 90s: cruising cyberspace. This understanding is also invaluable for those interested in creating their own documents to place on the Web.

Unlike many other books, *Netscape Virtuoso* goes beyond the common simple procedural documentation for each button and menu option, and provides the background conceptual information for how those features actually work. And there are real-world examples of different ways to use those features so that you can customize your use of Netscape to meet your own personal needs. (For example, someone who frequently demonstrates the Web to other people has different requirements from a person who wants to use Netscape's useful features for developers of World Wide Web documents, just as someone who uses a dialup IP connection with a

14.4 Kbps modem has different needs from a person whose networked office computer is connected to the Internet through a corporate LAN.) We've done everything we can to give you the tools and the knowledge to use them to make Netscape, and the Web, your own.

Who Is This Book for?

No matter what your background, *Netscape Virtuoso* seeks to give you all the skills and information you need to become a masterful, confident Web explorer with your vehicle's settings perfectly tuned to your individual needs. This book is for you if…

- You've heard about Netscape's latest advanced features, like Java applets and plug-ins, and want to find out what the buzz is about.

- You want useful technical information and discussion about advanced topics like memory and disk caching, MIME types, and security issues, presented in an accessible style instead of like an engineering document. We'll explain how the technology works and how to make it work best for you in plain, jargon-free English.

- You want to know what's really going on when you go from site to site on the Web, which requires more than just basic knowledge about how and why URLs are constructed. We go into detail about the use of the URL format and show you how to glean a surprising amount of information about a site just from its address, as well as how to identify bad URLs on sight.

- You want to better understand and control Netscape's navigational and configuration features and functions. (It's one thing to fill in all the fields in the Preferences section, but it's another thing altogether to know what that information means and how to use it.) *Netscape Virtuoso* not only contains complete information about the Web and the underlying Web protocols and standards that Netscape uses, but it also includes tips, tricks, and shortcuts for the fastest navigation and smoothest file transfers.

- You recognize that MIME types are crucial to handling the movies, graphics, and sounds that you encounter on the Web, but nothing in the run-of-the-mill documentation explains what MIME types actually are—they just tell you how to mechanically enter the names of helper applications in the predefined fields. We'll explain what MIME types are and why they were developed, and will show you how to apply this knowledge to ensure that your helper applications and FTP sessions work smoothly.

- You want to understand the relationship between the World Wide Web and the other Internet services that you can access through a Web browser. (Despite what you might think, Web browsers are far from being an ideal tool for accessing all Internet services.) We'll discuss how to get the most out of the email, Usenet News, and FTP capabilities of Netscape, and will explore its limitations in these areas.

- You're interested in online commerce—perhaps you'd like to buy something from an online storefront—but are concerned about whether your credit card number and other personal information are safe when they're broken down into packets whizzing invisibly across the Internet. We'll discuss the "how" and "why" of data encryption and other security techniques, and will explain how to determine when your information will stay confidential and when it won't.

- You use Netscape across a secure network and have to deal with settings for cryptic items like SOCKS, firewalls, and proxies. *Netscape Virtuoso* contains a complete explanation of how those technologies protect your site from unwanted intruders, as well as instructions for ensuring that your access to the Web is transparent despite these security measures.

- You're a new Netscape user and you need to get up and running quickly. *Netscape Virtuoso* has complete instructions for installation, configuration, and basic use of the Netscape software. When you're ready for more information, it's available. Also, please see our "A Note to Novice Users...You're *not* Dummies!" in the next section.

A Note to Novice Users…You're *not* Dummies!

There's an unfortunate tendency for people who are first learning how to use a software program to think of themselves as "dummies" or "idiots." To make matters worse, there are a lot of books on the market that perpetuate the idea that you're stupid just because you've never used a certain sophisticated, complex tool—like a piece of software—before. We've got nearly three decades of combined experience in the computer industry, so take it from us: No matter how elegant the interface, there's rarely anything that's truly intuitive about a piece of software unless you've already used similar products before.

We don't believe that people who haven't used a piece of software before are dummies. No one lacks the essential skills to use a software program like Netscape; all it takes is a little bit of time and a little bit of patience, mostly with yourself. We'll do everything we can in this book to show you that even a novice can navigate cyberspace with grace and confidence and can understand the technologies that make such travel possible.

What's in the Book

Part One: Working Smarter with Netscape

This section contains beginning, intermediate, and advanced information about how to customize and use Netscape's basic browser features.

- Everyone knows that URL stands for Uniform Resource Locator, and everyone has a pretty good idea of what the parts of a URL basically mean. But there's more information in a URL than just a protocol type and file name, if you know how to decode them. Chapter 2 covers everything there is to know about URLs, including how they relate to other kinds of Internet services (FTP, telnet, News, SMTP, and secure servers). It contains a complete explanation of how URLs indicate the nature of the client-server relationships on the Web. This chapter also explains why the URLs that you create for Web files on your own computer have different characteristics and uses than the URLs that are publicly accessible to others on the Web.

- It's easy to alter the appearance of documents in Netscape, but the subtle effects of the changes that you make may not always be obvious. In Chapter 3, you'll learn how to make the best use of screen "real estate" by choosing appropriate fonts and colors, by determining which button styles to use, and by choosing the best definitions for the various kinds of styled text supported by HTML. This chapter contains quick tips to modify Netscape for easier viewing in group settings or presentations.

- It's easy to add new bookmarks to the end of a simple list with the **Add Bookmark** command. But it's harder to organize them into submenus and to make the new bookmarks appear in the correct location. In Chapter 4, learn the advanced secrets of working with the bookmark manager, including how to sort bookmarks as well as how to import and export bookmarks to and from separate HTML files.

- Chapter 5 contains complete information about all of Netscape's features that keep track of what you visited and when, including the not-so-obvious history list in the Go menu, and the way that your global history list affects the techniques and procedures for disk and memory cache management which are crucial for optimizing Netscape's performance. You not only can speed up the display of pages that you revisit, but you can also retrieve URLs and even complete documents and graphics directly from the cache—without even being online!

- Wondering why sometimes the screen looks strange? In Chapter 6, we'll talk about two frequently used tools in the Web page layout arsenal: tables and frames. Most importantly, we'll explain how to navigate through a page with frames so that you can view the information you're looking for without getting lost.

- Chapter 7 gives you information about the not-so-obvious navigational tips and tricks that can help you navigate quickly through the Web. Learn the best use of the Drag and Drop features, the drop-down URL box, and more!

Part Two: Helper Applications, Plug-ins, and Java

Netscape itself can only display ASCII text, HTML documents, and certain types of graphics. But, because of a standard known as MIME, Netscape can pass items that it can't display on to plug-ins or helper applications that can.

- To get the best use of the other multimedia elements of the Web, you'll need to understand how Netscape identifies items that it can't handle and how it knows which helper applications to launch. Chapter 8 contains everything you need to know about MIME types (Multipurpose Internet Mail Extensions) and their role in bringing multimedia directly to your desktop.

- Chapters 9, 10, and 11 cover the essentials of choosing, obtaining, installing, and configuring the best helper applications for the Windows, Macintosh, and UNIX computers.

- Chapter 12 explores one of the latest technologies for browsers: plug-ins. Although they're similar to helper applications, plug-ins have some exciting new capabilities that can make the Web's multimedia presentations even more exciting.

- One of the most exciting new Web technologies is use of the Java programming language to create "applets"—small, cross-platform programs that are executed within the browser. In Chapter 13, we'll explain how Java works and talk about the way that it's changing the Web.

Part Three: Using Other Internet Services with Netscape

One of the most remarkable features of Web browsers is that they offer an interface to many of the popular Internet services which predate the Web. But configuring your browser to take full advantage of them can be a little tricky.

- Netscape has a rather sophisticated built-in mechanism for sending documents to other people via electronic mail. Chapter 14 discusses the best ways to use Netscape's email capabilities, including a thorough discussion of its benefits and disadvantages as compared to a dedicated mail program like Eudora.

- Chapter 15 contains complete information about using Netscape to read Usenet News, with a realistic analysis of its benefits and its very real disadvantages. Learn how to best configure the built-in news-reader, how to navigate among several different news servers, and how to post your own news articles and replies.

- Chapter 16 discusses the procedures and the pros and cons of using other popular Internet services through Netscape, including FTP, gopher, and WAIS.

Part Four: Transactions and Security on the Web

With all the controversy surrounding online security and privacy issues, it's a good idea to familiarize yourself with the basic concepts and models of how information is actually transmitted on the Web and how you can protect yourself when necessary.

- The most basic transaction that you'll encounter on the Web is the use of an unprotected form. Chapter 17 explains how to understand and correctly use the forms interface when you encounter it, and it contains information about CGI (Common Gateway Interface)—the technology that makes forms and other kinds of online programs possible.

- Considering taking the plunge and actually buying something on the Web? Chapter 18 talks about the issues involved with electronic transactions, and gives you some guidelines to consider before you send any sensitive information across the network.

- Wonder how to decode those messages that Netscape sends you about entering and leaving secure sites? Chapter 19 explains the technology behind the Secure Sockets Layer and includes practical tips on ensuring that your personal information remains confidential.

- If you work in an environment where security is an issue, your network administrator may have set up firewalls to protect company data. In Chapter 20, learn how to correctly configure Netscape for optimal use across a network that has firewalls and proxy servers.

Part Five: Self-Publishing on the Web

Given the relative ease of making information available on the Web, it's natural to want to start putting together your own documents.

- Interested in creating your own Web pages? Chapter 21 contains a thorough introduction to HTML, including the basic tags that you need to know, an HTML style guide, and a tutorial on using Netscape Navigator Gold, Netscape's full-featured HTML editor that's built into a Web browser.

- Seen something you like elsewhere on the Web? Chapter 22 provides complete information about collecting software, graphics, HTML, and multimedia files from other locations to use in your own pages, including details on controlling the downloading of files and building local copies of remote Web sites.

Part Six: Emerging Technologies and Trends on the Web

- Sometimes you're not in the mood for mindless cruising; you need specific information and you need it fast. Chapter 23 discusses the expert usage of the Web's most popular search engines, including how to pick the right service for the kind of information you're looking for, the differences between local and global searches, and how to structure your query to get the best results. We'll also give you a realistic analysis of the kinds of information that you will and won't find on the Web.

- The Web is already more than just text, pictures, and sounds. Take a look at today's cutting-edge sites in Chapter 24, including virtual worlds, real-time audio, "active pages," video- and newspapers-on-demand, and more. Is Netscape really the "killer app" of the Internet or a harbinger of things to come? Chapter 24 also looks at the next generation of Web browsers and Internet tools, as well as changes in telecommunications technology that may impact the way that you connect to the Internet in the not-so-far-off future.

Appendices

- Need a refresher or a quick start with Netscape essentials? Appendix A is a handy quick reference for basic Netscape functions.
- Just getting started with the Web? No worries. Appendix B contains all the background information that you need to configure a dialup IP connection from your office or home.
- Appendix C contains instructions for obtaining, installing, and configuring Netscape for Windows, Macintosh, and UNIX computers.

How to Use the Book

Depending on your needs, you can use *Netscape Virtuoso* in a variety of ways. If you're looking for a solid technical explanation of URLs and disk and memory caching, or a practical discussion of bookmarks and navigational shortcuts, you might start with Part One, "Working Smarter with Netscape." If you have specific interests in MIME types and their relationship to helper applications, the optimal use of Netscape for other Internet services, using forms and security functions, or just exploring the Web and the possibilities held in its future, you can go directly to those sections as well.

- If you're familiar with basic navigation using Netscape but want to manage your time and resources better, check out Part One, "Working Smarter with Netscape." The chapters in this section contain everything from a straightforward, informative explanation of URLs and memory and disk caches, to suggestions for picking the best fonts and colors, to a discussion of the most effective use of Netscape's often confusing bookmark manager.

- Feel like you're not getting as much out of the Web's multimedia capabilities as you should be? The chapters in Part Two, "Helper Applications, Plug-ins, and Java," explain exactly what MIME types are and why they're critical to Netscape's ability to handle multimedia. You'll learn why Netscape does what it does with sound, picture, movie, and application files, and how to ensure that you're getting the best possible performance out of your helper applications.

- Figured out that Java is more than a tasty beverage but not sure what it has to do with your Web browser? Chapter 13 explains everything you need to know about why this new programming language may change the ways that the Web is used.

- Confused in the jargon jungle of email, FTP, and Usenet News? Part Three, "Using Other Internet Services with Netscape," explains the relationship between the Web and other Internet services and provides all the information you need to confidently use these tools. We'll also discuss the potential drawbacks of using Netscape as an all-purpose Internet navigation tool.

- Cut through the confusion about whether it's safe to send your credit card number or any other kind of personal information to a person or company through the Web. In Part Four, "Transactions and Security on the Web," we'll talk about what really goes on when you send information and how to protect yourself from unscrupulous snoopers.

- Ready to create your own home page? Check out the chapters in Part Five, "Self-publishing on the Web," where we'll cover HTML basics as well as guidelines for design and style. Plus, learn how to "mine" Webspace for useful pictures and HTML codes.

- Interested in the future of the Web and Netscape's place in it? See Part Six, "Emerging Technologies and Trends on the Web," where we'll talk about the real value of information on the Web and how to find the good stuff. We'll look at some of today's most innovative sites and explore the potential of the latest technological developments and corporate strategic announcements.

- If you're a Netscape neophyte, start with the appendices. These contain all the information that you need to get up and running with Netscape, presented quickly and clearly.

Conventions Used in This Book

Writing about software that runs on three different platforms is a bit of a challenge; no matter how similar the applications are, they're bound to look and act slightly differently because of the inherent differences among the operating systems. The material in this book is appropriate for users of Windows 95, Macintosh, and UNIX platforms. However, because the majority of readers will be using Windows-based PCs, most of the screen shots are of Netscape for Windows. Don't worry if you're a Macintosh or UNIX user—pictures of each platform will be used in cases where the screens vary drastically. And, in sections where the wording of the dialog boxes differs only slightly, we'll let you know what to look for on your screen.

About Beta Software

When we wrote this book, the final version of Netscape Navigator 3.0 hadn't been released: instead, we used a *beta*, or pre-release, version of the software made available by Netscape. The good news is, using the beta software allowed us to deliver a book to you that covers Netscape's latest features. The bad news is that some of the commands may appear slightly different in your version of the software. However, you can be confident that the superficial changes will be minimal and that the conceptual information is still correct.

About Dialup IP

Frequently, we'll talk about how to use Netscape with a *dialup IP* connection. Dialup IP is a method of connecting your personal computer to the Internet using a modem, a telephone line, and some special software; most people who use Netscape from home are probably using one of the two forms of dialup IP: SLIP (Serial Line Internet Protocol) or PPP (Point to Point Protocol). So, don't be confused if you see the terms "dialup IP," "dialup connection," or "SLIP or PPP connection"—if you're using a telephone line and a modem to use Netscape, then the information in that section will be useful for you. (More information about getting starting with SLIP and PPP can be found in Appendix B.)

What the Icons Mean

Certain passages of this book are flagged with icons so you can find and use relevant information quickly.

NOTE

This part is especially interesting, relevant, or informative—be sure to read it!

SHORTCUT

This is a convenient tip that will save you time and trouble.

VIRTUOSO

Here's a little-known or advanced trick that the pros use.

WARNING

Pay special attention to this information to avoid encountering a serious problem.

Summary

Our goal is to empower you to understand the technology that's becoming ever more commonplace in today's society. Instead of just providing procedures and instructions, we've done everything we can to demystify the use of Netscape and the technology of the World Wide Web. We hope that as a result you'll become a more confident, technically aware consumer of the vast array of online offerings, able to separate the truly innovative from the overly hyped. Happy surfing!

CHAPTER 1

NETSCAPE AND
THE WORLD WIDE WEB

In the past few years, the Internet has changed from being a bastion and refuge of computer scientists and researchers to becoming the most talked-about and promoted technology in the world. You can reach millions of people all over the world with electronic mail. Updates to commercial software packages are available by downloading them using FTP. Television networks, newspapers, corporations, governments, nonprofit organizations, and even your neighbors' kids have "home pages" on the World Wide Web. As clichéd as the phrase has become, we really are in the midst of a telecommunications revolution...and the Web, with its elegant presentation of text and multimedia and its easy navigation to sites around the world, is right at the center of it.

Several events transpired to lead up to this huge shift in the way that we think about computers and communication, ranging from the beginnings of the Web as a communications tool for physicists, to the changes in governmental policy allowing the Internet to be used for commercial purposes, to the development of the protocols to support the graphical applications that make enjoyment of the Internet possible to millions who'd never touched a modem before. In this chapter, we'll talk about the events that shaped the Internet and the World Wide Web into their present forms, and we'll discuss the unique position held by Netscape Communications, developer of Netscape Navigator, the world's most popular graphical Web browser.

The Beginning of the Web

It's important to keep in mind that the Internet and the World Wide Web are *not* the same thing, despite the media's interchangeable use of the terms. The Internet is the network infrastructure of computers around the world that have agreed to share information with each other. By agreeing on a set of common protocols, or communications standards, computers on the Internet can exchange information no matter who manufactured the CPU and no matter what operating system is in use. These standards, known as TCP/IP (Transmission Control Protocol/Internet Protocol), are the *lingua franca* of the Internet; any computer adhering to the TCP/IP protocols can talk to any other computer, regardless of vendor or operating system in use. So, a Sun workstation running the Solaris operating system can communicate with an IBM mainframe running VM/CMS, and they can both share information even with personal computers, as long as all the machines agree to use the TCP/IP protocols to manage the exchange.

The Internet itself has been in existence in one form or another for more than a decade, providing services such as electronic mail and file exchanges to computer scientists and researchers around the world. Technically, the World Wide Web is just another service like email, telnet, FTP, and others that sit atop the infrastructure of the Internet.

The World Wide Web originated at CERN, the European Laboratory for High Energy Physics. (The acronym stands for Conseil Europeen pour la Recherche Neclaire.) Scientists at CERN were struggling to find a way to share a huge variety of documents—ranging from experimental data to computer documentation to up-to-the-minute news of scientific breakthroughs—with the large community of physicists who could benefit from such access.

Tim Berners-Lee, who now heads the World Wide Web Consortium, first conceived of the protocols that make it possible for Web documents to be accessible to desktop computers around the world. The first Web browser, a *line-mode browser* that could only run on text-only, VT-100 terminals, was released to the public in 1991. The idea of the Web was greeted with delight by the Internet community. Less than two years later, the first widely used World Wide Web browser—NCSA Mosaic, a graphical Web browser—was available for public distribution.

About Graphical Internet Applications

For decades, access to the Internet was through text-only terminals or terminal emulator programs. The graphical user interface revolution, which started with Sun's engineering workstations in the early 1980s and was implemented in personal computers with the Macintosh and eventually for the PC by Microsoft Windows, represented a huge leap in the usability of computers. You no longer needed to type arcane commands to perform simple operations like opening a file or creating an email message; instead, the now-commonplace features of using mice to select objects and commands from menus made it possible to concentrate on what you were working on instead of on how to access your own materials.

It was only a matter of time before Internet tools were developed to take advantage of the graphical user interface. While they were available in the 1980s for users of workstations, graphical Internet applications couldn't become available for personal computers such as IBM and the Macintosh until those computers could be connected to the Internet via the TCP/IP protocols. Although third-party software products allowed some TCP/IP support for personal computers in the mid-1980s, it wasn't until the early 1990s that Apple, Microsoft, and independent software developers recognized the strategic value of TCP/IP support and included it in their operating systems.

So, by the beginning of the decade, it was possible to use graphical Internet tools on your desktop computer...if it was directly connected to the Internet through a LAN at a corporation or university. The next logical step was to develop a way to let people use their personal computers to access graphical Internet applications from their home, using a modem and a telephone line to create a temporary but full-featured connection to the Internet. The result was SLIP (Serial Line Internet Protocol), followed by PPP (Point to Point Protocol), which in conjunction with TCP/IP made this possible.

VIRTUOSO

Want to really understand what SLIP and PPP are about? Looking for information about making your dialup IP connection run as smoothly and reliably as possible? Check out *Internet Direct: Connecting Through SLIP and PPP*, also published by MIS:Press. It covers everything you need to know about configuring dialup IP for Windows 95, Windows 3.1, Macintosh, and OS/2, from buying a modem and choosing a service provider to installing the software and troubleshooting your system if things go wrong.

To sum up, the combination of the graphical user interface, operating system support for TCP/IP, and the development of the dialup IP protocols combined to make it possible to surf cyberspace in a multimedia environment from your own home, small business, or any place where you can plug in a computer and a modem.

About NCSA Mosaic

As we mentioned earlier, NCSA Mosaic, developed at the National Center for Supercomputing Applications at the University of Illinois, was the first graphical Web browser. Mosaic made it possible for users with direct or dialup Internet connections to navigate through the Web viewing multimedia documents, complete with different fonts, styled text, and inline graphics. But the most important feature of the Mosaic browser was its ability to identify an object's MIME type (we'll talk about this more in Chapter 8). If it couldn't display an object directly, it would pass the object to an application on the user's own computer that could. This made it possible for people to access movies, audio, high-quality graphics, and more...right on the Internet. For the first time, an Internet service could support tangible style and visual appeal, something sorely lacking in the days of text-only information exchanges.

The overwhelming success of the freeware version of Mosaic led NCSA to license the code to other companies, such as Spyglass, Inc., who in turn provided the code for Spry's Air Mosaic browser. But other commercial competitors soon appeared, the most significant of which is none other than Netscape Communications Corporation.

The Birth of Netscape Communications Corporation

In April of 1994, Marc Andreessen, who conceived and spearheaded the development of Mosaic, left NCSA to cofound Mosaic Communications in Mountain View, California. (The company changed its name to Netscape Communications in November of that year.) Andreessen's partner was none other than Dr. James H. Clark, founder of Silicon Graphics, Inc., an extremely successful Fortune 500 manufacturer of high-tech workstations and associated software. The other members of the executive management team are from equally prestigious backgrounds. Besides Andreessen, the core technical team contains five out of six other developers of the original Mosaic—Eric Bina, Rob McCool, Jon Mittelhauser, Aleks Totic, and Chris Houck—as well as Lou Montulli, author of Lynx (a popular text-only browser for the Web).

In October, 1994, the first version of Netscape Navigator was made available on the Internet. In August of 1995, more than 80% of the people using the World Wide Web were using the Netscape browser. When Netscape Communications went public on August 9, the stock jumped from $28 to more than $75—one of the largest initial public offerings in history.

Although it may seem to the general public that the Netscape Navigator Web browser is Netscape's only product, that's absolutely not the case. The truth is that Netscape develops and sells a wide range of server software products to corporate customers who wish to provide information on the Web—after all, they're not staying in business by just giving away the browser.

But since so many people do use the Netscape browser, companies that want to be Web information providers may well feel compelled to use Netscape's server software. Netscape servers are guaranteed to support and work smoothly with all of their browser's special features, which we'll talk about in the next section (and cover in detail in the rest of the book).

NOTE Besides the Navigator Web browser, Netscape has developed a variety of additional consumer products, including: Navigator Gold, a browser with a built-in graphical WYSIWYG HTML editor; SmartMarks, a bookmark manager program whose features include automatically updating out-of-date bookmarks; and CoolTalk, an Internet telephony and collaboration software package. Presumably, this is part of an ongoing strategy to become a premier provider of commercial Web- and Internet-related software.

Another commercial area in which Netscape is making great strides is in the development of software for *intranets*: corporate-wide networks which are based on the same standards as the Internet.

NOTE

Why is Netscape So Great?

NCSA Mosaic set the first real standard for graphical Web browsers. Netscape Navigator, developed by almost exactly the same team as NCSA Mosaic, has risen to the challenge of following up such a groundbreaking product by improving on the original graphical browser features and introducing some very important new ones of its own. Some of Netscape's best features are listed below:

- Netscape is optimized for use over a low-bandwidth connection, making it ideal for users who connect using SLIP or PPP. In addition to hidden technical improvements, Netscape has features which are immediately obvious, such as allowing you to browse the text in a document while the graphics are loading, and handling *interlaced GIFs*—inline graphics that are displayed in a rough form and then filled in, so you can get an idea of what the picture is without waiting for it to load completely.

- Netscape uses HTML 3.0 (the markup language that lets a developer define what a Web document will look like). And, Netscape incorporates its own custom extensions, such as flashing text and tables, which it assumes will be incorporated into the next version of HTML when the new standard is released. The more features available to a developer, the better the page will look to a user. Many other Web browsers can't display pages that use Netscape's extensions to HTML; you may often see a warning on a Web document that the page won't look right unless you're using the Netscape browser.

NOTE   Some people go overboard in using Netscape's custom extensions. The Enhanced for Netscape Hall of Shame at http://www.meat.com/netscape_hos.html contains links to the sites that are considered to be the worst implementation of Netscape-only features.

- Netscape contains sophisticated, built-in security features that allow you to conduct electronic commerce over the Web (such as purchasing items with a credit card) without fear that your confidential information will be compromised.

- Netscape was the first browser to embrace new technologies like multimedia plug-ins and support for Java applets. Additionally, Netscape Communications is one of the major supporters of new standards for information delivery, contributing to the recent adoption of a standard for VRML (Virtual Reality Modeling Language), which lets you navigate three-dimensional representations with your mouse.

Becoming a Netscape Virtuoso

You've probably figured out by now that if you've chosen Netscape as your graphical Web browser, you're not alone—almost everyone out there is using Netscape, too.

But not everyone knows that Netscape's user interface is deceptively simple. You can use it for months or years without discovering Netscape's powerful hidden features. In the rest of this book, you'll learn how Netscape really works...and as a result, how to make Netscape really work for *you*.

CHAPTER 2

UNDERSTANDING URLs

If you've used Netscape or another browser to explore the Web at all, you know that a URL is a *Uniform Resource Locator*. URLs act as "universal addresses" for resources on the Web. In fact, they're a bit like telephone numbers—if you don't have the means to locate the URL of an item you're looking for, then you simply can't get to that information. Like telephone numbers, you can tell a great deal about a Web site based on its URL, in much the same way that you can determine in which part of the country—or even of the city—a certain telephone number is located. (And, like telephone numbers, there are directories and other kinds of indices to help you find the URL that you're looking for; this topic will be discussed at length in Chapter 23, "Strategies for Searching the Web.")

When you're done with this chapter, you'll be able to discern a surprising amount of information about a site based on its URLs; to identify bad URLs simply by reading them; to understand why URLs for files on your local machine look different from URLs for Web sites located elsewhere on the Internet; and to make educated guesses about what a correct URL for a site might be. Most importantly for developers, you'll know how to construct simple, easy-to-understand URLs for your own site so that your users don't encounter any problems.

Viewing a URL

Here's a quick review of how to view URLs. To see the URL of the page you're currently using, select **Show Location** from the Options menu. The **Location** field will be displayed at the top of the Netscape screen (Figure 2.1).

Figure 2.1 The **Location** field.

To see the URL that you'll go to if you click a link, position the pointer over the underlined link. The URL contained in the link will be displayed in the lower-left corner of the Netscape screen (Figure 2.2).

Figure 2.2 Clicking the link will go to the URL at the bottom of the screen.

Why URLs Fail

It's happened to all of us. You hear about a Web site on TV or in a newspaper article, or you click a link in someone else's document to a page you've never seen. But instead of finding a new site that's chock-full of useful or entertaining materials, you get error messages like those in Figures 2.3, 2.4, 2.5, and 2.6.

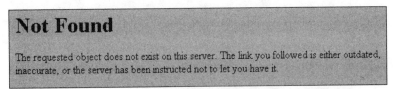

Figure 2.3 Too bad—the file you're looking for doesn't exist.

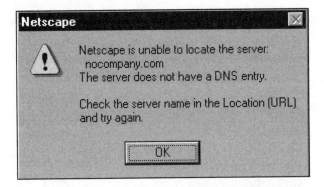

Figure 2.4 The site that's supposed to house the file doesn't exist.

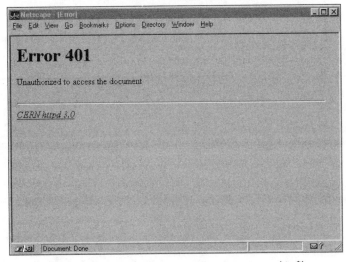

Figure 2.5 You don't have permission to access this file.

Figure 2.6 The server didn't respond—it's too busy or not available.

We'll discuss the specific causes for each of these kinds of error messages later in this chapter. But in general, if a remote URL fails you, it's for one of a few simple reasons:

- You entered the URL incorrectly; check your typing and try again.
- The site doesn't exist—either the files have been moved or they were never at that location.
- The URL provided to you contains incorrect information and the site can't be located on the Internet.
- You're trying to access a private Web site that's not open to the general public.

One of the most basic issues in working with URLs is that they are relentlessly unforgiving. Although URLs are often long and complicated, sometimes containing 50 or 60 characters as well as unusual spelling and capitalization (to say nothing of nonstandard punctuation, including underscores), there is simply no latitude whatsoever for error. If you type even one character incorrectly, you'll get an error message that the item can't be found.

NOTE For power users, typing URLs is almost always a last resort. There are a number of schemes to handle URLs so that you rarely have to touch them with your bare hands. However, it's important to make sure that you understand all the components of a URL discussed in this chapter so that you can make educated guesses about the site, the content, and the possible causes of any errors that you encounter.

What's even more frustrating than encountering an error as a result of your own typing is coming across incorrect URLs in other people's documents on the Web. This occurs when developers are sloppy about creating their documents or when they fail to keep them up-to-date. Another irritating way that bad URLs are perpetuated is when Web resources are described in television and print media; the combination of short line lengths and possible lack of knowledge in the production staff ensures that a number of URLs published in this way will be incorrect. However, after reading this chapter, you should be able to identify bad URLs in print or broadcast and to make reasonable guesses about what the correct URL is.

URLs versus HREFs

Once you start constructing your own Web documents, you'll start using the HREF tag in HTML to create links to other materials on the Internet. (Don't worry if this doesn't mean anything to you yet; this is completely covered later in the book.) This chapter only discusses the information included in a URL—the address of a document that, if necessary, you could type into the Open Location dialog box to go to that location. Although the information that you place in your documents' HREFs includes URLs, they're a little more complicated. However, regardless of whether or not you construct your own Web documents, you'll be well served by understanding the intricacies of the information comprising URLs discussed in this chapter.

Components of a URL

There are three basic components of a URL:

- Type specifier
- Host or machine identifier
- Path identifier and file extension

NOTE

It's important to know the difference between specifiers and identifiers. A *specifier* is simply a type or class used to describe categories of objects, while an *identifier* actually denotes a single unique item such as a machine or file name.

In the following sample URL

```
http://www.foobar.com/products/catalog.html
```

http is the type specifier, www.foobar.com is the host identifier, and products/catalog.html is the path identifier listing the exact file we're looking for (**catalog.html**) in the directory structure (it's in the /**products** directory).

Punctuation in URLs

There are very strict rules regarding punctuation of URLs. If any of the rules are violated, you'll fail to connect to the site. For any URL on a remote site, the punctuation is as follows:

```
specifier://hostname/pathname/filename.extension
```

WARNING

It's crucial that the specifier be followed with a colon and two forward slashes; that the elements in the pathname be separated by single forward slashes; and that there be no spaces or unusual characters. The only punctuation that's acceptable in a URL is the underscore (usually **Shift-hyphen** on the keyboard); the decimal (the period on the keyboard); and the hyphen. You may also see certain characters in URLs such as pound (**#**), question mark (**?**), and plus (**+**), but it's fairly uncommon for you to type them. (These characters are usually generated by CGI, which is discussed later in this chapter.) If you see a URL for a remote Web site that contains irregular characters or spaces between words, it's a good sign that the URL is incorrect.

About Type Specifiers

Type specifiers are used to identify the protocol class of the URL. To understand what a protocol class for URL means, we need to look back over the history of Internet protocol and the unique position of the World Wide Web in the history of the Internet, as well as to understand a little bit about client-server architecture and its implications for transactions across the Web.

Internet Protocols on the Web

Over the past decades, a number of distinct protocols, or communications standards, have evolved for services available over the Internet that allow dissimilar computers to share all kinds of information in different ways. If you picture the Internet as simply a network of roads and highways, every Internet service generates a unique kind of traffic—electronic mail, remote logins, file and data sharing, etc. All of these require participating machines to use special protocols so that the information can be managed correctly.

The common element among all Internet service protocols is that they share the same basic transport mechanism: TCP/IP (Transmission Control Protocol/Internet Protocol). However, the information that's being transported by TCP/IP and the way that it's handled are entirely up to the service's protocol. Any time a new Internet service is created, a new protocol class must be developed concurrently to handle the new kind of traffic.

Generally speaking, you'll use a different type of application for each service and its associated protocol on the Internet—for example, you use a mail program like Eudora to check your mail, an FTP program to transfer files remotely, and so on. A unique feature of Web browsers compared to other Internet application programs is a result of the early Web developers having the presence of mind to build an "umbrella" address mechanism (the URL) that allows the Web to incorporate other existing Internet service protocols related to file sharing. So, in addition to viewing Web pages, browsers can look at and handle files on gopher and FTP sites, and they can include a limited amount of support for other Internet protocols including telnet, Usenet News, and electronic mail.

Client-Server Network Architecture

To understand how software communications protocols work on the Internet, you need to examine the nature of client-server architecture.

Client-server architecture is a way of viewing the relationship between the users of network services and the providers of network services.

For practically all protocols on the Internet, including the ones discussed in this section, there are both client and server components that *implement*, or "speak," the same protocol. The server part of the protocol resides on the remote host machine, which is why the computers you connect to are called, for example, gopher servers or Web servers. The client part of the protocol runs locally on your desktop machine. Together, the client and server software exchange commands and responses according to the rules set forth by the protocol. Most protocols are associated with a specific client application for your desktop machine, such as the Macintosh TurboGopher client program that's used solely to access gopher servers. However, as we discussed earlier, Web browsers implement the client side of many Internet protocols to at least a limited degree.

One of the most important features of the client-server relationship is that it allows each type of computer to do what it does best. The client application lets the desktop machine deal with issues of display and user interface, while the host machine handles large data sets and issues of computational complexity without worrying about how the information it generates will ultimately be displayed. For example, you can run a weather simulation from your desktop in which the server, a Cray XMP supercomputer at the National Center for Supercomputing Applications, generates the results thousands of times faster than your 486-based PC possibly could, but the interface you used to send the commands to the Cray and the way the information ultimately appears are a result of your Windows operating system.

Another important feature of the client-server relationship that directly impacts your experiences on the Web is the idea of a "stateless" protocol. Most of the recently developed client-server protocols are *stateless*, meaning that the servers regard the clients in an impersonal fashion and don't keep any information about them beyond the duration of the time needed to handle an information request. In a stateless protocol, the client connects to the server and presents its request; after the server satisfies the request, which usually takes a second or less, it drops the connection between the two. You may have noticed that each time you click a new link on a Web page, there's a brief period when the status message says it's connecting to the server, even if you're accessing a document at the same site. This occurs because the server ended your previous connection as soon as you received all the necessary information.

Because of stateless protocols, a typical high-performance Web or gopher server can handle the requests of thousands of clients in a short period of time without generating any error or "busy" message. This is remarkable when contrasted with FTP, which, as the oldest information system protocol in use on the Internet, is not stateless. When you connect to an FTP site, you have an ongoing connection that won't be severed until you physically tell your Web browser to leave that site and go somewhere else (or until you're disconnected by the server after a specified period of idle time). There can be very real limitations on the number of simultaneous ongoing connections that can be supported by a nonstateless protocol, and as a result you may find that popular FTP sites are difficult to access during normal hours.

Kinds of Type Specifiers

The item that makes it possible for the Web browser to know when to expect different protocols is the type specifier in the URL, which is always the first item.

The type specifier lets the browser know, before it even starts to look for the item in cyberspace, what kind of object it's going to be working with: a Web page, a gopher site, or an FTP file archive.

Table 2.1 lists the type specifiers that you'll find in URLs on the Web.

Table 2.1 Type Specifiers in URLs

Type Specifier	Meaning	Syntax
http	Hypertext transport protocol for a WWW site	http://[hostname][pathname]
gopher gopher site	Gopher protocol to access a gopher://[hostname][pathname]	
ftp	File Transfer Protocol for retrieving remote files	ftp://[hostname][pathname]

Table 2.1 Type Specifiers in URLs (continued)

Type Specifier	Meaning	Syntax
news	Usenet News site	news:[newsgroup name]
mailto	Sends electronic mail message to specified address	mailto:[email address]
telnet	Uses telnet to emulate a terminal session	telnet:[hostname]
file	Displays a local file without invoking any Internet protocols	file://[pathname]

NOTE You may also see items in the Location field that begin with about: or javascript:. The about: specifier is used to display certain information about your version of Netscape, such as the license and release information or specific information about your cache. (Complete information about using about: to find out about your cache and link history can be found in Chapter 5.) The javascript: specifier is another special kind of specifier that you will never type yourself; it's used when an item you click on an HTML page causes a JavaScript item to be run. We'll talk more about JavaScript in Chapter 13.

About HTTP URLs

HTTP stands for Hypertext Transport Protocol, which is the primary protocol of the World Wide Web and is supported by so-called Web sites and Web servers around the world. (Although it's standard practice to type it in lowercase letters in a URL, *HTTP* as an acronym for the protocol name is commonly spelled in capital letters.) HTTP is the mechanism that allows hypertext Web pages and their associated links and graphics to be transported thousands of miles across the Internet to be displayed correctly on your desktop.

About Gopher URLs

Gopher is the protocol for an earlier type of information system developed at the University of Minnesota and widely used for public information systems at universities and colleges. Gopher is a menu-driven hierarchical system in which you navigate through titled directories to find the information you're looking for and download items to your own computer. As an early attempt to provide browseable media across the Internet, gopher allows links to other gopher sites around the world (called *gopherspace*) and supports a variety of MIME types for objects, including sounds, pictures, and formatted documents. Though it can only display plain text objects on the screen, other kinds of objects are downloaded to your computer for later viewing. (For more information on MIME types, see Chapter 8, "MIME Types, Helper Applications, and Plug-Ins.")

About FTP URLs

FTP is a file transfer protocol dating from the earliest days of the Internet. It was originally developed as a simple way for individuals to move files from one Internet host to another; hence, its primary verbs are *get* a file (retrieve it) and *put* a file (place it somewhere else). Over the years, FTP began to be used not only for file transfers by registered account holders but also for "anonymous FTP," in which system operators built large archives of shareable files that were widely available to anyone on the Internet. This convention of publicly accessible file archives is one of the most influential traditions on the Internet, fostering collaboration and a history of free or shareware access to sorely needed software tools. Web browsers typically use the anonymous FTP mechanism to let you view and navigate through the files at sites of interest and to download files directly to your machine.

About Telnet URLs

Telnet is a terminal emulation tool that lets you log on to shell accounts of Internet-connected systems. Despite what you may think, not everything interesting on the Internet is available with a graphical interface on the World Wide Web; in fact, most library catalogs and other kinds of public access information like freenets are only available through telnet sessions.

Although telnet is a real Internet protocol, Web browsers require that you install a separate telnet program and that you configure your browser to use it as a helper application. For more information, see Chapters 9 through 11.

About News URLs

Usenet News is a worldwide network of computers that carry thousands of discussion groups, called *newsgroups*, devoted to a vast and sometimes controversial array of topics. Although Usenet is predominantly a text-only network, it continues to be one of the leading methods of communication and up-to-date information dissemination on the Internet. URLs that take you to a newsgroup are in the format *news:group.specifier*, where the group specifier is the name of the Usenet newsgroup.

 Accessing newsgroups through the Web requires that you correctly configure Netscape to use an accessible news server. Complete information about this feature and about Usenet News in general can be found in Chapter 15, "All About **NOTE** Usenet News."

About Mailto URLs

Electronic mail is one of the Internet's most popular applications, allowing you to send messages and files to a specific user or to a distribution list of hundreds. Netscape supports the limited use of electronic mail to send messages from within the application. URLs with the *mailto* type specifier will send an electronic mail message to the address designated in the URL. URLs that generate an electronic message are in the format *mailto:username@hostname;* clicking the link containing that URL displays a blank window for you to type your message.

 Sending mail through the Web requires that you correctly configure Netscape to use an accessible mail server. Complete information about this can be found in Chapter 14, "Electronic Mail and Netscape."
NOTE

About File URLs

This type specifier is a unique case that doesn't actually invoke an Internet protocol—in fact, it doesn't use any part of the Internet or the client-server relationship at all. Unlike other kinds of URLs, which establish a connection and negotiate requests and exchanges with remote servers, this specifier simply says that the URL should be interpreted as the name of a local file on the user's machine. The Web browser presents the requested file name to the local file system, which returns it to the Web browser, which does its best to display the file correctly.

NOTE

We'll talk at length about this kind of type specifier later in this chapter.

About Host Name Identifiers

In all URLs that require accessing a remote server, the second part of the URL is always the name of the Internet host. (This component is also called an *Internet address*, *Internet identifier*, or *machine identifier*.) If the host name can't be found, you'll get a message like the one in Figure 2.4, letting you know that the host system couldn't be located on the Internet.

An Internet host name is a unique address for each computer connected to the Internet anywhere in the world. Host names can take the form of an IP number, such as 127.5.4.21, or the form of a more meaningful name, such as www.uh.edu.

About IP Numbers and the Domain Name System

The Internet is a packet-switching network. Information that you send is broken into several individual packets, each of which contains addressing information for its ultimate destination. The packets head off into the network, taking whatever routes are available to get to their final address, where they're reassembled into the correct order.

Packets are able to find their ultimate destination because every single computer on the Internet has a unique identifying address, called an *IP number*. Machines on the Internet called *routers* send your data packets along until they reach the machine with the specific IP number contained in the packet.

IP numbers contain four parts, separated by decimals, containing a number between 0 and 255. For example, 152.23.4.17 is a valid IP number that might exist, while 342.54.12.17 and 211.32.1 are not. (The first incorrect IP number contains a number larger than 255, while the second contains three parts instead of four.)

NOTE It's uncommon to see IP numbers in a URL instead of an Internet address (described below), but it can happen. If you attempt to use a URL that contains an IP number and it fails, first make sure that the IP number can actually be valid by ensuring that it conforms to the rules described above.

Because of the difficulty that people can have keeping track of long lists of numerals, such as IP numbers, the *Domain Name System* was devised so that any machine with an IP number could also have a more meaningful text-based name. The Domain Name System lets us use addresses like rtfm.mit.edu instead of 18.181.0.24. Not only is the first address easier to remember, but you learn a great deal about its location simply by looking at its name.

Like an IP number, an Internet address in the Domain Name System has several parts, each separated by a decimal. The first name or names identify a particular computer within an organization; in the example above, the machine's name is rtfm. The last two names in an address are especially significant, as they comprise the *domain name* of an Internet address. (In the above example, mit.edu is the domain name.) No matter how many machine names appear in front of a domain name—there may be one or more, or there may be nothing in front of the domain name at all—valid Internet addresses must contain a complete domain name.

SHORTCUT It's common on the Internet for a Web server to use www as the machine name preceding the domain name (for example, www.microsoft.com is the host name for Microsoft's Web server, and www.apple.com is the host name for Apple's). If you know what a company's domain name is—and it's not always companyname.com— then you can make a reasonable guess about what URL you could use to reach them.

The part of the domain name that appears at the very end of the address—in our example, edu—is known as the *top-level domain name*. This name roughly identifies what kind of organization the domain belongs to: a for-profit company or a nonprofit research institution or university. Table 2.2 lists the common top-level domain names of the Internet and their meanings.

Table 2.2 Top-Level Domain Names

Domain Name	Description
com	For-profit commercial organization
edu	University or research institution
gov	Government organization
mil	Military organization
net	Internet service facility or service provider
org	Not-for-profit organization

NOTE As more and more countries connect to the Internet, a new standard for domain names is emerging. Countries outside the United States generally have a two-letter country code as the last element in their domain name; for example, .ca is the code for Canada; .jp is the code for Japan, and .nl is the code for the Netherlands. You'll occasionally see codes for the United States (.us), though this is less common than for other countries.

The domain name of an Internet address is used to translate the simple Internet names that we understand into the numbers that are actually used by the Internet to route traffic. This process is managed by Domain Name Servers at various locations on the Internet. There is no single Domain Name Server that has global knowledge of every machine on the Internet; instead, each server knows how to contact other Domain Name Servers to look up information.

NOTE Despite the best efforts of system administrators, Domain Name Servers have been known to fail. If absolutely none of the URLs you use are working, and you're sure that your dialup IP or network connection is configured correctly, try connecting to a site like Microsoft (http://www.microsoft.com), which should always be available and is easy to spell. If you receive a DNS error when you try to connect to a reliable site like Microsoft, it's a sure sign that something is wrong with the Domain Name Server that you're using. Contact your service provider if this is the case.

Port Numbers in URLs

You may occasionally see URLs containing a colon and a number appended to the end of the host name, such as www.xyz.com:80. This number, known as a *port number*, plays an important part in making sure that the protocol class for the Internet service that you're using works correctly.

The transport mechanism that delivers packets across the Internet to a remote server is responsible for handing off the packets in such a way that the server knows what kind of packets they are (for example, a telnet request, an HTTP request). Certain ports on the server are designated by number to handle specific kinds of packets. When you use a URL to make a request of a remote server, the packets automatically go to the standard or well-known port number for the protocol specified in the URL. Table 2.3 contains a list of well-known port numbers for protocol classes used on the Web.

Table 2.3 Well-Known Port Numbers

Protocol	Port Number
HTTP	80
Gopher	70
FTP	21
Telnet	23
SMTP (mail)	25
NNTP (news)	119

However, some servers may request that packets of a certain type go to a different port number from the well-known port number. In this case, the host name in the URL is followed by a colon and the number of the port that should be used instead of the well-known port number.

One reason that port numbers are specified in URLs is that a site may be experimental, in development, or simply not ready for the general public yet. If you have a URL that specifies a nonstandard port and it doesn't work, it may mean that the site is no longer experimental and has been moved to the well-known port. So, try the URL again without the port number.

NOTE

If you look at URLs that are embedded in a list of bookmarks or URLs that were generated by another program, port numbers may be displayed. (Machine-generated URLs often contain port numbers.) However, these port numbers are unnecessary for you to include in a URL if they're the default well-known port numbers associated with the protocol class. For example, if you came across the URL

NOTE

```
http://www.foo.com:80
```

it wouldn't be necessary to include the **:80** if you retype it or share it with a friend, since that's the specifier for the standard port for the HTTP protocol.

About Pathnames

The *pathname* is the third item in a URL. Once you've used the correct protocol to arrive at the specified machine, the pathname tells the Web browser exactly where to find the file you're looking for in the host machine's directory structure. If the pathname is incorrect but the host could be found, you'll see an error message like the one in Figure 2.3.

Pathnames are a way of representing the name of a file in a hierarchical file system. Such hierarchical systems, which first appeared more than 20 years ago with the development of UNIX, have become standard on all operating systems for personal computers, including DOS, Windows, and the Macintosh OS. The basic idea of a hierarchical file system is that you can have any number of directories on a volume (in graphical operating systems like the Macintosh and Windows, directories take the form of folders), and that directories can contain not only files but also other directories. In order to find a specific file, you need to know not only its name, but also the path to the directory in which it resides. For example, a file named **foo** located in directory **x** within directory **y** on volume **D**, would be specified on a DOS Windows machine as **d:\y\x\foo**. A visual depiction of the hierarchical structure is shown in Figure 2.7.

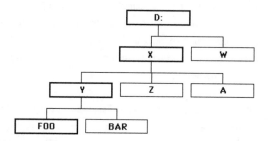

Figure 2.7 Hierarchical location of d:\y\x\foo.

NOTE UNIX uses forward slashes to separate files and directories in a pathname. Because the World Wide Web is part of the Internet, which evolved on predominantly UNIX-based computers, pathnames are specified in this way. However, since Microsoft uses backslashes for DOS and Windows, PC users may need to unlearn the instinct to type backslashes to separate directories in a pathname, as they'll fail. Macintosh users, who rarely identify a file by any means other than selecting it from the Finder or Mini-Finder, are less likely to have this problem.

This simple idea of the hierarchical file has become so commonplace that we take it for granted, but the power it provides in allowing the organization and tracking of immense numbers of different files on a machine can't be underestimated.

Web sites are sets of files grouped in a hierarchical structure. After you identify the protocol class and the machine on which the file is located, you must generally include the pathname for the specific page that you're interested in, or you'll simply land at the top level of a site and will have to click through several links to find the information you're looking for.

Web server software is usually configured so that only selected sets of files are accessible to browsers across the Internet, since system administrators aren't interested in letting you browse personnel files or other proprietary data. Material that's available for public viewing is usually housed on a separate drive or volume. Web server software allows the administrator to specify a directory on the server that forms the root or top-level directory of the hierarchy that's visible to Web browsers and that contains all the directories and files that can be accessed.

NOTE

The top-level directory usually contains a file called **index.html**. If you enter a URL that doesn't contain a pathname but does identify a protocol class and host name, the browser will look for the **index.html** file at the top level of the directory that's visible to Web browsers and display it by default.

SHORTCUT

You may occasionally see a URL whose pathname begins with the prefix /icons (such as http://hostname/icons). This prefix specifies a directory on the server that holds all the images and graphical elements that are used by the Web pages on the server. At many sites, you can browse that directory by including /icons as part of the URL, and you can retrieve the graphical elements for use in your own pages. (For more information, see Chapter 22, "Working With Public Web Pages.")

Another item that you may see in URLs is a tilde (~) as the first part of the pathname. This occurs when the Web server software is configured to allow many users to create personal Web pages and is typical of universities and Internet providers who supply personal accounts. The tilde signifies that individual account holders on a machine can share a portion of their home directory with Web browsers. The pathname of such URLs will begin with /~ followed by the user's login name or other personal identifier. The tilde in the pathname tells the browser to search all the home directories on the machine until it locates one with the specified name.

SHORTCUT

The same rules apply to URLs with tildes as to other URLs—if you don't identify a file within the directory, the default file **index.html** will be displayed if it's available. So, the URL

```
http://www.xxx.com/~jdoe
```

should display JDoe's top-level index page. This allows you to use some intuition in guessing the URLs for personal home pages. For example, if I know someone's user name and the name of the machine, I can make an educated guess about the URL for their home page, if they have one.

Combinations of the rules described above define every kind of pathname you might encounter. Interpreting pathnames can give you a great deal of information about the site you're using. For example, the pathname /~rmiller/kiosks/index.html tells me that this is a personal home page and that there is at least one level of subdirectories in the rmiller account. The fact that there are subdirectories should lead you to believe that information on other topics is available in other directories. If you came directly to this file via a link from another site and were interested in the other kinds of information provided by rmiller, you might enter a URL with the same type specifier and host identifier, simply followed by /~rmiller. This would take you to the top level of the directory and would display an index of all the contents.

About File Extensions

The last item in a pathname may be a *file extension*, appended to the name of the file after a decimal. (For example, in the file name **index.html**, the file extension is **.html**.) In general, file extensions provide important clues about the type of information contained in the file. In some operating systems, file extensions are required to let the operating system know what kind of file is being used; for example, DOS always treats a file with the **.txt** extension as a plain text file.

Understanding file extensions commonly used in URLs can help you determine what kind of material you're going to end up viewing in advance, as well as help you discern whether a helper application is going to be launched as a result of clicking a link. Table 2.4 contains a list of common file extensions and their associated file types.

Table 2.4 Common File Extensions

Extension	Meaning	Viewing Mechanism
.html, .htm	HTML file	Can be viewed directly by Netscape
.jpeg, .jpg	JPEG picture file	Can be viewed directly by Netscape
.gif	GIF picture file	Can be viewed directly by Netscape
.zip, .sit, .bin, .hqx, .tar, .Z	Various archive and encoding formats	Requires helper applications to view
.pict, .pic, .tif, .tiff	Various graphics formats	Requires helper applications to view
.qt, .mov, .mpeg, .mpg, .mpe, .avi	Various video formats	Requires helper applications to view
.eps, .ps	PostScript format	Requires helper applications to view

NOTE

Complete information about choosing, configuring, and using helper applications can be found in Part Two, "Helper Applications, Plug-ins, and Java."

WARNING

When you're developing your own Web pages, it's important to use appropriate file extensions. Browsers on some platforms require the information in the file extension to know which helper application to launch. We'll discuss all the issues in choosing path and file names in Part Five, "Self-Publishing on the Web."

Local versus Remote URLs

About the Local Mode of Operation

One of the most powerful features of Web browsers is that they support both local and network modes of operation. Not only can they be used to search remote sites around the world but they can also support viewing HTML documents that reside on your own personal system. If you're a relatively new user, it's possible that you've only used Netscape to look at Web pages on the Internet and you haven't explored the utility and power of the local mode of operation.

What makes the local mode of operation so useful is that you can have local copies of Web documents on your hard drive that contain links to other sites on the Internet. This allows you to construct your own personal "starting points" page containing all the links that you want to access regularly, without navigating through an ever-growing list of bookmarks to find the link that you want. (Just try managing a bookmark list that contains more than 40 items of interest!) You can build local sets or collections of hierarchically organized pages to systematically keep track of interesting information (we'll discuss this in detail in Chapter 4, "Managing Your Bookmarks") And, what's even more important for some people, you can create complete replicas of existing Web sites so that you don't always need to establish a network connection to view information. This is especially useful for online information that doesn't change frequently, such as software documentation and product catalogs; instead of logging on to the network each time you have a question, you can download the entire online manual and all its links to your own system! (Provided, of course, that you have enough disk space.) This isn't a good strategy for sites that are updated frequently, but it's ideal for browsing static information that you only need from time to time.

In Part Five, we'll talk about developing and managing collections of Web documents on your own computer system. Here, we're only going to discuss the basic concepts of local Web pages.

NOTE

Pros and Cons of Local Pages

As one might expect, there are advantages and disadvantages to using the local mode of operation to view Web pages on your own system. The biggest advantages of storing Web pages on your own computer are speed of access and the lack of a need for a network connection.

Obviously, when you're exploring new sites on the Web, you need to use your Internet connection, whether through dialup IP or another connection method. If you make a local copy of information that you need frequently, then you can access the item quickly any time you want. Your computer can directly access information on your hard disk thousands of times faster than it can receive information through a typical SLIP or PPP connection; you'll be amazed at how much faster it is to load a local page than to wait for it to download across the network.

Also important for dialup IP users is that accessing a local page doesn't require you to tie up your telephone line. Even people who connect through a faster, direct network connection can benefit from saving pages locally, as even the best-maintained networks are periodically unavailable due to repair or maintenance.

Saving pages to a local system can be crucial for anyone who plans to make a presentation that includes a demonstration of the World Wide Web. If the documents reside on your computer, then you can guarantee that you can display them anywhere—you don't have to worry about establishing a network connection in a conference room or auditorium or that the site you wish to show may become temporarily unavailable.

NOTE

One disadvantage of using local files only occurs when you make copies of existing Web sites. If the information at the original Web site changes, your files are not modified accordingly. So, saving local copies of a site that publishes industry news or a joke of the day isn't a good idea; although the original site gets updated frequently, your files will only change when you save new versions.

Another disadvantage of local pages is that they can't contain *dynamic elements* such as forms or image maps. We'll talk about static versus dynamic documents in great detail later in the book; the important issue for now is that the most interactive sites on the Web simply won't function if you attempt to save copies as local files.

Accessing a Local File

There are several ways to view a local file. The first and easiest way is to simply open the file by following these steps:

1. From the File menu, select **Open File**....
2. Locate and select the file you wish to open.
3. Click **OK**.

You may also add a local file to your bookmarks or to choose one to serve as your local home page.

NOTE

These topics are discussed at length in later chapters. Brief reviews of these procedures can be found in Appendix A: "Netscape Navigator Quick Reference."

Anatomy of a Local URL

Local URLs look a little bit different from those used to access sites elsewhere on the Internet. Because no Internet protocol is invoked to view files on a local system, the specifier is always *file* followed by a colon and three slashes. In general, local URLs follow this form:

```
file:///drive_name/pathname
```

NOTE Yes, those are three slashes after the colon—the first two slashes are the ones that always follow the type specifier, and the third is the one that would appear after the host name. Since there is no host name identifier for a local file, the three slashes simply appear together.

The way the name of the drive is handled depends on what kind of computer you're using. For Microsoft-based operating systems—that is, any flavor of Windows or Windows 95—the letter for the hard drive name is followed by a | character (on most keyboards, this character is created by pressing **Shift-backslash**). The usual colon can't appear in the pathname of a URL, as it's reserved for use after the type specifier. So, on a PC, the above URL might look like this:

```
file:///C|/pathname
```

Local URLs on the Macintosh

The first time you see a URL on the Macintosh that doesn't conform to the old DOS "8.3" rule (an eight-character name followed by a decimal and a three-character file extension) it may look very strange, with odd characters inserted into the name.

Although the Macintosh lets you create local files containing non-standard characters, URLs cannot contain spaces or punctuation besides the underscore and the decimal. To handle this case, Netscape automatically inserts a **%** sign followed by the ASCII code for the unacceptable character into the string.

For example, although my bookmarks file is located in the drive **Macintosh HD** in the folder **Netscape folder** the local URL for this item is

```
file:///Macintosh%20HD/Netscape%20folder/Bookmarks.html
```

As you can see, **%20** (20 is the ASCII code for a single space) appears in each location where a space appears between words in the pathname.

You'll probably never need to type a local URL, but it's good to be aware of this convention so you don't get worried if you see all kinds of weird characters in the name.

URLs and CGI

Originally, the Web could only display HTML documents and certain kinds of graphics formats, and interactions were limited to viewing documents and downloading files. The development of *CGI* (*Common Gateway Interface*) and support for forms has made it possible to perform more complicated operations such as searching databases.

Even as a Netscape power user, you'll never have to type a URL related to CGI; they're automatically created by the Web site that you're accessing. However, you'll probably see URLs that include CGI information any time you use services that generate information for you based on information that you enter, such as in search engines like Lycos or WebCrawler. After performing a search, the URL of the page that displays your results will contain the parameters—in the case of search engines, the character string or regular expression—that you searched for.

NOTE

More information about the CGI interface can be found in Chapter 17, "Forms, Image Maps and CGI."

What You Learned

After reading this chapter, you should be able to do the following:

- Use intuition to verify URLs that you receive from other sources by evaluating the syntax of the URL for obvious errors in punctuation or spelling and by spotting invalid host names (such as .edv as a top-level domain).

- Glean a great deal of information from a URL, such as what kind of organization it belongs to, whether it is an experimental site, and what kind of materials might reside there.

- Understand the difference between local and remote URLs.

- Make educated guesses about what a site's URL might be, based on the domain name and, if you're looking for a personal home page, the person's user ID.

- Create valid easy-to-remember URLs when constructing your own Web pages.

CHAPTER 3

CUSTOMIZING NETSCAPE'S LOOK AND FEEL

One of the most important and powerful features of the World Wide Web is that you can use your browser to control the way that documents are displayed. This is different from almost all other kinds of media—you have no direct control over the appearance of material in newspapers, books, and magazines, and while you can superficially modify characteristics of a television display such as brightness and contrast, you're not having a significant effect on the amount and kind of information that your set actually receives. Even compared to other forms of electronic communication, such as interactive multimedia delivered via a CD, the amount of control that you have in determining how materials appear in Netscape is remarkable.

The reason for this flexibility is twofold, related both to the nature of Hypertext Markup Language (HTML) as a page markup language, and to Netscape's built-in options for letting you modify the size and appearance of the Netscape screen.

WARNING Because developers of Web sites can't take into account all the ways that a person might configure their browser, documents tend to be based on the default characteristics of Netscape and Mosaic-based browsers. Although there's often good reason to modify the way that pages appear on your screen, you may occasionally find sites that don't read or scan correctly because of the choices that you've made. If you come across a site that appears particularly difficult to read, make sure that it's not a result of your browser configuration before you start cursing the site's Webmaster!

Markup versus Page Description Languages

Much of the flexibility in displaying Web documents is a result of the use of a markup language for creating documents, instead of a page description language. Page description languages, such as PostScript, painstakingly describe the way that each item should appear, regardless of the display device. If a document in a page description language says it should be in a 12-point Palatino font, that's the way that it's always going to appear. The problem with page description languages is that not every display or output device (such as monitors and printers) can necessarily handle what's called for by the document. Because there's no room for flexibility in a page description language, you can either see the document as its creator intended or you can't see it at all.

NOTE Although this sounds very negative, page description languages have a very real and definite use in creating printed output. It's simply not a good system for displaying documents on-screen if you don't know what kinds of platforms the viewers might be using.

Markup languages, on the other hand, take into account the fact that viewers might be using one of any number of combinations of computer platforms and display devices. Markup languages such as HTML, the language used for items on the Web, don't absolutely define how each letter should look on a page. Instead, markup languages use *tags* to identify each element of a document, such as body text, section headings, quotations, etc. As a user, you tell the display mechanism—in this case, your Web browser—how you want each type of item to appear. The Web browser then displays the document based on the choices that you made.

The beauty of this scheme is that you can choose the appearance of certain design elements that work best for you instead of relying on the design choices of the documents' creators—almost all popular graphical Web browsers allow you to change the font, size, and color of most items on the screen. So if you have vision problems and want to use a large font, or if you have red-green color blindness and need to modify your display accordingly, or even if you just like to tweak your display characteristics, you can make Web documents appear however you wish.

NOTE

More information about HTML can be found in Part Five, "Self-Publishing on the Web."

What Netscape Lets You Control

Netscape has built-in features for modifying not only document appearance but also the look and feel of the Netscape screen itself. The following items can all be controlled within Netscape:

- Whether your default home page or a blank page is displayed after launching the application
- Whether the Netscape browser, Netscape Mail, or Netscape News function is displayed by default after launching the application
- Window size and page width
- Text appearance
- Colors and appearance of links, screen, text, and background
- Amount of screen "real estate" allotted to the toolbar, location box, and directory options
- Whether certain information in Web documents (such as images) is displayed at all
- The preferred language for documents you receive

NOTE

In this chapter, the figures will be screen shots of Netscape 3.0 running on the Windows 95 operating system. However, the procedures that you follow will be correct no matter which operating system you're using, and the screens that you see will be very similar, if not exactly the same.

Choosing the Startup Functions

Choosing Default and Startup Pages

When you first launch Netscape, a browser window will be displayed, and Netscape will attempt to connect to the Netscape Communication Corporation's own home page. If you wish, you may choose another home page for your default home page. (You can always reach the Netscape home page by clicking the Netscape logo at the right corner of the browser window, or by selecting **Netscape's Home** from the Directory menu.)

To change the default home page, follow these steps:

1. From the Options menu, select **General Preferences**.... The General Preferences window will be displayed.

2. Click the **Appearance** tab. The Appearance screen will be displayed (Figure 3.1).

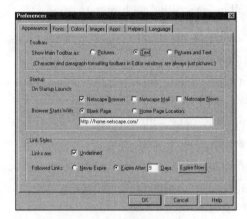

Figure 3.1 The Appearance screen.

3. In the Startup section, locate the **Home Page Location**: field and type the desired URL.

VIRTUOSO

Want to set a local page as your default home page? This is useful if you've got a local page that you use frequently, but, it can be complicated to figure out the URL of a local file. To display the pathname of a local file so you can use it as the default home page use the **Open File** command in the browser to locate and open the file. Then, select and copy the URL that's displayed for the local file in the Location field. You can then go to the Appearance section of General Preferences and paste the URL into the **Home Page Location** field. The next time you launch the browser, the local file will be displayed. You can even use your local Bookmarks file as your default home page—each time you launch the browser or go to your home page, you'll see a formatted page listing your current bookmarks.

Setting the Browser to Launch with a Blank Page

If you've chosen a default home page that is not a local file, Netscape will automatically try to connect to your default home page after launching the application. If you wish, you may set Netscape so that it opens with a blank page instead, so you can use Netscape for local browsing without it attempting to establish a connection. (You can still go to your default home page every time you click the **Home** button on the toolbar.) To set Netscape to show a blank page at startup, click **Blank Page** for the Browser Starts with: item in the Appearances section of General Preferences. To set Netscape to show the default home page, click **Home Page Location** instead.

Displaying Mail or News on Startup

If you wish, you can have Netscape display its Mail or News features on startup instead of a browser. If you choose to display something other than the browser, the settings that you chose for the default home page in the preceding section will come into effect as soon as you open a browser window.

To display Mail or News at startup, click **Netscape Mail** or **Netscape News** at the On Startup Launch item in the Appearance section of General Preferences.

Modifying Window Size and Page Width

By default, Netscape displays pages that are 6.5 inches wide. (This is based on the regular printed paper width of 8.5 inches with a one-inch margin on each side.) Because most color monitors for personal computers display items at 72 or 75 dots per inch, the 6.5 inch document width translates into a default screen width of approximately 480 pixels. (Seventy-five dpi is usually assumed as the display resolution because it's easier to perform arithmetic with round numbers.)

Most monitors have dimensions of at least 640 pixels horizontally and 480 pixels vertically, so the default page width of 480 horizontal pixels means that a certain amount of your monitor screen will be visible to the side of the browser.

The size of the Netscape screen is controlled in the same way as screen size for any other application for the operating system that you use. Use the regular features of your graphical user interface—including closing, zooming, resizing, and scrolling the window—to modify the size and appearance of the screen as needed.

Saving Changes to Screen Size

If you move the screen to a new position or modify its size and would like the new size and position to be the default, perform the appropriate operation:

- For Macintosh and Windows, set the window size, position it as desired, and select **Save Options** from the Options menu.
- For UNIX, invoke Netscape using the command line option

  ```
  -geometry =WxH+X+Y
  ```

  or set the X resource

  ```
  Netscape.TopLevelShell.geometry: =WxH+X+Y
  ```

  where W and H are width and height and X and Y are the location coordinates on the screen in pixels.

Changing the Appearance of Text

As a general rule, browsers let text flow to the right margin of the page, which is defined by how wide you set the screen using the steps in the preceding section. Words wrap automatically at the right margin, so the size of the screen and the size of the font that you choose affect how much text will appear on a line. Figure 3.2 shows a page displayed with the default 12-point Times font, while Figure 3.3 shows the same page displayed in 14-point Times; note how differently the same words appear on the screen.

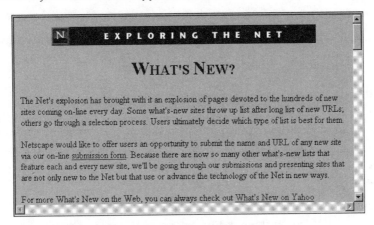

Figure 3.2 Page displayed in default font.

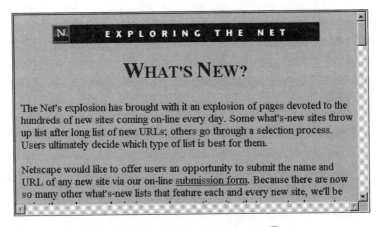

Figure 3.3 Page displayed in 14-point Times.

How Netscape Handles Fonts

Netscape assumes that there are two kinds of text that you'll encounter on the Web: text that requires a font with proportional spacing, such as Times or Palatino, and text that requires a font with fixed spacing, also known as a monospace font, such as Courier or Elite. Figure 3.4 compares the same text displayed in a proportional font and in a fixed font.

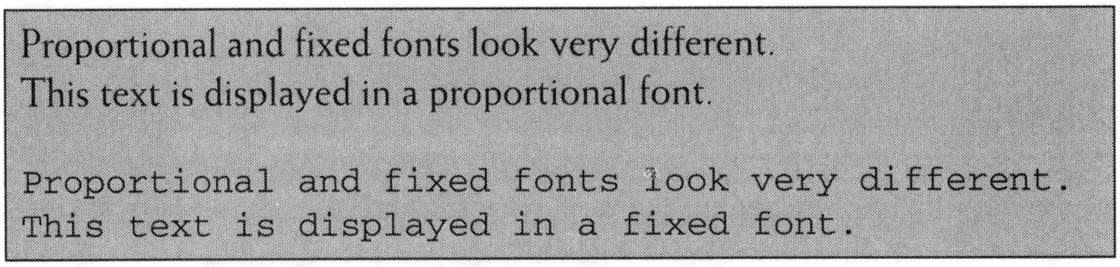

Proportional and fixed fonts look very different.
This text is displayed in a proportional font.

```
Proportional and fixed fonts look very different.
This text is displayed in a fixed font.
```

Figure 3.4 Text in proportional and fixed fonts.

Although proportional fonts are prettier than fixed fonts, fixed fonts are useful when displaying tables and other text that must be formatted in an exact way. Fixed fonts are also often used to note text that is generated by a computer or that you enter in a specific way. And, the fixed font that you choose will be the one used any time you enter information in an online form.

Font choices are modified in the Fonts section of the General Preferences dialog box. Netscape considers each font choice to be part of an *encoding set*. For each encoding set, you can choose the proportional and fixed fonts and the point size that you wish to be displayed. If you're a speaker of English, the "Western/Latin1" encoding set is the only one that you'll modify. Other choices include Japanese, Central European, traditional and simplified Chinese, Korean, Cyrillic, Greek, and user-defined sets (which we'll discuss later).

Here are the general steps for changing the font in Netscape for Macintosh and PC computers:

1. Select the encoding set whose features you're modifying.

2. Choose new fonts for the proportional and fixed fonts, as desired.

3. Make sure that the encoding set you modified is selected as the default document encoding set in the browser's Options menu.

Choosing an Appropriate Font Size

Netscape's default display font on Windows and on the Macintosh is a version of 12-point Times. If you have problems reading the screen or you're just not sitting very close to your monitor, consider changing the default size to 14-point Times or changing the font to a larger font such as Palatino or a similar font on your system. Other 12-point fonts can appear noticeably larger than 12-point Times.

For Windows...

To choose different fonts and point sizes for Windows, follow these steps:

1. From the Options menu, select **General Preferences**.... The Preferences window will be displayed.

2. Click the **Fonts** tab. The Fonts and Encodings options shown in Figure 3.5 will be displayed.

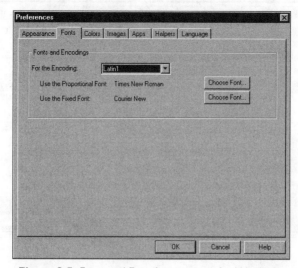

Figure 3.5 Fonts and Encodings options for Windows.

3. In For the Encoding, make sure that **Latin 1** is selected.

4. To select the proportional font, follow these steps:

   a. Select **Choose Font**... to the left of Use the Proportional Font. The Choose Base Font dialog box will be displayed.

   b. In the left column, select the desired font.

   c. In the right column, select the desired point size.

   d. Click **OK**.

5. To select the fixed font, perform the above steps using the items to the left of Use the Fixed Font.

6. To make sure that the encoding set you modified is in use, make sure that **Western (Latin1)** is selected in the Document Encoding item of the Options menu.

For the Macintosh...

To choose different fonts and point sizes for the Macintosh, follow these steps:

1. From the Options menu, select **General Preferences**....

2. Click the **Fonts** tab. The Fonts/Encodings options shown in Figure 3.6 will be displayed.

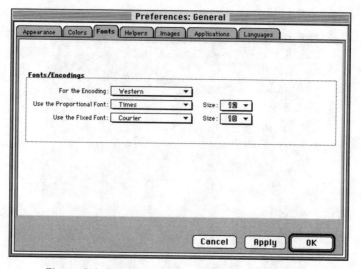

Figure 3.6 Fonts/Encodings options for the Macintosh.

3. In For the Encoding, make sure that **Western** is selected.

4. To set the proportional font, follow these steps:

   a. Hold down the mouse over the pop-up menu next to **Use the Proportional Font** and select the desired font.

   b. Hold down the mouse over the pop-up menu next to **Font size** and select the desired size.

5. To select the fixed font, perform the above steps using the pop-up menu next to **Use the Fixed Font**.

6. To make sure that the encoding set you modified is in use, make sure that **Western (Latin1)** is selected in the Document Encoding item of the Options menu.

Choosing Whether Links are Underlined (All Platforms)

Links to other items will always appear in the color that you choose for followed and unfollowed links (discussed below). By default, Netscape also underlines links to make them even more visible on the page. If you wish, you can turn off this feature so that links are not underlined. To do so, follow these steps:

1. From the Options window, select **General Preferences**...
2. Click the **Appearance** tab.
3. In the "Link Styles" section at the bottom of the screen, select or deselect **Links are Underlined** as desired.

Changing Colors in Netscape

There are four items whose colors you can control in Netscape:

- Links
- Followed links
- Text
- Background (for which you can set a color or a pattern)

VIRTUOSO

On the Macintosh, you can also control the pattern or color that Netscape uses for all items that aren't part of a document (e.g., the toolbar area and scroll bars). You can find information on using this feature in Chapter 7, "Advanced Tips, Tricks, and Shortcuts."

If you haven't changed the default settings, links that you haven't followed appear in blue, while links containing URLs that you have visited appear in purple. (For more information about how Netscape keeps track of the links you've visited, see Chapter 5.) Regular text appears in black, and most backgrounds appear as a pale gray unless a document specifically calls for a custom background.

Backgrounds in Netscape can be a solid color or a pattern of your choice. By default, backgrounds are a light gray color, which you can replace with any color that your computer can display. Even though you may have hundreds, thousands, or even millions of colors to choose from, whatever you select will be displayed as a single solid color throughout the background.

NOTE Your computer's hardware can display a background color choice quickly and efficiently, so there's no performance penalty associated with choosing another color for the background. However, you may experience slower performance if you select a custom background pattern.

Unlike colors, background patterns are small pictures which are replicated or *tiled* to cover the entire area of the background. They can be used to represent all kinds of surfaces, textures, or patinas such as brushed aluminum or Italian marble. Unfortunately, since they're pictures that must be loaded from a graphics file, a fair amount of processor power is required to fill the display screen with these drawings; using custom backgrounds can considerably slow down the speed at which Netscape displays pages.

WARNING Background patterns can make any text that appears on top of them difficult to read; if you use this feature, be sure to pick a pattern that doesn't overpower the rest of the elements of the page.

Some documents may specify certain colors for text and background, while others may not. (This is a choice made by the author of the document.) You can choose whether to let these documents' settings override the ones that you set, or whether your own settings should be used regardless of the authors' intent. If you let the document settings override your choices, documents which specify certain colors will be displayed as the authors intend, while documents that don't contain those specifications will be displayed according to your choices. If you set Netscape to always use your settings, then any specifications set by document authors will be ignored.

NOTE Since most sites don't have extra specifications for colors, and those that do tend to have a good reason for it, we recommend setting Netscape to let the document override your settings if additional information is available. On the other hand, if you have a slow dialup IP connection and frequently find yourself using sites that have slow-to-load custom backgrounds, you might choose the default background color or a custom color instead of a pattern and tell Netscape to always use your own settings.

Modifying Colors

Getting Started

To prepare to modify colors for Netscape follow these steps:

1. From the Options menu, select **General Preferences**.
2. Click the **Colors** tab. The Colors options (Figure 3.7 or 3.8) will be displayed.

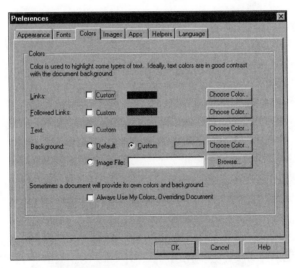

Figure 3.7 Colors options for Windows.

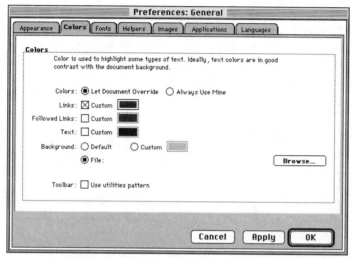

Figure 3.8 Colors options for the Macintosh.

Choosing Whose Colors to Use

On Windows...

If you want to always use your settings regardless of the document, click **Always Use My Colors, Overriding Document** at the bottom of the screen. If you want to let document specifications override your settings as described earlier, make sure that this item is *not* selected.

On the Macintosh...

If you want to always use your settings regardless of the document, locate the Colors: item and click **Always Use Mine**. If you want to let document specifications override your settings as described earlier, click **Let Document Override**.

Changing the Color of Unfollowed Links

To change the default color for links that you haven't followed, follow these steps:

1. To the left of Links, select **Custom** so that a check is displayed.
2. On Windows, click **Choose Color**.... On the Macintosh, simply click the box containing the current color.

   The color selection mechanism for your operating system will be displayed. In Windows, you'll see a box containing the available colors; on the Macintosh, you'll see a color wheel.

3. Select a new color, using the unique color handling capabilities of your operating system.
4. When you've chosen a new color, click **OK**.

When you return to the Colors screen, the new color will be displayed.

NOTE

If you remove the check that you placed in the Custom box, the links will revert to their default setting. However, the custom information that you entered for the color will not be lost; if you reselect the **Custom** option, it will reset to the last custom color that you chose.

Changing the Color of Followed Links

To change the default color for links that you have followed, perform the same steps as described above for changing the color of unfollowed links, except click the items to the left of Followed Links. The same note about deselecting the check box applies.

Changing the Color of Text

To change the default color for all text that appears on the page, perform the same steps as described above for changing the color of unfollowed links, except use the items to the left of Text. The same warning about deselecting the check box applies.

Changing the Background

To use the default gray background, simply select **Default**.

To use a custom color for your background, click **Custom** and select a new color as described above.

To use a custom image file as your background, follow these steps:

1. Select **Image File**. (On the Macintosh, select **File**.)
2. To the right of Image File (or File), click **Browse**.
3. Select the file you wish to use as your custom background.
4. Click **Open**.

NOTE

If the image file you select is smaller than the size of the screen, Netscape will use it as "wallpaper," repeating the graphic in rows until the entire screen is filled.

Controlling Netscape's Graphical Elements

Another significant way to control Netscape's look and feel is in the way that you choose to display the toolbar, the Location field, and the directory buttons.

NOTE

All these items provide useful navigation and management aids. However, keyboard shortcuts and/or menu commands are available for most of these functions. You may find that you can operate effectively without the toolbar, Location field, or directory buttons, in which case you can benefit from the increased amount of space used to display the Web page itself.

NOTE

All of the items in this section require selecting and deselecting items in the Options menu. Any change that you make will only be good for the duration of the session in the open Netscape window where you make the selection. If you want to permanently change any of these settings, select **Save Options** in the Options menu when the items are configured the way you like.

Working with the Toolbar

Changing the Toolbar's Appearance

The toolbar contains a variety of buttons that are used for navigating as you browse the Web. Depending on your wishes, the toolbar can be displayed as text only, as pictures only, or as a combination of pictures and text. Figures 3.9, 3.10, and 3.11 show how the different choices for the toolbar in Netscape for Windows affect the size of the screen available for displaying documents.

Figure 3.9 Toolbar displayed as text.

Figure 3.10 Toolbar displayed as pictures.

Figure 3.11 Toolbar displayed as pictures and text.

As you can see, displaying the toolbar with any kind of pictures takes up the greatest amount of space on the screen. If you want to preserve the greatest amount of display space for an actual document, select **Text**.

NOTE

To modify the display of the toolbar, follow these steps:

1. From the Options menu, select **General Preferences**.

2. Click the **Appearance** tab.

3. In the Toolbars section, locate Show Toolbar as: and select **Pictures**, **Text**, or **Pictures and Text**.

Displaying ToolTips (Macintosh)

On the Macintosh, you can choose to turn on the ToolTips feature. When this feature is turned on, moving the mouse over an item on the toolbar displays a text box containing a description of each button's function (Figure 3.12).

Figure 3.12 ToolTips display information about the item beneath the mouse.

To turn the ToolTips feature on or off, follow these steps:

1. From the Options menu, select **General Preferences**.
2. Click the **Appearance** tab.
3. In the Toolbars section, select or deselect **Show ToolTips**.

ToolTips information is generally limited to a few words that are similiar to the text displayed with the button. So, if you're displaying the toolbar with text or with pictures and text, you probably won't find this feature to be very helpful.

NOTE

Hiding the Toolbar

It's also possible to hide the toolbar entirely, which provides you with even more screen space.

To hide the toolbar, open the Options menu and deselect **Show Toolbar**. If the toolbar is set to be hidden, a check mark will not be displayed next to the item.

To show the toolbar, open the Options menu and select **Show Toolbar**. A check mark will once again be displayed next to the item.

Menu commands and keyboard equivalents for the items in the toolbar can be found in the File, Edit, View, and Go menus.

SHORTCUT

Working with the Location Field

The Location field is an extremely useful tool. Not only does it allow you to see the URL of the current page, but you can circumvent a few steps in opening a new URL to visit by simply typing the new location into the field and pressing **Return**.

VIRTUOSO

This is especially helpful when you want to visit a page that's a few levels higher at your current site. Simply delete the last parts of the pathname and press **Return** to go as many levels up as you specified.

N O T E

You may notice that when you type into the Location field, the label changes to Goto. This is to let you know that Netscape understands that you wish to visit whatever URL that you enter. A little less obvious is why the Location field is sometimes labeled Netsite and other times labeled Location. If the location field says Netsite, it means the displayed page is hosted on a Netscape server. If the field says Location, the displayed page is hosted on a non-Netscape server.

Although it's generally a good idea to keep the Location field visible, you can choose whether to hide or display it.

To hide the Location field, open the Options menu and deselect **Show Location**. If the Location field is set to be hidden, a check mark will not be displayed next to the item.

SHORTCUT

If the Location field is hidden, open a new URL by clicking **Open** on the toolbar, choosing **Open Location...** from the File menu, or using the keyboard command.

To show the Location field, open the Options menu and select **Show Location**. A check mark will once again be displayed next to the item.

Working with Directory Buttons

The directory buttons in Netscape don't provide any additional functionality for navigating the Web. Instead, they're simply links to information maintained by Netscape Communications. Of all the items that you can control through the Options menu, this is the one to consider permanently hiding if you're low on screen space.

To hide the directory buttons, open the Options menu and deselect **Show Directory Buttons**. If the directory buttons are set to be hidden, a check mark will not be displayed next to the item.

Menu selections for the items in the directory buttons can be found in the Directory menu.

SHORTCUT

To show the directory buttons, open the Options menu and select **Show Directory Buttons**. A check mark will once again be displayed next to the item.

Controlling Display of Items in Documents

Netscape lets you control the display of the following items in the browser:

- Whether inline images included in Web documents are automatically displayed on your screen.
- Whether graphics are displayed incrementally while they load, or hidden until they're completely available.
- In Windows and UNIX, you have additional control over how to handle the display of colors that are not in the system's palette.

About Automatic Image Loading

Controlling Image Loading

The **Auto Load Images** item in the Options menu determines whether an image's inline graphics will be interpreted and displayed or whether a placeholder will appear instead. Many sites are so graphics intensive that it can take a minute or more for the pictures to load across a 14.4 or 28.8 Kbps connection when you open a new document. In these cases, you might choose to turn off the automatic loading of images so that only the text related to the site will be displayed.

To turn off automatic image loading, open the Options menu and deselect **Auto Load Images**. When Netscape is set to not automatically load the files, no check mark will appear next to the item.

To turn automatic image loading back on, open the Options menu and select **Auto Load Images**. A check mark will once again be displayed next to the item.

WARNING Most graphics-intensive sites will provide you with some kind of alternate text-only navigational option, or will display text next to the graphics placeholder explaining the contents of the image. Others, however, may not be so enlightened—in the worst case, you may occasionally find yourself at a site where the only navigational possibility is a clickable image map, with no text options whatsoever. If this happens, you'll have to display images in order to navigate through the site. Should this occur, consider sending a politely worded complaint to the site's Webmaster, explaining the problems that you encountered.

Displaying Images without Automatic Loading

If you have automatic image loading turned off, you can still choose to display any or all graphics in a document.

To display all the graphics on a page, click **Images** on the toolbar or select **Load Images** from the View menu. The connection to the site will be reestablished and all the graphics will be downloaded to your machine.

To display an individual graphic on a page, click the placeholder for the graphic. The connection to the site will be reestablished, but only the selected image will be displayed.

About Displaying Images While or After Loading

A final option related to the display of graphics on your screen determines whether graphics are incrementally displayed as you load them, or whether Netscape waits until the entire image is downloaded to your system before placing the picture on the screen.

If you choose to display graphics while they're loading, you can actually see the picture being drawn. Many people prefer to have this "preview" of what they're going to see when the download is finished, which also gives you the chance to cancel the download if you decide you don't want to see that picture after all. (You can always cancel a download by clicking the **Stop** button, but this way you can choose based on the contents of the graphic.) On the other hand, the graphics will download and be drawn on the screen a little bit faster if you choose not to display them until after they're loaded.

To choose when downloaded graphics are displayed, follow these steps:

1. From the Options menu, select **General Preferences**.

2. Click the **Images** tab and locate the Display Images: item in the Images box.

3. To display the graphics while loading, select **While Loading**. To display the images after they've been loaded, select **After Loading**.

Controlling Dithering for Windows and UNIX

Most people's systems can't display every single color that might be called for in a graphic. On Windows and UNIX platforms, you can choose whether Netscape should approximate the called-for color with a process called *dithering*, or whether it should simply use the closest color in the available palette. (Dithering is a process by which dots of different colors are placed close to each other to approximate the appearance of a third color that can't be directly displayed.) If you choose to dither images, they will take a little bit longer to load on computers with slow processors, but the colors will be more like the originals; if you choose to use the nearest color, the images will be displayed quickly but the colors will not be exactly what the author intended.

To choose whether Netscape should dither images or use the closest available color, follow these steps:

1. From the Options menu, select **General Preferences**....

2. Click the **Images** tab and locate the Choosing Colors: item in the Images box.

3. Select one of the following options:

   - To let Netscape attempt to choose the most appropriate image display, select **Automatic**.

   - If you want graphics to appear dithered, select **Dither**.

   - If you want graphics to appear as the closest color available to the system, select **Substitute Colors**.

Setting the Language Preferences

Some Web servers are able to send pages in more than one language, depending on the language preferences of the requesting browser. On Macintosh and Windows, Netscape lets you set a language preference so that if you encounter a multi-language server, you're ensured of receiving pages in the language you request.

To set the languages that you can accept, follow these steps:

1. From the Options menu, select **General Preferences…** and click the **Language** tab. The following screen (Figure 3.13) will be displayed.

2. In the **Language/Region** field, select the language you wish to add to the list.

3. Click the right arrow to add the language. The language will be displayed in the Accept List on the right.

4. Repeat the procedure to add additional languages.

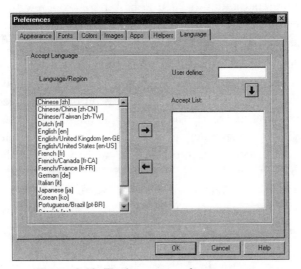

Figure 3.13 The Language preferences screen.

To delete a language from the Accept List, select it and click the left arrow. It will be removed from the list.

SHORTCUT

If you need to use a language code that isn't displayed in the Language/Region field, you can enter the code in the **User define** field and click the down arrow to add it to the Accept List. However, this advanced feature will only work if you define the entry correctly, using a two-letter primary tag that is the ISO 639 language abbreviation and an optional two-letter subtag that defines the ISO 3166 country code. Don't worry if this doesn't make any sense; chances are extremely slim that you'll ever need to do this, since so many common and less-common languages are represented in the Language/Region list.

NOTE

To view foreign-language Web pages, you'll also need to use a version of your operating system that supports the language's character set.

Configuring Netscape for Presentations

How you configure Netscape for personal use is up to you. However, if you're going to be using Netscape to make a group presentation in an office, conference room, or lecture hall, here are a few things to keep in mind to ensure that your presentation will be visible to your audience.

When making presentations, your biggest decision will be how to balance fitting a lot of information on the screen with making sure that the displayed text and pictures are comprehensible to the people in the audience. How to create this balance depends on the display technology that you plan to use. If you're using a high-quality LCD projector or panel, you won't suffer image degradation as a result of the projection system, and you can probably leave the settings any way you wish; for the most part, items that you can read on the screen will be readable on the projector, provided that the audience is fairly close to the display.

However, not everyone has access to such high-end equipment. It's entirely possible that you'll find yourself making a presentation using a scan-rate converter whose output is displayed on a large television monitor or video projector. In this case, it's crucial that you select a font size that's at least 14 or even 18 points.

NOTE

Of course, it goes without saying that any time you plan to make a presentation that uses computers in any way, you should make sure that everything works correctly and is adequately displayed well in advance of the scheduled time. In any given situation, experimentation with the actual equipment is the only way to ensure a good result.

VIRTUOSO

You might notice that projected text often looks "blocky"—the lines of the characters that appear smooth and straight on your screen look choppy when you enlarge them for display. If you're using Windows 95, the optional Plus Pack installation contains a feature that will incorporate font-smoothing techniques (also known as *anti-aliasing*) into all your applications, so text enlarged for display will look as good as it does on a small screen.

What You Learned

After reading this chapter, you should be able to:

- Select appropriate fonts, font sizes, and backgrounds for your viewing needs.
- Hide and display parts of Netscape's navigational system to optimize the amount of screen space available for documents.
- Control how and when images are loaded and displayed.
- Set language preference for multi-language servers.
- Configure Netscape appropriately for presentation purposes.

CHAPTER 4

MANAGING YOUR BOOKMARKS

If you've mastered the basics of navigating the World Wide Web with Netscape, you've discovered the Bookmarks feature, which allows you to save a reference to a frequently visited location so that you can access it with the click of a mouse. But more advanced features, like creating submenus and controlling the location of newly added items in the list, aren't as obvious as the simple Add Bookmark command in the Bookmarks menu. In this chapter, we'll talk about:

- Creating submenus and separators to help organize your bookmarks, and choosing which menus and submenus are visible
- Controlling where new items are placed in your bookmark list
- Exporting organized bookmark lists into HTML files for easy access to large sets of data

Concepts of Bookmark Management

As you gather treasures from various sites on the Web, your bookmark list will grow longer and more disorganized as new items are added to the end of the list. The more items you have on a variety of topics, the harder it is to locate the bookmarks that you're looking for. To handle this problem, Netscape has a built-in, sophisticated mechanism for editing book-marks that's very much like using the file system of your computer—you can add, delete, rename, and move items, and you can search for informa-tion in the entries.

(Of course, you don't have to organize your bookmarks in this way, just like you don't need to create folders or directories for different pro-jects on your hard drive or your filing cabinet; some people are perfectly happy with a long single list of bookmarks in the Bookmarks menu. But it'll be much easier to have frequently used materials at your fingertips if you do organize your bookmarks.)

In addition to its powerful organization capabilities, one of the best (and most underused) features of Netscape's bookmark management sys-tem is the ability to export your bookmark list of favorite locations directly to a fully formatted HTML file. All the information about the bookmarks will be part of the file, including not only the links themselves but also the organized headings and subheadings, and, best of all, any text annotations such as descriptions that you wish to add to any item! This feature allows you to create a completely organized custom home page of your favorite locations without ever touching an HTML editor with your bare hands. (You can also share this file with your friends and co-work-ers.)

The final feature of Netscape's bookmark management system is its ability to import bookmarks from any HTML file, whether it is a book-mark list from another person, a hotlist file created by a Web browser like Mosaic, or even just a Web document that you saved to your hard drive. The bookmark manager identifies every single URL included in the body of the file and adds them to your bookmark list. (If the file was a Netscape bookmark list in the first place, then the organizational structure and comments are even maintained!)

Combined, these features—powerful organization, the capacity to export formatted HTML documents, and the ability to import URLs as links from any other HTML document—make Netscape's bookmark man-ager an effective tool for virtuoso use of the Web.

Components of a Bookmark List

When you create a bookmark, Netscape saves the following information about the item:

- **Name.** The name assigned to the bookmark by default is the <TITLE> tag contents in the original HTML file. If there is no <TITLE> tag, then the URL of the item will be displayed instead. (For more information about HTML tags, see Chapter 21.)

NOTE One exception to this is when the bookmarked file is an untitled index.html file, as discussed in Chapter 2. In this case, the default name for the bookmark is "Index of directory_name," where directory_name is the directory the file is stored in.

Although a bookmark name is automatically assigned, you may change the name if desired.

- **Location.** The URL of an item is automatically saved when you create a bookmark for that page. If necessary, you can modify the URL; this can be useful if the site moves elsewhere but you wish to retain the rest of the information for the bookmark you created.

- **Description.** You can enter up to six lines of descriptive text for each URL. Although this information won't appear in the Bookmarks menu, it will be visible when you export your bookmarks into an HTML file.

- **Last Visited and Added On.** These items display the time and date that the item was added and when it was most recently visited. These dates cannot be modified and are provided for informational purposes only.

Creating and Modifying Bookmarks

Creating a Bookmark

When you're at a page that you wish to bookmark so you can return to it later, select **Add Bookmark** from the Bookmark menu. Later in this chapter, we'll discuss how to control where the item appears in your bookmark list.

Displaying and Modifying Bookmarks

To display and modify information about bookmarks, follow these steps:

1. From the Window menu, select **Bookmarks**. The Bookmarks window will be displayed, showing the directory structure of your bookmarks file (Figure 4.1).

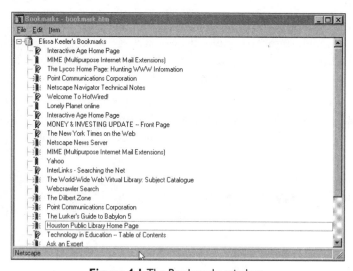

Figure 4.1 The Bookmarks window.

If you're using a Macintosh and your screen looks significantly different, then you're using an older version of Netscape. In Netscape 2.0 and later releases, the Bookmarks window should look similiar to this.

NOTE

2. Select the bookmark whose information you wish to view.

3. In the Item menu, select **Properties**....The Bookmark Properties window (Figure 4.2) will be displayed.

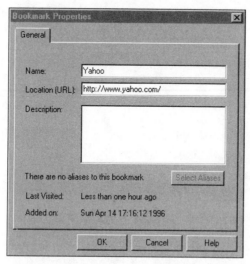

Figure 4.2 The Bookmark Properties window.

4. Modify any information as desired.

5. To return to the Bookmarks window, click **OK**.

6. When you're finished viewing or changing information, close the Bookmarks window to return to the browser, or click in the browser window to bring the browser back to the foreground.

Deleting Bookmarks

To delete an item from the bookmark list, follow these steps:

1. At the Bookmarks window, select the item you wish to remove.

2. From the Edit menu, select **Delete**.

Searching a List of Bookmarks

If you have a substantial number of bookmarks, you may find it difficult to find the item that you're looking for in the list. Netscape allows you to search the bookmarked items for character strings that you identify.

For Windows...

To search for a bookmark in Windows, follow these steps:

1. In the Bookmarks window, select **Find...** from the Edit menu. The Search Headers window will be displayed (Figure 4.3).

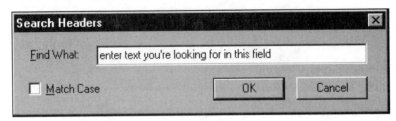

Figure 4.3 The Search Headers window.

2. In the **Find what:** field, type the word or a few letters of the word you're looking for.

NOTE

Despite the name of the window, Netscape does search more than the text of the headers.

3. To limit your search to items that exactly match the capitalization pattern of the text you entered, select **Match Case**.

4. Click **OK**. The next bookmark in the list containing that character string will be highlighted. (If the string is contained in the URL or the description and not in the name of the bookmark, you'll have to display the bookmark's properties to see why it was selected.)

If no items are found containing the string, the "Not Found!" message will be displayed.

5. To locate the next item containing the character string, select **Find Again** from the Edit menu, or press **F3** on the keyboard.

For Macintosh and UNIX...

To search for a bookmark, follow these steps:

1. At the Bookmarks window, select **Find...** from the Edit menu. The Find Bookmark window will be displayed (Figure 4.4).

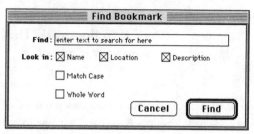

Figure 4.4 The Find Bookmark window.

2. In the **Find:** field, enter the word or a few characters of the word that you're looking for.

3. On the next line, select **Name** to search the names of the bookmarks as displayed in the Bookmark window; select **Location** to search the URLs of the bookmarks; or select **Description** to search the contents of the Description fields. You may choose any or all of these settings; however, you must select at least one.

4. To limit your search to items that exactly match the capitalization pattern of the text you entered, select **Match Case**.

5. To limit your search to items that exactly match the text you entered, select **Match Word**. For example, if you're searching for the word "shock," selecting this option will find bookmarks for "The Shock Me Home Page" but not for "The Shockwave Plug-In Center."

6. Click **Find**. The next bookmark in the list that meets your search criteria will be highlighted. If no bookmarks are found that match your criteria, the "Not Found" message will be displayed.

7. To locate the next item containing the character string, select **Find Again** from the Edit window.

Navigating at the Bookmarks Window

When the Bookmarks window is displayed, you can go directly to a book-marked location without returning to the browser window. To do so, follow these steps.

1. At the Bookmarks window, select the bookmark.
2. From the Item menu, select **Go to Bookmark**. The bookmarked loca-tion will be displayed in the browser window.

To open the the URL, you can also double-click the name of the bookmark in the list; drag the bookmark from the Bookmarks window to any location in the main browser; or easiest of all, just select the bookmark and press **Return**.

VIRTUOSO

Organizing Your Bookmark List

If you're like most people, you surf the Web looking for all kinds of differ-ent information, ranging from current events to professional and business news to technical innovations to leisure time hobbies. After only a few additions, your bookmark list can turn into a confused jumble! For exam-ple, after a few sessions of adding bookmarks for the information I found about travel resources and computer industry developments, my book-mark list was a mess, especially considering the number of other resources I'd marked, like search engines that I use frequently and entertainment items like comic strips. Figure 4.5 shows the unorganized, confused list of all the bookmarks I'd assembled.

Figure 4.5 Messy Bookmarks menu.

Luckily, Netscape provides some very powerful ways of organizing your bookmarks. You can rearrange the order of items in your list so that similar bookmarks appear together. You can use separator lines to further delineate differences in sections. And, you can create submenus of items within the Bookmarks menu so that related bookmarks appear grouped under the same heading, furthering organization and saving space on the screen.

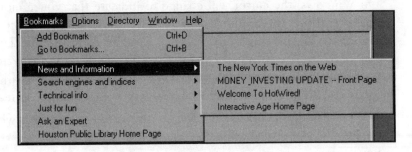

Figure 4.6 Organized Bookmarks menu.

Rearranging the Order of Bookmarks

When you first create a list of bookmarks, new items are simply added to the list. (We'll talk about controlling the location of new items a little later in this chapter.) It's likely that you'll want to rearrange the list so that similar items are grouped together.

If you haven't modified any settings yet, the Bookmarks window displays the bookmarks as "children" of the top-most Bookmarks folder. (If you've entered information about yourself in Mail and News Preferences, then the top-most Bookmarks folder will display the name you entered: e.g., "Elissa Keeler's Bookmarks."

There are two ways to move a bookmark in the window: by dragging the item to the desired location, or by cutting and pasting the bookmark.

Dragging Bookmarks to a New Location

To drag a bookmark to a new location, follow these steps:

1. Select the bookmark you wish to move.
2. On Windows, hold down the left mouse button. On the Macintosh, simply hold down the mouse button.
3. Keep the button held down as you begin to move the mouse.

   On Windows, the cursor will change to indicate that you're moving an item. Move the mouse so that the item you wish to place the bookmark after is highlighted. For example, to move the "Lycos Home Page" bookmark after the "Point Communications Corporation" bookmark, drag the "Lycos Home Page" bookmark on top of the Point Communications bookmark so that it's highlighted.

   On the Macintosh, a black line will be displayed that indicates where the item will be placed when you release the mouse.
4. When the item is located in the correct new location as described above, release the mouse. The item will appear in its new location.

Pasting Bookmarks in a New Location

To move a bookmark by cutting or copying and pasting into a new location, follow these steps:

1. Select the bookmark you wish to move.

2. From the Edit menu, select **Cut** or **Copy**.

3. Select the bookmark that appears *above* the location where you want to place the item.

4. From the Edit menu, select **Paste**. The bookmark will be placed after the item you selected.

To place an item at the top level of a Bookmarks folder, select the folder and then select **Paste**.

N O T E

Working with Submenus

Submenus allow you to place the items in your bookmark list into different categories. When you display the Bookmarks menu, the headings of the submenus appear so that you don't have to scroll through several unrelated bookmarks to find the one you want to use. For example, back in Figure 4.6, we chose to place links to the Yahoo and Tradewave Galaxy indices and the Lycos and WebCrawler search engines within a single submenu item called "Web Resources." This way, we can find them easily when we want them, without using up valuable space. While a menu of 20 items is difficult to scroll through, a menu containing just five submenus, each with only four items, is simple!

You can have multiple levels of submenus—in other words, you can have menus nested within menus nested within other menus, in the same way that you can nest directories or folders within other directories or folders on your hard drive.

An exception to this is the Macintosh, which allows you to create as many sub-menus as you want, but will only display up to five.

NOTE

It's up to you to decide how many submenus you want to have; keep in mind that multiple submenus can be as hard to navigate as a very long list of bookmarks.

Also keep in mind that it's not necessary to place every single bookmark within a submenu! If you have items which aren't assigned to a submenu, they'll appear at the first level of the Bookmarks menu along with the names of the submenus.

NOTE

In Netscape, the item that defines a submenu is called a folder. Folders can have names and descriptions like bookmark entries, and are moved in the same way. However, folders don't contain URLs, so they can't be used to navigate the Web.

Creating Submenus

The Bookmarks window shows all items in the bookmark list in a hierarchical structure similar to the file system of your personal computer's operating system. Submenus appear as folders in the window. The top level of the hierarchy is your Bookmarks folder, which contains all Bookmarks menu items. Items that appear as children of a submenu will be indented beneath the submenu's folder; items will appear as elements of the submenu in the Bookmarks menu of the browser. Items whose parent is the top-level Bookmarks folder will appear at the first level in the Bookmarks menu.

In the Bookmarks window in Windows, the line to the left of each item links the item to its parent header, so it's easy to follow the organizational structure of your bookmarks.

NOTE

To create submenus, follow these steps:

1. Select the item above the location where you wish to place the new header. If you want the header to appear as the first item in your Bookmarks menu, select the top-level Bookmarks folder. If you want the menu to appear as a subitem of another menu, select the folder for the menu where you wish to place the new item.

2. In the Item menu, select **Insert Folder**.... The Bookmark Properties window (Figure 4.7) will be displayed with the default name New Folder.

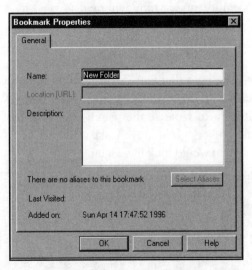

Figure 4.7 Bookmark Properties window for new folder.

3. Enter a new name for the folder. If desired, enter a description as well.

4. Click **OK** to return to the Bookmarks window. The new folder will be added beneath the item you selected.

Adding Items to Submenus

To move items into submenus, follow the same steps as for moving items in general. You can drag items into a submenu or cut/copy and paste them there. Bookmarks located within a submenu will appear as children of the folder. When you return to the browser, the menu will display the submenus you created containing the items you added.

Deleting Submenus

To delete a submenu and all of its contents, follow these steps:

1. Select the item you wish to remove.

2. From the Edit menu, select **Delete**. A warning message will make sure that you really want to delete all the contents of the item. (If the submenu was empty, no warning will be displayed.)

Creating Separators

Separators are plain lines that you can place anywhere in your Bookmarks file to act as visual aids to organization. For example, in my Web Resources submenu, I might want to separate the search engines (WebCrawler and Lycos) from the subject indices (Tradewave Galaxy and Yahoo). After adding a separator, the menu item would look like Figure 4.8.

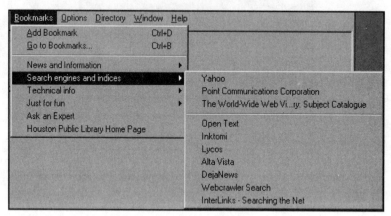

Figure 4.8 Use of a separator.

Separators can appear anywhere in a bookmark list, including bookmarks, headers, and submenu items.

To create a separator, follow these steps:

1. Select the item above the location where you wish the separator to appear.
2. In the Item menu, select **Insert Separator**. A new separator (Figure 4.9) will be displayed beneath the selected item.

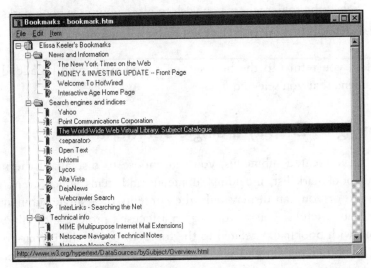

Figure 4.9 Newly created separator.

You can cut, copy, paste, move, and delete the separator like any other item.

Controlling the Bookmarks Menu

To further enhance your use of bookmarks, Netscape allows control of two additional items: which submenus are displayed in the Bookmarks menu, and where new bookmarks are added in the list.

Choosing Where New Bookmarks are Added

Netscape lets you choose a submenu in which to place new bookmarks. If you're searching for information on a certain topic, you can create a header for that material and ensure that all new bookmarks are added directly to that submenu. This saves you the time of reorganizing the items into their correct locations.

To choose which submenu will contain new bookmarks, follow these steps at the Bookmarks window:

1. Select the folder where you wish to place your new bookmarks.
2. From the Item menu, select **Set to New Bookmarks Folder**.

When you return to the browser, new bookmarks will be added to the submenu that you selected.

Choosing to Display a Single Submenu

If you've created submenus, you can choose to display all the items in your bookmark list, including submenus and items which aren't in submenus, or you can display only the contents of a single submenu. This might be useful if you're working on a focused project and only want to work with bookmarks related to the topic, or if you share your computer with another person and you wish to keep your bookmark information separate. It's also useful for demonstrations, where you might not want a large group of people to see the bookmarks that you create for personal enjoyment!

 When you display only the contents of a submenu, the items appear in the Bookmarks menu as individual listings. The heading for the submenu will not be visible.

NOTE

To display only the contents of a single submenu in the Bookmarks menu, follow these steps at the Bookmarks window:

1. At the Bookmarks window, select the folder whose contents you wish to display in the Bookmarks menu.
2. From the Item menu, select **Set to Bookmark Menu Folder**.

When you return to the browser, only the items in the selected submenu will be displayed in the Bookmarks menu.

NOTE

If you set an empty folder as the Bookmark Menu folder, nothing will be displayed in the Bookmarks menu.

WARNING

Displaying a single submenu in the Bookmarks menu doesn't affect the settings for where new bookmarks are added. No matter what submenu is displayed in the browser, new bookmarks will always be added to the folder that you selected at the New Bookmarks folder.

If you wish to display all the items in the bookmark list in the menu again, set the top-level folder in the Bookmarks menu as the Bookmark Menu folder.

Checking Your Bookmarks

The good news is that by now you probably have a menu full of bookmarks to all kinds of fascinating or useful places. The bad news is, you couldn't possibly visit all of them every day to see if new information has been added. Netscape takes care of this problem with its "What's New?" feature, which performs a quick check of all your bookmarked sites and lets you know which ones have new information, which ones are the same, and which ones are not accessible at the current URL for the site.

To check your bookmarks, follow these steps:

1. Make sure that the Bookmarks window is displayed.

2. If you wish to check only a set of bookmarks, select the desired set.

3. From the File menu of the Bookmarks window, select **What's New?** The What's New? dialog box will be displayed (Figure 4.10).

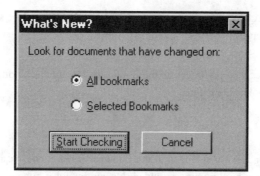

Figure 4.10 The What's New? dialog box.

4. If you selected a set of bookmarks in step 2, click **Selected Bookmarks**. (The default setting is to check all bookmarks, whether you selected a set of bookmarks or not.)

5. Click **Start Checking**. Netscape will attempt to connect to each site to determine if the site is still available and if the information has changed.

If a site has changed, emphasis marks will appear around the icon for the bookmark. If a site cannot be reached, a question mark will be displayed with the icon.

N O T E This feature doesn't make repeated attempts to contact a site, and it times out quickly to go on to the next bookmark, so it's not foolproof; it may mark a site as not being reachable when it simply takes a long time to connect. It will also report that a site has changed if the advertising banner displayed on the site has changed. Since many sites constantly change the displayed advertising, you may find that you never get a good answer about whether the information you're interested in has been updated.

Working with HTML Files of Bookmarks

Netscape provides an elegantly simple mechanism to turn your bookmarks file into a fully formatted HTML document, and to import other bookmark files into Netscape. You can use these features for a variety of reasons, including:

- Easily creating a customized home page containing all the links that you want quick access to. When your bookmark list contains several items, it can be much easier to click text that appears on a page than to try to select the right item from a menu! As an added bonus, any information that you typed into the description field is displayed with each item.

- Share your personal list of bookmarks with your friends! HTML files are platform-independent, so you can give the file to users of any Web browser on any kind of computer.

- If you use Netscape at home and at the office, you can make sure that both locations have the same set of bookmarks.

With a few simple mouse clicks, the bookmark file we've used in the examples so far becomes this document (Figure 4.11).

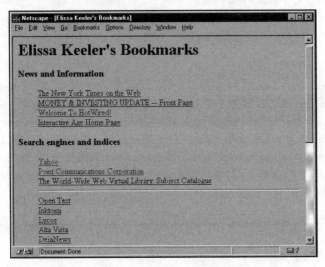

Figure 4.11 Bookmarks file viewed in Netscape.

Any information that you typed in the Description field will be visible on the page when you view your bookmarks.

NOTE

Viewing and Creating HTML Files of Bookmarks

When you create bookmarks with the **Add Bookmark...** command or make changes to your bookmarks as described earlier in the chapter, you're actually creating an HTML file without even knowing it. On the PC, this file is called **bookmark.htm**, and it's stored in the same folder as Netscape. On the Macintosh, the file is called **Bookmarks.html**, stored in System Folder/Preferences/Netscape. On UNIX, the file is **bookmarks.html**, stored in the .netscape directory in your home directory.

VIRTUOSO

Want to use your bookmark list as your home page? Use the **Open File...** command to locate the bookmark file on your system. Then, copy the URL for the file from the Location field (the URL should begin with **file:///**.) At the Options menu, select **General Preferences**, click the **Appearance** tab, and paste the URL for the bookmark file into the **Home Page Location** field. Every time you display your home page, the current list of bookmarks will be shown.

VIRTUOSO

And here's another bookmark strategy to consider if you have a list of bookmarks that you like and use especially frequently. Save the bookmarks as a custom HTML document that you assign to be your new home page using the procedures in the preceding Virtuoso tip. Then, delete all those items from your bookmark list. All the information is saved on an organized home page, and the list displayed in the Bookmarks menu is cleaned out so that you can easily locate new items that you add.

To save your bookmarks as a separate HTML file, follow these steps:

1. In the Bookmarks window, select **Save As...**from the File menu. (On the Macintosh, select **Save Bookmark File As...**). A dialog box for saving the bookmarks file will be displayed.

2. If you wish to save the file somewhere other than the Netscape folder, such as on a diskette, identify the location where you wish to store the file.

3. In the **File name** field, type a new name for the file you're creating. It's strongly recommended that you append .htm or .html to the name of the file so that it is readily identified as an HTML file.

In Windows, do not change the information in the **Save as type** field.

NOTE

4. Click **Save**. The file will be saved to the location you specified. You can now use it as your default home page or share it with your friends.

Importing Bookmarks and Other HTML Files

Netscape lets you add bookmarks to your existing list by importing any HTML document. When you import such a document, Netscape identifies all the URLs in the source document and adds them directly to the bottom of your bookmark list! This feature is useful if:

- You were given a hotlist or bookmark list by another person.
- You use Netscape on two computers and want to keep your bookmark lists in synch. (Because HTML is plain text and platform-independent, you can even transfer bookmarks between different kinds of computers.)

If you switch between Macintoshes and PCs, you may find that only the bookmarks in the first level of hierarchy are imported. If this occurs, use a text utility to add special line feed characters to the bookmark file, which will solve the problem.

WARNING

- You come across a page of URLs so good that you want to add them all to your list quickly, without visiting each location and adding them separately.

NOTE

As an added bonus, if you import a Netscape bookmark file, the description information for the bookmark is retained when it's added to your file!

SHORTCUT

If you've been using another browser like Mosaic, your hotlist files are not in HTML. Luckily, you can use a bookmark conversion program to turn those hotlists into Netscape-readable HTML. For the Macintosh, retrieve the HHConv Hypercard stack from http://www.interport.net/~laronson/HHConv.html. For Windows, Netscape provides the unsupported program Mozilize, available at ftp://ftp.netscape.com/unsupported/windows/oze.exe. For UNIX, use the "hot-convert" shell script that came with Netscape. (It should be in the same directory as the application. If you can't find it, you can retrieve it from http://home.netscape.com/people/jwz/hot-convert.)

To import a bookmark file, follow these steps:

1. In the Bookmarks window, select **Import**... from the File menu. (On the Macintosh, select **Import Bookmarks**....)

2. Locate and select the file containing URLs that you wish to import to your bookmark list.

3. Click **Open**.

What You Learned

After reading this chapter, you should be able to:

- Create bookmarks.
- Rename, reorder, and enter descriptions for items in your bookmark list.
- Create submenus and separators for your bookmark list.
- Choose which items are displayed in the Bookmarks menu.
- Control the location in the list where new bookmarks are added.
- Turn your bookmarks file into a formatted, custom HTML document without ever touching an HTML editor.
- Import and export HTML files of bookmarks.

CHAPTER 5

NETSCAPE REMEMBERS: LINK HISTORY AND CACHE MANAGEMENT

Some of Netscape's most powerful and least understood features deal with the way that it keeps track of places that you've visited, from the impermanent storage of followed links in the Go menu to the volatile memory cache to the more permanent history files and disk caches. Before delving into these topics in depth, let's review some basic terminology for these concepts:

- The *history list* is a list of URLs that you visited in a single session. The history list is automatically created for you as you navigate the Web and is displayed in the Go menu.

- *Followed links* (or visited links) are links to pages that you've visited during earlier Netscape sessions. In Chapter 3, we talked about changing the color of followed links. In this chapter, we'll talk about controlling when the links appear as followed and when they don't.

- *Cache memory* is a general computing technique for improving speed so that documents are retrieved as quickly as possible. (You may be using a RAM cache on your computer right now.) For Web browsers, knowledgeable use of the memory and disk caches can greatly improve performance.

About the Go Menu's History List

Because NCSA Mosaic (the first popular graphical World Wide Web browser) used a menu titled History to keep track of the links visited during a session, the items in Netscape's Go menu are referred to as a "history list." The way that Netscape chooses to display items in the Go menu isn't always clear; sometimes you'll have several items in the list, and then after one click you'll have only two!

Here's how the Go menu and history list work. Every single link that you visit is added sequentially to the history list, which is displayed in the menu. As long as you keep visiting new locations, every item you've displayed appears in the menu.

However, the history list gets complicated when you start using the Back button or selecting items in the Go menu to review documents that you recently saw. (If you look at the Go menu after using the **Back** button, you'll see that all the items you've visited are displayed, but the selection mark showing which document you're currently viewing is not at the bottom of the list.) Using the **Back** and **Forward** buttons or selecting a document from the Go menu doesn't immediately change the history list, so you can keep visiting items in the history list without changing things.

But if you revisit a page in your history list, and then branch off from the history list by clicking a link appearing on that page, all the items that appeared in the history list beneath the link you branched off from will be removed from the history list.

SHORTCUT

Want to see the URL of a page you visited recently without going back? In the Window menu, select **History**. A window will be displayed containing the names and URLs of all the items in the history list. You can select an item and go there directly by clicking the **Go to** button, or you can create a bookmark without returning to the page by selecting the item and clicking the **Create Bookmark** button (on Macintosh and UNIX it's the **Add to Bookmarks** button).

NOTE

Don't get the **Back** button on the toolbar confused with the **Back** buttons or links that you sometimes see in documents. The toolbar button retraces your personal path, taking you back through the items in the Go menu; where you end up depends on the items you visited recently. However, a **Back** button or link in a document is static and is designed to help you navigate at specific Web sites—the author will have linked it to one particular place, usually a higher level in the hierarchy.

WARNING

The information about the **Back** and **Forward** buttons in this section is only related to navigation between different Web pages; if you're navigating within frames (a special way that developers control the display of information on a single Web page), you'll need to use different commands. Complete information on working with frames can be found in Chapter 6.

About Link History

Link history is the mechanism that keeps track of the places you've visited on the Web. Links in a document are color-coded to let you know whether you've already visited the location. (We talked about setting the color of followed links in Chapter 3.)

Because link history keeps track of all URLs that you visit, you'll know whether or not you've visited a site even if you've never seen the current document containing the link before. This is helpful when authors provide links to other sites but place different text in the link; the URL is the same, but the wording of the link may be different. Even if you've never seen the words before, you'll know that you've visited the site because the text appears in a different color. (If you haven't changed the default settings, unfollowed links appear blue and followed links appear purple.)

For example, I recently searched for information about Thailand, which led me to Lonely Planet Publication's home page, among other locations. Later that day, I visited a document containing a link that said "click here for travel information about Thailand," which happened to be a link to the Lonely Planet information. Because I'd already visited that site, this link appeared in a different color, and I knew that I wasn't going to find any new information by following the link. However, I wouldn't necessarily have known that I'd seen the site just from the way that it was described or from looking at the URL, considering how many URLs might be visited in a search for information!

Netscape keeps track of all the links that you visit by storing the URL, along with time stamp information, in a separate file. For Windows, the **netscape.hst** file is located in the same directory as the Netscape application. On the Macintosh, the **Global History** file is in System Folder/Preferences/Netscape Preferences. On UNIX platforms, the **history.db** file is stored in the .netscape directory in your home directory. 4Unless you specifically issue the command to wipe out the information in the file (we'll talk about this in a moment), information about every link you've ever visited will be retained forever.

VIRTUOSO

Interested in finding the link for a site that you're sure you visited recently? In the Location field, type **about:global** and press **Return**. The URL and visitation date of each item in your Global History file will be displayed in the browser window.

Netscape lets you set an *expiration date* for followed links; this expiration date controls whether links appear as followed or unfollowed. For example, if followed links are set to expire in 15 days and you haven't visited a URL for longer than that, links to that URL will appear as if you haven't followed them. You can change the number of days that pass before links expire; because all link information is stored, you can easily go from showing only links that you visited yesterday as followed to showing all links that you ever visited as followed!

To change the expiration date for followed links on all platforms, follow these steps:

1. From the Options menu, select **General Preferences**....

2. Click the **Appearance** tab and locate the Followed Links: item in the Link Styles box.

3 If you want to change the number of days after which the links appear as unfollowed, select **After** and enter the desired number of days into the field. (For Windows, select **Expire After**.)

If you want all links that you've visited since the last time the history list was cleared (see below) to appear as "followed," select **Never**. (For Windows, select **Never Expire**.)

NOTE

Again, remember that as long as you don't clear the history list, you can change the amount of time before expiration with impunity! You can show every link you've ever visited or only the links that you visited today.

WARNING

However useful the link expiration feature is, keep in mind that the file containing your link history will grow and grow; its potential size is only limited by your storage capacity. Even if you set links to expire after only a few days, the information about the links will still be stored in the file! The *only* way to completely clear out the file is to expire all the links at once. If storage space is tight, you may need to do this frequently.

To clear out the global history list on all platforms, follow these steps:

1. From the Options menu, select **General Preferences...**.
2. Click the **Appearance** tab and locate the Followed Links: item in the Link Styles box.
3. Click **Expire Now**. (For the Macintosh, click **Now**.) The history list will be completely cleared.

WARNING

This action is irrevocable. Once the information has been cleared, it cannot be recovered.

One last thing to keep in mind about followed links: the link history file only keeps track of URLs that you visited, not the information that the sites contain. It's entirely possible that a link will appear as followed even though the site contains different information from the last time that you visited. For example, news services that are updated daily or weekly will almost always contain new information, though the links to the site appear as followed. Use your judgment and common sense in determining when it's worth revisiting a site.

About Memory and Disk Caches

You might have noticed that when you return to documents that you've visited recently, they tend to display more quickly than when you accessed them the first time. After a document is acquired from the network, Netscape stores it in a *cache* (pronounced cash) on your local system. When you return to the document, Netscape retrieves the document from the local cache instead of from the network. Since the interface between your computer and disk drive is much faster than the connection between your computer and the network (especially if you're using dialup IP with a 14.4 or 28.8 Kbps modem), the document will be displayed much more quickly.

There are two kinds of caching in Netscape—*memory caching*, in which the most recently accessed documents are stored in RAM, and *disk caching*, in which documents are stored in a group of files that can be as large as the amount of free space available on your disk drive. Figure 5.1 shows the relationship between Netscape, the memory cache, the disk cache, and the Web site where the original information is stored.

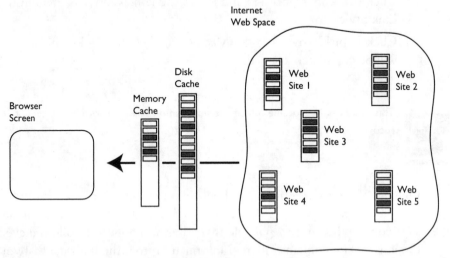

Figure 5.1 How caching works.

When you request a document, Netscape first checks to see if it's available in the memory cache. If the document is in the memory cache, Netscape then checks the time stamp of the document at the original site to see if the information in the document has changed. (We'll talk about how Netscape works with time stamps later in this chapter.) This is the fastest place to retrieve a document from. However, memory cache is volatile—it's not saved from session to session—and it usually can't be very large, unless you have an exorbitant amount of free memory on your system.

If the document isn't available in the memory cache, Netscape then checks the disk cache. If the object is there, Netscape establishes a network connection to check the time stamp of the original document. If a newer version is there, then the most recent document is downloaded; if the item in the cache is current, then the cached item is displayed. If the document isn't stored in either cache, then the item is retrieved from the server. As soon as a document is retrieved from the server, it's placed in both the memory cache and the disk cache.

The disk cache is a series of documents, each containing one object that Netscape has displayed. (An object can be an HTML file or a graphic element.) On Windows, the default location for disk cache files is the Cache folder in the Navigator directory. On the Macintosh, the default location is the Cache folder in Netscape's Preferences folder (in the System folder). On UNIX systems, the default disk cache directory is the cache directory in the .netscape directoy of your home directory.

VIRTUOSO

If you want, you can specify a different location for the cache file. For example, if you have an external hard drive which has 40 megabytes of free space, you could choose that as the default location for your disk cache and have huge amounts of storage allocated to caching your favorite Web documents. However, this may slow down the time it takes to quit Netscape; we'll talk about this a little later.

Wherever your cache files are stored, the folder or directory will contain several items with cryptic names (Figure 5.2).

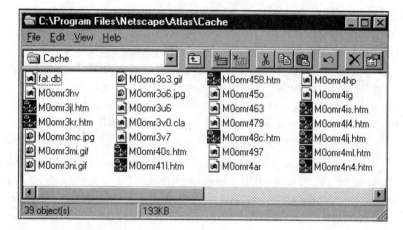

Figure 5.2 The cryptic contents of a disk cache directory.

These oddly named files are actually cached documents! As an experiment, use the **Open File...** command to view one of these files. Netscape will display a page that you visited in the past. (At the end of the chapter, we'll talk about how to use this feature to find lost URLs or to retrieve graphics.)

Changing Caching Information

Netscape lets you specify the size of the memory cache and the size and location of the disk cache.

Getting Started: All Platforms

No matter what kind of computer you're using, follow these steps to get started:

1. From the Options menu, select **Network Preferences....**
2. Click the **Cache** tab.

Modifying Cache Sizes

In general, you'll probably get by just fine with Netscape's default cache sizes, displayed in Table 5.1.

Table 5.1 Netscape's Default Cache Sizes

Platform	Default memory cache	Default disk cache
Windows	1024K	5000K
Macintosh	~500K (difference between suggested and minimum RAM allocation at Finder)	1 MB
UNIX	3000K	5000K

You can set your disk cache to be as large as you want, bearing in mind that the cache will grow to be as large as you allow it. Generally, something between 2000 kilobytes and 5000 kilobytes is sufficient to ensure that documents you've seen recently can be accessed quickly.

WARNING The larger your disk cache, the more time Netscape may need to "clean up" your cache when you quit the application. If the cache maintenance feature causes you more delay in closing the application than you want to deal with, set the disk cache to a smaller size.

Likewise, you can set the size of your memory cache to be the largest amount of memory that your system usually has free, but keep in mind that the more memory you let Netscape use, the greater the chance of affecting the performance of other applications that you are running simultaneously. If you're lucky enough to have a computer with a lot of RAM, you can set your memory cache as high as four or five megabytes and revisit documents in a session very quickly, without affecting other applications or being hindered by the disk cache management process when you quit Netscape.

For Windows and UNIX...

To change the sizes of your caches, follow these steps:

1. To change the size of the memory cache, type the new number (in kilobytes) in the **Memory Cache:** field.

2. To change the size of your disk cache, type the new number (in kilobytes) in the **Disk Cache:** field.

For Macintosh...

Changing the Memory Allocation

If you're using a Macintosh, the size of the memory cache is not controlled within Netscape; instead, you modify the amount of RAM allocated to the application in Netscape's Get Info window at the Finder. To display the Get Info window, follow these steps:

1. At the Finder, locate and select the icon for the **Netscape** application.

2. Press **Command-I** or select **Get Info** from the File menu. Netscape's Get Info window (Figure 5.3) will be displayed.

When you display the Get Info window, you'll see three boxes in the lower-right corner: Suggested size, Minimum size, and Preferred size. The Suggested size is the amount of RAM suggested by the application's developers. The Minimum size is the smallest amount of RAM required by the application to launch; if you reduce this number, you probably won't be able to launch the application. The Preferred size contains the amount of RAM that Netscape will use, if available.

Figure 5.3 Netscape's Get Info window.

NOTE

The size of your RAM cache is approximately equal to the difference between the Preferred size and the Minimum size. If you increase the Preferred size, you increase your RAM cache accordingly.

To change the allocation of RAM to the applications, enter a higher number in the **Preferred size** box. To determine how much free RAM is available, launch all the applications you typically like to have running, and then select **About this Macintosh...** from the Apple menu at the Finder. If you use Virtual Memory, turn it off before starting this procedure. And remember, you can't assign more memory to an application than is physically installed on your computer.

Changing the Size of the Disk Cache

To change the size of the disk cache on Netscape for the Macintosh, click the **Up** arrow or **Down** arrow next to **Cache Size:** to change the number of megabytes allotted to the disk cache.

Changing the Location of the Disk Cache

For Windows and UNIX...

To change the default location for the disk cache, type the name of the new directory into the **Disk Cache Directory** field.

For Macintosh...

To change the default location for the disk cache, follow these steps:

1. Click the **Browse** button to the right of the cache directory name. A dialog box similar to Figure 5.4 will be displayed.

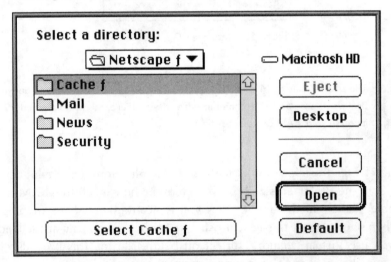

Figure 5.4 Dialog box to select disk cache directory.

2. Locate and select the folder which you want to use as the default. (Be sure not to open the folder but to simply click its name in the window.) When a folder is selected, its name will appear in the Select folder_name button at the bottom of the window. (The actual name of the folder will appear in the button.)

3. Click the **Select Folder_name** button at the lower left.

Document Time Stamps and Caches

As you recall from the model of how caching works, Netscape first checks the memory cache and then the disk cache when you ask to display a document. If the item is found in one of the caches, Netscape checks the time stamp of the original document on the remote site to make sure that the local copy isn't out of date, or *stale*. If the item isn't found, a copy of the document is retrieved from the site, displayed, and added to the cache.

To get the fastest performance, you want to avoid always having to connect to the remote Web site, especially if you have reason to believe that the information won't have changed very much. As we've described so far, even retrieving a document from a cache requires that a network connection be established to check the time stamp of the original against the time stamp of the locally stored item. To address this issue, Netscape gives you an additional level of control over the disk cache by letting you choose how often the original document on the Web site is checked for new information. The following is a list of Netscape's options that let you choose when and if the time stamps of the original document are actually checked:

- **Once per session**. The first time that you ask for a given document after launching Netscape, a connection will be established to the original site. If the time stamp of the document on the server has changed, then the new document will be retrieved from the server and displayed. If the time stamp hasn't changed, the cached document will be displayed. This is the setting that most people choose.

- **Always** or **Every Time**. Every time you ask for a document that's in the cache, a network connection will be established to the original site to check for changes in the time stamp. Although this setting can slow the display of documents since a network connection must be established each time, it ensures that you're always looking at up-to-date information. This is useful for automatically generated documents such as those containing real-time information. (For example, a page containing stock quotes that are updated every fifteen minutes is useless if the information isn't the most recent available.)

- **Never**. Every time you ask for a document that's in the cache, the item will be retrieved from the cache without checking to see if the information has changed. This setting is most useful if you want to browse files in your cache offline, without establishing a network connection.

To choose how often Netscape checks the original of a cached document for new information, select one of the above options next to **Verify Documents**. (On the Macintosh, it's **Check Documents**.)

Ensuring That You See the Newest Documents

If you're looking at a document retrieved from your cache and you suspect that it's not the latest version of the document, either because of the way you set the document verification options or simply because the information looks out of date, click the **Reload** button on the toolbar. Netscape will connect to the site and check to see if the time stamp of the document on the server is different. If the time stamp is later, the document will be retrieved from the server instead of from your cache; if the time stamp is the same, the document will be redisplayed from your cache.

If the time stamp information on the server is incorrect, which can happen for a variety of reasons, your browser may continue to retrieve stale documents from the cache. If you think this is the case, follow the instructions in the next section to clear your caches.

VIRTUOSO

You can force Netscape to retrieve a document from the server and ignore cached items by using the "Super Reload" feature. On the Macintosh, hold down the **Option** key while selecting **Reload** from the View menu; on Windows and UNIX, hold down the **Shift** key while selecting **Reload** from the View menu. This causes Netscape to ignore the cached document and retrieve the document from the server.

Clearing Cache Information

Sometimes your caches can get confused and refuse to display a new version of a page, even if you tell Netscape to verify the document's time stamp. (For example, if the server has been rebooted and the time and day information has not been correctly reset, documents on the server will contain invalid time stamp information.) If it seems that you're regularly viewing stale documents, you should clear your caches to remove the out-of-date files.

To clear your caches, click **Clear Memory Cache Now** and **Clear Disk Cache Now**. (On the Macintosh, only **Clear Disk Cache Now** is available.)

WARNING

Once you clear the caches, the information is permanently removed. There's no harm in this at all, but it may take longer to display Web documents that you've visited recently (as they'll be retrieved from the site and not from the cache) and you won't be able to retrieve information from the cache, as discussed later in this chapter.

What Happens When the Cache is Full?

If you don't periodically clear your caches, eventually they'll reach the size you allotted to them. (This happens more frequently to the memory cache, which tends to be much smaller than the disk cache.) When either cache is full, Netscape checks the time stamp which indicates the last time you viewed each cached entry. The oldest entries will be removed to make space for the newly cached items.

Recovering URLs, Files, and Graphics from the Cache

VIRTUOSO

Visited a great site the last time you cruised the Web but forgot to save the URL? Want to use a graphic that you saw earlier in the day, but don't want to go back online? If you saw the item you're interested in fairly recently, or if you set a large disk cache, you can use Netscape to view a list of cached files to find the item that you're looking for.

To see a list of all the items in your cache that's a lot easier to make sense of than the jumble of names shown in Figure 5.2, follow these steps:

1. In the Location field, type **about:cache**

2. Press **Return**, and be prepared to wait for several minutes while Netscape reads all the information in your disk cache.

Netscape will then generate a document containing information about all the items in your disk cache (Figure 5.5).

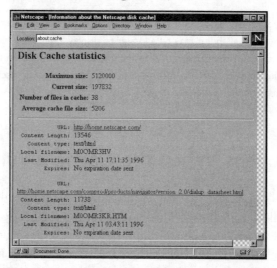

Figure 5.5 Information about the Netscape disk cache.

Scroll through the document until you find the item you're looking for.

When you've located an item you wish to retrieve, you'll find that there's an unexpected step! If you click the URL of the item in the Information window, the item itself is *not* displayed; instead, you see more detailed information about the document (Figure 5.6).

At this screen, you can click the URL of the document to view it in the browser. If you want to retrieve the cached document without launching a connection to the document's original site, be sure that you've set your file verification option to **Never**. If you want to work with the file itself, the information in the **Local filename:** field tells you the name of the file as it's stored in your cache directory.

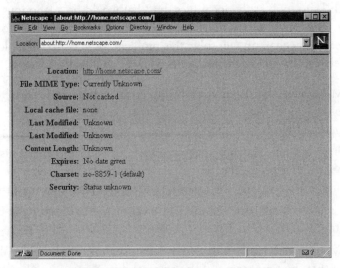

Figure 5.6 Detailed information about a cached document.

VIRTUOSO

Just want to find an image that you're sure is in the cache? At the Location field, enter **about:image-cache**. Only the cached images will be displayed in the listing.

SHORTCUT

If you remember any part of the URL, such as a unique company name, use the **Find** command in the Edit menu to look for the character string. (It's much easier than scrolling through a huge list.)

WARNING

Documents that you visit at secure sites will only be cached if you specifically request the caching of secure documents in the Cache options of the Network Preferences panel. If you choose not to cache secure documents, be sure to bookmark those pages if you wish to return to them, or save copies of the pages to your disk. (Security issues are discussed at length in Part Four.)

Creating Local Copies of Web Sites with the Disk Cache

Looking for a way to create all or part of a remote Web site on your local hard drive so you can conduct demonstrations without using a network connection? You could download every single page and inline image and modify the URLs to look at the local files, but that would be a laborious and error-prone approach. (If you don't believe us, try this a few times to find out.) The cache mechanism will solve this problem for you. To create local copies of Web sites in your cache for offline viewing, follow these steps:

1. Make sure that your disk cache is set sufficiently high to contain every single document and image that you wish to replicate.

2. Visit the Web site and display every single document that you want to view offline. (Be sure that you wait for each page to finish loading before you go to another page. If you go to another page while the first one is loading, the first one will not be placed in the disk cache.)

3. Create a bookmark for the top level of the site you wish to demonstrate.

4. When you're ready to do your demo, set your cache control to **Never** so that the time stamp of the original documents won't be checked.

When you select the bookmark for the top level of the site, that document and others linked to it will be retrieved from the cache. Just be sure that all the items you wish to display are still in the cache and haven't been bumped out *before* you begin your demonstration!

VIRTUOSO

Software products are now available that will perform these exhaustive searches to duplicate Web sites for you. The most popular of these is Web Whacker, available at: http://www.ffg.com/whacker.html.

Privacy Issues with Link History and Caches

WARNING

If privacy is a concern for you, and you don't want people to know what sites you've been visiting, consider clearing both your link history and disk cache frequently or turning off your disk cache altogether. You may think that no one at the office knows that you've been sneaking peeks at *Golf Digest* or searching online databases for another job, but if someone is nosy (and Netscape literate) enough to look through your disk cache or history files, they can find out every site that you've visited recently.

Network Buffer Size and Connections

The buffer size and network connections options are two odd Netscape parameters that aren't really related to caching, but they do work with the amount of memory allocated to the program.

Both of these items are related to what happens when you have multiple Netscape windows open.

VIRTUOSO

As you may know, there's no reason that you can't download a file and read Usenet News at the same time. Just choose **New Web Browser** from the File menu (it's **New Browser** on the Macintosh) to open another, separate TCP/IP connection.

However, the additional TCP/IP connections require additional memory, which can sometimes be hard to come by on a tight system. The buffer size parameter specifies the amount of memory allotted to hold incoming data while a page is being drawn. The larger the buffer size, the faster the page will be drawn.

The network connections parameter specifies the greatest number of windows you can have open simultaneously. Keep in mind that for each window you specify here, you reduce the amount of available memory by the size of the network buffer parameter.

The default values for buffer size and network connections represent a good tradeoff between performance and excessive memory use. Unless you're tight on memory, in which case you might want to decrease the number of potential simultaneous connections, you probably won't need to modify these settings, except in the following special circumstance.

NOTE

Netscape's technical notes suggest that some problems can be solved by increasing the buffer size. On a Windows platform, the default buffer size is 32K, while the default on the Macintosh is 8K. If you're using a Macintosh and seem to be experiencing an inordinate number of "404 Not Found" error messages, try raising the network buffer size. Then, quit and relaunch Netscape. If you weren't just constantly entering bad URLs, this should fix the problem.

What You Learned

After reading this chapter, you should be able to:

- Understand how the Go menu and **Back/Forward** buttons work.
- Manage the appearance of followed links and the size of the link history file.
- Choose an appropriate size for your memory cache, and the size and location of your disk cache.
- Control when items are retrieved from the cache and when they are retrieved from the server.
- Extract useful items like graphics and HTML files from your disk cache.
- Understand when to clear caches to resolve performance issues.
- Painlessly create local copies of Web sites.
- Understand privacy issues involved with caches and history files.
- Understand the buffer size and network connections options.

CHAPTER 6

TABLES AND FRAMES

Tables and frames are special elements that Web developers use to organize the information within a document. Although they're not technically related to each other, we've grouped them together because they can seem strange when you see them on the page, and you need to know how to navigate them with Netscape.

Both tables and frames started out as Netscape-developed extensions to the HTML specification. You'll often see Web pages that say they're "enhanced for Netscape"; they suggest that if you don't use the Netscape browser, you won't get the full impact of the page. However, tables and frames have proven so useful and popular that they're now supported in almost every graphical Web browser and have become part of the standard for HTML.

About Tables

As in any printed document, tables are a way to organize information in a grid. On the Web, tables can contain text, graphics, or any other kind of supported object. As a Web surfer, you can't actually interact with a table—it's just a page layout mechanism—but it has some important properties that affect the way your browser functions.

Uses of Tables in Web Documents

Until the development of newer HTML extensions such as column formatting commands and frames (which we'll talk about in the next section), tables were the only way for Web authors to control the placement of text in columns and grids on a page. Even with the advent of newer methods, tables are still frequently used to provide organization and meaning to text on a page. You'll often find them used for the following purposes:

- Emulation of published material. For example, the *Wall Street Journal*'s online Money and Investing Update uses tables to make their page look just like the front page of the physical newspaper's Money and Investing section, with short excerpts of articles appearing in the first two columns, and a summary of business news and features appearing in the third (Figure 6.1).

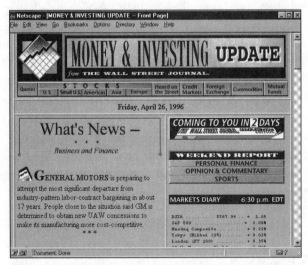

Figure 6.1 Wall Street Journal Money and Investing Update.

- Layout of information from a database. The regular grid of tables lends itself well to the presentation of database information; a developer can set up the table as a template to display the material that a user requests. For example, several stock quote services, such as PAWWS (http://www.pawws.com) display quotes and price information in easy-to-read tables such as those in Figure 6.2.

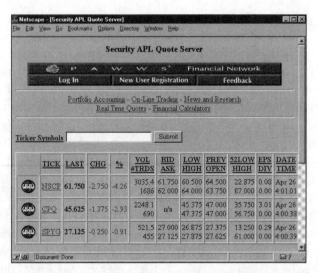

Figure 6.2 Multiple stock quotes from PAWWS, displayed in tables.

- Decision-making charts. As a visual aid, tables can make it easy to organize information so that online readers can make the correct choice for their needs. For example, Netscape's browser release notes (at http:/home.netscape.com/eng/mozilla/rel_notes) are organized by platform so you can easily determine the right link.

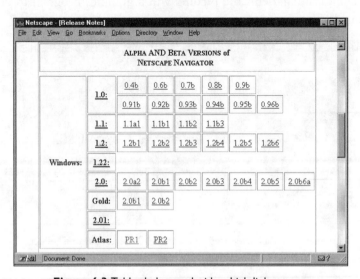

Figure 6.3 Tables help you decide which links to use.

User Issues for Tables

Because you can't interact with tables, there are only a few points about
them that you need to know. The most important issue regarding tables is
the impact they have on the way that a page is displayed. If there are no
tables on a page, all the text on the page is loaded before the graphics,
and you can start reading before the full page is loaded. But on a page
with tables, a great deal of the text might be included within the graphical
boundaries of the table. Such text will not be visible until after all the
information about the table and the text within it has been retrieved. For
example, at the Wall Street Journal's Money and Investing Update, the
entire front page appears within the boundary of a table; you won't be
able to read the text of the page until all of it has been retrieved. Since the
front page can often be as large as 25K and the site is often quite busy,
there may be a significant delay before you can read any of the news.

Another thing to keep in mind about tables is that they can contain
any kind of object that you might find on the Web: regular text, hypertext links, graphics, etc. A common developer trick that you'll sometimes
see is a table that only has a single cell with a thick boundary, containing
a graphic such as a photograph. This creates the effect of a three-dimensional "picture frame" around the graphic, without requiring that the
developer actually edit the picture with a graphics program to create the
"framed" effect.

Figure 6.4 Table cell used to create a 3D "picture-frame" effect.

Working with Frames

Frames are a relatively recent development in Web design that were introduced with Netscape 2.0 and have been quickly adopted by both Web site authors and companies who develop competing Web browsers.

Frames let the site developer divide a single page into a series of two or more rectangular windows that can behave independently of the other elements on the page. Each individual frame on a page has characteristics of an independent page—you can scroll it, click links, and so on.

Besides allowing the simple division of a page into windows, frames have additional features that make them a useful tool in the Web developer's arsenal. First, a frame can have a unique URL so that each frame can load information independently of other frames on the page. However, you'll rarely use the URLs of the individual frames, since you'll usually access the top-level page, or *frame-set*, at its own URL.

VIRTUOSO

Interested in finding out the URLs of the individual frames on a page? When you're on a page that has frames, select **Document Info** from the View menu. A new page will be displayed, similar to the one in Figure 6.5, that describes the elements of the page, including the URLs of the frames.

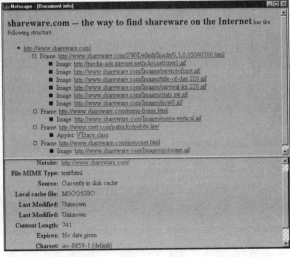

Figure 6.5 Document information for a page with frames.

Second, frames can be targeted by other URLs. In English, this means that frames can interact with each other—an action in one frame can cause something to occur in another frame on the same page. (If frames couldn't interact with each other, there wouldn't be much point to them; you could just open a new browser window for each page.)

Frames can contain any kind of information that you'd normally find on a Web page—in fact, they really are just mini-Web pages that each appear as a pane within the full browser window. To understand why frames are such an interesting and powerful tool, let's look at a few common ways that they're used:

- Frames can provide fixed navigational elements. Before there were frames, documents would usually have a set of navigational tools for moving around the Web site at the top and bottom of the page. This works fine for short pages, but it's a problem for long documents: you might have to scroll through several screens of text to find the navigational tools at the top or bottom of the document. But with frames, a developer can put a fixed navigation bar at the bottom of the page. You can scroll anywhere in the document while your navigation aids stay exactly in the same place. Frames are also often used for copyright notices and other items that should be visible to the user at all times.

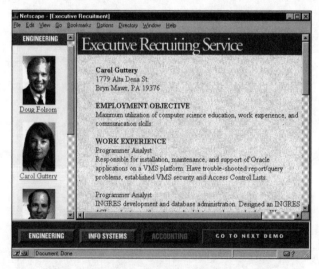

Figure 6.6 Frames provide fixed navigational aids.

- Frames can provide a permanent index or table of contents. This is really the same idea as the fixed navigational aid, applied to a more specific problem. If your site provides a great deal of information on a variety of topics (such as the Encyclopedia Mythica, at (http://www.pantheon.org/myth), your users might eventually get annoyed with having to reload a table of contents each time they want to view information on another topic. Frames allow the developer to place a fixed, scrollable table of contents directly on the page; when you click a topic, the information about it appears in the content area. No time is wasted in reloading the table of contents.

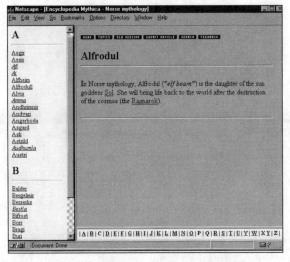

Figure 6.7 The Encyclopedia Mythica.

- Frames can let you enter a query and see a response on the same page, allowing you to enter another query without having to back up to the original search page. For example, HotWired's cocktail pages (http://www.hotwired.com/cocktail) let you search for the name of a drink and see the results on the same page. You can then choose to display the recipe for the beverage or search for something else.

Another way that frames are used is as containers for JavaScript, Java applets, or plug-in data. For example, Sean McGuire's HTML Interactive Editor (http://www.math.macalstr.edu/~smcguire/HIE/) lets you compose HTML in the top frame and then render it for immediate viewing in the bottom frame.

Figure 6.8 HotWired's cocktail page.

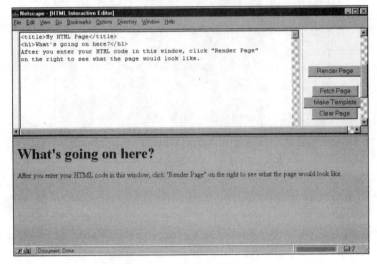

Figure 6.9 HTML Interactive Editor.

Another more commercial use of frames and Java can usually be found at large, corporate-sponsored sites, such as shareware.com, where a Java-based advertisement recently ran in the lower-right corner of the screen as soon as you click it.

Frames are still relatively new, and it's hard to say what kind of long-term impact they'll have on the overall design aesthetic of the Web. However, for the short term, their use is almost a litmus test for good Web design; while there are many great Web sites that don't use frames, you can really tell the difference between a professionally developed site that uses them and an amateur or hobbyist site.

Working with Frames

As you might imagine, frames can have some interesting (and often unexpected) effects on the way that you navigate Web pages.

Navigation Survival Tips

The thing that you will likely encounter that you won't know how to deal with the first time you hit a site that has frames in it is that the navigation buttons no longer perform as expected. The trick is to rely on the pop-up menu for navigation, instead of on the toolbar. Although the **Back** and **Forward** buttons on the toolbar in the recent releases of Netscape are now functional with frames (in the older versions, they took you back to the last page you were on before you entered the page with frames), they *only* work if you've selected a frame, as described below. In general, the best method for navigating a site with frames is to always use the pop-up menu.

If fames don't appear to be working for you at all, check to make sure that JavaScript isn't disabled. Frames often relay on JavaScript to interpret your mouse clicks and cause another action to occur. To enable and disable JavaScipt, click the Languages tab in Network Preferences; for more information about JavaScript, see Chapter 13.

Selecting Frames

Selecting a frame makes it possible to perform certain activities, like mailing the contents of the frame or navigating to something else that you've already displayed within the borders of the frame. To select a frame, click your mouse in the frame area. A thin black line around the border of the frame indicates that it's selected. (You'll often end up selecting a frame as an incidental result of clicking a link that appears in the frame; however, as you'll see in the sections about the menus, there may be times that you'll want to simply select a frame so that you can print it, view it full-screen, or mail the information to someone else.)

WARNING If you want to select a frame, make sure that you don't click your mouse on a navigational link or an image map; if you do, you might find that the frame you wanted to use has been replaced by the target of the link! To be sure that you can just select a frame without causing activity, check the status message area at the lower-right corner of the full Netscape window. If it doesn't display a URL or coordinates, then it's safe to click.

Changes in the Pop-up Menu

The pop-up menu that's displayed when you hold down the mouse button (on Windows, click the right mouse button) is different for frames than it is for regular Web pages. The following items are available:

- **Back** takes you back within the individual frame. This option is only active if you've displayed more than one item in the frame already.

- If you've gone back in the frame, **Forward** will become active. **Forward** takes you forward through the "history list" for the current frame, even though Netscape's regular history list will not reflect your navigation within the frame (it only keeps track of your entry and exit of the top-level page).

- If a frame has a unique URL, the pop-up menu will allow you to display the frame individually in a browser window. To return to the original page, click the close box in the upper-left corner of the new window.

NOTE If you hold down the mouse over a regular element within a frame, such as a hyper-text link or a graphic, the options for the items described above will be displayed in addition to the regular options for that kind of object.

WARNING On the Macintosh, where your mouse only has one button, be sure that you hold down the mouse over an area that doesn't contain a "hot" item like a link or a clickable image. You may end up navigating further into the site when what you really wanted to do was back up.

Changes in Netscape Menus

When a frame is selected, the following new items will be visible in the File menu:

- The **Mail Document** item changes to **Mail Frame**. If you select **Mail Frame**, then the Message Composition window will be displayed, with the URL for the frame in the text area of the message and the HTML file for the individual frame specified as an attachment.

- **Save as...** becomes **Save Frame as....** Choosing this item will display a dialog box so you can save the contents of the selected frame as a file on your disk drive.

- **Print...** becomes **Print Frame....** Choosing this item will send the selected frame to the printer.

The following items will be active in the View menu:

- **Reload Frame.** Choosing this item will reload the contents of the currently-selected frame.

- **Frame Souce.** Choosing this item will display the HTML source code of the currently-selected frame.

- **Frame Info.** Choosing this item will display information about the structure of the currently-selected frame.

Resizing Frames

One of the options available to developers is to choose whether frames are resizable or not. If a frame is resizable, then you can manually make it bigger or smaller. To see if a frame can be resized, move the mouse over the boundary of the frame and check to see if it changes into the cursor displayed in Figure 6.10.

Figure 6.10. The cursor indicates that you can resize this frame.

If you see this kind of cursor, then hold down the mouse button (the left mouse button for Windows users) and drag the boundary to the new location.

VIRTUOSO

If a frame is resizable, it will automatically grow or shrink if you resize the entire Netscape browser window.

Disadvantages of Frames

There's no doubt that frames can be used for good purposes. When properly designed, a page that contains frames can provide a consistent and easy-to-understand interface for viewing and manipulating many kinds of information. Unfortunately, there are a number of sites that use frames poorly: either the information doesn't require such sophisticated layout and the frames don't add anything to the site, or the frames are too big or too small by default, or they're just badly designed and make the site more difficult to understand.

To a certain extent, the use of sophisticated visual elements like frames on the Web is similar to the early days of desktop publishing: most people had never before had the ability to use several fonts on a page, or to easily format documents with columns or graphics, and poor taste often prevailed over good design and judicious restraint. (Frames can sometimes make Web pages so difficult to work with that a crop of personal "I Hate Frames" home pages can usually be found online at any given time; frames are hated about as much as the HTML tag that makes text blink incessantly.)

Let's hope that the novelty of a new format wears off and common sense and good design prevail; in lieu of that, let's at least hope that sites will continue to offer "frames-free" navigation, in the same way that you can choose a "text-only" path if you're using a low-bandwidth connection.

What You Learned

After reading this chapter, you should:

- Understand the unique elements of frames and tables.
- Understand the way that frames and tables can affect your browsing experience.
- Know the basics of navigating pages that contain frames.
- Be aware of the ways that frames and other page design tools can be misused.

CHAPTER 7

ADVANCED TIPS, TRICKS, AND SHORTCUTS

Netscape contains a wide variety of nearly hidden timesaving features that let you speed up almost every action you might perform, from displaying new pages to saving files to simply scrolling through windows. And there are several not-so-obvious ways to handle common problems and needs, from letting more than one person use Netscape on a single machine to ensuring that large documents actually make it into the cache so they'll be faster to display. This chapter contains a grab bag of shortcuts and techniques for the optimal use of Netscape's features.

NOTE

Nearly every item in this chapter is a Virtuoso tip. Use of the Virtuoso icon will be limited to marking the procedures that are the most advanced of the bunch.

Using the Pop-up Menu

In addition to the pull-down menus at the top of the screen, Netscape provides a pop-up menu containing advanced navigational choices that apply to the clickable parts of a document or to the document as a whole. This pop-up menu provides quick access to some items that are available from the menus or toolbar, but it also contains advanced options that aren't available anywhere else.

To display the pop-up menu on Windows and UNIX, position the mouse over a clickable element and click the right mouse button. The following menu (Figure 7.1) will be displayed.

Figure 7.1 Pop-up menu for Windows.

To display the pop-up menu on a Macintosh, position the mouse over a clickable element and hold down the mouse button without releasing it for a few seconds. The following menu (Figure 7.2) will be displayed.

NOTE

Netscape determines what kind of item you've selected and chooses as the menu's default selection what is considered to be the most likely choice. For example, if you displayed the pop-up menu for a regular link, the item in the menu selected by default will be to open the link. If you displayed the pop-up menu for a graphics placeholder, the item in the menu selected by default will be to display the graphic. Netscape also "grays out" the menu selections which are not appropriate for the item—if you selected a graphic which is not a link, items related to opening links will not be available.

```
Back
Forward

Open this Link
Add Bookmark for this Link
New Window with this Link
Save this Link as...
Copy this Link Location

Open this Image
Save this Image as...
Copy this Image
Copy this Image Location
Load this Image
```

Figure 7.2 Pop-up menu for Macintosh.

NOTE

If you're using Netscape Navigator Gold, most of the commands in the pop-up menu will appear slightly different.

Going Back and Forward

The **Back** and **Forward** items in the pop-up menu navigate you through your history list like the **Back** and **Forward** buttons on the toolbar. If a frame is selected, the **Back** and **Forward** items navigate you backward and forward within the selected frame.

Working with Links

The following options are available if the item beneath the mouse pointer contains a link:

- To open the link that you've selected, select **Open** (URL_of_link). On the Macintosh, the command is **Open this Link**.

- To create a bookmark for the link without retrieving the item, select **Add Bookmark for this Link**. (On Windows, use the **Add Bookmark** item at the bottom of the menu.)

- To display the document referred to in the link in a new window, select **Open in New Window** (Windows) or **New Window for this Link** (Macintosh).

- To save the document referred to in the link without displaying it, select **Save Link As...** (Windows) or **Save this Link as...** (Macintosh). You'll see the dialog box that lets you choose the name, location, and whether the file is saved as source (HTML) or plain text.

- To copy the URL of the link to the Clipboard so that you can paste it into another document without having to retrieve the document, select **Copy Link Location** (Windows) or **Copy this Link Location** (Macintosh). You may then use the **Paste** command to paste the URL into any other document.

On Windows, you can double-click the link icon at the left of the Location field to copy the URL of the current document to the clipboard.

SHORTCUT

Working with Graphics

The following additional options are available if the item beneath the mouse pointer contains a graphic:

- To display only the graphic in a new window, select **View Image** (Windows) or **View this Image** (Macintosh).

- To save the graphic to your disk drive, select **Save Image as...** (Windows) or **Save this Image as...** (Macintosh). The standard dialog box for saving a file will be displayed.

- On the Macintosh, to copy the graphic to the Clipboard so it can be pasted into another document, select **Copy this Image**. (This option is not available on Windows.)

- To copy the graphic's URL so you can paste it into another document, select **Copy Image Location** (Windows) or **Copy this Image Location** (Macintosh). You may then use the **Paste** command to paste the URL into any other document.

- If the selected item is a graphics placeholder, you may load the individual image without displaying the other graphics on the page by selecting **Load Image** (Windows) or **Load this Image** (Macintosh).

Creating an Internet Shortcut (Windows 95)

If you're using Windows 95, the pop-up menu lets you create an Internet shortcut, which lets you quickly access documents that you use often. Just double-click the Internet shortcut to launch Netscape and retrieve the page you created the shortcut for. To create an Internet shortcut, follow these steps:

1. From the pop-up menu, select **Internet Shortcut**. The Create Internet Shortcut dialog box will be displayed.

2. If you wish to change the name of the shortcut, enter the new name in the **Description** field.

3. Click **OK**. The new shortcut will be created on your Desktop.

Keyboard Commands

As discussed in Chapter 3, there are menu and/or keyboard shortcuts for every item that appears on the toolbar or list of directory buttons. To find the keyboard shortcuts for those items, display the menu containing the item and look for the keyboard equivalent to the right of the item.

However, there are also keyboard shortcuts for navigating within and among displayed documents, in case you don't wish to use the mouse. Table 7.1 contains a list of actions and their associated keystrokes.

Table 7.1 Common Keyboard Shortcuts

Location	Action	Keyboard command
Within a document	Scroll up	Up arrow
	Scroll down	Down arrow
	Display previous screen	Page Up
	Display next screen	Page Down
Between documents	Go back in history list	(Mac) Command-left arrow; (PC) Alt-left arrow
	Go forward in history list	(Mac) Command-right arrow
In a form	Go to next field	(PC) Alt-right arrow; Tab

Using Drag and Drop

The *Drag and Drop* concept is a fairly recent development for personal computers' operating systems, first introduced with Macintosh System 7.5 and Windows 95. While earlier applications like Microsoft Word were drag-aware to a certain degree (you could drag objects within a single document), the addition of this feature to the operating system allows you to use the mouse to move items from document to document and even from application to application without using any keyboard or menu commands.

Drag and Drop is a conceptual extension of the cut-and-paste metaphor. If you select an object (such as a chunk of text or a picture) and drag it over a drag-aware destination (another place on the page, another window, or another application), you can simply drop the object into its new location without having to issue the **Cut**, **Copy**, or **Paste** commands. This makes it simple to edit almost any kind of document with a minimum of keystrokes.

To drag an item, follow these steps:

1. Place the pointer over the item to be dragged. (In Netscape, you can place it directly over a link; in other applications, like word processors, you must select the item before you can begin to drag it.)

2. Hold down the mouse button over the object and keep it held down.

3. Without releasing the mouse button, move the pointer. Depending on your operating system, the icon for the pointer will change and there may be an outline box that moves with the pointer representing the selected object.

WARNING

If you're dragging a link in Netscape on the Macintosh, be sure to move the mouse quickly or you'll display the pop-up menu for the item instead of dragging the item.

4. Place the pointer in the location where you wish to put the object.

5. Release the mouse button. This will "drop" the item into the new location.

Because Netscape is a drag-aware application, you can perform all kinds of tricks and shortcuts using this feature.

Launching a URL from Another Application

If you have a drag-aware document that contains a URL, you can go directly to that location without pasting or retyping the URL. Just select the URL in the document and drag it onto the Netscape window. Netscape will open a connection and retrieve the item specified in the URL.

Drag-aware applications that ship as part of the operating system include the WordPad word processor in Windows 95, and the Stickies, NotePad, and SimpleText applications in Macintosh System 7.5. Several other packages, including the commercial version of the popular mail package Eudora, support Drag and Drop.

Uploading Files with Drag and Drop

As we'll discuss further in Chapter 16 and Chapter 22, Netscape supports the use of FTP to upload files to other locations. If you wish, you can use Drag and Drop to upload a file instead of using the **Upload File...** command in the File menu. First, make sure that you're at a location where you have *write privileges*—that is, where you're allowed to create new files—such as your own account or an FTP site that accepts user contributions. Then, drag the icon for the file you wish to upload over Netscape's window. When you release the mouse, the upload process will begin.

Drag and Drop Tricks for Windows

With Bookmarks...

The Bookmark Properties window is drag-aware, allowing you a quick way to access bookmarked sites, as well as a simple way to add new bookmarks to the list.

To go directly to a bookmark displayed in the window, drag the URL to Netscape's browser window. Netscape will open a connection to that site.

To add a link displayed on a document to the bookmark list without going to that location, drag the URL to the Bookmark Properties window. It will be added to your bookmark list in the location that you drop it.

NOTE Within Netscape, you don't need to select the URL before dragging it. Just hold down the mouse over the link and move the mouse away from the location before the pop-up window appears.

With the Link Icon...

The link icon that appears to the left of the Location field can be used for various Drag and Drop functions. If the Bookmark window is open, just drag the link icon into the window to create a bookmark for the current page. To open the current file in the editor, drag the icon into the open editing window.

Drag and Drop Tricks for the Macintosh

On the Macintosh, dragging a link from Netscape into the open window of another application simply places the URL of the link into the new document. But dragging a link from the Netscape window onto the Desktop or onto a folder at the Finder saves a copy of the actual document onto your disk drive in the location where you dropped the link. This action is performed in the background so you can continue browsing.

VIRTUOSO

Using this trick at FTP sites lets you choose the destination for the file you're downloading. If you just click the link to begin the download, the file will be placed by default in your temporary directory. By dragging the link directly to the folder where you wish to store the file, you can place files directly into various locations without having to navigate through the operating system to relocate items.

Working in a Multi-Window Environment

This section contains information about using Netscape with more than one window open at a time.

Managing the Download Window

When you're downloading a file through FTP, gopher, or just by choosing **Save As…** from the File menu, Netscape automatically creates a separate dialog box that monitors the progress of the download and gives you the option to cancel at any time (Figure 7.3).

This window is obviously much smaller than the regular Netscape window. As a result, the window will be hidden by Netscape as soon as you click something on the full-screen document and the browser window will be brought back to the foreground.

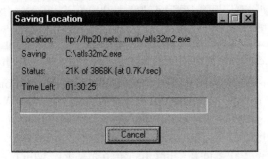

Figure 7.3 The Download window.

To make sure that you can watch the progress of your download while you continue to browse, perform one of the following actions:

- For Macintosh and UNIX, drag the download window to the side of the screen, beyond the browser window. When you return the browser window to the foreground, you can continue to see your progress.

- For Windows, minimize the download window. It will be displayed in your Taskbar with constant updates regarding the percentage of completion.

Using More than One Browser Window

As you undoubtedly know by now, you can have more than one Netscape window open at the same time. To open a new window, select **New Web Browser** from the File menu. The maximum number of possible windows is controlled by the **Connections** item in Network Preferences. (For complete information on these settings, see Chapter 5.)

The multiple window feature is often underused by beginning and intermediate users, since for the most part it doesn't seem that you could possibly need to have two windows open at once. After all, you can only read one page at a time.

But there are several kinds of items that you might retrieve that take a long time to load, such as large graphics files, indices at a gopher or FTP site, or the results of a complicated search engine query. Once Netscape is engaged in a protocol exchange, you won't be able to do anything but switch to another window without canceling the transfer in progress. In these cases, if you don't open a new window before you begin the transfer, you can't do anything but wait until the transfer is finished. But if you create a new window before you start the exchange, you can continue to browse in the new window while the items are being loaded into the first window.

Another reason you might want to have more than one window open is if you're reading a series of related, but separate, Web documents. Instead of using the **Back** and **Forward** buttons to navigate through the pages, which requires that you wait for each item to reload, it may be easier to just have all the documents open at once, which allows you to go back and forth between pages with no delay at all.

If you're using multiple windows to keep browsing during a complicated file transfer, you may want to keep an eye on your progress. The
best way to do this is to simply resize or move the window that you're
browsing in so that you can see the messages and the progress gauge at
the bottom of the first window, and the development of the scroll bar at
the right side of the screen.

NOTE The scroll bar will be usable as soon as the first screen of data has been loaded; as
soon as it's visible, you can start browsing the information that you retrieved. More
information about the scroll bar for Windows users appears in "Other Tricks for
Windows" later in this chapter.

Working in a Multi-User Environment

If you share your computer with coworkers or family members, Netscape
has a mechanism to allow each person to use his or her own bookmarks,
preferences, and cache files.

NOTE Because UNIX is a multi-user operating system by design, every person must
always have his or her own personal directory. So, setting up Netscape for multiple
users is not an issue for this platform.

Multiple Users in Windows 95

To allow more than one person to use Netscape with their own preferences, follow these steps:

1. Open the **Passwords** control panel.

2. Click the **User Profiles** tab.

3. Select **Users can customize their preferences and desktop settings**
   (the second item from the top). This allows each user to customize
   his or her own version of Netscape and any other application that
   contains preferences.

NOTE

Once you change User Profiles to this setting, every person who uses the computer will have to log in individually each time he or she uses the machine.

Initially, the default settings for directories and other items will be the same for each user. However, users may then specify different locations and information for all configurable options.

Multiple Users on the Macintosh

To allow more than one person to use Netscape with their own preferences, follow these steps:

1. At the Finder, make a copy of the Netscape Preferences folder (located in System Folder/Preferences) for each person who wishes to use Netscape.

2. Rename the folders individually for each user. (For example, at our house we'd create folders called "Elissa's Netscape" and "Robert's Netscape," each of which would contain our own bookmarks, global history lists, cache information, etc.)

3. To open Netscape, each person should double-click the **Preferences** file in their own copy of the Preferences folder. This launches the Netscape application using each person's individual information.

Ensuring that Documents are Cached

One of the greatest advantages of Netscape over earlier versions of NCSA Mosaic is that you can scroll and navigate within a document while it's still loading. However, that doesn't mean that everything will function normally if you start attempting to browse in the same window in which the document is loading.

One of the most important things to keep in mind is that if you click a link on a page that's still loading, Netscape will not cache the document.

If you want to return to the document later, it will be retrieved in its entirety from the server. As impatient as you may be to continue browsing, it's not always worth it to click a link if it means you'll just have to wait on that page again. So, if you want to ensure that the document can be redisplayed quickly, don't click a link, press the **Back** or **Forward** buttons, or select an item from the Go or Bookmarks menus while a document is loading. The only thing that will let you continue browsing while ensuring that the document is cached is to use another window, as described in the preceding section.

A common example of this problem occurs with large information files such as Netscape's online documentation. These files are often 50K or more in size and can take some time to load. However, the first page displayed contains a menu of hot links to other locations in the same document. A natural tendency is to click one of these links as soon as it's visible. But if you do so before the document is completely loaded and cached, then Netscape will reload the *entire* document just to display the location that you requested. It's often worth the patience to wait or to browse in another window while such documents are being loaded.

Other Tricks for Windows

This section contains some Windows-specific shortcuts and tips.

Viewing Network Information

You can view details about the number of open connections and other network information by pressing **Control-Alt-t**. A dialog box like Figure 7.4 will be displayed, showing the number of URLs waiting for an open socket or connection (which is limited by your entry in Network Preferences); the number of URLs waiting for fewer connections to be active so that the information requested from the URL can be retrieved; the total number of open connections; and the number of currently active URLs. (An active URL is a URL displayed in a browser window.)

Figure 7.4 Network information.

Hiding the Status Message Area

Under certain circumstances, you might want to temporarily hide the status message area at the bottom of the screen. For example, if you're trying to fit a large part of a document into the window and you need to conserve "screen real estate," hiding the status message area can let you display with at least one extra line of text, if not more. Or, if you're giving a presentation that uses local pages but you want it to appear as if you're using a live connection, hiding the status message area will keep your audience from seeing the telltale "Reading file..." messages. To hide or display the status message area, press **Control-Alt-s**.

Estimating Document Length

In Windows 95, you can estimate the length of a document by looking at the size of the *thumb* in the scroll bar. (The thumb is the rectangle that you drag to display different parts of the document.) The size of the thumb represents the percentage of the entire document represented by the part of the document currently visible in the window.

If a document is fully loaded, this allows you to estimate the length of the entire document. For example, if the thumb takes up half of the scroll bar, then you know that the document is twice as long as the part that's visible in the screen.

This feature is also useful in estimating how much of a file is available for viewing while it's being downloaded. For example, if you're retrieving a very long file and the thumb takes up one-third of the screen, you know that you have only loaded about three pages of the entire document. As the download progresses, the thumb will get smaller and smaller, indicating how much more of the document is available.

Other Tricks for the Macintosh

This section contains some Macintosh-specific shortcuts and tips.

Opening Netscape from Another Application

If you're reading your mail or another document while Netscape isn't running, and you come across a URL that you'd like to visit, there's now a way to launch Netscape and immediately display the selected URL. A Control Panel called URLKey lets you select any text containing a URL, copy it to the Clipboard, and press a hot-key combination. URLKey will find the URL in the text that you selected, open Netscape, and establish a connection to the site in the URL.

URLKey is available at http://www.city.net/cnx/software/urlkey.html.

Using Internet Config

If you use any Internet applications besides Netscape, you've probably noticed that each of them requires you to enter the same information as you did in Netscape's various Preferences windows. If you're sick and tired of retyping your name, server, signature, gateways, and other information each time you set up a new application, you might want to try the Internet Configuration System, generally referred to as "Internet Config." This Control Panel lets you enter all your preferences and identity information in a central location that can be accessed by all Internet applications that have been modified to use it; starting with Netscape Navigator 3.0, the Netscape browser supports the use of Internet Config. (Check Internet Config's documentation for a current list of other products supporting its use.)

For more information about obtaining and using Internet Config, see the Internet Config FAQ at: ftp://ftp.share.com/pub/internet-configuration/IC_FAQ.html.

To set up Netscape to use Internet Config, follow these steps:

1. From the Options menu, select **Mail and News Preferences...**.
2. Click the **Identity** tab.
3. At the lower-left corner of the window, select **Use Internet Configuration System**.

WARNING Support for Internet Config was first implemented in beta releases of Netscape 3.0. At this time, it's not clear from Netscape's documentation how much of the information from the Internet Config database will actually be used by the browser; chances are good that at least some configuration information will still need to be entered into Netscape.

Resizing the Document Window

Is the document you're looking at too big for the size of your Netscape window? Click the **Resize** button in the upper-right corner of the window. The screen will automatically be redrawn at the same size as the widest element in the document. To return to the default size, click the button again.

Opening Any Local File

By default, the **Open File...** command only displays HTML, text, JPEG, and GIF files on your system. But what if you want to view another kind of file that you have on your disk drive? To force the dialog box to display all types of files, hold down the **Option** key while selecting **Open File...** from the File menu. All files in the selected folder will be displayed, regardless of their type.

Understanding the Status Indicators

One of the most useful features of Netscape's screen is the status indicators that appear at the bottom of the page. During file retrieval, the status message area at the lower left contains textual information about the progress of the transfer. After a document is loaded, the status message area displays information about the item that the mouse pointer is currently located above. The progress indicator in the lower right shows a graphical representation of how much of the current document has been retrieved. Both the status message area and the progress indicator refer to the component elements of the document being loaded, as opposed to the document as a whole. For example, if a document consists of an HTML file and two inline images, the status indicators will move from zero to 100% three different times.

To understand the information displayed in the status indicators, it's important to know the order in which Netscape retrieves the different elements of a document. Netscape first loads the entire HTML file before it attempts to load any of the inline images and builds a "framework" for the document leaving appropriately sized spaces in the text for the graphics that will be loaded later.

When the status message area says "Layout complete," the HTML portion of the document has been completely loaded. You can scroll from the beginning of the document to the end while the inline images are being loaded.

You can tell that a document has been completely loaded when the status message area displays "Done" and the Netscape icon in the upper-right corner of the screen is no longer animated.

NOTE   The information above is true for all URLs beginning with HTTP. For gopher and FTP URLs, the status indicators can only tell you how much of the document has been loaded, as the protocol does not provide any information to Netscape about the size of the file. For these kinds of transfers, the status message area will show the amount of the file, in kilobytes, that's been loaded, and the progress indicator will simply show activity. In these cases, there's no way to estimate how much longer the document retrieval will take.

Really Useless Tricks

The Amazing Fish Cam

Want to see the current activity in the fish tank at Netscape's corporate office? Press **Control-Alt-f** (On the Macintosh, **Control-Option-f**) and you'll be on your way.

NOTE

This fish tank is allegedly in the shared office of Garrett Blythe and Lou Montulli, and, according to coworker Jamie Zawinski, the fish have a short life span and are replaced with alarming frequency.

Visit the White House

A built-in keyboard shortcut to the White House Web site is **Control-Alt-w** (on the Macintosh, **Control-Option-w**).

The World According to Mozilla

For wit and wisdom from Netscape's mascot Mozilla, type **about:mozilla** in the Location field.

Meet the Folks at Netscape

If you know the account name of someone who worked on the Netscape development team, you can visit their home pages by typing **about:name** in the Location field, where **name** is the person's login name. For example, **about:jwz** takes you to Jamie Zawinski's pages, where you can learn (among other things) why his cubicle is draped in camouflage netting. A list of names that you can access in this way can be found at http://www.yikes.com/fun/netscape/people.html. (To give credit where it's due, much of this last bunch of useless Netscape tricks comes from the Netscape Tricks site at http://www.yikes.com/fun/netscape.)

What You Learned

After reading this chapter, you should have learned a variety of advanced tricks and shortcuts for using Netscape.

CHAPTER 8

MIME TYPES, HELPER APPLICATIONS, AND PLUG-INS

One of the unique features of graphical World Wide Web browsers is that they know when you click on links to graphics, movies, animations, or formatted text (such as Adobe Acrobat documents). Because Netscape can identify the kind of object that you've retrieved from the Web, it knows whether it can display the item directly (text, HTML, JPEG, GIF, and XBM files) or whether it must rely on a "plug-in" or a helper application to correctly handle the file.

Netscape knows what kind of file it's working with because all items available on the World Wide Web have a *MIME type* associated with them (such as text/html for text-only HTML documents, or video/x-mpeg for MPEG videos) which lets client applications retrieving them know what they're working with. When you configure Netscape, you identify *helper applications* to work with each MIME type, so that if you come across something that Netscape can't handle, it knows what external application to launch and pass the object to.

In this chapter, we'll talk about:

- How and why MIME types developed
- Why MIME types make the multimedia capabilities of the Web possible

- Common MIME types that you'll encounter
- Different kinds of helper applications that you should understand

How MIME Types Came About

Although most of us know about MIME types from configuring our Web browsers, the truth is that MIME types—Multipurpose Internet Mail Extensions—were developed to make it possible to send different kinds of files through Internet email. They were adopted by graphical Web browsers because they were a pre-existing, elegant solution to a rather thorny problem.

History of Computer-Based Multimedia

To understand why MIME types exist at all, it's useful to look at the history of displaying images and playing sounds on the computer. This can provide insight into why things happened the way they did.

Back in the Dark Ages of computing (before the late 1970s), computers didn't deal with *media* like pictures or sounds at all—they only handled *data*, which is information represented as arrays of numbers or text. During these early years, data was displayed on text-only terminal screens or in the form of printed reports. No effort was made to display data in other forms, as the large mainframe computers simply had no way to handle any kind of graphics, audio, or video output.

With the rise of engineering workstations and personal computers in the early 1980s, the text-only *display terminals* and printers, which could only display the ASCII or EBCDIC (IBM's standard for text) characters sent directly by the main processor, were replaced by *memory-mapped, frame buffer display terminals*, which are the foundation of the graphical user interface so prevalent today on personal computers and workstations. Unlike video display terminals, which display rows and columns of alphanumeric characters transmitted by the controlling program on the mainframe, memory-mapped displays can show *bitmapped images*—two-dimensional arrays of points on the screen, not just arrays of text—that make it possible to actually show graphics on the screen.

The way that images are created on a computer screen is somewhat similar to photography. When you take a picture, each point in the real world is translated through the lens to a corresponding point on the film. The picture is a method of displaying the array of points, all of which have arbitrary values that may be black, white, shades of gray, or one of millions of discrete colors. To show a photograph or any image, a computer's video display must be able to interpret what color the computer says each point should be and to show those points on the screen.

The technology that made this possible was the development of the *frame buffer display*, which allows the output of any software to be displayed as two-dimensional arrays of points. Even the fonts that you see on your screen as you type aren't displayed as they were in the days of video display terminals. When you press a letter on the keyboard, the ASCII character you request is used to look up the proper entry in the font table, which sends the correct sequence of 1s and 0s to display the character in 12-point Palatino or 14-point Bookman. Figure 8.1 shows a bitmapped 12-point Palatino letter, enlarged so you can see that it's just an array of dots.

Figure 8.1 Enlarged bitmap of a 12-point Palatino letter.

The computer actually tells the monitor exactly how every picture element—or *pixel*—that appears on your screen should look, regardless of whether it's text or a graphic. As a result, you have a great deal more control over fonts, screen colors, and other graphical items. (On basic video display terminals, the color and font of text was determined by the manufacturer of the terminal; the only thing that you could change was the screen's brightness, contrast, and its position on your desk.)

The development of the frame buffer display and the increase in computing power resulting from the concurrent microchip revolution led developers to think about new ways to display computer-based information graphically and audibly, to use images and icons for operating systems in addition to plain text, and to come up with ways to represent user-defined images, graphics, and audio.

You might think that just one standard for pictures and audio should have been the result, but the fact is that many people were involved in the early efforts to deal with multimedia, and they were working on different platforms and operating systems. As a result, a variety of different standards, or formats, emerged. In any given area, such as sound or video, there are three or four primary file formats and up to ten times as many proprietary formats for specialized uses.

In a heterogeneous computing environment like the Web, there are a number of accepted standards in use for each different kind of media. Through the use of helper applications, we can prepare Netscape to handle the two or three most popular formats for each major type of media, including moving pictures, still images, audio, and archive formats.

Formats and File Extensions

File extensions—those three or four characters that appear after the decimal at the end of a file's name—have historically been the critical identifier of what kind of information is held in the file. Application programs generally look at files' extensions to determine which files are appropriate for them to open. (An early exception to this scheme is the Macintosh operating system, which stores the file type as part of the file's properties, allowing you to name files however you wish. This freedom in naming files has been more or less adopted by Windows 95.)

The Problems of Electronic Mail

What you've got so far is the ability to display multimedia on a computer screen, and methods to let a computer know what kind of file is being used, whether text, image, or a proprietary format like a spreadsheet or a word processor. The next logical step was finding some way to share the information with other computers.

Wide-area networks such as Usenet and the Internet and point-to-point file transfer methods such as Kermit have been a common way to send information to people at remote sites for years. Unfortunately, standard transfer methods only send a stream of bytes or characters across the network. Often there were limitations on the size and content of a transmission, making it impossible to reliably transmit long binary files like pictures. Furthermore, file names, types, and other attributes were notoriously nonportable from one computer to another, and were often lost during transfers. A solution needed to be developed to let you send an image or an application file like a word-processed document or spreadsheet to a remote location. Basically, there were four problems that needed to be solved:

- While binary data files use all eight bits in a byte for each character, many communication channels can only send seven bits per character. (In the early days of network development, only ASCII or IBM's EBCDIC was ever transmitted. These character sets only required seven bits, so the eighth bit in the byte was often used in an error-checking routine called *parity checking*.) There needed to be a way to send 8-bit information through a communication channel that couldn't necessarily support it.

- Files needed to be reconstructed at the other end with the original name and file type, despite the fact that file attributes may be represented in different ways on different computers.

- The structure of files varies from platform to platform. For instance, even files as simple as plain text files require different characters to note the ends of lines on different platforms. To complicate matters more, every file on the Macintosh consists of two separate parts, known as a *resource fork* and a *data fork*, as opposed to the simple file model used by most other operating systems.

- When networks are used for the distribution of software, reports, and other items, there's often a need to distribute large collections of files. But the more files you send, the more tedious handling them becomes and the more likely it is that they'll get damaged in transit. Archiving techniques needed to be developed so that many separate files could be combined into one file, which could easily be sent across the network and then broken up into its component parts on arrival.

All of these problems were initially addressed with platform-dependent ad hoc solutions, such as the UNIX uuencode and the Macintosh binhex utilities that translate eight-bit information into seven-bit data that can be correctly transmitted, and archiving and file compression utilities like ZIP, StuffIt, or tar that create file archives. Unfortunately, these approaches were platform dependent and required expertise and judgment on the part of the user to determine how to handle the files; the mechanism for delivering the data simply wasn't smart enough to know what kind of files it was working with.

The MIME standard was developed as a way to address these limitations for the area of electronic mail and messaging. MIME is a platform-independent way to handle those problems so you can send messages across the Internet that will arrive intact, regardless of the sender, the receiver, and any intervening communications channels. Although most email is still ASCII text, MIME makes it possible to define extensions (tags or codes) that are embedded in the header of the message, indicating the kind of encoding that was used for the data stream that follows.

Structure of MIME Types

MIME types have two components: a main type and a subtype. The main type tells you in general what kind of file you're dealing with. The seven main MIME types currently defined are:

- Text
- Application
- Image
- Audio
- Video
- Multipart
- Message

The last two MIME types—multipart and message—are more closely associated with MIME's original usage for email and are not, as yet, incorporated for use on the Web.

The subtype specifically identifies what kind of application or format was used. For example, the MIME type **image/gif** means that the item is a GIF graphic, while **image/jpeg** means that the item is a JPEG graphic.

MIME Types and the World Wide Web

When the designers of HTTP (the protocol that defines the World Wide Web) needed a general-purpose, platform-independent, unambiguous scheme for shipping data from Web servers to Web browsers, they evaluated the existing schemes for encoding, transporting, and identifying multimedia information. Because the MIME scheme already handled the problems that they would encounter in sending multimedia, text, and binary objects, the HTTP developers adopted it for their needs.

If you're connecting to a site using the HTTP protocol, Web browsers handle MIME types in the following way:

1. The Web browser issues the connection request to the server, indicating the object that it wants from the URL that you entered or the link that you clicked.

2. Using its MIME type mapping table, the server looks at the object and determines what its MIME type is, usually based on its file extension.

3. The server sends the object as a MIME-encoded data stream back to the browser.

4. When the file arrives, the browser checks the MIME headers to find out what kind of MIME type the item is. It uses its MIME type mapping table to decide whether to display the item, launch an associated helper application, or ask the user what it should do.

MIME Types, Plug-Ins, and Helper Applications

Netscape is able to directly display ASCII text, HTML files, and GIF, JPEG, and XBM graphics. If the object is one of these items, it will be displayed directly in the browser. If it's another kind of object, Netscape checks to see if there's a plug-in application available to handle it; if there isn't, Netscape then checks your settings to see if you have identified a helper application to launch and interpret the file. If you didn't identify a helper application for the MIME type, then Netscape asks if you want to save the file; pick an application to associate it with; cancel the operation; or see more information about MIME types.

NOTE

If you're working with a local URL or are using FTP to request an object, the browser doesn't receive any specific instructions about what kind of file it is since the object isn't MIME-encoded. Instead, the browser decides what kind of object it's looking at based on the object's file extension. (Objects that you receive from the network using the FTP protocol are handled this way because the FTP protocol predates the use of MIME types.)

One of the most important ways that you improve your use of Netscape is in providing a full suite of plug-ins and helper applications to handle all the MIME types that you're likely to encounter and configuring your browser accordingly. Table 8.1 shows a list of some of the most common MIME types and file extensions.

Table 8.1 Common MIME Types on the World Wide Web

Type/Subtype	File Extensions	Type of File
image/gif	.gif	GIF graphic
image/jpeg	.jpg, .jpeg, .jpe	JPEG graphic
image/pict	.pict	PICT graphic
image/tiff	.tiff, .tif	TIFF graphic
image/x-bitmap	.xbm	X-bitmap graphic
audio/basic	.au, .snd	Basic sound
audio/x-wav	.wav	WAV sound file
audio/x-aiff	.aiff, .aif	AIFF sound file
video/quicktime	.qt, .mov	QuickTime movie
video/mpeg	.mpeg, mpg	MPEG movie
text/html	.html, .htm, .mdl	HTML file
text/plaintext	.txt	ASCII text file
application/rtf	.rtf	Microsoft's Rich Text Format file
application/mac-binhex40	.hqx	Binhex-encoded binary
application/macbin	.bin	MacBinary-encoded Macintosh binary
application/x-zip-compressed	.zip	Zip archive

Table 8.1 Common MIME Types on the World Wide Web (continued)

Type/Subtype	File Extensions	Type of File
application/x-stuffit	.sit	StuffIt archive
application/postscript	.ai, .epx, .ps	PostScript file
application/octet-stream	.exe, .bin	Executable file

NOTE

Interested in finding out even more about MIME types? Check out RFCs 1521 and 1522, which propose and define MIME types. The RFCs are available at http://www.oac.uci.edu/indiv/ehood/MIME/MIME.html and elsewhere on the Internet. For less technical, more user-friendly information, check out Usenet's comp.mail.mime FAQ (frequently asked questions list), available at ftp://ftp.uu.net/usenet/news.answers/mail/mime-faq/ and elsewhere on the Internet. (An explanation of RFCs appears in Chapter 2.)

Common Graphics Formats

Formats for computer graphics vary in a number of significant areas, including how many colors the image contains, the kind of compression (if any) used to reduce the size of the file, and the type of computer with which they're primarily associated.

We've already said that an image is just a two-dimensional array of picture elements, a concept which is demonstrated by the Impressionist painters such as Seurat. Pixels (picture elements on your monitor) can vary from the simple monochrome, in which each point is either off (black) or on (the color of the monitor), to a system where each pixel can be chosen from a palette of millions of colors. While the schemes for handling pixel depth vary tremendously, here's a list of several of the most common pixel formats:

- 1 bit per pixel. In this scheme, each pixel typically represents either black or white. This scheme is also known as *monochrome*. It is still commonly used for bitmaps to be sent to printers or fax devices, but it is not as common on computer displays anymore. However, older one-piece Macintoshes all have built-in monochrome monitors. In this scheme, eight pixels can be stored in one byte of memory, since each pixel contains only one bit, which can either be on or off. (Remember, there are eight bits in a byte.)

- 4 bits per pixel. This is a fairly common scheme on VGA monitors. Two pixels can be stored in one byte of memory, as each pixel requires four bits. The greater the number of bits in a pixel, the more color or grayscale values can be represented by each pixel. The number of colors or shades of gray increases exponentially by the number of bits, each of which has two possible values. So, a 4-bit pixel can display 2^4 different values, or 16 colors or shades of gray.

- 8 bits per pixel. This is an extremely common format, in which each pixel represents one of 256 (2^8) possible colors or shades of gray. When used for grayscale images, 8 bits per pixel produces lovely images, because 256 grays gives you a smooth gradation of shades from pure black to pure white. However, it's not ideally suited for photographic images, as a naturalistic photograph generally has many more than 256 distinct colors in its palette, when all the variables including hue, saturation, and brightness are considered. In an 8-bit image, each pixel takes up one byte of space.

- 24 bits per pixel. This is the most common format on high-end multimedia displays, and it will probably become the eventual standard in another few generations of equipment. 24 bits per pixel is usually accomplished by separating each pixel into its red, green, and blue components, and assigning eight bits worth of information to each component color. This gives you 256 possible shades in each of the red, green, and blue components. (In fact, if you've ever worked with a color wheel in a program like Photoshop or just to pick a new background color for your Macintosh, you might have noticed that each color you select has three numbers assigned to it. These are the values of the red, green, and blue components that make up the pixels of the color you choose.) With this scheme, you have 2^{24}, or 16.7 million, colors.

Compression is a technique used to reduce the size of graphics files so that they take up less space and require a shorter time to transmit. Technically speaking, you could just store a two-dimensional array in a file; this is called a *raw bitmap*. BMP files on PCs are raw bitmaps. However, raw bitmap formats are not particularly common, as they're highly inefficient. If you look at an image, you'll notice that many adjacent pixels have the same value. For example, in a photograph of the Grand Canyon, the hazy blue color above the horizon might fill half the frame of the picture. Many, if not all, of those hazy blue points are exactly the same color. It would be wasteful to store that color value in memory hundreds of thousands of times in a row when you could simply record the number of adjacent pixels that share a common value and the color value in question. Compression recognizes the necessity of using elaborate schemes to keep track of adjacent groups of pixels with common values, thereby reducing the number of bytes of data needed to represent a picture.

Two of the most common picture file formats—GIF and JPEG—both use built-in compression; the difference is the degree of compression that they use. GIF files use a technique called *lossless compression*, which ensures that the original array of pixels is reconstructed identically to the original when displayed. JPEG, on the other hand, uses an even more extreme form of compression called *lossy compression*, which only approximately reconstructs the original array of pixels when the image is redisplayed. When you create a JPEG graphic, you choose the degree of compression to be used. The more compression you use, the smaller the file becomes, but the loss of fidelity in the image is increased. Nonetheless, in many cases, the stored image can be compressed to one tenth the size of the raw bitmap with little perceived degradation of the image.

The following is a brief description of the most popular image formats that you're likely to find on the Web:

- GIF (Graphics Interchange Format). This 8-bit, lossless compression format was originally developed by CompuServe, and has become one of the most widely used graphics formats on the Internet. GIF images are directly displayed by Netscape; no helper application is needed.

- JPEG. This 24-bit, lossy compression format was developed by the Joint Photographic Experts Group, a subgroup of the International Standards Organization. JPEG is a favorite on the Web, because it can represent millions of colors in relatively small files without perceptible loss of image quality. However, more complex compression requires longer times to draw the image, as it must decompress the image based on a more complicated algorithm. JPEG images are directly displayed by Netscape; no helper application is needed.

- XBM (X-bitmap). This is the native bitmap file format for X-Windows systems. XBM images are directly displayed by Netscape; no helper application is needed.

- TIFF (Tagged Image File Format). Jointly developed by Aldus and Microsoft, TIFF supports a variety of compression techniques. TIFF is most frequently used for grayscale images.

155

- PICT. This is the native bitmap file format for the Macintosh.

Common Audio Formats

Like graphics file formats, audio formats trade off between the quality of the sound and the size of the file necessary to contain it. 8-bit sound is acceptable for speech, but two-channel, 16-bit sound is necessary for true musical reproductions. Sound file formats tend to be platform-specific; if you work with a sound file that's native to your system, you won't need special tools to play the audio. But in the heterogeneous world of the Web, you'll probably end up wanting to listen to audio formats that aren't designed for your platform and that require special tools.

The following is a list of the most common audio formats found on the Web:

- AU files. The actual name for files with this extension is µlaw (pronounced mew-law). This is the native sound format for Sun and many other UNIX workstations, and is becoming increasingly popular on other platforms because of its sophisticated compression techniques.
- WAV. This is the native sound format for Microsoft Windows, and it is probably going to be an industry standard for a while. (After all, an 800-pound gorilla can sleep anywhere it wants.)
- AIFF. This common sound format is used for entertainment-quality reproductions. Its greatest corporate proponents are Apple and Silicon Graphics.
- SND. This is the native format for sounds on the Macintosh.

Common Video Formats

One of the more exciting things about computer-based multimedia is the comparatively recent ability to display video clips directly on the computer. However, there's still a long way to go before desktop video looks as good as television or movies. Although some high-end computers can display full-motion video at 30 frames per second like your television set, most movies that you'll find on the Web will play at about 10–12 frames per second or less in a fairly small window on your screen. And because each frame is actually a separate picture, the size of movie files can become immense—just one second of video requires the display of 12 different images! Compression is even more crucial in video formats than it is in graphics formats, because the pictures have to be drawn quickly enough to fool the eye into perceiving motion.

Although there are a growing number of video standards in use today, the following is a list of the most common video formats found on the Web:

- QuickTime. This is Apple's standard for digital video. It is gaining general popularity with their release of QuickTime for Windows.
- MPEG. This format was developed by the Motion Picture Experts Group, a subgroup of the International Standards Organization. With its good compression and wide availability of players, many industry watchers think MPEG is going to become the predominant standard for future multimedia products, both on the Internet and on CD-ROM.

About Helper Applications

The next three chapters contain specific information about choosing and configuring helper applications for Windows, Macintosh, and UNIX computers. The following is a general discussion of how Netscape works with helper applications.

There are three different ways that Netscape uses helper applications:

- To let you view or play objects on the Web
- To handle the downloading and decoding of applications and data files
- To launch supporting applications for other kinds of network sessions

Viewers and Players

If configured to do so, Netscape will automatically launch viewers and players to let you work with items that you encounter on the Web. These items, which may be graphics, movies, or sound files, are downloaded to your computer and stored in a temporary file. Netscape then launches the helper application that you identified and sends it the contents of the temporary file so that you can see the movie or hear the sound.

WARNING

Items in temporary files will be frequently deleted by the browser. If you want to save the object that you downloaded for future use, you must use the Save feature of the helper application.

NOTE

Viewers and players are the kinds of helper applications that are most commonly available as plug-ins.

Archive, Compression, and Decoding Tools

Other items that you'll find on the Web are intended for permanent use instead of for temporary viewing. These are generally archived or encoded data or application files that you download and that you may or may not use in conjunction with your Web browser.

Netscape's responsibility in this case is to deliver the file to your hard drive in a usable format. If you identified a helper application for Netscape to use when handling certain types of archives (like tarred, zipped, or stuffed files) or encoding techniques (like uuencode or binhex), then Netscape launches the helper application to decode and unarchive the files. However, Netscape will not launch the item that you downloaded.

NOTE

You may come across self-extracting archives on the Web. These files are self-contained archives which include a small expander program within the archive, and which therefore don't require an external helper application for expansion—you simply launch the file. (However, Macintosh archives—whether self-expanding or not—are stored on Web servers in an encoded form, most likely binhex. When you download these files, Netscape hands them off to a helper application to decode the file. StuffIt Expander, a popular helper application, will also automatically expand the archive, though other utilities that handle binhex, like DeHQX, will only decode the archive.) On the Macintosh, the common file extension is .sea; on Windows, the common suffix is .exe. (These items are handled somewhat differently; we'll discuss this more in the chapters for each platform.) Self-extracting archives often become a set of several files containing an installer or setup program that you launch to make sure the files are placed in the correct locations, but they may also simply contain a number of other files.

Other Kinds of Supporting Applications

Besides configuring your browser to handle different MIME types, you must also identify three other supporting applications for Netscape: telnet and TN3270 emulators, and a viewer for HTML source documents.

Telnet and TN3270

There's still a great deal of information on the Internet which requires a traditional text-only terminal to view. For example, most university and public library catalogs, as well as most *freenets* (local free computer networks dedicated to community service), require you to emulate an old-fashioned telnet or TN3270 terminal session to connect to these sites. (Telnet is an Internet-based terminal emulator for traditional VT-100 ASCII terminals, while TN3270 is an Internet-based terminal emulator for the IBM 3270 and related video display terminals. There are still enough of these 3270-based IBM machines available on the Internet to make TN3270 a useful helper application, even though you don't hear about it as much as telnet.) To access these sites from the Web, you must make the appropriate applications available to Netscape.

Viewer for HTML Source Documents

When you start writing your own HTML documents, you might find that you're suddenly a lot more interested in how other Web authors achieve their effects. You can view the HTML code for a document simply by selecting **Document Source** from the View menu.

VIRTUOSO

Netscape will allow you to view the source code of a document directly in the browser window, or to choose another viewer such as a simple text editor like NotePad, WordPad, SimpleText, or xedit. If you view the source in Netscape, you won't be able to save or edit the document, but if you view it in another application, the HTML file will be downloaded separately to your computer so you can manipulate it directly. If you've started using full-featured HTML editors like BBEdit, HotMeTaL, or Microsoft Word's HTML extensions, you might want to change the default application so you can display the file directly in a useful application. Or, if you're using Netscape Navigator Gold, you can display the HTML directly in Gold's editor window.

WARNING

If you think you'll be working with large documents, don't set your HTML viewer to SimpleText on the Macintosh or NotePad on Windows; these applications can not open files larger than 32K.

About Plug-Ins

Support for plug-ins was one of the most exciting new features of Netscape 2.0. Basically, plug-ins are a special class of helper applications that have the following additional characteristics:

- Unlike helper applications, you don't need to go through any special configuration steps to get plug-ins to work. You simply install them in Netscape's special Plug-ins folder and you're ready to go.

- Plug-ins have the unique ability to display or play data directly in the Netscape window. For example, a helper application for QuickTime must launch and play the movie in a separate window, while a QuickTime plug-in can play the movie right on the Netscape page. This greatly increases the Web's potential to deliver seamless multimedia, because it makes it possible to have the same kinds of video, animation, and sound that we've come to expect from CD-ROMs delivered directly across the Web. (That is, if you have an incredibly fast connection, a reasonably fast computer, and a lot of free RAM and disk space.)

In Chapter 12, we'll discuss some of the most popular plug-ins in more detail.

Helper Applications vs. Plug-Ins: What Should I Use?

With all the excitement that the recently-developed plug-in technology has generated, you might wonder why you should even bother using helper applications. If plug-ins are the cutting edge of Internet multimedia, what's the point in working with anything else?

All the industry hype aside, there are some very compelling reasons to use helper applications instead of plug-ins.

Excessive RAM Consumption

Plug-ins require a significant amount of memory that needs to be available in addition to the memory required solely by the Netscape browser. Unlike independent helper applications, who receive their RAM allocation from the operating system, plug-ins get their memory allocation directly from Netscape. This means that Netscape has to "grab" enough RAM at launch to be able to support not only itself but also the greediest plug-in that you have installed.

The trouble is, some of the plug-ins that add the the most interesting multimedia functionality require huge amounts of memory. For example, the most recent version of Shockwave for the Macintosh, which is in beta at the time of this writing, requires that you increase Netscape's minimum RAM allocation to 8 MB (instead of the default 4 MB) and the disk cache to 5 MB (which you could otherwise set to any level you want.) This means that having 8 MB of installed RAM, a common amount for personal computers, is no longer enough.

And for some people, the problem gets worse. On the Macintosh, where memory allocation is still assigned statically (see Chapter 5 for information about increasing Netscape's memory allocation), you need to manually provide enough memory to satisfy Netscape as well as the most RAM-intensive of the plug-ins that might be simultaneously active. That memory is permanently assigned to Netscape while it's open, whether Netscape is using it or not. So, no other programs can get the memory while Netscape is running, regardless of whether it's being fully used. (This isn't quite as big a problem on Windows; although you still need to worry about whether you have enough installed RAM to handle the plug-ins, you don't have to manually change the allocation to the Netscape application. Windows dynamically assigns as much memory as an application needs, and always uses virtual memory, so it'll always try to give enough memory to your applications without you getting involved).

Problems With Beta Software

You can assign any kind of application to be a helper application, as long as it can handle the kind of data that you ask it to work with, but plug-ins have to be specially designed to work with the browser. As a technology, plug-ins have only been around since the second half of 1995, while other text, graphics, audio, and video applications have been in existence for years. The first generation of plug-ins are only now (as of this writing) in the beta stage of software development; since beta software has not been subjected to rigorous quality control testing, and is not considered to be of good enough quality to sell commercially, the best that you can hope for is that most of the bugs in the software have been found and documented in release notes. (For example, at the time of this writing, the Adobe Acrobat Reader had been a commercial product for months, but the Amber plug-in was still in beta development.)

Lessened Ability to Manipulate Data

Lessened ability to manipulate data. When a helper application handles data, such as a sound or an animation, it usually downloads it to your computer as an individual file. When you're using the interface of a helper application, you can manipulate, replay, save or edit the file. But in some cases, if the data is handled "invisibly" by a plug-in, you don't have easy access to an interface that will let you save the file for future use, unless the plug-in provides one for you. In short, they're not very good for collecting files and other resources to use later.

What You Learned

After reading this chapter, you should be able to:

- Understand why MIME types were developed and their importance to the multimedia capabilities of the World Wide Web.
- Identify common MIME types and file extensions.
- Know how and why helper applications are used.
- Know how and why plug-ins are used.

CHAPTER 9

HELPER APPLICATIONS FOR WINDOWS

In Chapter 8, we discussed how MIME types came to be and why they're so important for transmitting and displaying multimedia across a heterogeneous, distributed network like the Internet and, of course, the World Wide Web. In this chapter, we'll learn to configure Netscape to use helper applications and will describe some of the most popular packages.

NOTE

To make best use of this chapter, please read Chapter 8 first. It contains background material about MIME types and helper applications.

NOTE

Wondering whether to use plug-ins or helper applications? See "Plug-ins vs. Helper Applications: What Should I Use?" in Chapter 8 to help you make your choice.

First, we'll discuss the general procedure for associating helper applications with MIME types. Then, we'll cover some specific packages that you may wish to use.

Configuring Netscape for Helper Applications

There are two general procedures in configuring Netscape to work with helper applications: identifying the MIME type and attaching the MIME type to an application, a file type, and an action for Netscape when it encounters that kind of file. For common MIME types such as TIFF graphics or QuickTime movies, the MIME type is already defined in Netscape, so you can skip the first part of the procedure. (A table of some common MIME types defined in Netscape appears in Chapter 8.)

However, new MIME types are often created for specific purposes. For example, RealAudio Progressive Networks defined a new MIME type and associated helper applications and plug-ins that allow you to listen to a sound file while it's being downloaded (in "real time") instead of waiting for several minutes for the entire file to be retrieved to your desktop. (We'll talk more about the RealAudio plug-in in Chapter 12.)

If you encounter a helper application for a MIME type that isn't already defined, you'll need to add an entry for the type to Netscape, to which you'll assign the application.

About the Helper Applications Configuration Window

All configuration of helper applications for Netscape occurs in the Helper Applications section of Preferences. To display this window, follow these steps:

1. From the Options menu, select **General**....
2. Click the **Helpers** tab. A window similar to Figure 9.1 will be displayed.

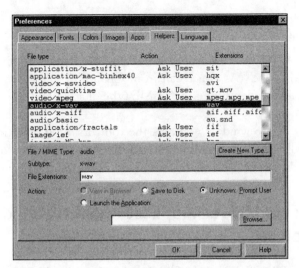

Figure 9.1 Helper Applications configuration window.

NOTE

At the time of this writing, it seemed likely that the screens and procedures for configuring Netscape 3.0 for Windows to use helper applications would change to be similiar to the procedures described for the Macintosh in Chapter 10. If your screen does not look similar to the one in Figure 9.1, check Chapter 10 to see if the screens and procedures there are corrrect for your version of Netscape. However, the information in this chapter about locating various helper applications for Windows will still be correct.

Here's a description of the items on the window:

- The **File type** section contains all the MIME content types that are currently defined in Netscape. (You'll recall from Chapter 8 that MIME types consist of the general MIME type and a unique content type identifier.) If you create a new MIME type, it will be added to this list.

- The **Action** section describes what Netscape will do when it encounters that kind of file. The options are: to view it in the browser, which is only available for items that Netscape can display directly; to save it to the disk so that you can work with the file later; to prompt the user for instructions as to whether it should save the file, delete the file, or open it with an application that you identify on the fly; or to launch the assigned application.

- The **Extensions** section lists the file extensions associated with that MIME type. (As you recall from Chapter 8, file extensions are often crucial for identifying the MIME type of a file.)

The rest of the window contains the tools for modifying information for the MIME type that you select in the top part of the window and for creating additional MIME types.

Associating a Helper Application with an Existing MIME Type

This section contains instructions for associating an application with an existing MIME type. You'll need to do this if you download helper applications for the MIME types that are already defined in Netscape but that can't be displayed directly in the viewer. For example, if you've retrieved LView so that you can display TIFF files, you'll need to associate the LView helper application with the MIME type **image/tiff**. (If you need to add a MIME type or modify a MIME type's associated file extensions, go to the next section.)

To associate a helper application with a MIME type, display the Helper Applications window as described above, then follow these steps:

1. Locate and select the MIME type that you wish to identify with a helper application. The bottom half of the window will update to display the current information about the MIME type that you selected.

2. In the area next to **Action**, choose the action that Netscape should take when it encounters a file of that type.

VIRTUOSO

For large documents and other material that you're likely to need later, the most appropriate action is to save the file to your disk so you can work with it after your Netscape session. For example, if you configure the **application/x-zip-compressed** MIME type to work with WinZip and to simply save the file, any ZIP archives that you download will be stored instead of launched.

- If you want Netscape to save the file to your storage disk, click **Save to Disk**.

- If you want Netscape to ask you what to do with the file so that you may identify an application on the fly or simply save or delete the file, click **Unknown: Prompt User**.

- If you want Netscape to launch an application associated with that MIME type, select **Launch the Application**.

NOTE The first item in the list—**View in Browser**—is only selectable for MIME types such as GIF and JPEG that Netscape can display directly. It is also the default for these files. Generally you won't need to associate these types with external applications, though you can if you desire.

3. To associate a helper application with a MIME type, follow these steps:

   a. Click **Browse....** A dialog box for selecting an appropriate helper application will be displayed.

   b. Navigate through your files until you locate and select the application you wish to associate with the currently selected MIME type.

   c. Click **Open**.

4. When you're finished, select another MIME type to modify or click **OK** to return to the main browser window.

NOTE Be sure to click **OK**; if you click **Cancel**, all changes that you made since opening the Preferences window will be lost.

Creating or Modifying a MIME Type

If you wish to configure Netscape to use a helper application with a MIME type that is not displayed by default, then you'll need to add information about the new MIME type to the browser before you can associate a helper application with it. Also, you may need to modify the information that appears for an existing MIME type, such as the file extensions associated with it.

Creating a New MIME Type

If you're creating a MIME type for a special Web-related helper application such as RealAudio, instructions will be provided containing the exact information to enter for the MIME type, subtype, and file extensions for the procedures described below.

If you wish to create a new MIME type, display the Helper Applications window in Preferences, then follow these steps:

1. Click **Create New Type**.... The Configure New MIME Type window (Figure 9.2) will be displayed.

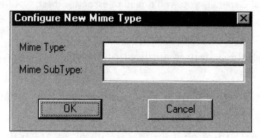

Figure 9.2 Configure New MIME Type window.

2. In the **Mime Type** field, type the general MIME classification (usually text, application, image, audio, or video).

3. In the **Mime SubType** field, type the specific MIME subtype that you're identifying. This uniquely identifies the new MIME type.

4. Click **OK** to return to the Apps window. The MIME type you created will be selected and will appear at the bottom of the list.

5. In the **File Extensions** field, enter the file extensions associated with the MIME type. If there's more than one file extension, separate them with commas.

Do not include the period that separates a file extension from a file name. For example, for the .exe file extension, only enter **exe**.

NOTE

6. In the area next to **Action**, choose the action that Netscape should take when it encounters a file of that type.

   - If you want Netscape to save the file to your storage disk, click **Save to Disk**.

   - If you want Netscape to ask you what to do with the file so that you may identify an application on the fly or simply save or delete the file, click **Unknown: Prompt User**.

   - If you want Netscape to launch an application associated with that MIME type, select **Launch the Application**.

7. To associate a helper application with the MIME type, follow these steps:

   a. Click **Browse**.... A window for selecting an appropriate viewer will be displayed.

   b. Navigate through your files until you locate and select the application you wish to associate with the currently selected MIME type.

   c. Click **Open**.

8. When you're finished, select a MIME type to modify, create another MIME type, or click **OK** to return to the main browser window.

Be sure to click **OK**; if you click **Cancel**, all changes that you made since opening the Preferences window will be lost.

N O T E

Modifying an Existing MIME Type

If you wish to modify information for an existing MIME type, select the MIME type in the top of the Helper Applications window and modify information as desired. Use the instructions in the preceding sections for an explanation of your options.

Popular Helper Applications

Just as there are many different kinds of spreadsheets, word processing programs, and even Web browsers, there are many different helper applications available for every kind of MIME type that you might encounter. In this section, we'll discuss the most popular helper applications for the MIME types that you'll encounter most frequently on the Web. This list is far from definitive—you should feel free to experiment with other helper applications to see which ones best suit your preferences and your needs. And, it's important to keep in mind that helper applications frequently come and go, often being replaced by the latest great utility. It's best to be flexible in your search for and use of helper applications to support your Web surfing.

NOTE Netscape's Web site contains information and FTP links for several popular helper applications at http://home.netscape.com/assist/helper_apps/windowhelper.html. Another good place to look for helper applications is at NCSA's Web site; since they created the first graphical Web browser, they maintain a great deal of information that is relevant to Web browsers in general. Check them out at ftp://ftp.ncsa.uiuc.edu/Mosaic/Windows/viewers. Also, Stroud's Consummate Winsock Apps List, at http://www.cwsapps.com/, is justified in its name: you'll find more information than you can imagine about the vast spectrum of Winsock applications that you can use, including product reviews.

NOTE FTP information for the helper applications listed below is in the form of a URL, as you can use Netscape to retrieve these files. If you can't find the files at the sites listed below, try an Archie search for an up-to-date listing of several sites that do have copies of the files. (For more information about FTP and Archie, see Chapter 16.)

WARNING After you download a file, you should always look for a README file. These files contain installation instructions specifically for the software package, as well as information about registration and any associated shareware fees.

VIRTUOSO Want to make sure that your helper applications are configured correctly? Check out the WWW Viewer Test page at http://www-dsed.llnl.gov/documents/, where samples of the most common Web files that you'll encounter are conveniently located on a single page.

Decompression Utilities

Since most of the files for Windows that you'll encounter on the Web are compressed with a ZIP utility, an "unzipper" is far and away the most important helper application to obtain and install before trying to retrieve any other software. Associate the helper application for ZIP files with the MIME type **application/x-zip-compressed** (also sometimes **application/zip**).

A variety of tools are available to extract and decompress ZIP files. Our favorite is the WinZip utility, because of its easy-to-use graphical interface and wide range of options. An evaluation version of WinZip can be obtained directly from the company at http://www.winzip.com/download.htm.

Graphics Utilities

Nearly every graphics format that isn't handled directly by Netscape can be viewed with LView, a popular image editor for Windows. LView not only lets you view most kinds of graphics files, but also lets you edit and manipulate them. A 16-bit version of LView for Windows 3.1 is available via anonymous FTP at ftp://ftp.ncsa.uiuc.edu/Mosaic/Windows/viewers/lviewp1b.zip; a 32-bit version for Windows 95 and Windows NT is available at ftp://ftp.ncsa.uiuc.edu/Mosaic/Windows/viewers/lviewp1c.zip. You can associate this application with a variety of graphics MIME types, notably **image/tiff**.

Sound Utilities

Netscape Communications distributes their own sound plug-in called LiveAudio with each copy of the Netscape browser. So, by virtue of the fact that you have installed Netscape for Windows, you already have a plug-in that will handle the **audio/basic**, **audio/x-aiff**, **audio/wav**, and **audio/midi** MIME types by default. For more information about using LiveAudio, see Chapter 12.

If you decide to use helper applications instead, a popular sound utility is WHAM, which lets you modify and manipulate nearly every kind of

sound file in addition to playing them. WHAM is available at ftp://
gatekeeper.dec.com/pub/micro/msdos/win3/sounds/wham133.zip.

Video Utilities

The most common formats for video on the Web are QuickTime
(**video/quicktime**), MPEG (**video/mpeg**), and AVI (**video/x-msvideo**).
Some plug-ins may be available for different kinds of video; for complete
information, see Chapter 12.

Netscape Communications distributes their own AVI plug-in called
LiveVideo with each copy of the Netscape browser. So, by virtue of the
fact that you have installed Netscape for Windows, you already have a
plug-in that will handle the **video/x-msvideo** MIME type by default. If
you wish to use a regular AVI player as a helper application, you can find
one at ftp://gatekeeper.dec.com/pub/micro/msdos/win3/desktop/
avipro2.exe.

The Chinese University of Hong Kong has created extensions that let
you play QuickTime movies through the Windows 3.x and Windows 95
Media Player (MPLAYER.EXE). These extensions can be found at
http://www.ncsa.uiuc.edu/SDG/Software/WinMosaic/Viewers/qt.htm. Or,
you can get Apple's real QuickTime for Windows at http://quicktime
.apple.com/qt/sw/licensew.html.

A shareware player for MPEG movies is MPEGPLAY, available at
ftp://gatekeeper.dec.com/pub/micro/msdos/win3/desktop/mpegw32g.zip.

Adobe Acrobat PDF Files

Adobe, the company that brought us PostScript, Photoshop, Illustrator,
FreeHand, and other high-end graphics processing tools as well as many
of the fonts that we use today, has created an application called Acrobat,
which allows developers to create perfectly formatted cross-platform documents that contain advanced features like color, graphics, fonts, and navigation options.

Acrobat files are commonly referred to as PDF (Portable Document
Format) files, and they use PDF as their file extension. A free reader for
Adobe Acrobat is available at http://www.adobe.com/acrobat/windows.html.

(Or, you can download and use the Adobe Acrobat Amber plug-in at http://www.adobe.com/Amber/, but at the time of this writing, it was a special "pre-release" version—in other words, it was too full of bugs to ship as a commercial product.)

NOTE You'll have to create a MIME type for PDF files. Use the MIME type **application/pdf** and the file extension **pdf**. See Adobe's instructions at http://www.adobe.com/acrobat/helpers/netscape-win.html for complete information.

VIRTUOSO Because PDF files are typically large documents containing a great deal of information, you might want to configure Netscape to simply save PDF files so you can review them later.

RTF Utilities

RTF is Microsoft's Rich Text Format, a method of converting any binary created by a Microsoft word processor to an encoded text file that can be reconstructed to contain the original information. RTF is a popular way to transmit formatted Microsoft Word documents across the Internet, since turning them into text documents makes it possible to mail them without further need of encoding.

If you're using Windows 95, you can associate the MIME type **application/rtf** with WordPad; this built-in word processing utility can read and write RTF files. If you're using another version of Windows, you'll need to associate RTF files with Microsoft Word or another product that supports RTF.

Using Other Supporting Applications

As we discussed in Chapter 8, Netscape handles supporting applications for telnet, TN3270, and for viewing the source code of HTML documents separately, as they are not associated with any MIME types.

To configure Netscape for these helper applications, follow these steps:

1. At the General Preferences window, click the **Apps** tab. The following window (Figure 9.3) will be displayed.

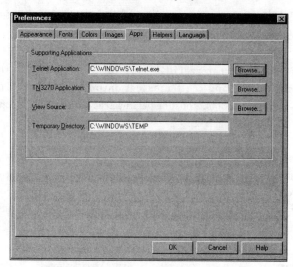

Figure 9.3 Applications configuration screen.

2. Next to each application that you wish to associate with Netscape, follow these steps:

   a. Click **Browse....**

   b. Locate and select the application you wish to use.

   c. Click **Open**.

3. When finished, click **OK**.

Telnet Applications

Windows 95 is distributed with a rudimentary telnet application called Telnet.exe, which should be located in the Windows folder. If you're not using Windows 95, a popular shareware telnet application for Windows is WinQVT, available at: ftp://hubcap.clemson.edu/pub/pc_shareware/windows/Comm/winqvt.exe.

TN3270 Applications

It's fairly rare to come across a link to a TN3270 session, but if you do, you can retrieve QWS3270, a shareware TN3270 application, from ftp://hubcap.clemson.edu/pub/pc_shareware/windows/Comm/qws3270.zip.

Applications for Viewing Source

You can look at the HTML source code of any document by selecting **Document Source** from the View menu. If you don't specify an application, Netscape will launch an internal text viewer, which will not allow you to edit documents directly.

NOTE

If you're using Netscape Navigator Gold, you can edit a local copy of the document by selecting **Edit Document** from the File menu.

If you wish to view documents on the Web in another application, such as an HTML editor, you'll need to specify the application in the **View Source** field.

HoTMetaL Free—a freeware version of SoftQuad's popular HoTMetaL Pro—is available at ftp://ftp.ncsa.uiuc.edu/Web/html/hotmetal/Windows/hotm1new.exe.

What You Learned

After reading this chapter, you should be able to:

- Associate helper applications with MIME types.
- Create new MIME types.
- Obtain and configure popular helper applications for your platform.
- Choose appropriate actions for Netscape when it encounters identified MIME types.
- Associate telnet, TN3270, and source viewers with Netscape.

CHAPTER 10

HELPER APPLICATIONS FOR
THE MACINTOSH

In Chapter 8, we discussed how MIME types came to be and why they're so important for transmitting and displaying multimedia across a heterogeneous, distributed network like the Internet and, of course, the World Wide Web. In this chapter, we'll learn to configure Netscape to use helper applications and will describe some of the most popular packages.

To make best use of this chapter, please read Chapter 8 first. It contains background material about MIME types and helper applications.

NOTE

Wondering whether to use plug-ins or helper applications? See "Plug-ins vs. Helper Applications: What Should I Use?" in Chapter 8 to help you make your choice.

NOTE

First, we'll talk about the general procedure for associating helper applications with MIME types. Then, we'll talk about specific packages that you may wish to use.

Configuring Netscape for Helper Applications

There are two general procedures in configuring Netscape to work with helper applications: identifying the MIME type and attaching the MIME type to an application, a file type, and an action for Netscape when it encounters that kind of file. For common MIME types such as TIFF graphics or QuickTime movies, the MIME type is already defined in Netscape, so you can skip the first part of the procedure. (A table of some common MIME types defined in Netscape appears in Chapter 8.)

However, new MIME types are often created for specific purposes. For example, RealAudio Progressive Networks defined a new MIME type and associated helper applications and plug-ins that allow you to listen to a sound file while it's being downloaded (in "real time") instead of waiting for several minutes for the entire file to be retrieved to your desktop. (We'll talk more about the RealAudio plug-in in Chapter 12.)

If you encounter a helper application for a MIME type that isn't already defined, you'll need to add an entry for the type to Netscape, to which you'll assign the application.

About the Helper's Configuration Window

All configuration of helper applications for Netscape occurs in the Helper Applications section of Preferences. To display this window, follow these steps:

1. From the Options menu, select **General Preferences**....

2. Click the **Helpers** tab. A window similar to Figure 10.1 will be displayed.

Here's a description of the items on the window:

- The **Description** section contains a description of each of the MIME types that Netscape is configured to handle. To see the actual MIME type for an item, select its name and click **Edit**....

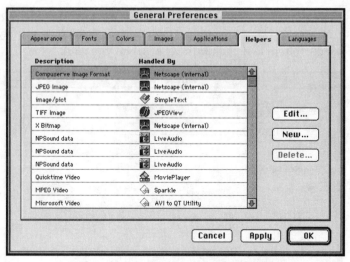

Figure 10.1 Helpers configuration window.

- The **Handled By** section shows which application is configured to handle the MIME type and what will happen when the MIME type is encountered. The options are: to save it to the disk so that you can work with the file later; to launch the assigned application; to view it in the browser, which is only available for items that Netscape can display directly; or to prompt the user for instructions as to whether it should save the file, delete the file, or open it with an application that you identify on the fly.

- Netscape for the Macintosh "prefers" to associate certain file types with common applications. For example, it assumes that you'll be using JPEGView to look at TIFF files and SimpleText to look at PICT files, and places those items in the Handled By section. If you do not have a copy of the preferred application installed on your machine, then the icon will appear grayed out.

NOTE

You don't have to use the applications that Netscape recommends; they're just included so that if you do choose to install them, you won't need to perform any additional configuration steps.

All of the steps in configuring Netscape to work with helper applications occur in the Edit Type window (Figure 10.2), which is displayed when you select an item and click **Edit...**, or when you click **New...**.

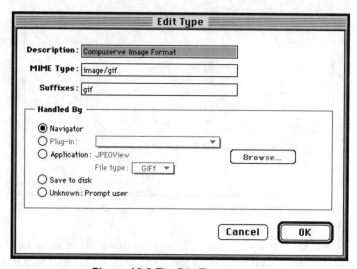

Figure 10.2 The Edit Type window.

- The **Description** field contains the description of the MIME type that appears in the first Helpers window.
- The **MIME Type** field contains the MIME type that you're currently working with. (You'll recall from Chapter 8 that MIME types consist of the general MIME type and a unique content type identifier.)
- The **Suffixes** section lists the file extensions associated with that MIME type. (As you recall from Chapter 8, file extensions are often crucial for identifying the MIME type of a file.)
- The **Handled By** section contains information about which application program should be associated with the MIME type and what should happen if such a MIME type is encountered.

The most unusual item on this window is the **File type** pop-up menu, which is unique to the Macintosh.

About the File Type Pop-up Menu

While other operating systems use file extensions to determine what kind of application to associate with a file, the Macintosh uses a pair of tags called a *signature*. The signature—which consists of a TYPE tag and a CREATOR tag, each containing four unique characters—is considered by the operating system as the authoritative identification mechanism for file types. If you use Netscape to open a file that's located on your hard drive, the Macintosh will look at the signature to determine what MIME type and/or application to associate with the file.

Each time you add a new helper application, Netscape checks to see which file types are associated with that application (which is considered the creator) and adds them to the File type pop-up menu. By default, Netscape selects the file type which is most common for the application. However, if you create a new MIME type or select an application that is not normally associated with that kind of file, no file type will be associated with the MIME type by default. (All the associated file types will appear in the pop-up menu, but none will be displayed as selected. You'll have to choose the file type that's appropriate for the type of document that you'll be retrieving.)

VIRTUOSO

To view the signatures associated with common file types, try an application like FileTyper, available at http://hyperarchive.lcs.mit.edu/HyperArchive/Archive/disk/filetyper-422.hqx. FileTyper is an invaluable tool for understanding the way that the Macintosh associates file types with applications.

Associating a Helper Application with an Existing MIME Type

This section contains instructions for associating an application with an existing MIME type. You'll need to do this if you download helper applications for the MIME types that are already defined in Netscape but that can't be displayed directly in the viewer. For example, if you've retrieved JPEGView so that you can display TIFF files, you'll need to associate the JPEGView helper application with the MIME type **image/tiff**.

To associate a helper application with a MIME type, display the Helpers window as described above, then follow these steps:

1. Locate and select the MIME type that you wish to associate with a given helper application.

2. Click **Edit**.... The Edit Type window will be displayed.

3. In the **Handled By** section, select one of these items:

   • To let Netscape display data of this type, select **Navigator**. This item is only selectable for MIME types such as GIF and JPEG that Netscape can display directly; it is also the default for these files. Generally you won't need to associate these types with external applications, though you can if you desire.

   • To associate the MIME type with a plug-in, select **Plug-in** and choose the desired plug-in from the pop-up menu. Complete information on plug-ins can be found in Chapter 12.

   • To associate the MIME type with a helper application, select **Application** and proceed to step 4.

   • If you want Netscape to simply save the file to disk, select **Save to disk**.

VIRTUOSO

For large documents and other material that you're likely to need later, the most appropriate action is to save the file to your disk so you can work with it after your Netscape session. For example, if you create and configure the **application/pdf** MIME type to work with Adobe Acrobat Reader and to simply save the file, any PDF files that you download will be uncompressed and stored, instead of launched.

4. If you chose **Application** in step 3, follow these steps to associate a helper application with the MIME type:

   a. On the Application line, click **Browse**.... A window for selecting an appropriate viewer will be displayed.

   b. Navigate through your files until you locate and select the application you wish to associate with the currently selected MIME type.

   c. Click **Open**.

   d. If it is necessary to select a four-character file type other than the default, hold down the mouse over the **File type** pop-up menu and select the new type from the list.

See "About the File Type Pop-up Menu," in the preceding section.

NOTE

5. When you're finished, click **OK** to return to the Helpers window.

Be sure to click **OK**; if you click **Cancel**, all changes that you made since opening the Preferences window will be lost.

NOTE

6. At the Helpers window, click **OK** to save your modifications and return to the browser, or click **Apply** to save your modifications and remain at the Helpers window.

Creating or Modifying a MIME Type

If you wish to configure Netscape to use a helper application with a MIME type that is not displayed by default, then you'll need to add information about the new MIME type to the browser before you can associate a helper application with it. Also, you may need to modify the information that appears for an existing MIME type, such as the file extensions associated with it.

Creating a New MIME Type

If you see an error message that Netscape doesn't know what to do with a certain file, it means that there isn't a MIME type configured for that kind of file. The error message will contain the exact spelling of the MIME type and subtype to use during this configuration.

If you're creating a MIME type for a special Web-related helper application such as RealAudio, instructions will be provided containing the exact information to enter for the MIME type, subtype, and file extensions.

NOTE

If you wish to create a new MIME type, display the Helpers window in Preferences, then follow these steps:

1. Click **New**.... The Edit Type window will be displayed.

2. In the **Description** field, type a description of the MIME type. The text that you enter will describe the MIME type at the Helpers win-

dow. (If you don't enter anything, you won't be able to tell what the MIME type is for the helper application you identify.)

3. In the **MIME Type** field, enter the MIME classification (usually text, application, image, audio, or video) and the subtype for the new type, separated by a slash.

Remember, MIME types are in the form **type/subtype**; for example, **application/pdf** or **image/tiff**.

NOTE

4. In the **Suffixes** field, enter the file extensions associated with the MIME type. If there's more than one file extension, separate them with commas.

Do not include the period that separates a file extension from a file name. For example, for the .exe file extension, only enter **exe**.

NOTE

5. In the **Handled By** section, select one of these items:

- To let Netscape display data of this type, select **Navigator**. This item is only selectable for MIME types such as GIF and JPEG that Netscape can display directly; it is also the default for these files. Generally you won't need to associate these types with external applications, though you can if you desire.

- To associate the MIME type with a plug-in, select **Plug-in** and choose the desired plug-in from the pop-up menu. Complete information on plug-ins can be found in Chapter 12.

- To associate the MIME type with a helper application, select **Application** and proceed to step 5.

- If you want Netscape to simply save the file to disk, select **Save to disk**.

VIRTUOSO

For large documents and other material that you're likely to need later, the most appropriate action is to save the file to your disk so you can work with it after your Netscape session. For example, if you create and configure the **application/pdf** MIME type to work with Adobe Acrobat Reader and to simply save the file, any PDF files that you download will be uncompressed and stored, instead of launched.

6. If you chose **Application** in step 4, follow these steps to associate a helper application with the MIME type:

   a. On the Application line, click **Browse**…. A window for selecting an appropriate viewer will be displayed.

   b. Navigate through your files until you locate and select the application you wish to associate with the currently selected MIME type.

   c. Click **Open**.

   d. If it is necessary to select a four-character file type other than the default, hold down the mouse over the **File type** pop-up menu and select the new type from the list.

NOTE

See "About the File Type Pop-up Menu," earlier in this chapter.

7. When you're finished, click **OK** to return to the Helpers window.

NOTE

Be sure to click **OK**; if you click **Cancel**, all changes that you made since opening the Preferences window will be lost.

8. At the Helpers window, click **OK** to save your modifications and return to the browser, or click **Apply** to save your modifications and remain at the Helpers window.

Modifying an Existing MIME Type

If you wish to modify information for an existing MIME type, select the description of the MIME type at the Helpers window, click **Edit**…, and modify information as desired. Use the instructions in the preceding sections for an explanation of your options. When you're finished, be sure to click **OK** or **Apply**; if you click **Cancel**, all changes that you made will be lost.

Popular Helper Applications

Just as there are many different kinds of spreadsheets, word processing programs, and even Web browsers, there are many different helper applications available for every kind of MIME type that you might encounter. In this section, we'll discuss the most popular helper applications for the MIME types that you'll encounter most frequently on the Web. This list is far from definitive—you should feel free to experiment with other helper applications to see which ones best suit your preferences and your needs. And, it's important to keep in mind that helper applications frequently come and go, often being replaced by the latest great utility. It's best to be flexible in your search for and use of helper applications to support your Web surfing.

NOTE Netscape's Web site contains reasonably current information and FTP links for several popular helper applications at http://home.netscape.com/assist/helper_apps /machelpers.html. Another good place to look for helper applications is at NCSA's Web site; since they created the first graphical Web browser, they maintain a great deal of information that is relevant to Web browsers in general. Check them out at ftp://ftp.ncsa.uiuc.edu/Mosaic/Mac/Helpers/.

NOTE FTP information for the helper applications listed below is in the form of a URL, as you can use Netscape to retrieve these files. If you can't find the files at the sites listed below, try an Archie search for an up-to-date listing of archive sites that will have copies of the files. (For more information about FTP and Archie, see Chapter 16.)

WARNING After you download a file, you should always look for a README file. These files contain installation instructions specifically for the software package, as well as information about registration and any associated shareware fees.

VIRTUOSO Want to make sure that your helper applications are configured correctly? Check out the WWW Viewer Test page at http://www-dsed.llnl.gov/documents/, where samples of the most common Web files that you'll encounter are conveniently located on a single page.

Decompression Utilities

As we discussed in Chapter 8, most applications that you'll find on the Web will be encoded as binhex files, with a .hqx extension. You'll also encounter files that have been compressed with StuffIt Lite or Compact Pro.

StuffIt Expander, a shareware utility by Aladdin Systems (the developers of the StuffIt product line), will decode and decompress any files that have been encoded with binhex and/or compressed with StuffIt Lite or Compact Pro. It's available via anonymous FTP from Aladdin at ftp://ftp.aladdinsys.com/Pub/stuffit_exp_40_installer.bin; you can also find it at NCSA's FTP site (the URL is at the beginning of this section).

WARNING

This file is encoded in the MacBinary format, which Netscape can't handle directly. Unfortunately, there's no point in downloading the binhexed version of the file, since the point is to retrieve a utility that can decode binhex. To obtain this file, use a graphical FTP application like Fetch or an old-fashioned terminal emulator for the Macintosh like ZTerm, either of which can correctly download MacBinary files to your computer without additional helper applications.

Netscape is automatically configured to use StuffIt Expander with the MIME types **application/mac-binhex40**, **application/x-stuffit**, and **application/x-macbinary**.

VIRTUOSO

Although Netscape is preconfigured to use other applications for **application/x-compressed** and **application/x-tar**, if you download a file called DropStuff from Aladdin Systems, you can configure StuffIt Expander to decode these files as well.

Graphics Utilities

Nearly every graphics format that isn't handled directly by Netscape can be viewed with JPEGView, a popular image viewer. JPEGView is available via anonymous FTP at ftp://ftp.ncsa.uiuc.edu/Mosaic/Mac/Helpers/jpeg-view-331.hqx. JPEGView is the default application for **image/gif**, **image/jpeg**, and **image/tiff**. (While GIF and JPEG files can be directly displayed by Netscape without a helper application, TIFF files cannot.)

Sound Utilities

Netscape Communications distributes their own sound plug-in called LiveAudio with each copy of the Netscape browser. So, by virtue of the fact that you have installed Netscape, you already have a plug-in that will handle the **audio/basic**, **audio/x-aiff**, **audio/wav**, and **audio/midi** MIME types by default. For more information about using LiveAudio, see Chapter 12.

If you decide to use helper applications for sound, a popular sound application is SoundMachine, available at ftp://ftp.ncsa.uiuc.edu /Mac/Mosaic/Helpers/sound-machine-21.hqx. A good utility for WAV files that can also handle several other file types is SoundApp, available at ftp://ftp.utexas.edu/pub/mac/sound/soundapp-20-fat.hqx.

Video Utilities

The most common formats for video on the Web are QuickTime (**video/quicktime**), MPEG (**video/mpeg**), and AVI (**video/x-msvideo**). Some plug-ins may be available for different kinds of video; for complete information, see Chapter 12.

Sparkle, Netscape's default application for MPEG movies, will play QuickTime movies as well. Sparkle can be obtained at ftp://ftp.ncsa.uiuc.edu/Mac/Mosaic/Helpers/sparkle-245.hqx.

WARNING Viewing QuickTime movies requires not only a helper application but also Apple's QuickTime System Extension. QuickTime 2.1 is shipped with new Macintoshes, and you can always get the latest version of QuickTime directly from Apple at http://quicktime.apple.com/qt/sw/sw.html. Meanwhile, an older version—QuickTime 1.6.2—can be obtained at ftp://ftp.cac.psu.edu//pub/mac/quicktime /QuickTime162.hqx.

AVI is Microsoft's Video for Windows format. While there is no AVI player for the Macintosh, a utility to convert AVI files to QuickTime movies can be found at ftp://mirrors.aol.com/pub/info-mac/gst/mov/avi-to-qt-converter.hqx.

NOTE By the time you read this, Netscape may have made their LiveVideo plug-in available for the Macintosh; this plug-in handles AVI video.

Adobe Acrobat PDF Files

Adobe, the company that brought us PostScript, Photoshop, Illustrator, FreeHand, and other high-end graphics processing tools as well as many of the fonts that we use today, has created an application called Acrobat, which allows developers to create perfectly formatted cross-platform documents that contain advanced features like color, graphics, fonts, and navigation options.

Acrobat files are commonly referred to as PDF (Portable Document Format) files, and they use PDF as their file extension. A free reader for Adobe Acrobat is available at http://www.adobe.com/acrobat/mac.html (Or, you can download and use the Adobe Acrobat Amber plug-in at http://www.adobe.com/Amber/, but at the time of this writing, it was a special "pre-release" version—in other words, it was too full of bugs to ship as a commercial product.)

NOTE You'll have to create a MIME type for PDF files. Use the MIME type **application/pdf** and the file extension **pdf**. See Adobe's instructions at http://www.adobe.com/acrobat/helpers/netscape-mac.html for complete information.

VIRTUOSO Because PDF files are typically large documents containing a great deal of information, you might want to configure Netscape to simply save PDF files so you can review them later.

RTF Utilities

RTF is Microsoft's Rich Text Format, a method of converting any binary created by a Microsoft word processor to an encoded text file that can be reconstructed to contain the original information. RTF is a popular way to transmit formatted Microsoft Word documents across the Internet, since turning them into text documents makes it possible to mail them without further need of encoding.

If you have a Microsoft application such as Word or Works, associate the MIME type **application/rtf** with it. If you're using another kind of word processor, check to see if it has extensions or filters which allow it to handle RTF files.

For this MIME type, be sure to select **TEXT** from the File type pop-up menu. RTF files must be handled as text in order to be interpreted correctly.

NOTE

Using Other Supporting Applications

As we discussed in Chapter 8, Netscape handles supporting applications for telnet, TN3270, and for viewing the source code of HTML documents separately, as they are not associated with any MIME types.

To configure Netscape for these helper applications, follow these steps:

1. In Preferences, select **Applications and Directories**. The following window (Figure 10.3) will be displayed.

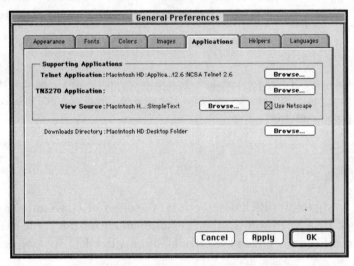

Figure 10.3 Applications configuration screen.

2. Next to each application that you wish to associate with Netscape, follow these steps:

   a. Click **Browse**....

   b. Locate and select the application you wish to use.

   c. Click **Open**.

3. When finished, click **OK**.

Telnet Applications

NCSA Telnet is a robust and popular telnet application for use with direct and dialup IP connections. NCSA Telnet 2.6 is available via anonymous FTP at ftp://ftp.ncsa.uiuc.edu/Mac/Telnet/Telnet2.6/Telnet2.6.sit.hqx. NCSA Telnet 2.7 was still in final beta testing at the time of this writing.

NOTE

You can download the User's Guide in a variety of formats, including PDF, at ftp://ftp.ncsa.uiuc.edu/Mac/Telnet/Telnet2.6/Telnet2.6UserGuide/.

TN3270 Applications

It's fairly rare to come across a link to a TN3270 session, but if you do, you can retrieve the TN3270 application in a variety of Macintosh formats from ftp://ftp.ncsa.uiuc.edu/Mac/Telnet/contributions/tn3270/.

Applications for Viewing Source

You can look at the HTML source code of any document by selecting **Document Source** from the View menu. If you don't specify an application, Netscape will default to TeachText or SimpleText, depending on which you have on your system (if SimpleText is available, Netscape and other Macintosh applications will always use it by default).

NOTE

If you're using Netscape Navigator Gold, you can edit a local copy of the document by selecting **Edit Document** from the File menu.

If you wish to view documents on the Web in another application, such as an HTML editor, you'll need to specify the application in the **View Source** field.

You'll definitely need to do this if you want to view files larger than 32K, as SimpleText cannot open files larger than that.

NOTE

BBEdit Lite with HTML Extensions is a popular shareware HTML editing utility. For information about obtaining BBEdit Lite and the HTML extensions (the extensions are provided separately from the BBEdit Lite application), see http://www.uji.es/bbedit-html-extensions.html.

If you just want to look at the HTML code for a file and don't want to edit it directly, you can use Netscape to view the HTML of any file that's displayed in the browser. To do so, just click **Use Netscape** at the right of the **View Source** item at the Appearance window.

VIRTUOSO

What You Learned

After reading this chapter, you should be able to:

- Associate helper applications with MIME types.
- Create new MIME types.
- Obtain and configure popular helper applications for your platform.
- Choose appropriate actions for Netscape when it encounters identified MIME types.
- Associate telnet, TN3270, and source viewers with Netscape.

CHAPTER 11

HELPER APPLICATIONS FOR UNIX

In Chapter 8, we discussed how MIME types came to be and why they're so important for transmitting and displaying multimedia across a hetero-geneous, distributed network like the Internet and, of course, the World Wide Web. In this chapter, we'll learn to configure Netscape to use helper applications and describe some of the most popular packages.

To make best use of this chapter, please read Chapter 8 first. It contains back-ground material about MIME types and helper applications.

NOTE

Wondering whether to use plug-ins or helper applications? See "Plug-ins vs. Helper Applications: What Should I Use?" in Chapter 8 to help you make your choice.

NOTE

First, we'll talk about the general procedure for associating helper applica-tions with MIME types. Then, we'll talk about specific packages that you may wish to use.

Configuring Netscape for Helper Applications

There are two general procedures in configuring Netscape to work with helper applications: identifying the MIME type and attaching the MIME type to an application, a file type, and an action for Netscape when it encounters that kind of file. For common MIME types such as TIFF graphics or QuickTime movies, the MIME type is already defined in Netscape, so you can skip the first part of the procedure. (A table of some common MIME types defined in Netscape appears in Chapter 8.)

However, new MIME types are often created for specific purposes. For example, RealAudio Progressive Networks defined a new MIME type and associated helper applications and plug-ins that allow you to listen to a sound file while it's being downloaded (in "real time") instead of waiting for several minutes for the entire file to be retrieved to your desktop. (We'll talk more about the RealAudio plug-in in Chapter 12.)

If you encounter a helper application for a MIME type that isn't already defined, you'll need to add an entry for the type to Netscape, to which you'll assign the application.

Changes in Netscape 3.0

In earlier versions of Netscape (all versions of 1.x and 2.x), configuration of MIME types took place in a separate file called *.mime.types* and configuration of helper applications took place in a separate file called *.mailcap*. With Netscape 3.0, manual editing of these files is no longer necessary; a graphical interface is provided within the General Preferences section to identify MIME types and helper applications for use by Netscape.

About the Helpers Configuration Window

All configuration of helper applications for Netscape occurs in the Helper Applications section of Preferences. To display this window, follow these steps:

1. From the Options menu, select **General Preferences**....
2. Click the **Helpers** tab.

Here's a description of the items on the window:

- The **Description** section contains a description of each of the MIME types that Netscape is configured to handle. To see the actual MIME type for an item, select its name and click **Edit**....

- The **Handle By** section shows which application is configured to handle the MIME type and what will happen when the MIME type is encountered. The options are: to save it to the disk so that you can work with the file later; to launch the assigned application; to view it in the browser, which is only available for items that Netscape can display directly; or to prompt the user for instructions as to whether it should save the file, delete the file, or open it with an application that you identify on the fly.

All of the steps in configuring Netscape to work with helper applications occur in the Netscape Helper window, which is displayed when you select an item and click **Edit...**, or when you click **New....**

- The **Description** field contains the description of the MIME type that appears in the first Helpers window.

- The **Mime Type** field contains the MIME type that you're currently working with. (You'll recall from Chapter 8 that MIME types consist of the general MIME type and a unique content type identifier.)

- The **Suffix** section lists the file extensions associated with that MIME type. (As you recall from Chapter 8, file extensions are often crucial for identifying the MIME type of a file.)

- The **Handle By** section contains information about which application program should be associated with the MIME type and what should happen if such a MIME type is encountered.

Associating a Helper Application with an Existing MIME Type

This section contains instructions for associating an application with an existing MIME type. You'll need to do this if you download helper applications for the MIME types that are already defined in Netscape but which can't be displayed directly in the viewer. For example, if you wish to use xview to display TIFF files, you'll need to associate the xview helper application with the MIME type **image/tiff**.

To associate a helper application with a MIME type, display the Helpers Configuration window as described above, then follow these steps:

1. Locate and select the MIME type that you wish to associate with a given helper application.

2. Click **Edit**.... The Netscape Helper window will be displayed.

3. In the **Handle By** section, select one of these items:

   - To let Netscape display data of this type, select **Navigator**. This item is only selectable for MIME types such as GIF and JPEG that Netscape can display directly; it is also the default for these files. Generally you won't need to associate these types with external applications, though you can if you desire.

   - To associate the MIME type with a plug-in, select **Plug-in** and choose the desired plug-in from the pop-up menu. Complete information on plug-ins can be found in Chapter 12.

   - To associate the MIME type with a helper application, select **Application** and proceed to step 4.

   - If you want Netscape to simply save the file to disk, select **Save to Disk**.

VIRTUOSO

For large documents and other material that you're likely to need later, the most appropriate action is to save the file to your disk so you can work with it after your Netscape session. For example, if you create and configure the **application/pdf** MIME type to work with Adobe Acrobat Reader and to simply save the file, any PDF files that you download will be decoded and stored, instead of launched.

   - If you want to decide what to do with the file on the fly, select **Unknown:Prompt User**.

4. If you chose **Application** in step 3, follow these steps to associate a helper application with the MIME type:

   a. Type the command path to invoke the helper application, or click **Browse** to locate and select the desired application.

   b. Type any flags that must be used for the application to run correctly. (For example, proper use of the **tar** command might require you to enter **tar -xvf**.)

   c. Type **%s** (the temporary file place-holder) so that the helper application knows which file to open when invoked.

5. When you're finished, click **OK** to return to the Helpers Configuration window.

Creating or Modifying a MIME Type

If you wish to configure Netscape to use a helper application with a MIME type that is not displayed by default, then you'll need to add information about the new MIME type to the browser before you can associate a helper application with it. Also, you may need to modify the information that appears for an existing MIME type, such as the file extensions associated with it.

Creating a New MIME Type

If you see an error message that Netscape doesn't know what to do with a certain file, it means that there isn't a MIME type configured for that kind of file. The error message will contain the exact spelling of the MIME type and subtype to use during this configuration.

NOTE If you're creating a MIME type for a special Web-related helper application such as RealAudio, instructions will be provided containing the exact information to enter for the MIME type, subtype, and file extensions.

If you wish to create a new MIME type, display the Helpers Configuration window in Preferences, then follow these steps:

1. Click **New**…. The Netscape Helper window will be displayed.

2. In the **Description** field, type a description of the MIME type. The text you enter will describe the MIME type at the Helpers Configuration window. (If you don't enter anything, you won't be able to tell what the MIME type is for the helper application you identify.)

3. In the **Mime** field, enter the MIME classification (usually text, application, image, audio, or video) and the subtype for the new type, separated by a slash.

NOTE Remember, MIME types are in the form **type/subtype**; for example, **application/pdf** or **image/tiff**.

4. In the **Suffix** field, enter the file extensions associated with the MIME type. If there's more than one file extension, separate them with commas.

NOTE

Do not include the period that separates a file extension from a file name. For example, for the .exe file extension, only enter **exe**.

5. In the **Handle By** section, select one of these items:

- To let Netscape display data of this type, select **Navigator**. This item is only selectable for MIME types such as GIF and JPEG that Netscape can display directly; it is also the default for these files. Generally you won't need to associate these types with external applications, though you can if you desire.

- To associate the MIME type with a plug-in, select **Plug-in** and choose the desired plug-in from the pop-up menu. Complete information on plug-ins can be found in Chapter 12.

- To associate the MIME type with a helper application, select **Application** and proceed to step 6.

- If you want Netscape to simply save the file to disk, select **Save to Disk**.

VIRTUOSO

For large documents and other material that you're likely to need later, the most appropriate action is to save the file to your disk so you can work with it after your Netscape session. For example, if you create and configure the **application/pdf** MIME type to work with Adobe Acrobat Reader and to simply save the file, any PDF files that you download will be uncompressed and stored, instead of launched.

- If you want to decide what to do with the file on the fly, select **Unknown:Prompt User**.

6. If you chose **Application** in step 5, follow these steps to associate a helper application with the MIME type:

a. Type the command path to invoke the helper application, or click **Browse** to locate and select the desired application.

    b. Type any flags that must be used for the application to run correctly. (For example, proper use of the **tar** command might require you to enter **tar -xvf**.)

    c. Type **%s** (the temporary file place-holder) so that the helper application knows which file to open when invoked.

7. When you're finished, click **OK** to return to the Helpers Configuration window.

Popular Helper Applications

Just as there are many different kinds of spreadsheets, word processing programs, and even Web browsers, there are many different helper applications available for every kind of MIME type that you might encounter. In this section, we'll discuss the most popular helper applications for the MIME types that you'll encounter most frequently on the Web. This list is far from definitive—you should feel free to experiment with other helper applications to see which ones best suit your preferences and your needs. And, it's important to keep in mind that helper applications frequently come and go, often being replaced by the latest great utility. It's best to be flexible in your search for and use of helper applications to support your Web surfing.

NOTE FTP information for the helper applications listed below is in the form of a URL, as you can use Netscape to retrieve these files. If you can't find the files at the sites listed below, try an Archie search for an up-to-date listing of several sites that do have copies of the files. (For more information about FTP and Archie, see Chapter 16.)

NOTE Netscape's Web site contains information and FTP links for several popular helper applications at http://home.netscape.com/assist/helper_apps/unix_helpers.html. Another good place to look for helper applications is at NCSA's Web site; since they created the first graphical Web browser, they maintain a great deal of information that is relevant to Web browsers in general. Check them out at ftp://ftp.ncsa.uiuc.edu/Mosaic/Unix/viewers.

NOTE Want to make sure that your helper applications are configured correctly? Check out the WWW Viewer Test page at http://www-dsed.llnl.gov/documents/, where samples of the most common Web files that you'll encounter are conveniently located on a single page.

Decompression Utilities

For most flavors of UNIX, the system will already have built-in software tools to handle the UNIX compression and archiving formats that you'll encounter on the Web. The standard UNIX uncompress utility can be configured to work correctly for decoding files with the .Z extension. Netscape can also be configured to handle GNU Zip compressed files correctly, but you'll need to obtain the helper application gzip, available at ftp://oak.oakland.edu/pub /misc/unix/gzip124.tar.Z. Gzip can also handle compressed and regular tar files as well. Associate it with **application/x-gtar** or **application/x-tar**, respectively.

Graphics Utilities

Nearly every graphics format that isn't handled directly by Netscape can be viewed with xv, a popular image viewer available at ftp://ftp.ncsa.uiuc .edu/Mosaic/Unix/viewers/xv-3.00.tar.Z.

Sound Utilities

Audiotool, which is often distributed with X, can play nearly every audio type that you'll encounter on the Web. You might additionally wish to explore: AudioFile, available at ftp://ftp.dec.com/pub/DEC/AF, which can also play a variety of audio types; or showaudio, at ftp://ftp.ncsa.uiuc.edu/Mosaic/Unix/viewers/mm.tar.Z (this file also contains a metamail application).

Video Utilities

The most common formats for video on the Web that can be played on a UNIX workstation are QuickTime (**video/quicktime**) and MPEG (**video/mpeg**). A variety of MPEG players for common architectures are available at ftp://ftp.crs4.it/mpeg/programs/.

If you wish to view QuickTime movies as well as MPEG, try Xanim, which runs on several platforms and supports QuickTime as well as several

other animation and video formats. Xanim is available at http://www.
portal.com/%7Epodlipec/home.html.

Improving Sound and Video with X Play Gizmo

If you've chosen to use a helper application that's a simple filter without
control panels, like showaudio or mpeg_play, X Play Gizmo is a utility
that's definitely worth installing. X Play Gizmo creates a graphical user
interface for those applications that don't have a user interface. With X
Play Gizmo, you can start and stop movie and sound files as desired, and
save them locally without multiple retrievals. (Without X Play Gizmo, the
files are played as soon as they're downloaded and cannot be saved or
replayed without retrieving them again from the buffer or the network.)

X Play Gizmo still requires the use of regular helper applications, but
it'll definitely improve the quality of your interactions with multimedia on
the Web. To use X Play Gizmo, configure the desired MIME type to
invoke X Play Gizmo as well as the regular helper application. For example, to use X Play Gizmo in conjunction with mpeg_play for the MIME
type **video/mpeg**, you'd select the description for MPEG at the Helpers
Configuration window. click **Edit…** and enter the following in the application field of the MIME type editing window:

```
xplaygizmo mpeg_play %s
```

X Play Gizmo can be obtained at ftp://ftp.ncsa.uiuc.edu/Mosaic/
Unix/viewers/xplaygizmo/.

Adobe Acrobat PDF Files

Adobe Systems, the company that brought us PostScript, Photoshop,
Illustrator, FreeHand, and other high-end graphics processing tools as
well as many of the fonts that we use today, has created an application
called Acrobat, which allows developers to create perfectly formatted
cross-platform documents that contain advanced features like color,
graphics, fonts, and navigation options.

Acrobat files are commonly referred to as PDF (Portable Document
Format) files, and they use PDF as their file extension. Free readers for

Adobe Acrobat for Sun OS, Solaris, HP-UX, Silicon Graphics' IRIX, and AIX platforms are available at http://www.adobe.com/acrobat/others.html; follow the link for your operating system.

NOTE

You'll have to create a MIME type for PDF files. Use the MIME type **application/pdf** and the file extension **pdf**. See Adobe's instructions at http://www.adobe.com/Acrobat for complete information. (Even though the instructions are for Mosaic, they are accurate for Netscape as well.)

VIRTUOSO

Because PDF files are typically large documents containing a great deal of information, you might want to configure Netscape to simply save PDF files so you can review them later.

RTF Utilities

RTF is Microsoft's Rich Text Format, a method of converting any binary file format created by a Microsoft word processor to an encoded text file that can be reconstructed to contain the original information. RTF is a popular way to transmit formatted Microsoft Word documents across the Internet, since turning them into text documents makes it possible to mail them without further need of encoding.

If you have an application that can handle RTF files, associate it with the MIME type **application/rtf**.

Using Other Supporting Applications

As we discussed in Chapter 8, Netscape handles supporting applications for telnet, TN3270, rlogin, and viewing the source code of HTML documents separately, as they are not associated with any MIME types.

To configure Netscape for these helper applications, follow these steps:

1. In Preferences, select **Applications and Directories**. The Applications and Directories configuration window will be displayed.

2. Next to each application that you wish to associate with Netscape, enter the path to the application you wish to use or click **Browse...** to locate and select the desired application.

Telnet, TN3270, and Rlogin Applications

UNIX's built-in xterm application can handle both telnet and TN3270 terminal emulation sessions; the rlogin application can handle the supported rlogin options (rlogin and rlogin user).

Applications for Viewing Source

You can look at the HTML source code of any document by selecting **Document Source** from the View menu. The default is usually xedit. However, if you wish to view documents on the Web in another application, such as an HTML editor, you'll need to specify the application in the **View Source** field.

HoTMetaL Free—a freeware version of SoftQuad's popular HoTMetaL Pro that runs on Sun OS—is available at ftp://ftp.ncsa.uiuc.edu/Web/html/hotmetal/SPARC-Motif/sq-hotmetal-1.0b.tar.Z.

What You Learned

After reading this chapter, you should be able to:

- Associate helper applications with MIME types.
- Create new MIME types.
- Obtain popular helper applications for your platform.
- Associate telnet, TN3270, rlogin, and source viewers with Netscape.

CHAPTER 12

WORKING WITH PLUG-INS

An exciting feature that was introduced in Netscape 2.0 and improved upon in later versions is the ability of the browser to handle *plug-ins* for certain data types, in addition to helper applications. As we discussed in the preceding chapters, helper applications are programs external to Netscape that you configure to handle different data, such as sounds and video. By contrast, plug-ins actually extend the capability of the browser itself to display new kinds of objects: instead of launching another program, plug-ins let Netscape display data directly in the browser window (and in the case of sounds, invisibly).

NOTE   As with Java applets and other technologies that extend the browser's capabilities, don't expect to get good performance from plug-ins unless you have 2–4 MB of additional physical RAM over and above what you're using for your operating system, for Netscape, and for any additional applications that are open at the same time.

Plug-ins are an exciting technology for several reasons:

- They make Web pages more extendible. With helper applications, the contents of a Web page are still limited to text and certain kinds of graphics; however, plug-ins let developers display any kind of object—including sounds, movies, graphics, formatted documents, even spreadsheets—directly within a document. Plus, the developer can control additional elements, such as the size of the display area for the item, how much you can control the action, and more.

- For regular users, plug-ins make navigating the Web an easier experience. Because the data is displayed in the browser, you don't have to switch between windows and applications as you do when you use a helper application.

- Plug-ins are easier to configure than helper applications. Basically, you just drop the plug-in in the correct location and you're set to go. Since many plug-ins come with installers, adding a plug-in can sometimes be as easy as double-clicking an icon on your desktop.

In the rest of this chapter, we'll look at how plug-ins work in general, discuss how to configure Netscape to use plug-ins, and explore some of the most popular plug-ins available for your browser from Netscape Communications as well as third-party developers.

How Plug-ins Work

Like helper applications, plug-ins use MIME types to determine which kind of data they're supposed to work with. (Whether a plug-in is used instead of a helper application is up to you; we'll talk about installing and configuring plug-ins later in this chapter.) When Netscape encounters a MIME type that's associated with a plug-in, the data is handed off to the plug-in, which displays it in a way defined by the developer.

Since the advent of plug-ins, there are several ways that a developer can include objects such as sound or video in an HTML document:

- Separate window. This commonly occurs when the browser encounters a link to a multimedia object for which there is a plug-in. In this case, a separate window is opened which contains the default controls for the kind of plug-in that's being used.

- Full-screen. In this case, which is common with PDF documents displayed with Adobe's Amber, the data that's being handled by the plug-in expands to take up the whole screen, effectively turning the browser into a viewer for another kind of application.

- Partial screen. In this case, the developer embeds the plug-in data within a region on the page. The developer can also choose which controls—such as stop, start, and volume controls—are associated with the object.

- Invisible. In this case, the plug-in plays the data without providing any interface or controls. For example, some pages now contain sounds that will start to play when you access the page, and won't stop until you leave the page because there's no way for you to control it.

Knowing When a Plug-in is Needed or In Use...

If you encounter data on the Web that requires a plug-in which is installed, all you have to do is wait for the data to be downloaded. (For plug-ins that use *streaming* techniques so that you can view information while still downloading the rest of it, you won't even need to wait.)

If you encounter data on the Web that requires a plug-in which you don't have installed, Netscape will generate a dialog box asking if you want to get further information about the missing plug-in (Figure 12.1).

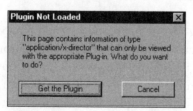

Figure 12.1 You don't have the plug-in for this data.

If you click **Get the Plugin** in this dialog box, a new browser window will be opened that contains information from Netscape about plug-ins. You can follow the links in this window to get to Netscape's list of available plug-ins.

NOTE The information displayed in the dialog box is often specific to the kind of plug-in that's needed. For example, if you're trying to view a QuickTime movie and you don't have the QuickTime plug-in installed, the dialog box contains a link to Apple's QuickTime site to download the missing software.

If you choose **Cancel**, you'll return to the page, where a placeholder image for plug-in data (Figure 12.2) will be displayed.

Figure 12.2 Placeholder for plug-in data.

Installing Plug-ins

One of the best features of plug-ins is their ease of installation and configuration. Unlike helper applications, which you must specifically configure Netscape to use, getting Netscape to use a plug-in is as easy as making sure the files are stored in the correct directory.

WARNING

The plug-ins folder will be created when you install Netscape. This folder *must* be stored in the correct location or Netscape won't be able to locate the plug-ins; be sure not to move it. On both the Macintosh and Windows, the folder is stored in the same directory as the Netscape application itself.

You'll obtain plug-ins for Netscape in one of two ways: either they'll be shipped with your version of Netscape and automatically installed correctly when you install the browser, or you'll download them from the Internet and install them yourself. If the plug-ins came with Netscape, they won't require any additional configuration to work (though in the case of QuickTime, you may need to download additional system extensions).

If you downloaded a plug-in, chances are extremely good that once you decompress the archive (using tools such as WinZip, discussed in Chapter 9, or StuffIt Expander, discussed in Chapter 10), you'll find an installer application instead of the actual plug-in itself.

NOTE

On Windows, installers are usually called Setup.exe. On the Macintosh, installers are usually named with the name of the plug-in, followed by the word "installer."

If there's an installer, life couldn't be simpler—just launch the installer and follow any prompts to install the files.

NOTE

If for some reason you obtained a plug-in that doesn't come with an installer, be sure to look at the Read Me file and any other associated documentation to make sure that you put all the pieces in the right place.

After Installing a Plug-in...

It's crucial that you restart Netscape after installing any new plug-ins. Netscape identifies and loads available plug-ins during its initialization step; it's simply not aware of anything added after Netscape is launched.

Seeing What Plug-ins Are Installed

To see what plug-ins are installed and currently available to Netscape, perform the appropriate action for your computer platform:

- On the Macintosh, select **About Plugins…** from the Apple menu.
- On Windows, select **About Plug-ins** from the Help menu.

NOTE

On any platform, you can type **about:plugins** in the Location field.

A screen of information about the plug-ins that are currently installed will be displayed (Figure 12.3).

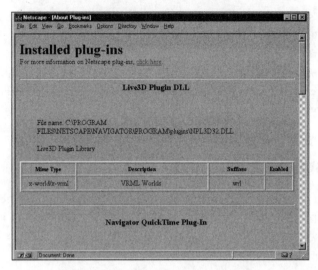

Figure 12.3 Information about plug-ins.

Information for each plug-in includes a list of each MIME type associated with the plug-in; a description of the data; the suffixes associated with the MIME type; and information about whether the plug-in is enabled.

Assigning and De-Assigning MIME Types to Plug-ins

By default, plug-ins are enabled simply by their presence in the plug-ins folder. If you take no additional steps to associate a plug-in with a MIME type, the plug-in will still automatically handle data of the MIME types that it's associated with by default—even if the plug-in handles a MIME type that isn't predefined in Netscape, the information about the MIME type will be loaded when you launch Netscape; you won't have to go through the step of creating a new MIME type as you do for helper applications.

So, if you install a plug-in or use the plug-ins that come with Netscape, you won't have to take any additional steps to make the plug-in work. In fact, if you're like most people, you may never want to associate plug-in data with another action or application. However, there may be some cases when you'll want to use a helper application to view a file (for example, if you want more control over a sound), or you'll want to save a file such as a movie to your disk drive for later use. In these cases, you might want to associate the MIME type with some other type of action.

To change a MIME type from being associated with a plug-in to being associated with another action, follow the steps in Chapter 9 (Windows), 10 (Macintosh), or 11 (UNIX). In general, the procedure will be similar to the following:

1. From the Options menu, select **General Preferences**....

2. Click the **Helpers** tab.

3. Select the line for the MIME type whose association you wish to change.

4. Click **Edit**.... The Edit Type window (Figure 12.4) will be displayed.

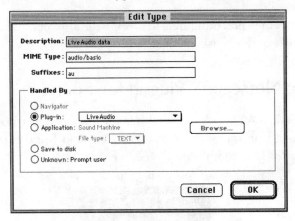

Figure 12.4 The Edit Type window.

5. Select the desired action for the MIME type as described in Chapters 9-11. (If you're reassociating a MIME type with a plug-in, select **Plug-in** and then choose the desired plug-in from the pop-up menu.)

6. Click **OK** to return to the Helpers window.

WARNING
At the time this book was written, the way that Netscape for Windows handled plug-ins and helper applications was problematic: there was no way to delete a MIME type once it was entered into the table, and if you assigned data that was once associated with a plug-in to another action, you couldn't reassociate it with the plug-in again. Presumably, this bug in the interface will be fixed by the time you read this; chances are good that the interface will end up looking like the one described in Chapter 10.

Disabling Specific Plug-ins

To disable specific plug-ins because they take up too much memory, you'll have to physically remove them from the plug-ins folder—even if their MIME type is associated with another action, Netscape will load the plug-in anyway. Be sure to restart Netscape immediately, as the decrease in memory won't take place until Netscape's restarted.

About Netscape's Plug-ins

Netscape comes preconfigured to work with a number of useful plug-ins that are part of the Netscape installation set.

LiveAudio: Netscape's Plug-in for Sound

Netscape's LiveAudio plug-in will handle the four most popular kinds of sounds found on the Web: WAV, AIFF, AU, and MIDI files. The default controller for LiveAudio is displayed in Figure 12.5.

Figure 12.5 Default controller for LiveAudio.

You may use the controller to change the volume, pause, and play the sounds.

LiveVideo and QuickTime: Netscape's Plug-ins for Video

Netscape provides two plug-ins for handling video: a version of Apple's QuickTime for QuickTime movies, and LiveVideo for AVI movies. The default controllers for each of these are displayed below.

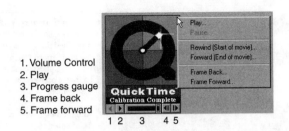

1. Volume Control
2. Play
3. Progress gauge
4. Frame back
5. Frame forward

Figure 12.6 QuickTime controller.

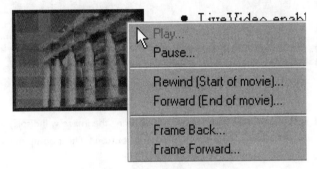

Figure 12.7 LiveVideo AVI controller.

NOTE

The QuickTime plug-in also lets you play QuickTime VR movies, in which you can navigate within special videos simply by dragging your mouse in different directions. The navigation feature set isn't as complicated as that of VRML, below, but the two don't really do the same thing; in VRML, all the objects are rendered by the computer, while a QuickTime VR movie can actually be a video of a real location.

Live3D: Netscape's Plug-in for VRML

VRML, or Virtual Reality Modeling Language, lets developers create electronic renderings of three-dimensional worlds. Similar to navigating complex graphics-oriented games like Doom, you can walk through a VRML world, turn around, change your perspective, and examine objects from every angle. Figure 12.8 shows a sample Live3D world.

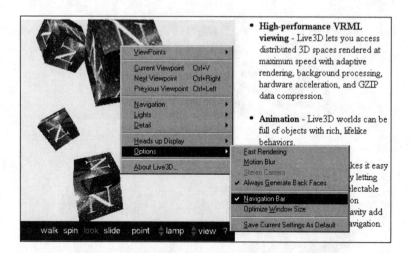

Figure 12.8 Live3D world.

In Live3D, as with many plug-ins, right-clicking the image will display a pop-up menu. (On the Macintosh, hold down the mouse button.) This pop-up menu provides precise control over the behavior of the plug-in.

To display a navigation bar containing simple but useful commands at the bottom of the Live3D region, use the pop-up menu command shown in Figure 12.8. The navigation bar provides a readily accessible way to control your exploration of the VRML environment.

Other Plug-ins

Dozens of plug-ins are already available to extend Netscape's capabilities, and more and more are becoming available every day. In this section, we're only going to discuss a few of the most popular; you can always check Netscape's plug-in information to get the latest news about available plug-ins. To get to the information quickly, select **About plugins...** from the Help menu (on the Macintosh, select it from the Apple menu) and click the link for more information that appears at the top of the page.

NOTE

Not all plug-ins will be available for all platforms.

VIRTUOSO

Some plug-ins have added functions beyond what's visible on the screen, such as Live3D's pop-up controller. For complete information on each plug-in's advanced features, be sure to look at the Read Me file that comes with the software.

Shockwave for Director

One of the first plug-ins to be wholeheartedly embraced by the multimedia development community, the Shockwave for Director plug-in lets you view presentations, or "movies," created with Macromedia Director. Director is one of the leading development tools for commercial CD-ROM projects; Netscape's ability to support Director movies means that a huge number of multimedia developers can now create content for the Web in a development environment that they've already mastered. Additionally, Shockwave supports a number of functions that you won't find in static CD-ROMs, such as links to other Web pages embedded within a movie.

Shockwave is available at http://www.macromedia.com/Tools/Shockwave/Info/index.html.

NOTE

All of Macromedia's plug-ins will probably be called Shockwave; currently, their other available plug-ins are Shockwave for Authorware (a tool for developing computer-based training) and Shockwave for Freehand (a graphics program). Be sure you're getting the right Shockwave!

Amber

As we discussed in the chapters about helper applications, Adobe has created an application called Acrobat, which allows developers to create perfectly formatted cross-platform documents that contain advanced features like color, graphics, fonts, and navigation options. Adobe's Amber is a plug-in that lets you view these perfectly designed documents directly in the browser. More and more information is being made available in the PDF format these days, including technical information, software documentation, and even corporate annual reports.

NOTE Interestingly, Amber supports an Adobe feature called WebLink, which supports hypertext links from within a PDF document to other documents anywhere on the Web; for this reason, some designers theorize that the PDF format, with its complete control over document appearance, might replace HTML.

Amber can be found at http://www.adobe.com/Amber/Download.html.

PointCast

The PointCast Network broadcasts up-to-the-minute news from a variety of sources; you not only can choose which news you want delivered to your desktop, but also how often the news should be updated. The PointCast plug-in can be found at http://www.pointcast.com. (We'll talk a little bit more about PointCast in Chapter 24.)

Word Viewer

Inso Corporation has developed this plug-in viewer for documents created in Microsoft Word 6.0 or 7.0; Word Viewer also lets you copy and print Word documents from the Web without losing any formatting information. Word Viewer can be found at http://www.inso.com/plug.htm.

Formula One/NET for Excel

Formula One/NET provides a Microsoft Excel-compatible plug-in viewer for viewing Excel spreadsheets on the Web; in addition to viewing spreadsheet data, Formula One/NET can let you manipulate the data in the document and link to other Web sites. The Formula One/NET plug-in can be found at http://www.visualcomp.com/f1net/download.htm.

Problems with Plug-ins

In general, plug-ins are really great things. They make it possible to use Netscape to view and manipulate all kinds of data without having to launch other applications. However, as we discussed in Chapter 8, plug-ins have some very real drawbacks. (For complete discussion of some of these items, see "Plug-ins vs. Helper Applications: What Should I Use?" at the end of Chapter 8.)

- Excessive RAM consumption. Plug-ins require a significant amount of memory that needs to be available in addition to the memory required solely by the Netscape browser. Unlike independent helper applications, which receive their RAM allocation from the operating system, plug-ins get their memory allocation directly from Netscape. This means that Netscape has to "grab" enough RAM at launch to be able to support not only itself but also the greediest plug-in that you have installed. Since Netscape itself has a fairly sizeable RAM requirement *before* accounting for plug-ins, you might find that you simply don't have enough RAM to run your application.

- Most plug-ins are beta software, or in the earliest stages of release. As a technology, plug-ins have only been around since the second half of 1995, while other text, graphics, audio, and video applications have been in existence for years. The first generation of plug-ins is only now (as of this writing) in the beta stage of software development; since beta software has not been subjected to rigorous quality control testing, and is not considered to be of good enough quality to sell commercially, the best that you can hope for is that most of the bugs in the software have been found and documented in release notes.

- Lessened ability to manipulate data. When a helper application handles data, such as a sound or an animation, it usually downloads it to your computer as an individual file. When you're using the interface of a helper application, you can manipulate, replay, save or edit the file. But in some cases, if the data is handled "invisibly" by a plug-in,

217

you don't have easy access to an interface that will let you save the file for future use, unless the plug-in provides one for you. In short, plug-ins are not very good for collecting files and other resources to use later; if you encounter something that you want to save, you'll have to reconfigure Netscape to save items of that MIME type instead of playing them with the helper application.

- The interface to plug-ins can often be less responsive than the interface to a helper application. Although the data from a plug-in appears in your browser window, it's actually being handled by the software in the plug-in; depending on the speed of your computer, it may take some time for your mouse clicks or keyboard commands to be sent to the plug-in, interpreted, and responded to in a fashion that shows up on your screen. VRML is particularly bad in this respect; unless you have a top-of-the-line Pentium or Power Macintosh with 16 or 32 MB of RAM, navigating complex worlds through your browser can become a very frustrating experience.

What You Learned

After reading this chapter, you should be able to:

- Understand the difference between plug-ins and helper applications.
- Configure Netscape to work with plug-ins.
- Work with some of the most popular currently available plug-ins.

CHAPTER 13

ABOUT JAVA AND JAVASCRIPT

If you've been following any of the recent developments in the Web industry, you've undoubtedly heard of a programming language called "Java," which has become not only the darling of the online world but also the latest computing rage in general. In this chapter, we'll discuss what Java is, its implications for the kinds of materials that can be distributed on the Web, and how to understand and work with any Java programs that you may encounter.

What is Java?

In brief, Java is a programming language created by Sun Microsystems that lets developers create small applications that can run on any kind of computer. For example, a developer can create a familiar game like Tetris using Java and embed it in a Web page; anyone who viewed the page could play Tetris right there in the Web browser, regardless of whether their computer is a Macintosh, Windows, or UNIX machine.

In this section, we'll talk about the mechanics of how and why Java programs work the way they do; if you just want to know about Java's implications for the Web, skip ahead to "Java and the Web."

The Problems of Multiple Computer Platforms

As anyone who's ever purchased (or just worked with) a computer knows, there are a variety of computers to choose from. For personal computers, the choices fall into two main categories: computers whose processing hardware is based on Intel's x86 or Pentium chips and whose operating system software is a version of Microsoft's Windows, and computers whose processing hardware and operating system software is created by Apple Computer. (To confuse matters a little more, there are actually two different kinds of processor chips in the Macintosh realm: the 68000 series and the newer PowerPC series. Even though PowerPC and 68000-based Macintoshes use an operating system that looks the same on both computers, the chip on which the OS runs is actually quite different.)

In the world of software development, the programming tools used to create any software program consist of two parts. First, there's the programming language itself, such as Pascal, C++, or Basic. Programming languages are fundamentally the same from platform to platform, so C programming is basically C programming whether you write your code on a UNIX workstation, a Macintosh, or a PC.

But the programs that you write in a standard high-level language like C still aren't portable from one kind of computer to another because of the second component of programming environments: specific items that deal with the interface of the operating system on which the application will eventually run, known as the Applications Programming Interface, or API. The elements of the user interface that you control must conform to the requirements of the specific operating system; for example, Windows applications can interpret the use of the right mouse button, while Macintosh computers don't even have a right mouse button.

Java addresses this problem so well that it's a viable solution for cross-platform programming. Instead of using a compiler to create stand-alone binary executable files, Java has an interpreter for each supported platform that allows the execution of any Java program on any supported computer; and instead of using the prescribed graphical user interface for each computer, Java lets the developer create a user interface that will work on any supported system. We'll talk more about these items in the next sections.

The Advantage of Interpreters

Most application programs that you use on your computer have been *compiled* specifically for that kind of system; in other words, the executable program is specifically designed so that it contains instructions that only work with a specific combination of processor hardware and operating system software. (This is why you can't install Microsoft Word for Windows on a Macintosh, or vice versa.) Compiling large application programs for specific applications makes a lot of sense, as it allows developers to take advantage of the unique characteristics of each platform. But, if you want to deliver a program in a cross-platform medium, like across the World Wide Web, you need some way to deliver code that isn't already specifically designed to run on a unique hardware/software combination.

The answer to this problem is the use of an *interpreter* instead of a compiler. While compilers turn a programmer's code into a stand-alone application, an interpreter is a software tool that must be present on a computer in order for an application to run. The interpreter reads the code for the program statement by statement and generates the appropriate output. As you might imagine, interpreted programs run somewhat more slowly than compiled programs, as the application has to "think" about how to perform every action; the difference is almost like the difference between knowing how to perform a certain action, like changing the toner cartridge in the printer, and having to look up the procedure every single time.

However, for cross-platform applications, the minor downside of slower performance is greatly outweighed by the following advantage: an interpreter can be created *for any platform*, so that the source code can be interpreted—that is, executed—on any platform that has an interpreter. If there is a Java interpreter available for your computer and operating system, then you can run any Java program that you encounter, whether you're on a Power Macintosh, a Compaq Presario, or a Sun SparcStation.

Java Source Code and Java Byte Code

It's interesting to note that the cross-platform Java code that's interpreted on your computer isn't exactly the raw source code that the programmer originally wrote. Although the interpretation step is the most important one for you, the user, there's actually a step that the developer takes before placing a Java program on the World Wide Web.

In general, source code of any kind is written in plain old ASCII text. If the program is to be compiled, that ASCII text is turned into a platform-specific binary executable file by the compiler. Although Java applets aren't compiled by the developer to create a platform-specific application, they *are* processed through a special compiler that turns the raw ASCII source code into something called Java *byte code*. This byte code isn't a stand-alone application—it still needs to be run by a Java interpreter—but because it's been changed to a binary format instead of an ASCII format, it's a little bit faster for the interpreter to read and execute. This information shouldn't have much impact on you as a regular Netscape user, but it might help you understand what people are talking about if you come across a discussion of byte code.

The AWT Interface Solution

So, we've talked about how Java interpreters make it possible for non-platform-specific byte code to be used on any kind of platform. What we haven't addressed yet is the second cross-platform problem: the user interface. All platform-specific applications take advantage of the unique requirements of the operating system (which is why, for example, many procedures in this book are different depending on whether you're using Netscape for Macintosh, Windows, or X-Windows on UNIX). Among other things, a computer's operating system determines how things like windows will be drawn, how menus are selected, and how mouse clicks are interpreted. If you're writing a program that isn't specific to a single operating system, what are you going to do for a user interface? All the built-in commands to create windows, etc., aren't there.

Sun's answer to the interface question is the Abstract Windows Toolkit (known as the AWT, which is sometimes also called the Advanced Windows Toolkit). This toolkit lets you create the standard elements of a graphical user interface—windows, menus, methods of handling keyboard and mouse input, etc.—without confining you to a specific platform. A cross-platform program whose interface is defined by the Abstract Windows Toolkit will look and act more or less the same, no matter what platform it's running on.

Platform-Specific Java Items

As we discussed above, the fact that Java is an interpreted language and the use of the Abstract Windows Toolkit for creating an application interface are the primary foundation of Java's cross-platform functionality. However, there are still some platform-dependent issues about a computer's processor and operating system that can't be avoided. Although the byte code that creates the Java program on your computer can be interpreted on any platform, the interpreter itself and the associated class libraries are platform specific.

A *class library* is a set of common commands that can be used by any program. The use of class libraries lets the developer assume that common commands such as those for calculating mathematical functions are available on the target computer and don't need to be included in the byte code for the program. This means that the code for the program can be smaller than if the programmer had to include the instructions for common actions in each applet. Additionally, some of the class libraries for each platform also contain specific instructions for how to work with that combination of hardware and operating system software.

So, even though Java byte code itself is platform independent, many of the tools you need to run it are platform specific. This is why Java-aware versions of the Netscape browser weren't all available at the same time; the tools needed to be created separately for each platform. (In fact, at the time of this writing, a Java-aware version of Netscape was not yet available for the 68000-based Macintosh—only for Windows, X-Windows, and Power Macintosh.)

The Future of Java

In May, 1996, all major developers of operating systems for personal computers—Apple, Microsoft, and IBM—announced that future releases of their operating systems would contain support for Java. Presumably, this means that they're banking on the use of Java as a critical component of Internet strategy; in fact, many industry players even posit that the network browser will become the interface to the local operating system as well as to the rest of the networked world. (Microsoft has announced that the Internet Explorer browser software will be integrated with what's currently known as Microsoft Explorer, a graphical front-end to the Windows 95 operating system.)

The immediate implication of this announcement for Web browsers will probably be moderately enhanced performance, as the interpreter will be part of the operating system, and, if nothing else, smaller installation packages to download from Netscape, since the interpreter and class libraries will already be installed on your system.

Java and the Web

The Java programming environment was originally developed simply as a cross-platform language; its incorporation into browsers is a relatively recent repurposing of an existing product to benefit from the popularity of the world's largest cross-platform network: the World Wide Web.

Although Java wasn't developed specifically for the Web, it's a viable solution to certain problems that have plagued Web site developers since the beginning: how to create interactive documents that aren't static presentations of text, graphics, and other media elements. The Common Gateway Interface, or CGI (discussed in Chapter 17), allows for certain kinds of interactions, but all the computation is handled by the server; the client computer, that powerful machine you paid thousands of dollars for, is still just acting as a document viewer.

What Java offers the Web community is the ability to harness the computational power of your desktop computer and make it work in conjunction with the media and information resources available on the Web. By embedding small applications, called *applets*, in a Web document—the same way that you'd embed a graphic or a sound—the kind of interaction that you can have with a Web site is limited only by the imagination (and the programming talent) of the site's developers. It's important to note that applets are not the same as stand-alone applications—they can only be executed by a Java-aware application, such as a Java-enabled Web browser or an application like Sun's Applet Viewer.

The Promise of Java vs. Java Today

Of the many ways that Java can be used, the idea that has more marketing visionaries drooling than any other is to use Java as a new method of software distribution. Instead of creating several different versions of the same application, companies can create a single cross-platform program, minimizing development, documentation, and packaging costs.

But the stakes have changed considerably with the combination of Java and the Web. Now, some visionaries are imagining a future where everyone has an inexpensive computer with a network connection…and little, if any, storage space on a disk drive. If you want to use an application like a spreadsheet or a word processor, you'll use one that you access across the network—and you'll be charged for the time that you use it.

However, the current reality is quite different. In the real world, Java is being used to write small applets that provide some additional functionality to a Web document, like an animated advertisement that takes you to another Web site if you click it, or a program that lets you graph complicated trigonometric functions. Like any other object on the Web, Java programs have to be retrieved to your computer, and developers need to balance the current issues regarding limited transfer speeds with the potential to build exciting but cumbersome large applets. At this time, you'd probably be hard pressed to find any examples of Java in use on the Web that provide critical functions that you couldn't live without and that couldn't be provided by some other kind of software.

Java vs. Plug-ins

You might be wondering what roles will be played by plug-ins and helper applications if Java is such a great cross-platform development tool. While Java does have the significant advantage of being a built-in feature—you don't need to download, install, or configure any additional software for Java applets to work—there are certainly strong reasons why Java is just another tool in the Web development arsenal.

The major difference between Java and plug-ins is that Java is an all-purpose programming language that can be used for anything, while other applications such as Director or Excel are very good at performing specialized functions. For example, Director is such an advanced tool for creating interactive multimedia that it would be foolish to attempt to build certain kinds of presentations in Java; instead, the smart choice is to create a Director movie that Web surfers can display using the ShockWave plug-in. Similarly, Microsoft Excel is such a widely used, powerful spreadsheet that there's no point in creating a competing spreadsheet in Java. For the most part, it's safe to say that Java will be used for small, custom applets to create interactions that can't be handled by existing plug-ins.

Working with Java Applets

Encountering Applets on the Web

As we mentioned earlier, applets on the Web are embedded in HTML documents just like inline images. The paired HTML tags used to embed an applet in a document are <APPLET> and </APPLET>; the pathname to the applet itself appears between the tags.

Because HTML documents are loaded from the top of the file to the bottom of the file, a Java applet that's embedded toward the end of a document won't be loaded until all the HTML preceding it has been displayed. When your Java-aware browser encounters an applet, the byte code is downloaded and sent directly to the interpreter, which creates whatever kind of interactions and displays are specified by the developer.

Handling Applets with Netscape

Knowing that You're Running an Applet

While an applet is being loaded, a placeholder will be displayed in the area where the applet will run. However, this placeholder is often the same one that is used when data for plug-ins is being downloaded. To be sure that you've encountered an applet, place the mouse over the item and check the status message area in the lower-left corner of the window. If it says that an applet is running, then you're looking at an applet and not at an item that's being handled by a plug-in. For example, in Figure 13.1, we know that the applet Qpa is running because of the message "Applet Qpa running."

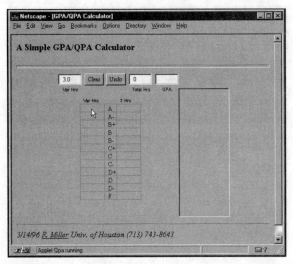

Figure 13.1 The status message area indicates that an applet is running.

Disabling Java-Awareness

There may be times when you want to "turn off" Netscape's ability to display Java applets. For example, if you're using a slow connection, you might not want to waste the time necessary to download the programs; if you're using a computer that's not very powerful, you might find that the performance of certain Java programs is so poor that there's no point in working with them. And, if truth be told, it's entirely possible that you'll encounter Java applets on the Web that haven't been tested and debugged correctly; you might end up needing information from a page which happens to contain a Java applet that generates nothing but error messages.

For this reason, Netscape has provided a way to disable and enable Java at will. To do so, follow these steps:

1. From the Options menu, select **Network Preferences**....
2. Click the **Languages** tab. The Languages Preferences window (Figure 13.2) will be displayed.

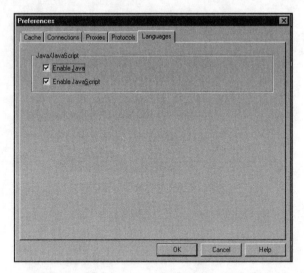

Figure 13.2 Languages Preferences window.

3. To disable Java, deselect **Enable Java**. To enable it again, reselect the item.

WARNING

Unlike images, which you can choose to display individually if Auto Load Images is turned off, you can not choose to display individual Java applets—it's an all-or-nothing proposition. If **Enable Java** is selected, Netscape will interpret and display all the Java it encounters; if Java is disabled, you'll see nothing but a blank area where the applet would be.

Showing the Java Console

Like most other programming languages, Java adheres to the convention that error messages should be displayed if a program encounters problems while running. In the Java environment, the messages are sent to the Java Console, which you can choose to display. If you encounter an applet that doesn't appear to be functioning correctly, the Java Console might contain messages providing clues about what went wrong; however, please keep the following items in mind:

- Even if there are errors in a Java applet, there's nothing that you as the user can do about it, except possibly send the information to the developer of the applet.

- It's entirely possible that the error messages displayed in the Java Console will be so cryptic that they'll be meaningless to anyone but a Java programmer.

With this in mind, you still might find the information displayed in the Java Console interesting. To display the Java Console, select **Show Java Console** from the Options menu so that a check mark appears next to the item. To hide the Java Console again, reselect the item so that the check mark is no longer displayed.

Java Applets in the Cache

Like any other item that Netscape downloads, Java applets are stored in the disk cache, where they can be identified by the **.class** extension at the end of their file name. However, it's important to note that unlike many other objects from the Web, Java applets *can not* be retrieved or run from the disk cache. Java applications aren't handled the same way that MIME objects are; instead, Netscape must encounter the <APPLET> tag embedded in an HTML document in order for the byte code to be passed off to the interpreter.

Even though you can't run Java applets from your cache in the same way you'd view an image, the overall advantage of the disk cache still works: when you revisit a site that has an applet which is in your cache, the applet will be interpreted and available for use more quickly than otherwise.

Finding Sites that Use Java

In a perfect world (or at least on a perfect Web), all the elements of a page—text, images, data handled by plug-ins, applets, etc.—would be so seamlessly integrated that it wouldn't matter to you what tools were used to develop the materials. However, since this is being written in the first year that Java became available, Java's use on the Web is still a bit of a novelty. If you're interested in finding examples of sites that use Java for specific purposes, such as gaming, educational software, or any other category, a good place to start looking is Gamelan: Earthweb's Java Directory, at http://www.gamelan.com, which does an admirable job of cataloging instances of Java applets on the Web.

Security Issues and Java

If you were using a program created with Java in the same way you use most programs that you'd download (such as freeware or shareware), then the only security threat you'd need to worry about is the same one you should always worry about when installing new software: the fact that it might contain malicious code or a virus that will infect your system.

However, Java applets on the Web add a new wrinkle to security fears, since you're not just downloading the program and using it while you're not connected to a network. Theoretically, Java programs that you download while connected to the Internet could analyze your system resources and communicate all kinds of information to entities on the network, or could even gain control of your system resources.

Luckily, Netscape's implementation of Java-awareness in the browser addresses this issue. Applets are currently written in a secure subset of the Java language and are not allowed to perform most operations that can affect the file or operating system of your computer. At this time, Java applets may only do the following: perform calculations; display output within a portion of the Navigator window as defined by the developer in the HTML file for the document; create and display output in special windows outside Navigator that are clearly marked as Java windows; and communicate with the host from which you downloaded the applet.

This implementation by Netscape attempts to ensure that no viruses can infect your computer and no sensitive information can be obtained by the use of Java applets. According to Netscape, future versions will eventually allow you to verify that an applet was created by the people who claim they created it (for a complete discussion of authentication, see Chapter 19) and will let you control which sites and which applets you "trust" enough to download.

WARNING Unfortunately, despite Netscape's best efforts, a number of well-publicized flaws in their implementation of Java have been uncovered in the past year. If you hear of a verified breach in the browser's security related to Java, you should disable Java until Netscape issues a patch for the problem.

VIRTUOSO

Interested in knowing where Netscape plans to go next with Java? Check out the document at http://developer.netscape.com/standards/java-security2.html, which clearly summarizes Netscape's security strategy for Java and contains links to further information.

About JavaScript

What is JavaScript?

Another Netscape-related buzzword that you might have heard is "JavaScript," which, despite its name, isn't actually the Java language at all. (In fact, the beta versions of JavaScript were called LiveScript; although JavaScript can communicate with Java applets—more on this in a second—it's also possible that the name was changed to capitalize on Java's marketing blitz.)

Unlike Java, which is a programming language, JavaScript is a *scripting language*, which has the following characteristics:

- There are a limited number of commands that a developer can use, and their functions are mainly limited to controlling the appearance of a document or the browser window. So, the tasks that you can perform with JavaScript are limited to the commands that Netscape has decided to create and support.
- Unlike Java, whose source code must be translated into byte code before it can be interpreted by your browser, JavaScript is written directly in plain ASCII text and is embedded within the actual HTML of a Web document.

The advantage of JavaScript is its simplicity: it provides developers with easy, predefined ways to write scripts that enhance and customize their Web pages and the browser's interface while on those pages. For example, JavaScript can be used to do the following: display the current date and time; choose an appropriate picture or background to display (for example, if it's evening, you might see a picture of the moon and stars, while during the daytime a picture of the sun would be displayed); generate text messages in different languages; and more.

Additionally, JavaScript provides the "glue" that makes it possible for frames to work. When you click your mouse in one frame and see an action in another, you can rest assured that JavaScript was used to interpret the mouse click and send the appropriate message to the other frame about what to display. JavaScript can also be used to send information to plug-ins or Java applets.

Recognizing JavaScript

JavaScript scripts are written in plain ASCII text and are written directly into an HTML document using the <SCRIPT> and </SCRIPT> matched tags. Because they're ASCII, and because they can be written directly into an HTML document, chances are good that you may see JavaScript scripts in the HTML of documents whose source code you choose to view. It's fairly simple to recognize JavaScript: it's the text that neither appears on the browser screen nor defines the way that text is displayed. And, in a complicated JavaScript script, the text that you see may well read like a computer program. For example, Figure 13.3 shows the HTML source code containing the JavaScript script for the interest calculator shown in Figure 13.4.

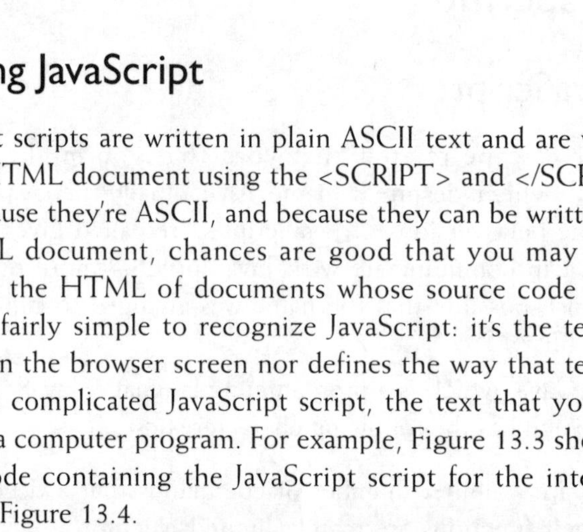
Netscape - [Source of: http://home.netscape.com/comprod/products/navigator/ve...

```
<HTML>
<HEAD><TITLE>Interest Calculator</TITLE>

<SCRIPT LANGUAGE="JavaScript">

<!-- hide this script tag's contents from old browsers

function checkNumber(input, min, max, msg)
{
    msg = msg + " field has invalid data: " + input.value;

    var str = input.value;
    for (var i = 0; i < str.length; i++) {
        var ch = str.substring(i, i + 1)
        if ((ch < "0" || "9" < ch) && ch != '.') {
            alert(msg);
            return false;
        }
    }
    var num = parseFloat(str)
    if (num < min || max < num) {
        alert(msg + " not in range [" + min + ".." + max + "]");
        return false;
    }
    input.value = str;
    return true;
}
```

Figure 13.3 JavaScript within an HTML document.

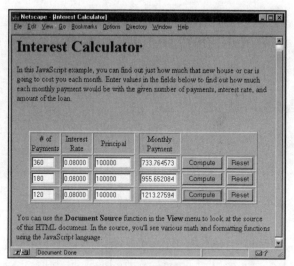

Figure 13.4 The interest calculator created with JavaScript.

Disabling JavaScript

In general, you won't ever have to worry about working with JavaScript; its interpreter is built into the browser and, if the scripts are written correctly, you'll never even know that it was there. However, you may encounter certain sites where the JavaScript hasn't been debugged very well, in which case you could see multiple error messages that are difficult to get rid of and that may cause you to be unable to leave the site. For example, the message in Figure 13.5 was displayed when we tried to use a frame-based HTML wizard whose JavaScript wasn't quite right. (We'll spare you the name of the site to protect the guilty.)

If you need to view information at a site that has buggy JavaScript, you can disable JavaScript using the following steps:

1. From the Options menu, select **Network Preferences**....

2. Click the **Languages** tab. The Languages Preferences window will be displayed.

3. To disable JavaScript, deselect **Enable JavaScript**. To enable it again, reselect the item.

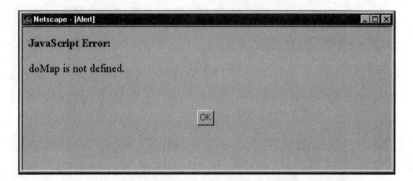

Figure 13.5 JavaScript error message.

WARNING

In general, you should only disable JavaScript if you're trying to use a site that has buggy JavaScript *and* that doesn't require JavaScript to use the information at the site. Unfortunately, you may find that the offending site relies on JavaScript to provide information to you. For example, if you received error messages when you clicked in a frame, turning off JavaScript will simply disable the ability of the frames to communicate with each other, in which case you won't be able to get to the information you were trying to reach. Additionally, if you do disable JavaScript, remember to turn it back on: otherwise, the next time you're at a site that requires JavaScript, you won't be able to use all the features.

NOTE

For a list of sites that are using JavaScript in interesting ways, check out Gamelan's JavaScript index at http://www.gamelan.com/frame/Gamelan.javascript.html.

What You Learned

After reading this chapter, you should be able to:

- Understand why Java applets can run on any platform.
- Identify Java applets when you encounter them on the Web.
- Configure Netscape to handle Java applets as desired.
- Know the security issues related to downloading Java applets.
- Understand what JavaScript is.

CHAPTER 14

Electronic Mail and Netscape

Electronic mail is easily one of the Internet's most popular applications. It can be used to send text messages or files to a specific user or to a distribution list of hundreds. Businesses, universities, and individuals rely on electronic mail as a primary means of communication with others both locally and around the world.

With an old-fashioned shell account, reading your email meant logging on to the host computer, launching a mail client application like VMS Mail, Pine or Elm, and reading the messages online. If you wanted a copy of the message or file sent to you on your own computer, you had to save the file to a directory within your account and then download the file to your hard drive using a file transfer protocol like Kermit or ZModem. Sending a file meant that you had to encode it with Binhex or PKZIP and upload it to your account before mailing. Composing a new message meant learning a text-only editor like pico or vi, which are very unlike the word processors that we're all accustomed to using.

Reading your mail with a graphical mail client application is much easier—you simply launch the application and ask it to retrieve your messages. Any mail that's arrived since the last time you checked is downloaded to your hard drive; any attached files that have been sent to you are automatically downloaded (and decoded, if necessary) to your hard drive in the location of your choice.

As part of an ongoing attempt to become a "Swiss Army knife" tool for all Internet services, Netscape Navigator provides the capability to send, receive, and organize electronic mail from within the application. Netscape's email functions allow you to send and receive mail and attached files at your desktop; to use cut, copy, paste and other familiar commands when composing a message; to organize the mail you receive into folders that you name; and to use address books and nicknames for commonly used electronic addresses and distribution lists. In the course of a Netscape session, you might use various mail functions to:

- Dash off a note to a friend or colleague about a great Web site you found. Netscape will automatically include the URL and, if you request it, the HTML code of the document.
- Send a note directly to a Web developer who requested feedback by including a "mailto" link in their document.
- Mail a message to a friend or colleague that has nothing to do with the Web page, using the mail feature as a time-saving convenience for simple outbound email.
- Read your incoming electronic mail.

All of these are actions you're likely to want to do while exploring the Web. Netscape lets you do them without the tedious (and RAM-consuming) steps of launching another application.

NOTE Much of the configuration information that you enter for electronic mail is also necessary for responding to messages in Usenet News. We'll talk about configuring and using Netscape to read Usenet News in detail in the next chapter, but in this chapter, we'll tell you when the email information that you enter will affect your use of Usenet.

About Electronic Mail

Unlike earlier versions of Netscape, which let you send mail but did not allow you to receive incoming mail, Netscape 2.0 and later support the retrieval and management of incoming electronic mail.

Netscape's mail retrieval and management features are typical of programs called *POP mailers*. POP, which stands for Post Office Protocol, is the protocol that lets you retrieve mail from your electronic mailbox on an Internet host to your desktop computer. Other popular mail programs, such as Eudora, are also examples of POP mail programs. Netscape currently supports POP3—the most recent version of the protocol at the time of this writing. However, not all service providers are using POP3 on their mail hosts; if you ever see a message like Figure 14.1, it's a good bet that your service provider isn't using POP3 (and might not be using POP at all). If you see this kind of message, consider talking to your service provider about upgrading to a more recent version of the protocol.

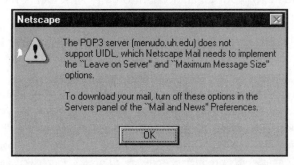

Figure 14.1 Your email is stored on a computer that doesn't support the POP3 protocol.

To receive electronic mail, you need more than just Netscape and a connection to the Internet; you also need a personal electronic mailbox on a computer that's connected to the Internet 24 hours a day. Your email address may or may not be the same as your login name on the system (which you probably entered if you configured your computer to use dialup IP from a modem at home). An email address always consists of the three following parts:

- Your unique user name on the host machine, such as RMiller or EKeeler;
- The @ symbol (pronounced "at"), which signifies the end of the user name and the beginning of the domain name;
- The unique domain name of your mail host. (Complete information about domain names can be found in Chapter 2.)

While POP is the protocol that lets you retrieve electronic mail, *SMTP* (Simple Mail Transport Protocol) is the protocol that lets you send electronic mail to others. To send mail from Netscape, you'll need to know the name of your *sendmail server* (which may be the same as your POP server). The sendmail server acts as a "post office" where you can deposit outgoing mail messages to be delivered to their proper destinations.

In summary, to send and receive electronic mail, you'll need to know the following three things:

- The name of the SMTP server that handles your outgoing mail;
- The name of your email account on a POP server, which functions as the email address you give to others;
- The name of the POP server allowing you to retrieve mail to your desktop computer.

WARNING

Some service providers may give you an electronic mailbox that conforms to the model described above, but that isn't housed on a computer that runs the POP protocol. For example, even though CompuServe provides PPP access to the Internet, all CompuServe mailboxes are hosted on a computer that requires you to use CompuServe's proprietary software to access your electronic mail. So, even though you have some kind of access to electronic mail, you can't use Netscape to read it. However, you may still be able to use Netscape to send mail—for example, CompuServe will let you use the sendmail server "mail.compuserve.com" to handle outbound mail from applications like Netscape, even though you can only retrieve incoming mail with the CompuServe Information Manager.

Configuring Netscape for Electronic Mail

Getting Started

All configuration of Netscape for electronic mail takes place in the Mail and News Preferences window. To get ready to configure Netscape for use with email, perform this step:

- From the Options menu, select **Mail and News Preferences**.... The Mail and News Preferences window will be displayed.

Identifying Yourself

Getting Started

To enter personal identification information, follow these steps:

1. At the Mail and News Preferences window, click the **Identity** tab. The following screen (Figure 14.2) will be displayed.

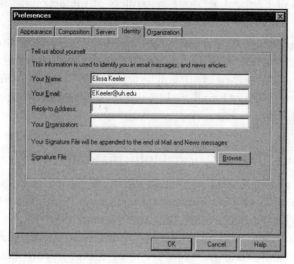

Figure 14.2 Identity options.

2. Enter information in the displayed fields as described in the rest of this section.

Entering Your Name

The information that you place in the **Your Name:** field will be displayed to the reader of any message that you create. Most people use their full names, or their first initials and last name. Others include their title or other professional designation. There's no limitation on the kind of characters that you can use in this field, so spaces and punctuation are considered acceptable.

To fill in this field, type your name as you wish it to appear in any messages that you send.

Entering Your Email Address and Reply-To Address

Enter your complete email address in the **Your Email:** field. If you don't know what your email address is, contact your service provider for more information.

If you have multiple email addresses, you may wish to receive your mail at a different address than you send it from; for example, if you have a personal account and a business account, you may wish for all mail to be sent to your personal account, regardless of the account that you used to create the message.

If you wish responses to your mail to be sent to a different address from the one you entered in the **Your Email:** field, type the address in the **Reply-to Address:** field. If you leave this field blank, the address you entered in the **Your Email:** field will be used for other people's replies to your mail.

Entering Your Organizational Information

If you're affiliated with a university, school district, or company, you can place the name of your sponsoring institution in the **Your Organization:** field. SMTP servers consider this to be a required field; if you don't enter information here, then your service provider will more than likely fill in this field with its own name. (For example, if your account is from Computize, leaving this field blank will result in "Computize, Inc." appearing in the Organization field of all messages that you send.)

Appending a Signature File

A signature file is a small text-only file that's appended to the end of any message that you send. Generally, a signature file contains your name, email address, title, work telephone number, and the company that you work for, though many people also include the URL for their home page and sometimes quotations or artwork. Many people whose addresses reflect a company or institution include a disclaimer stating that any opinions expressed represent their personal views, not those of their organization. A sample of a signature file is displayed in Figure 14.3.

```
John Q. Doe                  |Disclaimer: Any opinions expressed
Manager, Foobar Corporation  |are in no way the opinions of the
JQDoe@foobar.com             |Foobar Corp. I don't speak for them,
http://www.foobar.com        |and they sure don't speak for me.
```

Figure 14.3 Sample signature file.

Signature files are useful because you don't have to worry about typing your name and contact information at the end of every message that you create. You can simply type your message and send it, knowing that Netscape will correctly append your signature file.

VIRTUOSO

This is a good place to include a URL to your company's or your own home page; not only does it make the information readily available to your readers, but the URL will appear as a hot link in any articles that you post to Usenet News.

Creating a Signature File

NOTE

These are general instructions for creating a signature file. Simply creating the file will not automatically append it to your documents; you need to configure Netscape's Mail and News Preferences to use this file. Instructions on configuring Netscape appear at the end of this section.

To create a signature file, follow these steps:

1. Launch a simple ASCII text editor, like NotePad (Windows), SimpleText (Macintosh), or vi (UNIX).

2. Type the information that you wish to include in your signature file, following these brief rules:

   • Each line must contain fewer than 80 characters.

   • You must press **Return** at the end of each line.

   • Be considerate of your readers and network resources. Don't create a signature that's longer than three or four lines.

3. Save and close the file. (If you used a word processor instead of a text editor, be sure to save the file as ASCII text.) If you're using UNIX, name the file **.signature** (if you don't have a **.signature** file already).

Including the Signature File

If you wish to append a signature file, follow these steps:

1. Click **Browse....** at the right of the **Signature File**: field.

2. Navigate your file system until you can select the signature file you created.

3. On the Macintosh, you must select the field next to **File**: in order for the file to be used.

Entering Server and Directory Information

Getting Started

To enter information about your mail server and to choose local directories to store mail, follow these steps:

1. At the Mail and News Preferences window, click the **Servers** tab. The following screen (Figure 14.4) will be displayed.

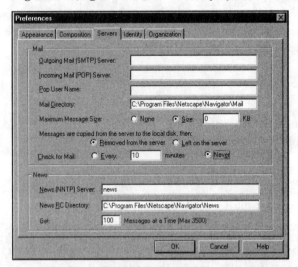

Figure 14.4 Server and directory options.

2. Enter information in the displayed fields as described in the rest of this section.

Identifying the SMTP and POP Servers

To identify the mail servers that you'll use, follow these steps:

1. In the **Outgoing Mail (SMTP) Server:** field, enter the name of your SMTP server as supplied by your service provider.

2. In the **Incoming Mail (POP) Server:** field, enter the name of your POP server as supplied by your service provider.

Entering Your POP User Name

Your POP user name is the unique account name on the POP server that identifies you as the owner of your mail. Your POP user name is the part of your email address that appears to the *left* of the @ symbol; for example, in the email address "EKeeler@uh.edu," "EKeeler" is the POP user name.

Enter your POP user name in the **POP User Name:** field.

Specifying a Mail Directory

Incoming messages that are retrieved with Netscape are stored locally on your computer. In Windows, the default Mail directory is stored in the same folder as the Netscape application; on the Macintosh, the default Mail directory is in the Netscape Preferences folder in the System Folder.

If you wish to store your mail messages in another directory, use the appropriate procedure:

- In Windows, type the name of the new mail directory in the **Mail Directory:** field.
- On the Macintosh, click the **Browse** button to the right of **Mail Directory:** and locate and select the desired location.

Choosing a Maximum Size for Messages

Netscape allows you to set a maximum size for messages to download. If a message is larger than the size you specify, it will simply be left on the server and ignored.

On the positive side, this feature can keep your system from getting bogged down with a lengthy file download. But, you need to make sure that you eventually download your long messages—either with Netscape's mail program or the mail reader of your choice—so that you don't overload the file storage area for your mail account.

VIRTUOSO

If you don't wish to set a maximum message size, make sure that **None** is selected at the right of **Maximum Message Size**. If you need to specify a maximum size, click **Size** and then enter the size, in kilobytes, in the field. (On the Macintosh, click the **up** and **down** arrows to increase or decrease the maximum message size by 1K.)

Choosing to Leave Messages on the Server

Netscape allows you two options when retrieving mail: you can leave messages on the server after retrieving them to your desktop, or you can delete them from the server after retrieving them to your desktop.

Whatever mail program you use most often should be set to delete messages from the server. If you subscribe to mailing lists or simply have an active professional or social life, you may find that you'll soon exceed the limitations of your disk space on the server!

WARNING

Use the following guidelines to make a decision about how to set this option:

- If Netscape is the *only* application that you use to read your mail, set Netscape to remove the messages from the server. (Click **Removed from the server**.) This ensures that you don't take up too much space on your service provider's computer by letting mail messages pile up without being deleted.

- If Netscape is *not* the primary application that you use to read your mail, set Netscape to leave the messages on the server. (Click **Left on the server**.) For example, if your primary mail reader is Eudora or cc:Mail or another commercial package with advanced mail handling capabilities, you should select this option. This allows you to check your mail from Netscape without launching another RAM-consuming application, but ensures that you can still retrieve and manage your mail with the other mail program of your choice.

Controlling When Netscape Checks for Mail

If desired, you can set Netscape to automatically check for new incoming mail at a time interval that you enter. Or, you can set Netscape so that it only checks mail when you specifically request that it do so.

WARNING

This option has some serious disadvantages, especially if you're using Netscape with a dialup modem connection from your office or home. One of the great features of a desktop mail program is the ability to read and compose messages even when you're not connected to the Internet—this leaves your telephone line free and can save you a *lot* of money if your service provider charges you for the amount of time you spend online. But, setting Netscape to automatically check your mail can cause the program to establish a dialup connection, even if you'd prefer to read your mail or review an HTML document when you're offline. For this reason, we strongly recommend that dialup users not use this feature. (It only takes a few keystrokes to check your mail any time you wish.)

To set Netscape to check your mail automatically, follow these steps:

1. To the right of **Check for Mail:**, select **Every**.
2. In the **minutes** field, enter the desired number of minutes for Netscape to wait between attempts to check the mail.

To set Netscape so that mail is never checked automatically (the recommended setting), select **Never**.

Special Notes for UNIX Users

Netscape for UNIX lets you select whether to use POP3 or a movemail utility. If you select **POP3**, the fields for server and user name are enabled, and you don't have anything else to worry about. However, if you do not have access to a POP3 account and you wish to use Netscape to read your mail, you can use Netscape's built-in movemail utility to move messages from your mail spool to a place where Netscape can read them.

WARNING

Before you attempt to configure the movemail utility, you *must* read the special note at http://home.netscape.com/eng/mozilla/2.0/relnotes/demo/movemail.html. This note contains critical information about how to configure Netscape to access your mail without causing potentially devastating damage to any of your messages. (If you don't want to type that URL by hand, scroll to the bottom of the default mail message from Mozilla and click the link in the last paragraph that says "Unix users, especially those who use procmail, should be sure to read this document.")

Controlling Composition and Management Options

Getting Started

To enter information about mail composition and management, follow these steps:

1. At the Mail and News Preferences window, click the **Composition** tab. The following screen (Figure 14.5) will be displayed.

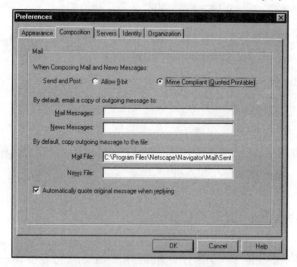

Figure 14.5 Composition options.

2. Enter information in the displayed fields as described in the rest of this section.

Choosing Send and Post Options

About Send and Post Options

The options in this section are related to sending items other than plain text files. To mail graphics, executable software, HTML, and any other kind of formatted documents, Internet email standards require that the material be encoded in a *transportable* form—one that can be read and understood by the wide variety of machines that may come into contact with your document on the way to its final destination.

The limitations of SMTP and other mail transport systems prohibit the use of certain kinds of control characters in a file. The safest strategy to ensure that you send a readable file is to follow the rules specified by the MIME standard, which defines the ways that email messages can be encoded so that they can be handled by a variety of different machines without being damaged. The MIME standard, which we discussed in Chapter 8, also specifies several transfer encoding formats that are compatible with SMTP transport limitations so that MIME objects can be sent as electronic mail without corruption.

The two primary encoding options that are available to you in Netscape are **Allow 8-bit** and **MIME-Compliant (Quoted Printable)**. The 8-bit setting is more efficient than the MIME-compliant setting because each byte of the file or message is transmitted directly, without encoding. But when you're sending messages across the Internet, there's no guarantee that all the machines you contact are going to be able to handle 8-bit data streams. Some mail servers that your message passes through will inevitably corrupt your data if you send it without the MIME-compliant transfer encoding. The only circumstance in which it's appropriate to use the 8-bit option is if you're using a local mail server which you know to be *8-bit clean* to send messages to another person on the same system, or if you're using a local news server which you know to be 8-bit clean to post messages only on local newsgroups. In other words, the 8-bit option is generally inappropriate for communicating with anyone who isn't part of your organization and located at the same site.

MIME content-transfer encoding solves the 8-bit clean problem by using one of several encoding schemes which are independent of an object's MIME type. These transfer-encoding schemes ensure that the data reaches its destination intact, regardless of the machines that it encounters on the way. Currently, Netscape primarily uses one kind of MIME content-transfer encoding—the *quoted printable* scheme. This encoding scheme sends all the characters in a message that are normal printable ASCII characters in an unaltered, printable form. However, control characters and characters in the extended ASCII character set are preceded by special tags and replaced with printable characters. The receiving application identifies the special characters by the tags and decodes them so that the document is returned to its original state.

The MIME developers created the quoted printable encoding scheme so that encoded files would be largely readable by humans—the normal parts of the message aren't altered by the encoding, so you can still read any English text that's embedded in the message, even if the message also contains binary information like a GIF file. When appropriate, Netscape will use another kind of content-transfer encoding called *base64*, which can be a more efficient encoding system but which creates files that are entirely unreadable to humans in their undecoded form.

NOTE An additional encoding option available to users of Windows 95 is **Use Exchange Client for Mail and News**, which we'll discuss in the section titled "Controlling the Appearance Options."

Setting Send and Post Options

To set send and post options for normal Internet email usage, click **Mime Compliant (Quoted Printable)**.

Managing Your Outgoing Messages

The Netscape mail program lets you keep track of your outgoing messages in two ways:

- You may mail copies of all outgoing messages to another email address. You might find this useful if you use another application such as Eudora as your primary application for managing mail, since it allows you to keep track of all your outgoing mail in one place.

- You may keep copies of all mail that you send in a local file. This lets you keep track of messages that you've sent.

To email copies of outgoing messages to another account, enter the email address of the account in the **Mail Messages**: field.

By default, Netscape will save copies of outgoing messages in a local file. The default location for mail messages on Windows is the Mail\Sent folder, located in the same directory as the Netscape application. The default location for mail messages on the Macintosh is System Folder:Preferences:Netscape *f*:Mail:Sent Mail.

To change the directory where copies of outgoing messages are stored, enter the full pathname of the directory in the **Mail File**: field. (On the Macintosh, click **Browse** and select the desired location.)

Quoting Messages that You Reply To

When you're replying to email messages, it's courteous to quote all or part of the message you're responding to. This reminds your correspondents of what they originally wrote so that they understand your reply in context. Text that's quoted is usually preceded by brackets so your correspondents can easily follow the thread of the conversation. For example, in the text below, the sentences preceded by brackets are from the message that I'm replying to; the text without brackets is the new message that I'm writing.

```
In your message of April 17, you wrote:
>I'm looking for information about vacation rentals
>in the Texas Hill Country. Can anyone give me a
>recommendation?

We very much enjoyed the Foxfire cabins, near Leakey, TX.
The facilities were nice, they're near our favorite state
parks, and the owners have a unique menagerie of semi-
domesticated animals roaming the grounds.
```

If you want Netscape to automatically quote the text of messages you're replying to, make sure that **Automatically quote original message when**

replying is selected at the bottom of the Composition window. If you don't want to automatically quote the message, deselect the item.

NOTE

Standard email netiquette is to delete as much of the original message as you can, leaving just enough so that your correspondent can understand the context of your comments. This way, messages don't get long and unwieldy.

VIRTUOSO

Even if you deselect this item, you can still quote individual mail messages at the time that you reply to them by selecting **Include Original Text** from the File menu when you have the mail composition window open. (Don't worry, we'll talk about this in later sections.) If you write a lot of mail, you might find it easier to not worry about paring down the original text in all the messages that you respond to.

Controlling the Appearance Options

Getting Started

To enter information about the display font, the appearance of quoted text, and the mail client, follow these steps:

1. At the Mail and News Preferences window, click the **Appearance** tab. The following screen (Figure 14.6) will be displayed.

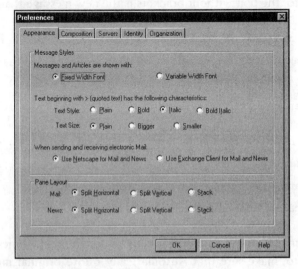

Figure 14.6 Appearance options.

2. Enter information in the displayed fields as described in the rest of this section.

Choosing a Font

You can choose to display messages in either the fixed-width font or the variable-width font that you chose in General Preferences. (Information on choosing fonts can be found in Chapter 3.)

To use the fixed-width font, select **Fixed Width Font**. To use the variable-width font, select **Variable Width Font**.

VIRTUOSO

Even though the variable-width font may be visually appealing, we strongly recommend using the fixed-width font to display messages. A fixed-width font will make it easier to keep track of how long your lines really are, because each character takes up the same amount of space. In certain circumstances, it can be very important that lines not exceed a certain length; we'll talk about this more when we discuss composing messages later in this chapter.

Setting Characteristics of Quoted Text

As discussed previously, Netscape allows you to quote text of messages that you reply to. In addition to placing brackets in front of the quoted text, you may choose the style and the size of the quoted text.

To set the style of quoted text, select the desired option (**Plain**, **Bold**, **Italic**, or **Bold Italic**) next to Text Style:.

To set the size of quoted text, select the desired option (**Plain**, **Bigger**, or **Smaller**) next to Text Size:.

Choosing a Mail Client (Windows 95)

Microsoft Exchange is a software package that you can choose to install with Windows 95. It acts as an umbrella under which all forms of messaging can be included. If you have correctly installed and configured Exchange per the Microsoft documentation and you wish to use it as the mechanism to transport your mail and news, you may select **Use Exchange Client for Mail and News** at the bottom of the screen. Otherwise, keep the default selection of **Use Netscape for Mail and News**.

WARNING

If you enable Exchange, all the other mail and news configuration data that you enter is superseded by the corresponding settings in Exchange. If you choose the option, be sure that Exchange is configured correctly.

Organizing Your Incoming Messages

To enter information about how you want your mail organized, follow these steps:

1. At the Mail and News Preferences window, click the **Organization** tab. The following screen (Figure 14.7) will be displayed.

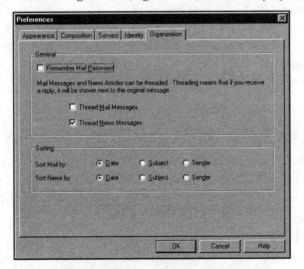

Figure 14.7 Organization options.

2. Enter information in the displayed fields as described in the rest of this section.

Setting Netscape to Remember Your Password

If you want Netscape to remember your mail password so you don't have to enter it every time you check your mail during a session, select **Remember Mail Password**.

WARNING

This feature is useful if you set Netscape to check your mail automatically, since it allows Netscape to log into the POP server and retrieve your messages without requiring additional input. But be careful! Letting Netscape remember your password means that anyone who uses your computer can check your incoming mail as long as Netscape is open. If you aren't positive that you're the only person who can use your computer, and privacy is important to you, then you should enter your password every time and not let Netscape store it.

Threading and Sorting Your Mail

If you want, you can choose to thread your incoming mail messages. If you thread messages, then replies to a message will be displayed beneath the original message. This makes it easy to keep track of a conversation, but makes it difficult to determine the order in which mail was received. To thread your mail messages, select **Thread Mail Messages**.

You can also control the default way that messages are sorted in the Netscape Mail window. Messages can be displayed by the date sent, by the subject of the message, or by the sender of the message. To choose the default sorting option, select the desired setting next to **Sort Mail by**:.

VIRTUOSO

We recommend sorting messages by date as the default setting so you can always identify the most recent messages when you read your incoming mail. As we'll discuss later in the chapter, you can resort messages on-the-fly at the Netscape mail window.

About the Netscape Mail Window

The Netscape Mail window can be displayed two different ways:

- By clicking the envelope icon at the lower-right corner of the browser window.
- By selecting **Netscape Mail** from the Window menu.

VIRTUOSO

If you want Netscape to automatically display the Netscape Mail window when you launch the application, select **On Startup Launch Netscape Mail** from the Appearances section of General Preferences.

If you've configured the Mail and News options correctly, you'll be prompted to enter the password for your POP3 account as soon as the Netscape Mail window is opened. We'll talk more about this in the next section, "Reading Your Mail."

Contents of the Window

The following illustration shows the components of the Netscape Mail window:

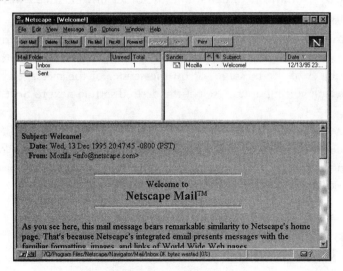

Figure 14.8 Netscape Mail window.

Here's a brief description of the elements in the window:

- Mail menus. Except for the Window and Help menus, these menus contain different items from the similarly named windows in the Netscape browser.

- Toolbar. These buttons provide shortcuts to several useful mail features.

- Panes. In this illustration, the pane on the left displays your mail folders and provides information about their contents; to display the contents of a folder, click its name. The pane on the right displays individual messages in a folder. To display an individual message, click its name. The headers in each pane can be sized or dragged to new positions.

- Message display area. When you select a message to display, it's shown in this section.

Customizing the Appearance of the Window

You can use the following procedures to modify the appearance of the Mail window:

- To resize any item in a pane or any pane itself, hold down the mouse over its boundary and drag to the desired size. Adjacent items will be resized accordingly. You may resize the headings within the panes, and the side and bottom boundaries of the panes themselves.

- To move headings within the panes, hold down the mouse over the heading and drag the item to its new location.

- The toolbar uses the same display settings (**Pictures**, **Text**, or **Pictures and Text**) that you set in the Appearance section of General Preferences. You can change the appearance by modifying the Preferences accordingly.

VIRTUOSO

In general, we recommend displaying the toolbar as text, which takes up less vertical space on the screen than displaying pictures (either with or without text), and ensures that you can immediately identify the buttons' meaning.

- By default, the Mail screen displays folders on the left, messages on the right, and the text of messages at the bottom of the screen. You may choose to show both the folders and the messages at the left of the screen with the text of the messages appearing on the right (Figure 14.9), or you may display the folders on top, the messages in the middle, and the text of the messages at the bottom of the screen (Figure 14.10). To choose the appearance of the panes, click the **Appearance** tab in Mail and News Preferences. In the Pane Layout section (on Macintosh, the Mail Pane Configuration section), select **Split Horizontal** (the default), **Split Vertical** (Figure 14.9), or **Stacked** (Figure 14.10). (On the Macintosh, the first two items are **Split Horizontally** and **Split Vertically**.)

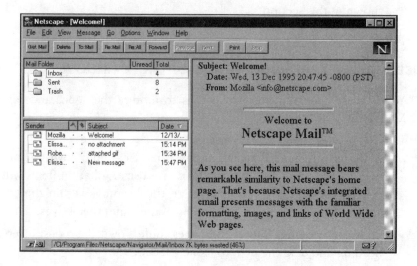

Figure 14.9 Mail window with panes split vertically.

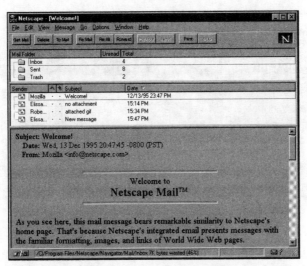

Figure 14.10 Mail window with stacked panes.

Reading Your Mail

This section contains instructions about how to retrieve and read your mail. For more detailed information about managing your mail, see the section titled "Managing Your Mail."

Retrieving Your Mail

The first step in reading your mail is to get Netscape to retrieve it from your mail server. To retrieve your mail, follow these steps:

1. Open the Netscape Mail window in one of these ways:

- Click the envelope icon at the bottom of the browser window.

- From the Window menu, select **Netscape Mail**.

- If you select **On Startup Launch Netscape Mail** from the Appearances section of General Preferences, Netscape will attempt to retrieve your mail as soon as you launch the application.

No matter how you open the Netscape Mail window, you'll be prompted to enter your password (Figure 14.11).

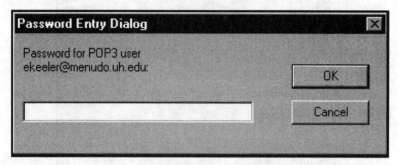

Figure 14.11 Password dialog box.

2. To retrieve your mail, enter your password in the field and click **OK**. To go to the Netscape Mail window without retrieving new mail, click **Cancel**.

NOTE

Problems getting your mail? Passwords for mail accounts are usually case-sensitive, so make sure that you enter them with the correct combination of upper- or lowercase letters. If you continue to have problems, make sure that you entered your POP server and POP user name correctly in the Servers section of Mail and News Preferences. If you still can't retrieve your mail, contact your service provider for further assistance.

All incoming mail is automatically stored in your Inbox folder at the Netscape Mail window. (More information about the Inbox folder appears in the section "Managing Your Mail.") The number displayed under the **Unread** heading lets you know how many messages are in the folder that you haven't looked at yet; the number displayed under the **Total** heading lets you know the total number of messages in the folder.

VIRTUOSO

If you set Netscape to automatically check your mail, then the envelope icon at the browser window will display information about the status of your mail. If the envelope is displayed by itself, then you don't have any new messages. If an exclamation mark is displayed, then you have new mail waiting for you. If a question mark is displayed, then Netscape couldn't check your mail automatically—make sure that you entered your password during this session.

Displaying Your Messages

To display a list of the messages in the Inbox, click the icon for the Inbox. The messages will be displayed in the pane on the right.

To read a message, click its title in the pane on the right. The contents will be displayed in the message area at the bottom of the screen. You can use the scroll bar at the right of the message display area to show different parts of the message.

VIRTUOSO Want to see more of the message? You can make the message display area bigger by placing the mouse over the bar separating the message area from the top panes, holding down the mouse button, and dragging the separator bar higher in the window.

Viewing Headers

The headers of mail messages contain a great deal of information, such as who sent the message; when the message was sent; the subject of the message; the type of mailer used to send the message; and some information about the path that the message took in arriving. You can choose to display normal headers containing basic information about the message; all headers attached to the message; or "brief-headers," which contain minimal information about the message.

To change the way that headers are displayed, select **All**, **Normal**, or **Brief** from the **Show Headers** item in the Options menu.

Working with Attachments

Controlling the Display of Attachments

Your correspondents may send you separate files as attachments to mail messages. Attachments may be any kind of document that can be transmitted across the Internet—HTML files, archives of spreadsheets or word processing documents, graphics, movies, etc. Attachments will be stored as part of the mail message in your Inbox; you'll need to extract the items to your desktop system if you want to work with them outside of Netscape.

Netscape lets you display attachments one of two ways: as inline parts of the document or as links. If you choose to display attachments inline, attachments such as graphics or HTML files that can be displayed as part of the message will be displayed as part of the message. (HTML files will be interpreted and displayed as if you were viewing them with the browser, instead of as HTML.)

If attachments are displayed as links, a link to the attachment file on your system will be displayed at the bottom of the message. If the attachment is an HTML file, clicking the link will display the formatted contents of the file in the message display area.

To change the display of attachments, select either **Attachments Inline** or **Attachments as Links** from the View menu of the Netscape Mail window.

Viewing Attachments

Attachments that Netscape Can Display Directly

If an attachment is of a MIME type that Netscape can display directly (such as a GIF graphic or an HTML page), and you've chosen **Attachments Inline** from the View menu, then the attachment will be interpreted and displayed at the bottom of the message (Figure 14.12).

If an attachment is of a MIME type that Netscape can display directly (such as a GIF graphic or an HTML page), and you've chosen **Attachments as Links**, then a link for each attachment will be displayed at the bottom of the message (Figure 14.13).

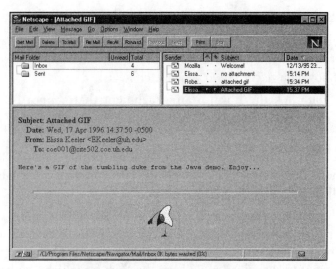

Figure 14.12 Attached GIF displayed inline.

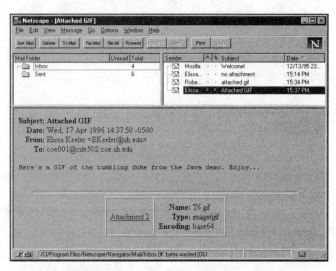

Figure 14.13 Attachment viewed as a link.

If you click the link, then the attachment will be displayed.

Attachments that Cannot be Displayed Directly

If an attachment is of a MIME type that Netscape cannot display directly, the attachment will appear as a link at the bottom of the window, regardless of how you've chosen to view attachments.

If you click the link for an attachment that cannot be displayed directly, one of two things will happen:

- If you've configured a helper application for that kind of MIME type, the application will be launched. (For complete information about MIME types and helper applications, see Part Two of this book.)
- If you haven't configured a helper application for that kind of MIME type, Netscape will display a dialog box asking what you want to do with the file. This is the same dialog box that you see when you attempt to download a file from the Web for which you haven't configured a MIME type—Netscape considers the action of extracting the item from the Inbox to be the same as downloading it.

Sending Mail

About the Message Composition Window

There are several ways that you can generate a mail message in Netscape: by clicking a mailto: link, by replying to email that someone sent you, or by simply deciding to send a mail message to someone you know. All mail that you originate in Netscape is created in the Message Composition window (Figure 14.14).

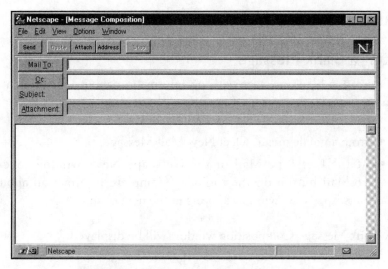

Figure 14.14 Message Composition window.

The components of the Message Composition window are listed below:

- Menus. The contents of the menus in the Message Composition window are different from the items available elsewhere in the browser.

- Toolbar. The buttons in the toolbar provide a simple interface to the most common mail functions, such as sending mail; including the text of a message you're replying to as a quote; choosing an email address from your Address Book; or stopping the process of sending a message.

- Information fields. These fields let you specify important information about the message such as the email address of the recipient; additional email addresses of people who should receive copies or blind copies; the subject of the message; and any attached files. You can hide or display information fields by toggling the selection of the item in the View menu.

- Message composition area. Compose your mail message in the area at the bottom of the Message Composition window. If you chose to quote a message, the text will be displayed here preceded by brackets.

Creating a Message

Creating a Blank Message

To create a blank message with no information about the recipients, the subject, or attachments, perform one of these actions:

- From any File menu, select **New Mail Message**.
- At the Netscape Mail or the Netscape News window, click the **To:Mail** button on the toolbar. (Complete information about the Netscape News window appears in the next chapter.)

A blank Message Composition window will be displayed.

Creating a Message with Some Information Filled In

To create a message in which some information is automatically included in the Message Composition window, perform one of these actions:

- From the File menu of the browser, select **Mail Document**.... A Message Composition window will be displayed with the title of the document in the subject field; the name of the current document in the Attachment field; and the URL of the document as the first line of the message.
- At a Web document, click a **mailto:** URL. A Message Composition window will be displayed with the email address of the recipient filled in.

VIRTUOSO

Mailto: URLs are usually displayed to the reader in the form of an email address; you can always be sure it's a mailto: link by looking at the status message at the lower-left corner of the screen when the pointer is over the link.

- At the Netscape Mail or the Netscape News window, select a message and click the **Re:Mail** button. (Complete information about the Netscape News window can be found in the next chapter.) A Message Composition window will be displayed containing the email address of the person you're replying to and the subject of the original message with "Re:" appended to the beginning. If you chose to automatically quote messages in the Composition section of Mail and News Preferences, then the complete text of the message will be displayed with brackets in front of it.

- At the Netscape Mail window, select a message and click the **Re:All** button to send your response to everyone who received a copy of the message you're replying to, instead of just the person who sent the message.

- At the Netscape News window, select a message and click the **Re:Both** button to send your response to the newsgroup and to the person who wrote the original message.

- At the Netscape Mail or Netscape News window, select a message and click the **Forward** button. The Message Composition window will be displayed with the Subject field containing the original title of the message with "Fwd:" appended to the beginning; the Attachment field will show that the message is being forwarded as an attachment.

Entering Header Information

A mail *header* is the text associated with a mail message that contains information about the message needed to route it to its correct destination. While a great deal of header information is created by the computers your mail passes through en route to its destination, you're responsible for some header information, which lets you specify the sender, the recipients, the subject, and attachments.

The fields in which you can enter header information are displayed beneath the toolbar and above the message composition area. You can control which fields are displayed by toggling their names in the View menu of the Message Composition window.

NOTE

Because mail messages and news messages are composed in the same window, there are some news header fields that aren't relevant for mail, and vice versa. Header fields for news messages will be discussed in the next chapter.

Table 14.1 Header Fields for Mail

Header item	Purpose	Required	Notes
From:	Identifies the sender.	Yes	Automatically filled in with information from Mail and News Preferences; you can't edit this field directly. On the Macintosh, this information is always displayed in the upper-right corner of the Message Composition window; not available in the Macintosh View menu.
Reply To:	Sends replies to a different address from the one the mail was sent from.	No	If you entered a Reply To: address in Mail and News Preferences, the field is automatically filled in. However, you can enter information for individual messages.
Mail To:	Identifies the recipient(s) of the message. Enter the email address of the recipient or use the information in your Address Book. (See "Using the Address Book" later in this section.)	Yes	Automatically filled in if you're responding to a message.
Mail Cc:	Identifies additional recipients of a message. Enter the email addresses of the recipients or use the information in your Address Book. (See "Using the Address Book" later in this section.)	No	Useful in business correspondence to identify the primary person who should respond to the message.

Table 14.1 Header Fields for Mail (continued)

Header item	Purpose	Required	Notes
Mail Bcc:	Identifies people who should receive a blind copy of the message (no other recipients will know that they received it).	No	If the recipient chooses an option like Re: All to send a response to everyone who received the message, the names of people who received blind copies will not be displayed or used.
File Cc:	Identifies a local directory to store a copy of the messages.	No	Useful if you're not automatically storing copies of all your messages.
Subject:	Identifies a topic for the message. Type the topic of the message here.	Yes	Field is automatically filled in if you reply to or forward a message. Field is always visible on the Macintosh; not available in Macintosh View menu.
Attachment:	Identifies additional files sent with the message. (See "Adding an Attachment" later in this section.)	No	Field is automatically filled in when you identify the file to attach; never enter information directly into this field. Field is always visible on the Macintosh; not available in Macintosh View menu.

To enter header information for a message, follow these steps:

1. Make sure the fields you wish to enter information for are displayed by selecting their names from the View menu. (To show all fields, select **Show All**.)

2. Enter information as desired, using Table 14.1 as a guide. Remember, the Mail to: and Subject: fields are required.

NOTE

To specify more than one recipient in the Mail to:, Cc:, or Bcc: fields, simply separate each entry with a comma.

Using the Address Book

Complete information on creating an Address Book appears at the end of this chapter. To use the information in your Address Book, follow the steps in the next sections.

SHORTCUT

If you remember the lowercase nickname you created for an entry, you can type that directly into a field. Or, you can type the name of the person exactly as you entered it in the Address Book.

For Windows...

To use addresses or mailing lists in your Address Book, follow these steps:

1. Click the **Address** button on the toolbar or click any button in the header area related to addresses (**Mail To:**, **Cc:**, or **Bcc:**). The Select Addresses window will be displayed.

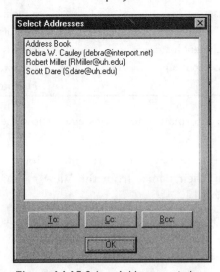

Figure 14.15 Select Addresses window.

2. Select the address or mailing list you wish to use.

3. At the bottom of the window, click the button for the field in which you wish the address to appear (**To:**, **Cc:**, or **Bcc:**).

Even if you displayed the Address Book by clicking the name of a field, you must click the name of the desired field at the Address Book.

WARNING

You can't select a field that isn't displayed in the header area for the message. For example, if you assign an address to the Bcc: field but the Bcc: field isn't displayed for the current message, that information will not be used.

WARNING

4. When you're finished, click **OK**.

The nicknames of the people or mailing lists you added will be displayed in the appropriate fields.

For Macintosh...

To use addresses or mailing lists in your Address Book, follow these steps:

1. Click the **Address** button on the toolbar. The Address Book itself will be displayed.

2. Drag an entry for a person or mailing list from the Address Book to the appropriate field in the Message Composition window.

3. Release the mouse.

The nicknames of the people or mailing lists you added will be displayed in the appropriate fields.

Adding an Attachment

Netscape lets you send files as attachments to the text you write in a mail message. You can send the following types of items as attachments:

- Files that reside on your computer.
- Files that are available somewhere on the Web.
- The text of mail or news messages displayed in the Netscape Mail or Netscape News window.

NOTE

When you work with attachments, keep in mind that your correspondents might not be using Netscape to read their mail—the files may simply be downloaded to their disk drive instead of being displayed as part of the message that you send.

You can add as many attachments as you wish.

Sending a File from Your Computer

To send a file that resides on your computer as an attachment to a mail message, follow these steps:

1. At the toolbar of the Message Composition window, click the **Attach** button. (Or select **Attach File…** from the File menu at the Message Composition window.) The Attachments window (Figure 14.16) will be displayed.

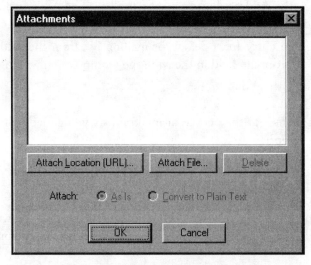

Figure 14.16 The Attachments window.

2. Click **Attach File**... A dialog box will be displayed.

3. Locate and select the file you wish to attach.

4. Click **Open**. You'll return to the Attachments window.

5. Click **OK**. (On the Macintosh, click **Done**.) You'll return to the Message Composition window, where the name of the file will be displayed in the Attachments field.

Sending a Web Document as an Attachment

Netscape allows you to send a Web document as an attachment to your mail message. You can send the file as the HTML source code or simply as the text of the document.

VIRTUOSO

If you're only interested in conveying the content of the document and not any of its associated links, then choose to send the document as text. That way, the recipient can read the document even if they're using a mail program that doesn't automatically interpret HTML.

SHORTCUT

If you're browsing the Web and you want to attach the current document to a mail message, just select **Mail Document...** from the File menu. The Message Composition window will be displayed with the document already added in the Attachments field. You can still use the steps below to choose whether the document is sent as HTML source or as plain text.

WARNING

Netscape attempts to load the selected Web document into the message. Therefore, the document must be available to Netscape at the time that you select this option. The document must be displayed in the browser window or you must have established (or be able to establish) a network connection so that Netscape can retrieve the contents of the document.

To send a Web document, follow these steps:

1. At the toolbar of the Message Composition window, click the **Attach** button. (Or, select **Attach File**... from the File menu at the Message Composition window.) The Attachments window will be displayed.

2. Click **Attach Location (URL)**.... A dialog box requesting that you enter the URL of the document to attach will be displayed. If you were currently displaying a document, the URL for the document will be displayed in the field.

3. If no URL is displayed in the field, or you wish to send a different document than the one specified, enter the correct URL in the field.

4. Click **OK**. You'll return to the Attachments window.

5. If you want to send the document as HTML, select **As Is** (on the Macintosh, click **Source**). If you want to send the document as plain text, click **Convert to Plain Text** (on the Macintosh, click **Plain Text**).

6. Click **OK**. (On the Macintosh, click **Done**.)You'll return to the Message Composition window. The status message area for the window will indicate the progress of Netscape's attempt to load the document into the message.

Removing an Attachment

To remove an attachment, follow these steps:

1. Display the Attachments window.

2. Select the attachment you wish to remove.

3. Click **Delete**.

Writing Your Message

To write a message, type the message in the message composition area at the bottom of the window. If you're replying to a message and you haven't set Netscape to automatically quote messages you reply to, you can add the text of the message to your mail by clicking the **Quote** button on the toolbar or by selecting **Include Original Text** from the File menu of the Message Composition window.

Sending Your Mail

Choosing Delivery Options

Netscape gives you two options for sending your mail:

- Immediate delivery. As soon as you click the **Send** button, Netscape attempts to establish a network connection (if not already present) and the mail is sent.
- Deferred delivery. As soon as you click the **Send** button, the mail is placed in an Outbox folder and isn't mailed until you issue the command to do so.

VIRTUOSO

Using the deferred delivery option lets you compose all your messages offline, which is useful if you use a dialup connection and want to free your telephone, or if your service provider charges you for connect time. It's also useful if you travel with a laptop computer—you can write your mail in transit and mail it when you arrive at a destination with a telephone. Plus, this option gives you the chance to change your mind about a message!

To change delivery options for a message, select **Immediate Delivery** or **Deferred Delivery** at the Options menu of the Message Composition window. If your toolbar displays pictures and text, or just pictures, choosing **Deferred Delivery** will display a clock in the picture for the **Send** button. If your toolbar is only displayed as text, no changes to the button will be visible.

Sending the Message

When you're finished with your message, make sure of the following:

- The addressing information is correct.
- Any attachments you wish to send are identified correctly.
- The text of your message is complete.

Then, click the **Send** button.

About Deferred Delivery

If you chose the deferred delivery option, clicking **Send** will create an Outbox folder at the Netscape Mail window and place any outgoing mail for deferred delivery in the Outbox.

To send the mail in your Outbox, select **Send Mail in Outbox** from the File menu of the Netscape Mail window.

Managing Your Mail

Working with Folders

After you've retrieved a few messages, you will find that having all your mail in the Inbox is unwieldy and that it's difficult to find the messages that you're looking for. Netscape lets you create folders to store mail that are similar to the folders or directories that you create on your computer.

For example, you might have folders called "Personal," "Humor," "Research," and "Business." After your mail arrives, you can move or copy the messages into the right place to keep your Inbox organized.

Creating a Folder

To create a folder, follow these steps at the Netscape Mail window:

1. From the File menu, select **New Folder**. A dialog box will be displayed asking you to name the new folder.
2. Type the name of the folder in the field.
3. Click **OK**. When you return to the Netscape Mail window, the new folder will be displayed.

Placing Messages in Folders

There are two ways to place a message in a folder:

- *Moving* the message to a folder means that the message is removed from the current folder and placed in the target folder.

- *Copying* the message to a folder means that a copy of the message is placed in the target folder and a copy of the message remains in the current folder.

Copying Messages

To copy a message into a folder, follow these steps:

1. Select the message or messages in the pane at the right. (You may copy more than one message at a time if the messages appear next to each other in the window.)
2. Display the Message menu and move the mouse to the **Copy** item. A list of existing folders will be displayed to the right of **Copy**.
3. Select the folder you want to copy the message to.
4. Release the mouse. A copy of the message will be placed in the folder, and the number of items in the folder will be updated in the Netscape Mail window.

Moving Messages

To move a message into a folder, follow these steps:

1. Select the message or messages in the pane at the right. (You may move more than one message at a time if the messages appear next to each other in the window.)
2. Display the Message menu and move the mouse to the **Move** item. A list of existing folders will be displayed to the right of **Move**.
3. Select the folder you want to move the message to.
4. Release the mouse. The message will be moved from the current folder to the target folder, and the number of items in both folders will be updated in the Netscape Mail window.

You can use Drag-and-Drop to move messages to folders! Just select the message in the window at the right and drag it into the desired folder at the left. As soon as you release the mouse, the message will be moved to the target folder.

SHORTCUT

Displaying the Contents of a Folder

To display the contents of a folder, simply click the name of the folder in the pane on the left. The messages in the folder will be displayed on the right.

Compressing Your Folders

You may notice that each time you display the contents of a folder, the status message at the bottom of the window shows the full directory path to the folder and a message that says "xK bytes wasted (y%)," where x and y are zero or other numbers (an example is shown in Figure 14.17).

/C|/Program Files/Netscape/Navigator/Mail/Inbox 3K bytes wasted (30%)

Figure 14.17 Status message alerting you that a folder needs compression.

Every time you delete a message or move a message to a folder, a few bytes of space on your disk drive are still allotted to the message that's no longer there. While it's usually only a few bytes per message, these "wasted" bytes can really add up if you use the mail program a lot! Netscape provides a simple way to reclaim the disk space that's wasted when you move files around; conceptually, compressing folders is similar to optimizing a disk drive.

To reclaim disk space from a folder, follow these steps:

1. Select a folder. If the status message states that there is wasted space in the folder, continue with the procedure.
2. From the File menu, select **Compress This Folder**. As Netscape compresses the folder, the status message area will provide information about the process and a progress gauge will be displayed.

It's a good idea to get in the habit of regularly compressing your folders, and not wait until you run out of disk space!

VIRTUOSO

276

Sorting Your Messages

You can sort the messages in a mail folder in a variety of ways: by date, by subject, or by sender. (You can also choose to sort by message number, but that option is primarily a carryover from Netscape's News options, much like the "flag message" feature.)

To sort messages within a folder, select the desired sorting option from the **Sort** submenu in the View menu.

SHORTCUT

Or, click the **Sender**, **Subject**, or **Date** header in the message panel to sort by that topic.

NOTE

Netscape sorts the messages based only on the information in the message headers. This means messages sorted by sender will be sorted by the first letter that appears in the sender field, which may or may not be the sender's actual name, and messages sorted by subject will simply be arranged in alphabetical order.

By default, messages are shown in descending order—messages sorted by date are shown from newest to oldest; messages sorted by subject or sender are shown in alphabetical order. If desired, you may choose **Ascending** from the Sort submenu to display the messages in ascending order (if the messages are sorted by date, the oldest message is first in the list; if sorted by sender or subject, the items are shown in reverse alphabetical order).

SHORTCUT

When messages are sorted, the heading that corresponds to the kind of sort is displayed with a triangle next to it (Figure 14.18). If the triangle points upward, the messages are sorted in ascending order; if it points down, the messages are sorted in descending order.

Sender	△	❦	Subject	Date ▽
📧	Elissa...	·	·	no attachment	15:14 PM
📧	Robe...	·	·	attached gif	15:34 PM
📧	Elissa...	┌	┌	New message	15:47 PM

Figure 14.18 The triangle indicates that messages are sorted in descending order.

Flagging Messages

You may "flag" messages so that they can be readily identified for you to return to at a later time. To flag a message, click the mouse beneath the flag icon on the same line as the message, or select a message and choose **Flag Message** from the Message menu. You can navigate among flagged messages by choosing **First Flagged**, **Next Flagged**, or **Previous Flagged** from the Go menu. To work with all flagged messages, choose **Select Flagged Messages** from the Edit menu. You can then move, copy, or delete all the selected messages at the same time.

Flagging messages and using the **Select Flagged Messages** option is the only way to select more than one message at a time in Netscape Mail. If you try to select messages by clicking them, you'll just display each message in the window.

VIRTUOSO

Deleting Messages

It's important to delete mail from time to time so that you don't fill up your disk drive. Deleting mail is a two-step process. You must:

1. Move the mail into the Trash folder (more on this in a minute).
2. Specifically choose to empty the Trash folder.

About the Trash Folder

The Trash folder is created the first time that you attempt to delete mail. It appears in your list of folders like any other folder. When you move a message to the Trash folder, it isn't deleted—it's just stored in the Trash until you delete it (much like a paper that you throw in the garbage can that isn't actually gone until you empty the trash). You may read messages in the Trash folder or move them out of the trash ... that is, until you empty the Trash folder.

To move mail to the Trash folder, follow these steps:

1. Select the message you want to delete.

2. Click the **Delete** button on the toolbar. The message will be moved to the Trash folder.

To empty your Trash folder, select **Empty Trash Folder** from the File menu.

Once you empty your Trash folder those messages are completely gone, so review your Trash folder before emptying it to make sure you're not throwing away something important.

WARNING

Working with Address Books

Just like your real-world address book that lets you keep track of the names and contact information of your friends and acquaintances, Netscape's Address Book lets you keep track of people's email addresses. You can type a name or nickname of a person as you entered it in the Address Book, and their email address will appear in the address field of your message! (After all, it's much easier to just type **bob** than to type **Robert@pdts.uh.edu**.) You can also create mailing lists so that you can messages to a group of people just by entering the name of the mailing list.

To display your Address Book, select **Address Book** from the Window menu. The Address Book (Figure 14.19) will be displayed.

To create an entry for your Address Book, follow these steps:

1. From the Item menu, select **Add User**. The Address Book entry window (Figure 14.20) will be displayed.

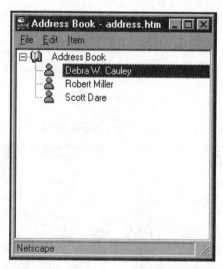

Figure 14.19 An Address Book with some information.

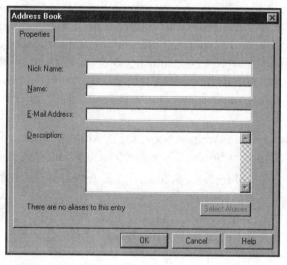

Figure 14.20 The Address Book entry window.

2. In the **Nick Name** field, type a one-word nickname for the entry you're creating. The nickname must be in lowercase letters or it will be rejected. (Use of this field is optional.)

3. In the **Name** field, type the name of the person you're creating an entry for. You can enter a first and last name, and use capital letters as desired. (This field is optional, but if you don't enter anything, you'll see a blank icon at the Address Book window.)

4. In the **E-Mail Address** field, type the exact email address of this person.

5. If you wish to enter a description of the person, type it in the **Description** field. (You can also use this field to store other information, like the person's mailing address or telephone number.)

6. Click **OK**. You'll return to the Address Book window, where a new icon will be displayed for the entry you created.

SHORTCUT

If you have mail from someone in your folders and you want to create an Address Book entry for that person, select the message and choose **Add to Address Book** from the Message menu. An Address Book Properties window will be displayed with the name and email address already filled in.

About Mailing Lists

If you regularly need to mail messages to more than one person, you can create mailing lists to store the names of the people on the list. Then, when you create a message, simply use the name of the mailing list in the **To:** field. Netscape will automatically send the message to everyone on the list. (You can also use mailing lists in the **Cc:** and **Bcc:** fields.)

To create a mailing list, follow these steps:

1. From the Item menu, select **New List**. The Address Book Properties window will be displayed. It will look just like the Properties window used to create single entries, but "New Folder" will be displayed in the Name field.

2. If desired, enter a nickname for the mailing list in the **Nick Name** field.

3. If desired, replace "New Folder" in the **Name** field with a more descriptive name.

4. If desired, enter a description of the mailing list in the **Description** field.

5. Click **OK**. You'll return to the Address Book window, where a new folder representing the mailing list (and displaying the name you entered in the Name field) will be displayed.

To add a person to the mailing list, follow these steps:

1. Make sure that you've created a regular Address Book entry for the person.

2. At the Address Book window, drag the icon for the person you wish to add to the mailing list over the icon for the mailing list. When you release the mouse, the icon for that entry will be copied into the new location. This creates an alias of the original entry; if you change any information for the entry, it'll be changed in the copy of the entry in the mailing list as well.

To delete entries in a mailing list, select the item and choose **Delete** from the Edit menu. Deleting entries in a mailing list does not delete the original entry or any other alias to the entry in other mailing lists. However, if you delete the original entry for a person, you'll get a warning message that you're also deleting the item from the mailing lists that it's a part of.

Importing and Exporting Address Books

Like bookmarks, Address Books are stored as regular HTML files on your computer. You can import other people's Address Books or export your own with ease.

To import another address book, follow these steps:

1. At the File menu of the Address Book window, select **Import**.... A standard file dialog box will be displayed.

2. Locate and select the Address Book you wish to import.

3. Click **Open**.

You'll return to the Address Book window with the new items displayed.

To export your Address Book, follow these steps:

1. At the File menu of the Address Book window, select **Save As**.... A standard save file dialog box will be displayed.
2. Enter a name for the file.
3. If desired, select a location.
4. Click **Save**. The file will be saved in the location you selected.

What You Learned

After reading this chapter, you should be able to:

- Understand how electronic mail is transmitted and received using POP and SMTP protocols.
- Understand and configure Netscape's configuration options for electronic mail.
- Create a signature file.
- Send and receive email messages from Netscape.
- Attach Web documents and files to mail that you send.
- Use Address Books to simplify sending mail to individuals or mailing lists.

CHAPTER 15

ALL ABOUT USENET NEWS

As we've mentioned, one of the powerful features of graphical Web browsers is that they integrate some of the most popular protocols for other network services so that you have at least a degree of access to the offerings of the Internet besides the World Wide Web. In this chapter, we'll talk about how you can read and reply to messages on Usenet News with Netscape's built-in newsreader.

What is Usenet News?

Long before the Internet, there was Usenet. In the 1980s, most businesses couldn't become part of ARPAnet—the Internet's Department of Defense–funded predecessor—because of an Acceptable Use Policy that prohibited the use of the ARPAnet backbone for most kinds of commercial endeavor. (Until the late 1980s, you could only get an account on the Internet if you were at a university or an organization that was conducting federally sponsored research and development, particularly projects for the Department of Defense.) Usenet came about in the early 1980s. It served as a common store-and-forward network for both news and mail, and it was entirely independent of the Internet. Electronic mail and Usenet News reached millions of people around the world, long before the real Internet changed its policy regarding acceptable use. Anyone who wants to place their computer on Usenet can do so; it just requires a computer (usually UNIX-based) and permission from someone who is already part of Usenet to use them as a server.

Besides the facilitation of electronic mail and file transfers, Usenet's most lasting and ongoing contribution to the online community has been Usenet News. Usenet News is an internationally distributed set of discussion groups, known as newsgroups. Several thousand newsgroups already exist, dedicated to every kind of computing, scientific, educational, business, interpersonal, entertainment, or prurient interest that you can imagine; and more newsgroups are being added every day. Although the sheer number of newsgroups and articles posted to them is daunting, Usenet News remains one of the best places online to get the most recent information or advice on a staggering array of topics.

To read Usenet News, you use a program called a newsreader. Originally, newsreaders were text-only mainframe programs like rn, trn, and tin that you operated while logged into a terminal session. Then, when graphical network applications came into being, you could use dedicated newsreaders like Newswatcher (Macintosh) or Trumpet News (PC). Following the model of NCSA Mosaic, and in order to maintain their reputation as the Swiss army knife of network tools, Netscape provides you with a set of built-in tools to access Usenet News.

Usenet Terminology

To understand what's going on when you use Netscape to read Usenet News, it's necessary to know the meaning of a few basic Usenet-related terms. This section contains a brief introduction to the key terms and concepts that you'll come across related to Usenet News.

News/NNTP Servers

Just as there are underlying protocols to support Internet services like HTTP for the Web and SMTP for electronic mail, NNTP—the Network News Transfer Protocol—is the communications standard for the distribution of Usenet News articles across the Internet-connected portion of Usenet.

To read Usenet News, you'll have to configure Netscape with the name of your Internet service provider's NNTP server, which is often commonly referred to as a news server. NNTP servers almost always require some kind of authentication—a procedure which ensures that only registered users can access News. The most common form of authentication is for news servers to verify that you're within the server's domain. For example, to access the news server at foo.edu, your IP number must be within the domain of foo.edu. However, other service providers may require an additional login procedure with another user name and password. In this case, you cannot use Netscape to read news, as the software can't handle this kind of login procedure. (Luckily, this form of authentication is rare, and you probably won't encounter it. If you do, investigate the use of a dedicated newsreader.)

If You Don't Have a News Server...

Many service providers supply some kind of access to Usenet News as part of their basic package. Others require additional fees or simply don't offer the service at all. You might have to pay extra for access to a news server or have to go to a different source altogether. If you don't have any access to a news server through a service provider, you do have other options for reading Usenet News:

- You can search for publicly accessible news sites. Some locations do not require authentication in order to use their news server. However, these sites don't generally make this fact public.

- You can read Usenet newsgroups mirrored through gopher or elsewhere on the Web. You won't be able to post new articles, but at least you can read and search through articles and send private mail to the authors. The gopher sites of many large universities will often contain mirrors of several Usenet newsgroups. For example, the URL gopher://sun4.bham.ac.uk:70/11/Usenet/ will let you access the many newsgroups mirrored into gopherspace at Birmingham University in England. Although it's a bit tortuous to use a Web browser to look at

Usenet News mirrored into a gopher site, this is a good way to access the information if other tools and servers are not available.

- If you're looking for specific information on a topic, you can't beat the Deja News service at http://dejanews.com. Deja News maintains a searchable archive of all Usenet News postings for the past year; they plan to "expand backward" and eventually archive all Usenet postings since 1979. With its powerful search engine, Deja News can actually be more useful in finding specific information than reading the current Usenet News.

About Newsgroups

Newsgroups are the conference-like discussion groups that constitute Usenet News.

About Newsgroup Hierarchies

Newsgroups are organized into hierarchies, which are primarily considered to be world newsgroups, regional newsgroups, and groups which are strictly local to a specific news server, such as an Internet service provider supplying newsgroups just for its subscribers. Most world newsgroup hierarchies are described below:

- **Comp**. The comp hierarchy contains newsgroups dedicated to the discussion of news and issues relating to computer science as well as the computing industry. The latest news about product releases, as well as hot tips and hotter criticism, can almost always be found here.

- **News**. The news hierarchy is devoted to discussion and information about Usenet News itself. Useful groups in this hierarchy include news.answers, which contains current versions of every newsgroup's *FAQ list*. (FAQs, or Frequently Asked Questions, are compendiums of the most commonly asked questions and answers for a newsgroup. Generally, the answers to most beginning and intermediate questions can be found in a FAQ.) If you're new to Usenet, check out news.announce.newusers and news.newuser.questions for help with common problems and questions.

- **Sci**. The sci hierarchy contains information about all aspects of science, from research and theoretical discussion to practical applications.

- **Soc**. The soc hierarchy contains newsgroups dedicated not only to topics related to socializing, like soc.couples and soc.singles, but also to discussions of various kinds of cultures and sociological issues. For example, the soc.culture.* newsgroups contain discussions, information, and general support for persons of various cultures.

- **Rec**. The rec hierarchy is home to newsgroups primarily about recreational topics, which range from books to sports to radio-controlled airplanes.

- **Talk**. The talk hierarchy contains newsgroups devoted strictly to chat and to the discussion of a variety of topics.

- **Misc**. This catch-all hierarchy contains discussions of topics that don't fit into any of the above categories.

- **Alt**. This is the most notorious of all the Usenet hierarchies because of its unmoderated, chaotic nature. (Anyone can create an alt newsgroup, and many people do so simply because they've thought of a clever name.) The alt hierarchy is home to many fringe elements, ranging from political extremists to sexually oriented groups to historical revisionists. However, keep in mind that the alt hierarchy can also have timely and useful information. Before a newsgroup is created in the world hierarchy, there's often an alt newsgroup dedicated to discussion of the topic. So, this hierarchy is where much of the most cutting-edge technical information can be found.

- **Clari**. Short for ClariNet, the company providing the service, the clari newsgroups contain news and current events from around the world. Sites must pay to carry clari newsgroups; if your site doesn't subscribe, then you won't have access to the information.

- **K12**. The K12 hierarchy contains information, discussion, and general chat for teachers and students in primary and secondary education.

- **Bionet**. The large bionet hierarchy is dedicated to disseminating information and discussing topics related to the biological and environmental sciences.

- **Bit**. Bit newsgroups are a carryover from the days of BITNET, a networking technology once in competition with the Internet. Members of BITNET engaged in discussions through a special mailing list program called LISTSERV; though BITNET is gone, LISTSERV mailing lists are still in wide use today. The mailing lists are often copied into Usenet newsgroups so that people can read information without having to personally subscribe and receive the huge amounts of mail that can be generated by a popular mailing list.

NOTE For more information about LISTSERV mailing lists, send an email message to listserv@uhupvm1.uh.edu that only contains the word "help" in the body of the message. You'll receive an automatic response via email containing instructions about other commands to use to get more information.

Which hierarchies and newsgroups are available depends on your Internet service provider. Most commercial service providers that offer Usenet News carry all the newsgroups within the world hierarchies, though many corporate sites restrict access to only the comp, sci, and news hierarchies. Other sites, such as regional educational networks, limit the newsgroups carried to those that are directly relevant to education.

About Newsgroup Names

The thousands of newsgroups in Usenet News are organized hierarchically. Newsgroup names begin with the name of the hierarchy, followed by other subgroup names separated by periods, until a unique name is reached. (There can be any number of subgroup names following the top-level hierarchy.) For example, newsgroups that begin with *comp.sys* are all discussions of computer systems; newsgroups that begin with *comp.sys.mac* are all discussions of various aspects of the Macintosh; *comp.sys.mac.os* groups are discussions of the Macintosh operating system itself.

To indicate that there are more newsgroups that begin with a given name or names, an asterisk (*) is used. For example, if you see a referral to the *comp.sys.mac** hierarchy, it refers to all the newsgroups whose names begin with *comp.sys.mac*.

Who Creates Newsgroups?

World newsgroups are created as a result of votes by the Usenet community after a process called a CFV (call for votes). Alternative newsgroups, on the other hand, can be created in a number of ways. For example, anyone who can read a FAQ can create an alt newsgroup that will be carried around the world.

Where are Newsgroups Distributed?

Another important concept in Usenet News is the geographic distribution of newsgroups. News sites in a region can agree to distribute certain newsgroups of local interest only among themselves; for example, there are many regional newsgroup hierarchies—ba.* for the California Bay Area, ny.* for New York, and so on—that are carried only by sites in that geographical area. And, many sites provide local newsgroups that are only for their users. For example, most universities have a hierarchy devoted to issues that are only of interest to faculty, staff, and students, while many service providers use local newsgroups to provide information only of interest to their customers. For example, Panix, an Internet service provider in New York, maintains a panix.* hierarchy of newsgroups only available to their subscribers.

NOTE

Netscape does not let you modify the geographical distribution of the articles that you write. They default to whatever distribution the news administrator has set for that newsgroup.

Another way that you can obtain access to local or special interest newsgroups is by switching to a news server that carries those local groups. For example, one hierarchy that will be useful to you is the Netscape hierarchy, which is hosted at Netscape's corporate location. It provides a forum for users to share information, advice, and problems that they encounter with the software.

NOTE

Incidentally, Netscape's news site uses its own extended protocol called snews (secure news, which we'll discuss more in the chapter about security), so you can only read, respond to, or post articles there if you're using the Netscape browser. Netscape's news site can be reached at snews://secnews.netscape.com.

Who Controls What Appears?

In most newsgroups, there is no central control over what gets posted. Anything that you submit is made publicly available almost immediately. However, some newsgroups are *moderated*—what you write is sent by electronic mail to the person in charge of moderating the group, who must read and approve the article before making it publicly available for others to read. Although moderated newsgroups don't have the same free-for-all attitude as unmoderated ones, the quality of the information is generally much higher in the moderated groups.

About Articles

The information that appears within newsgroups is called postings or articles. You can either write a new article or post a follow-up to an article that someone else has written. When follow-ups are posted in response to an article, the original article and the related follow-ups are called *threads*. You can follow the threads of a conversation from its inception down through the various paths that a discussion may take.

The newsreader in Netscape is a threaded newsreader, which means it presents newsgroup articles to you organized by topic, instead of by the date of the article. Responses to an article are displayed indented beneath the original article. This is advantageous, as it makes it possible for you to see all the titles of related articles. Unlike Netscape, older newsreaders display articles chronologically, making it difficult to determine which articles are responses to previous items.

Parts of an Article

Newsgroup articles are divided into two parts—the header and the body. The *header* contains all the descriptive information about the article, including the subject, the author, the author's organization, the geographical distribution, the title, what previous articles (if any) it's in reference to, and the newsgroups to which it will be distributed. (Placing the same article in more than one newsgroup is called *cross-posting*. Before you cross-post an article, be absolutely certain that the topic is relevant for all the newsgroups.)

The *body* of the article contains the actual text of the message, including any appended binaries.

Article Expiration Dates

Because tens of thousands of messages are posted to newsgroups every day, it's necessary for system administrators to clear out older messages to create enough disk space for new ones. The news administrator at your site sets article expiration dates for each newsgroup; if articles are set to expire every two weeks, then you won't be able to read any articles that were posted more than two weeks ago. However, since a thread of discussion generated by an expired article may still be going on, it's not unusual to find a thread that refers to an article that you can no longer view.

Configuring the Netscape Newsreader

Now that you've got a handle on some of the basic Usenet terms and concepts, it's time to put the information to use in context. But first you need to configure Netscape to access your NNTP server or servers.

Before You Start

Although they appear different on your screen and are used for different purposes, electronic mail and Usenet News are very close relatives. They share some common standards—RFCs—that define encoding rules and header formats. Also, the news system implicitly makes use of email in many ways. For example, if you post to a moderated newsgroup, the news server forwards the posting to the moderator via email; and, in News, you can send mail directly to someone who posted an article. Many of the features that you specify as Mail options, including your organization, email address, signature file, and send and post options, are very important to Netscape for handling how you post and respond to items in news. Be sure that you've read the preceding chapter before sending mail or posting news from the newsreader.

The Newsrc File

Newsreaders maintain information on your local system about the groups you've subscribed to and the articles you've read. This information is stored in the Newsrc file. By default, Newsrc files in Windows are stored in a news directory in the same directory as the Netscape application; on the Macintosh, they're stored in System Folder/Preferences/Netscape; and on UNIX they're stored as **.newsrc** in your home directory.

Configuring the Newsreader

To get ready to configure Netscape to read Usenet News, follow this step:

- From the Options menu, select **Mail and News Preferences**.... All configuration will be performed in this Preferences window.

Choosing Server Options

To choose the NNTP server that will be used, the location of the .newsrc file, and the number of articles that will be displayed at a time, follow these steps:

1. Click the **Servers** tab. The Servers options screen will be displayed.

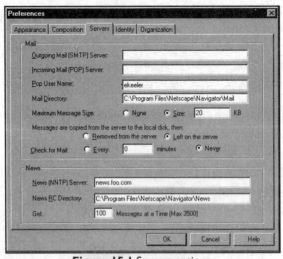

Figure 15.1 Servers options.

2. In the **News (NNTP) Server** field, type the name of the NNTP server supplied by your service provider.

WARNING

By default, Netscape displays the word **news** in the News (NNTP) Server field. This is because the Domain Name Servers at some locations will attempt to resolve a host name by appending one or more top-level domains to see if it produces a valid machine identifier. For instance, if your news server is **news.myprovider.com** and *if* the Domain Name Server is willing to resolve addresses without domain names, then leaving **news** in the field will allow you to access Usenet News on that server. However, this won't always work—it depends on how your TCP/IP software is configured. Worse, if it does work, Netscape ends up thinking that the server **news** and the server **news.myprovider.com** are different machines with different news servers, and will act as if you've subscribed to more than one server. The smart choice is to remove the default and replace it with the fully qualified name of your news server.

3. On Windows and UNIX, you can change the directory in which your Newsrc is stored. However, this is only useful if you're using UNIX and you already have a **.newsrc** file from the use of another news-reader. If so, make sure that the **News RC Directory** field contains the name of the directory where your **.newsrc** is stored to ensure that you don't lose continuity between newsreaders.

4. The **Get ___ Messages at a Time** field controls the number of articles that are displayed on each article selection in the newsreader. A setting somewhere between 100 and 500 should be adequate, as it will retrieve enough articles to provide information, but not so many that you wait a long time to download each set of titles. We recommend that you not change this number from the default until you've read News a few times and are accustomed with how it works. (To retrieve additional articles during a session, select **Get More Messages** from the File menu.)

5. Continue with the configuration as described in the next sections, or click **OK** to save your changes and exit the Preferences window.

Choosing Composition Options

You may set Netscape to save copies of News messages that you create in a local directory, or to email them to an address that you specify. To set these options, follow these steps:

1. At the Mail and News Preferences window, click the **Composition** tab. The Composition options screen (Figure 15.2) will be displayed.

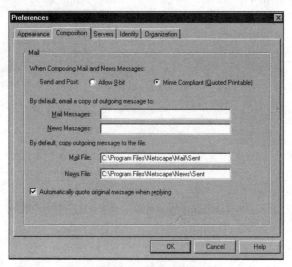

Figure 15.2 Composition options.

2. To make an email copy of your News messages, type the email address of the recipient in the **News Messages**: field (typically this will be your own email address). This option is useful if you post messages from a computer other than your primary machine and want to keep copies of what you've written.

3. To keep a local copy of your News messages, type the pathname of the directory where you wish to store them in the **News File** field. (There is no default directory on Windows.)

   On the Macintosh, select **News File** to enable the feature. If you want to store articles in a location other than the default, click the **Browse** button to locate and select a new directory.

Choosing Organization Options

As with electronic mail, you can choose the way that messages are displayed by default in the newsreader. Messages can be displayed threaded, and they can be sorted by date, subject, or sender. (You can resort messages on the fly in the newsreader window.)

We recommend that you do thread News messages, since it makes it easier to follow a discussion when all the contributions can be easily located.

VIRTUOSO

To set these options, follow these steps:

1. At the Mail and News Preferences window, click **Organization**. The Organization options screen (Figure 15.3) will be displayed.

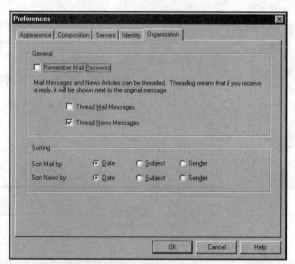

Figure 15.3 Organization options.

2. To set messages to appear threaded, select **Thread News Messages**. (This is the default setting.)

3. To sort messages by date, subject, or sender, select the desired setting at the bottom of the window.

Getting to Usenet News

There are several ways that you can view Usenet newsgroups in Netscape:

- Click a link containing a URL that points to a Usenet newsgroup. This will always display the list of articles in that newsgroup obtained from the default News server configured in Preferences.
- From the Window menu, select **Netscape News**.
- Type **news:** in the location box.

About the Netscape News Window

As soon as you perform any of the actions that will display newsgroups, the Netscape News window (Figure 15.4) will be displayed.

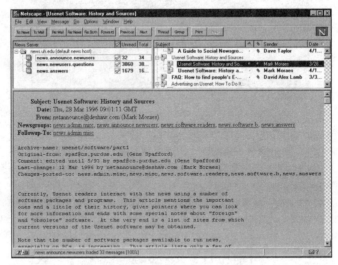

Figure 15.4 Netscape News window.

The following is a brief description of the items in the window:

- **News menus**. Except for the Window and Help menus, these menus contain different items from the similarly named windows in the Netscape browser.

- **Toolbar**. The toolbar contains useful items for displaying and creating articles.

- **News servers and newsgroups** are displayed in the pane on the left. Servers appear as computer icons; newsgroup hierarchies appear as folder icons; and newsgroups appear as document icons. To connect to a server, double-click its name. To display the contents of a newsgroup hierarchy folder, double-click the name of the folder. To display the articles in a newsgroup, click the name of the group. The headers in this pane can be resized or dragged to new positions.

- **Articles** are displayed in the pane on the right. To display an article, click its title. The headers in this pane can be resized or dragged to new positions.

- **Pane headings**. In the newsgroup pane, headings show the names of the current newsgroups, whether or not you're subscribed to the group, the total number of messages in the group, and the number of messages that you haven't read; in the article pane, headers show the name of the author, whether the article has been flagged, whether you've read the article, the subject of the article, and the date the article was created.

- **Article display area**. When you select an article to display, it's shown in this section.

Customizing the Appearance of the Window

You can use the following procedures to modify the appearance of the News window:

- To resize any item in a pane or any pane itself, hold down the mouse over its boundary and drag to the desired size. Adjacent items will be resized accordingly. You may resize the headings within the panes, and the side and bottom boundaries of the panes themselves.

NOTE

When you resize items, the mouse pointer should change to indicate that you can drag the item. Figure 15.5 shows the shape of the mouse pointer when it's in the correct location to resize an item.

Figure 15.5 The pointer indicates that you can resize the header.

- To move headings within the panes, hold down the mouse over the heading and drag the item to its new location.

- The toolbar uses the same display settings (**Pictures**, **Text**, or **Pictures and Text**) that you set in the Appearances section of General Preferences. You can change the appearance by modifying the Preferences accordingly.

VIRTUOSO

In general, we recommend displaying the toolbar as text, which takes up less vertical space on the screen than displaying pictures (either with or without text) and ensures that you can immediately identify the buttons' meanings.

- By default, the News screen displays servers and newsgroups on the left; articles on the right; and the text of articles at the bottom of the screen. You may choose to show both the server/newsgroup pane and the article titles at the left of the screen with the text of the articles appearing on the right (Figure 15.6), or you may display the folders on top, the messages in the middle, and the text of the messages at the bottom of the screen (Figure 15.7). To choose the appearance of the panes, click the **Appearance** tab in Mail and News Preferences. In the Pane Layout section (on Macintosh, the News Pane Configuration section), select **Split Horizontal** (the default), **Split Vertical**, or **Stacked**. (On the Macintosh, the first two items are **Split Horizontally** and **Split Vertically**.)

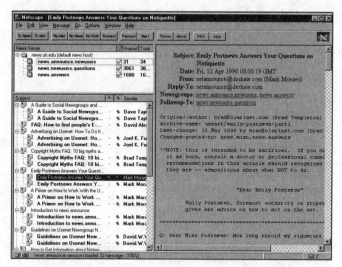

Figure 15.6 News window with panes split vertically.

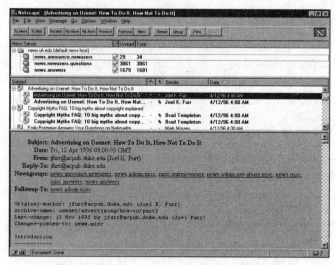

Figure 15.7 News window with stacked panes.

Displaying and Subscribing to Newsgroups

Once the News window opens, all the servers that you're subscribed to will be displayed. To display the newsgroups that you're subscribed to on a server, double-click the icon for the server. Netscape 2.0 automatically subscribes you to news.announce.newusers, news.newusers.questions, and news.answers by default.

Selecting from a Full List of Newsgroups

If you're new to Usenet News, you might want to look at all the available newsgroups to decide which ones you want to subscribe to. To view all the available newsgroups, follow these steps:

1. Make sure that you've selected a server in the list.

2. From the Options menu, select **Show All Newsgroups**. A message saying that it may take a few minutes to retrieve the list from the server will be displayed.

3. Click **OK**. After a few moments, a complete list of hierarchies available on the server you selected will be displayed.

4. Navigate through the hierarchies until you locate a newsgroup you wish to subscribe to. To navigate, double-click a folder to display its contents. (On the Macintosh, click the arrow to the left of the folder.) You can tell that you've finally reached a newsgroup when the icon changes to a document instead of a folder, and a box is displayed in the check mark column.

NOTE Because there are often several levels of hierarchy in a newsgroup name, you may have to continue to click links to find an actual newsgroup that you're interested in. This process of exploring the hierarchy can be tedious in Netscape; this is an area for which you might want to investigate dedicated newsreaders.

5. When a newsgroup you wish to subscribe to is displayed, click the mouse in the box in the check mark column. The next time you connect to the server, this newsgroup will be displayed without requiring you to navigate to it.

To unsubscribe from a newsgroup, click the box in the check mark column so that it's blank again.

Going Directly to a Specific Newsgroup

If you know the name of the newsgroup you wish to read, you can access it directly. To do so, follow these steps:

1. From the File menu, select **Add Newsgroup**....

2. At the prompt, type the name of the newsgroup.

3. Click **OK**. The newsgroup will be displayed in the window. If the server responds that there is no such group, verify that you typed the name correctly. If it fails again, try to find the newsgroup by displaying all the newsgroups and searching for it; for whatever reason, your site may not carry that specific group.

General Newsgroup Display Options

You may use the following items in the Options menu at the News window to control the display of newsgroups.

- To show only the newsgroups you've subscribed to, select **Show Subscribed Newsgroups**.

- To show only the newsgroups you've subscribed to that have received new articles since the last time you read it, select **Show Active Newsgroups**.

- To show all the newsgroups available on the current server, select **Show All Newsgroups**.

- To show only the newsgroups that have been created since the last time you showed all the newsgroups, select **Show New Newsgroups**.

Displaying and Reading Articles

To display articles in a newsgroup, click the name of the newsgroup. Unread articles will be displayed in the next pane. Articles whose names are in bold type have not been read; articles whose names are in plain type were read during this session.

To read an article, click its title. The text of the article will be displayed in the bottom window.

About Article Threading

By default, the list of articles will display not only the titles of threads but also the titles of the articles in the threads themselves. The article titles will appear indented, denoting which articles were in response to which other articles. This means that for an active thread, your screen might contain nothing but indented articles with the same topic line. To hide the individual articles in a specific thread so that you can more easily scroll through the list of articles, click the - to the left of the article so that a + is displayed (the + indicates that there are more articles in the thread); to display the articles again, click the + so that a - is displayed. To hide the articles in a thread on the Macintosh, click the triangle to the left of the folder so that it points at the folder; to display the articles in the thread again, click the triangle again so that it points down.

Understanding the Parts of an Article

Here's a picture of a typical Usenet article:

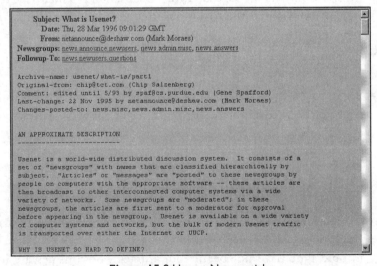

Figure 15.8 Usenet News article.

Articles consist of two parts: the header (which is described below) and the body of the article. The body of the message usually contains text, though it may also contain graphics, video, links to other Web pages, or binary files. (We'll discuss this later in the chapter.)

About Article Headers

Article headers contain a great deal of information: such as who wrote the message; when the message was written; the subject of the article; the type of program used to send the message; and some information about the path that the message took in arriving. You can choose to display normal headers, containing basic information about the article; all headers attached to the article; or brief headers, containing minimal information about the article.

To change the way that headers are displayed, select **All**, **Normal**, or **Brief** from the **Show Headers** item in the Options menu.

VIRTUOSO

We recommend showing **Normal** headers which displays information that's useful to you in identifying the author of the article and any other articles that are referenced. If the article you're viewing is a follow-up to previous articles, you can display any of the available previous articles by clicking a number in the References line in the article's header. If the article is cross-posted to other newsgroups, you can go directly to the other newsgroups by clicking the names of the other newsgroups in the header.

Marking Articles, Threads, and Newsgroups

Marking Articles

Marking Articles as Read or Unread

Newsreaders allow you to mark articles as "read" or "unread." By default, articles you haven't viewed will be considered "unread" and articles you have viewed will be considered "read." If you wish to mark an article that you've read as unread, or vice versa, follow these steps:

1. Select the article.

2. From the Message menu, select **Mark as Read** or **Mark as Unread**.

To display unread articles, choose **First Unread**, **Next Unread**, or **Previous Unread** from the Go menu, or click the **Next** or **Previous** button on the toolbar.

Flagging Articles

If you come across an article of interest to you, you may "flag" it so you can easily return to it at a later time. To flag an article, follow these steps:

1. Select the article.

2. From the Message menu, select **Flag Message**. (To unflag an article, select **Unflag Message**.)

SHORTCUT

Or, click the mouse in the Flag column of the articles pane to flag or unflag the article.

To display flagged articles, choose **First Flagged**, **Next Flagged**, or **Previous Flagged** from the Go menu.

Marking Threads

If you have read as much of an article thread as you care to, and don't want to see any more articles on that topic during this session, you can mark an entire thread as being read. To do so, follow these steps:

1. Select an article in the thread you wish to mark.

2. From the Message menu, select **Mark Thread Read**.

SHORTCUT

Or, click the **Thread** button on the toolbar.

Marking Newsgroups

If you don't want to read any more of the articles in a newsgroup, you can mark all the articles as read so that they won't be displayed the next time you visit the group. To mark an entire newsgroup as read, follow these steps:

1. Make sure that the contents of the newsgroup are displayed.
2. From the Message menu, select **Mark Newsgroup Read**.

SHORTCUT

Or, click the **Group** button on the toolbar.

General Sorting Options for Articles

The following is a description of the many ways you can sort and modify the display of articles in the selected newsgroup:

- To thread messages so that all articles appear grouped by topic, select **Thread Messages** from the **Sort** item in the View menu. (This item is selected by default.) If articles are threaded, then other sorting options will be applied within the threads.

- To view the most recent articles at the top of the list, select **Ascending** from the **Sort** item in the View menu.

- To sort articles by date, subject, or sender, select the desired setting from the **Sort** item in the View menu.

SHORTCUT

Or, click the pane heading for that item. A triangle in the pane heading shows that articles are sorted by that item.

- To show articles that are marked as read because you read them in a previous session, select **Show All Messages** from the Options menu.

To only show articles that you haven't read, select **Show Only Unread Messages** from the Options menu.

- To make sure that articles are added in the order you wish, select **Add from Newest Messages** in the Options menu to show the newest articles at the top of the list or **Add from Oldest Messages** to show the oldest articles at the top of the list. (This setting only applies to the way that articles are displayed as soon as you retrieve them; sorting the articles by date will change the order of their display on the fly.)

Decoding Articles in Rot-13

On Usenet, there's a convention for posting text articles which contain information that may be considered inflammatory (this convention is usually only followed in the world newsgroups). Newsreaders have a built-in simple encoding and decoding mechanism called *rot-13*, which is a simple letter-substitution mechanism used by the author or the moderator to obscure an article containing material that might be considered offensive. (Each letter is replaced with the letter 13 letters away in the alphabet. For example, in rot-13, each "a" appears as an "n.")

If you wish to read an article that's been encoded in rot-13, display the article and select **Unscramble (ROT-13)** from the View menu.

Viewing Attachments

Netscape supports the ability to display certain kinds of attachments to news articles directly in the News window. This ability is similar to the way that attachments are handled in Netscape's mail program; a complete discussion of the topic appears in Chapter 14.

Netscape lets you display attachments in one of two ways: as inline parts of the document, or as links. If you choose to display attachments inline, attachments such as graphics or HTML files that can be displayed as part of the message will be displayed as part of the message. (HTML files will be interpreted and displayed as if you were viewing them with the browser, instead of as HTML.)

If attachments are displayed as links, a link to the attachment file on your system will be displayed at the bottom of the message. If the attachment is an HTML file, clicking the link will display the formatted contents of the file in the message display area.

To change the display of attachments, select either **Attachments Inline** or **Attachments as Links** from the View menu.

WARNING Netscape will only correctly handle the kinds of MIME-encoded attachments that it is capable of displaying directly; basically, you can only be assured that it will handle small graphics, sound, or HTML files. A complete discussion of the limitations of the Netscape newsreader appears at the end of this chapter.

Visiting URLs Mentioned in Articles

Sometimes people will include URLs in their articles, either as part of their original article or as items in their signature file. (More information about your signature file appears in Chapter 14, "Electronic Mail and Netscape.") The Netscape newsreader is smart enough to recognize URLs that appear in articles and to display them as active, clickable links.

To visit a URL that appears in a Usenet article, just click the link. To return to the article, select it from the history list in the Go menu.

Saving Articles

To save articles to a local file on your disk drive, follow these steps:

1. Select the desired article or articles.

VIRTUOSO To select several articles at once, use the **Select Thread**, **Select Flagged Messages**, or **Select All Messages** options in the Edit menu.

2. From the File menu, select **Save Message(s) As...**.

3. Follow the prompts for your operating system to save the item as a local file.

Creating and Responding to Articles

Posting a New Article

To post a new article to a newsgroup, follow these steps:

 Articles are created in the Message Composition window, just like electronic mail. For a complete discussion of items in the Message Composition window, see Chapter 14.

NOTE

1. Make sure that the newsgroup you wish to post to is selected.

2. Click the **To:News** button on the toolbar. A Message Composition window will be displayed, with the name of the current newsgroup in the Newsgroups fields.

3. If you wish to specify additional information for the article, such as a newsgroup where follow-up articles should be posted, follow these steps:

   a. From the View menu, select the desired fields to display.

   b. Enter the information as desired.

4. If you wish to post the article to additional newsgroups, type a comma after the existing newsgroup and type the name of the additional newsgroup.

5. In the **Subject** field, type the subject of the article. Be as specific as possible.

6. If you wish to attach a document, click **Attach**, then locate and select the document you wish to attach.

7. In the large blank field, type the text of your message.

8. When you're ready to send the message, click **Send**.

Replying to an Existing Article

You may reply to an existing article by posting an article, by posting an article and sending it by mail to the author of the original article, or by simply sending mail to the author of the original article. To reply to an article, follow these steps:

1. Make sure the article you wish to reply to is displayed in the window.
2. At the toolbar, click the appropriate button:
   - To mail your response privately to the original author, click **Re:Mail** or click the author's name in the header of the article.
   - To post your reply to the newsgroup, click **Re:News**.
   - To post your reply to the newsgroup and mail it to the original article's author, click **Re:Both**.

   A Message Composition window will be displayed. If your reply will be posted, the newsgroup information will be displayed; if your reply will be mailed, the name and address of the original author will be displayed.
3. If you wish to specify additional information for the article, such as a newsgroup where follow-up articles should be posted, follow these steps:

   a. From the View menu, select the desired fields to display.

   b. Enter the information as desired.
4. If you wish to post the article to additional newsgroups, type a comma after the existing newsgroup and type the name of the additional newsgroup.
5. In the **Subject** field, type the subject of the article. Be as specific as possible.
6. If you wish to attach a document, click **Attach**, then locate and select the document you wish to attach.
7. In the text entry field, type the text of your message.

WARNING Save network bandwidth! Keep your citations of other articles to a minimum—delete any information in the original article that isn't relevant to your response. Otherwise, that useless information will be reposted to thousands of machines throughout the world.

8. When you're ready to send the message, click **Send**.

Canceling an Article

If you've posted an article to a Usenet newsgroup and regret your action, you may cancel the article. To cancel an article, follow these steps:

1. At the News window, select the title of the article that you wish to cancel.
2. From the Edit menu, select **Cancel Message**. A dialog box confirming your action will be displayed.
3. Click **Yes** to cancel the article.

NOTE

You may only cancel the articles that you posted.

WARNING

If you posted the article to more than one newsgroup, you must cancel the article in each individual newsgroup where it was posted. Also, remember that someone may have read and even saved your article during the time that it was available online; in general, you should always consider your words carefully before posting.

Ensuring Up-to-Date Information

Because Netscape retrieves information from the news server and stores it or displays it on your computer, you need to take certain steps to ensure that your list of newsgroups and lists of articles are current.

Making Sure Newsgroups are Up-to-Date

The first time that you access News, Netscape retrieves the full newsgroup list from the server. However, new newsgroups are frequently created. To ensure that your list of newsgroups is up-to-date, select **Show New Newsgroups** from the Options menu.

You should check for new newsgroups at least once a week. The more frequently you check, the less time it'll take to download the new newsgroups from the server, since the number of newsgroups will be smaller.

NOTE

Making Sure that Article Titles are Up-to-Date

If you think new articles have been posted while you've been reading a newsgroup, or you want to display more articles than the default number that you set in Mail and News Preferences, select **Get More Messages** from the File menu. (If you've posted an article, this is the way to view it without exiting News and coming back in.)

Working with Multiple Servers

As we discussed in Chapter 2, a news URL should be in the form news:[newsgroup]. When you click a URL that's written in this form, Netscape will look up the specified newsgroup on the news server that you entered in your Preferences.

However, an extension to the URL format has emerged, news://[news_server]/[newsgroup_name], which lets you access newsgroups at servers other than your default. While URLs that are written news:[newsgroup] will access the newsgroup on your server, URLs in this extended form will actually contact the named news site and display their articles.

One of the most common examples of this is Netscape's own news site, accessible from their home page, which allows you to read newsgroups that are only located on their news server at snews://secnews.netscape.com.

NOTE

When you've viewed newsgroups on a site other than your configured default server, Netscape keeps a record of the site. A separate Newsrc file is created for every server that you access. Each news host that you've visited will be displayed when you open the Netscape News reader.

However, the server that you entered in the Mail and News Preferences section will be listed as your default news server.

NOTE If you see an icon for a server that simply says *news* in the list, then at some point you accessed News without putting the fully qualified name of the news server in your configuration area. (For more information, see "Configuring the Newsreader" earlier in this chapter.) If you configure Netscape correctly before attempting to use it, this will never occur. But if you didn't, don't despair—just click the news item in the list and select **Remove News Host** from the File menu.

Adding New Servers to the List

To manually add a news server to your list, follow these steps:

1. From the File menu, select **Open News Host...**.
2. Enter the name of the news server.
3. Click **OK**.

Removing Extraneous Servers

You may find that there are servers in your list which you don't access anymore. To remove these extra servers (and their associated .newsrc files, which may be very large), follow these steps:

1. Select the icon for the server.
2. From the File menu, select **Remove News Host**.

Limitations of the Netscape Newsreader

For basic purposes, Netscape provides an integrated, convenient way to browse and post messages to Usenet News. However, there are some important features of Usenet News for which Netscape simply cannot be used. To take advantage of these features, you need to use a dedicated newsreader program like Newswatcher (for the Macintosh) or Trumpet News and News XPress (for Windows).

Posting and Extracting Binary Files

Another important feature missing in the Netscape newsreader is the ability to handle the extraction of binary files that are split across articles. Netscape does let you view pictures that are appended to Usenet articles, as long as they don't span more than a single article. But there's no way to handle large postings or binary files, which tend to be split across several different articles because of their size. (When a large binary file is attached to a news article, it's automatically posted as multiple consecutive messages. It's usually obvious from the title of an article, which will be numbered "1/7," "2/7," etc.)

There is a long-standing tradition of posting encoded binary files on Usenet, which makes them accessible to anyone who can read Usenet News, regardless of whether they're directly connected to the Internet. Several newsgroups are still dedicated to the distribution of such binary files, which include software, databases, spreadsheets, formatted documents, sound clips, and pictures.

NOTE

You're almost certainly looking at an article which contains a binary file if it displays nothing but cryptic numbers and text, like Figure 15.9.

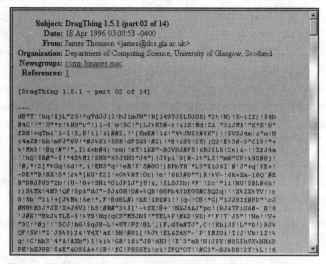

Figure 15.9 A binary file on Usenet News, displayed in Netscape.

Even though Netscape lets you work with other kinds of binaries on regular Web sites, Netscape does not provide tools to extract and save the binary files in Usenet News to your disk in any simple way, though dedicated newsreaders do.

VIRTUOSO

If you wish to download any of the binaries that are posted in Usenet, the best solution is to use a dedicated newsreader, which not only has commands for extracting all the parts of a binary file (even when split across articles), but which will usually launch an appropriate decoder.

Tips for Better Usenet Living

Usenet has been around for years and has developed its own unique culture, including some very specific social rules and norms. Depending on the newsgroups you choose to read, Usenet culture isn't always kind to newbies (beginners); if you accidentally violate a Usenet taboo, you may find yourself on the receiving end of a vitriolic public or private verbal attack called a *flame*. To decrease the chances of getting flamed, and to fit in with Usenet culture more quickly, please consider the following basic rules of *netiquette*:

- Read the introductory documents available in news.announce.newusers and news.newusers.questions before you consider posting an article. Good ones to start with include "A Primer on How to Work With the Usenet Community," "Answers to Frequently Asked Questions about Usenet," "How to Find the Right Place to Post," and "Hints on Writing Style for Usenet." It's definitely worth the time to take a look at these materials, which were designed to make it easier for new users to understand what's going on.

- If you're going to ask a question, always check the FAQ for a newsgroup first. These contain the answers to the most commonly asked questions in the newsgroup, and might include yours. FAQs can be found both in the newsgroup and in news.answers.

- Read a newsgroup for a few days before you join a discussion to get an idea of the tone of conversation. For example, most newsgroups will ignore you or flame you out of existence if you include ASCII smileys at the end of a line, while others may think you aloof if you don't include little <hug> statements.

- Where possible, try not to waste network resources by posting unnecessary messages. If you see an article that would be appropriate to respond to privately, please simply send email to the author. (Newsreaders support this function.) This way, an "I feel the same way!" or "If you find that information, please forward it to me" message only goes to the appropriate person and isn't carried around the world.

- Keep in mind that there's no way to guess who reads Usenet. Many more people *lurk* in newsgroups—read without posting anything— than you can possibly imagine. Hence, it's probably unwise to discuss your employer or your mother-in-law in a public newsgroup.

- No matter what your personal or political bent, you will undoubtedly encounter viewpoints different from your own, especially in the alt, talk, soc, and rec hierarchies. Although you'll notice that other people don't follow this particular rule, you might consider not being bombastic in expressions of your belief.

- If you come across a topic that distresses you at a deeply personal level, just don't read that newsgroup anymore. (Usenet News is so large that it's guaranteed to contain something to offend everyone, no matter how open-minded you think you are.) Freedom of expression and the right to free speech are dearly held principles, and they apply to the people who disagree with you as well as to you.

What You Learned

After reading this chapter, you should be able to:

- Understand the basic concepts and terminology used in Usenet.
- Configure Netscape to access your NNTP server.
- Subscribe to, read, and post articles to Usenet newsgroups.
- Evaluate whether a dedicated newsreader is more appropriate for your needs.
- Understand the basics of Usenet culture.

CHAPTER 16

USING OTHER INTERNET SERVICES WITH NETSCAPE

In this chapter, we'll discuss FTP and gopher, two of the most popular Internet services which are fully available to you through your Netscape browser. We'll also talk about the terminal emulators TN3270 and telnet, and we'll briefly explore WAIS.

About FTP and Netscape

FTP, or file transfer protocol, is a protocol that allows you to place or retrieve files from a remote system. Dedicated FTP sites are still extremely popular despite the growing predominance of the World Wide Web because of their reputation as being the major point of distribution for software, utilities, documentation, and other kinds of materials. Some of the most notable sites are listed below:

- To obtain Windows software, check out a publicly accessible mirror of the venerated SimTel software repository at ftp://oak.oakland.edu

- To find Macintosh software, try the Info-Mac archive, mirrored and easily accessed at ftp://mirror.apple.com/mirrors/Info-Mac.Archive/

- NCSA has a remarkable FTP site for all things related to the World Wide Web, especially Web server software for the UNIX platform. Use the URL ftp://ftp.ncsa.uiuc.edu/

Using FTP to Retrieve Files

There are two ways that FTP can be used to retrieve files—*anonymous FTP*, in which you log onto a remote site as an anonymous user to retrieve publicly accessible files, and *authenticated FTP*, where you must be a registered account holder on the machine containing the files in order to log in. Further information about each of these methods appears later in this section.

No matter which way you use FTP, the appearance of items on your screen will be the same. A sample screen from an FTP session is displayed in Figure 16.1.

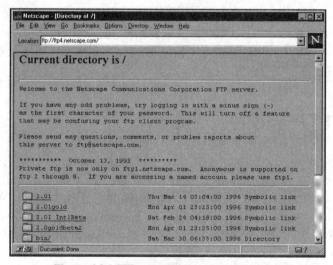

Figure 16.1 FTP session displayed in Netscape.

Each screen that you display will be an index of the items in the current directory of the server that you're logged into. Each item in the directory is accompanied by an icon that denotes what kind of object it is. Table

16.1 contains a list of FTP objects, their associated icons and file extensions, and Netscape's response to selecting the item.

Table 16.1 Icons and Actions for Common FTP Objects

Kind of Object	File Extension	Icon	Netscape's Action
Text	.html, .htm, .txt, etc.		Display in viewer
Image	.jpg, .jpeg, .gif, .tiff, .tif, etc.		Display in viewer
Directory	(none)		Display contents of new directory
Binary executable	.bin, .exe		Download and decode with appropriate helper application

NOTE Netscape looks up the type of object in your MIME types table according to the file extension, as described in Chapter 8. If you didn't configure Netscape for a certain file extension, the blank document icon will be used.

If the FTP protocol can't recognize what type of object is being displayed, then a blank document icon will be used.

NOTE Because there's no MIME encoding for FTP (the protocol was developed long before MIME), your Web browser must rely on file extensions as a clue to determine the content type of the information being displayed. This is why entries in the MIME type configuration screen contain both the MIME type and the associated file extensions.

VIRTUOSO By default, items that you download will be stored in the temporary directory you identify in the Temporary Directory field of the **Apps** panel in General Preferences. (on the Macintosh, it's the Downloads Directory in the **Applications** panel in General Preferences.) If you want individual control over where files are stored when downloaded, drag the file's link from the Web page to the folder on your disk drive where you want to store the item. (More information about using Drag-and-Drop features can be found in Chapter 7, "Advanced Tips, Tricks, and Shortcuts.")

About Anonymous FTP

Anonymous FTP is an extremely useful resource for obtaining new software or updates to existing software. Anonymous FTP sites exist for almost any kind of application and platform that you can think of. In fact, updates and new releases of the Netscape software can be obtained via anonymous FTP from Netscape Communications' FTP servers.

You'll probably come across the term *mirror site* in your search for software retrievable via anonymous FTP. The contents of sites which are extremely popular—for example, Netscape's FTP site—are often replicated at other locations to relieve congestion at the original site. (You may recall from our discussion in Chapter 2 that FTP is not a stateless protocol, so there are very real limits to how many people can log into a site at once.) Mirror sites are structured exactly like the original sites; they're simply located at a different address. Most popular FTP sites will list their mirror sites in the message they send when they reject your request to connect to the site.

To log onto an anonymous FTP site using Netscape, enter the site's URL in the following format:

```
ftp://[machine_name]/[directory_path]
```

The directory path is optional, but the machine name is required.

VIRTUOSO

If the first part of the machine name is ftp (for example, ftp.netscape.com), you can just type the machine name without the type identifier ftp:// in front of it. Netscape is smart about determining what kind of protocol should be used to connect to a site; if the machine name begins with ftp, it assumes that the FTP protocol should be used.

If you didn't enter a directory path, you'll be logged onto the top-level directory of the FTP site, where you can navigate through directories to find the files you want. If you entered a directory path, you'll be logged into the directory that you specified in the URL.

About Authenticated FTP

Besides using anonymous FTP to retrieve software from various locations, you can also use the FTP protocol to retrieve your own files from a shell account on a machine where you have login privileges. To protect the users' information, computers containing private directories almost never allow anonymous access. But you can use the FTP protocol to log in as a registered user and retrieve any files that you have permission to use.

To use Netscape to log into your own account using authenticated FTP, enter the URL in the following format:

```
ftp://username:password@machine_name/directory_path
```

VIRTUOSO

If you don't feel like entering your password directly into the URL, where it'll be visible to anyone passing by as well as being maintained temporarily in your history list and the drop-down location field, construct the URL in the following format:

```
ftp://username@machine_name/directory_path
```

Netscape will ask you to enter your password in a special box, and will display symbol characters instead of your password as you type it. If you plan to create a bookmark for logging into your own account with FTP, you should definitely bookmark the URL without the password included, since anyone who can access your bookmark file can retrieve that information.

After you enter the URL (and your password, if desired) you'll be logged into the machine that hosts your account. If you entered a directory path, you'll be at the top level of the specified directory; if you only specified the machine name, you'll be at the top level of the machine.

VIRTUOSO

Want to find out what the correct path to your home directory is? If you have an account on a UNIX or UNIX-like system, launch a terminal emulator session, such as with telnet, and log into your shell account. At the system prompt, enter **pwd**. The complete pathname to your home directory will be displayed.

You may navigate through directories and retrieve information in the same way as for anonymous FTP.

Continuing to Browse While Downloading Files

One of the best new features of Netscape is its ability to create a separate window for monitoring the download of files via anonymous FTP. Since files can be up to several megabytes in size, it can take several minutes (or even hours) to retrieve a complete file to your desktop. You can exploit the potential for parallel sessions provided by modern operating systems by creating multiple windows to handle different tasks at the same time.

In general, your TCP/IP connection is a shared resource that is accessible to any graphical Internet application at the same time. Unlike an old-fashioned terminal session, in which only one telecommunications application can be active at a time, you can now run as many graphical Internet applications as you have sufficient memory to launch. (Your use of multiple applications may, however, be limited by bandwidth if you're using a SLIP or PPP connection, as there's only so much information that can be simultaneously transmitted through a 14.4 or 28.8 Kbps connection.)

Netscape lets you begin a lengthy FTP transfer and continue to browse while the transfer is taking place. Beginning a download creates a dialog box that displays the URL of the item you're retrieving, the destination on your disk drive, and a Cancel button, as well as a gauge showing the progress of the transfer. You can continue to browse the Web in the Netscape window while the transfer occurs.

NOTE Performing network-intensive operations while downloading a file can greatly decrease Netscape's speed and performance in both sessions. Every time you load a new page in the browser, you're slowing down the FTP transfer. But if you're planning to be online for a while, there's no reason not to let the transfer proceed in the background, even if it ultimately takes longer to download the file.

Locating an FTP Site

There are thousands of anonymous FTP sites located around the world. How will you know where you can find the software you're looking for? In most cases, Web search engines are extremely good (we'll talk about them in Chapter 23) and you won't need to use anything else to locate and connect to an FTP site. However, in some cases, you may want to limit your searches strictly to the information on FTP sites. In this case, Archie is the tool to use.

Archie, developed in the late 1980s by researchers at McGill University, is a search mechanism that helps you locate specific files available via anonymous FTP. To use Archie, you enter the name of the software that you wish to use; Archie quickly returns with a list of titles and anonymous FTP locations where the item is stored.

NOTE Archie is not a protocol, like HTTP or FTP; instead, it's simply a database and search engine. Using Netscape, you can only access the Archie servers that have been specially modified to allow Web browsers to access them. Many Archie sites have added a Web interface to their Archie server so that you can enter and read the results of your request through a regular Web browser, as well as connect to the FTP site hosting the software.

To find an up-to-date list of Archie sites that have Web interfaces, check the Yahoo index for Archie at http://www.yahoo.com/Computers_and_Internet/Internet/Searching_the_Net/Archie/.

Figure 16.2 shows a sample Archie request form at http://www-ns.rutgers.edu/htbin/archie.

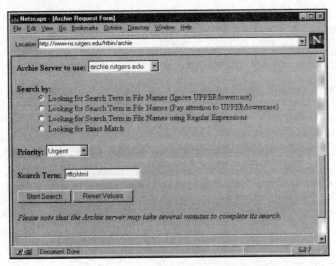

Figure 16.2 Filled-out Archie request form.

Figure 16.3 shows the results of this request.

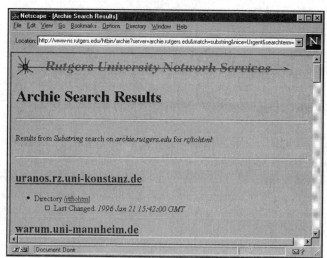

Figure 16.3 Results of an Archie search.

NOTE

Archie is only useful if you know the name of the software that you're looking for—it won't help if you only know the general category of software, like "graphics" or "HTML." To find names of software packages that are relevant to your needs, try some of the search strategies that are discussed in Chapter 23.

Using Netscape to Upload Files

A feature recently introduced to Netscape is the ability to upload files from your own desktop computer to a host machine. Among other things, this means that you can use Netscape to upload HTML files to your Web site.

To upload a file using Netscape, you must use authenticated FTP, as discussed earlier in this chapter. (If uploading files wasn't authenticated, then anyone could dump new files on other people's computers.) You must also have the privilege to add files to the directory where the files will be stored.

NOTE

When you're uploading files, you also need to worry about using appropriate file formats and naming conventions. Pay special attention to the way that file names and extensions are handled—for example, if you have a local file that's called xyz.gif on your machine, make sure that it doesn't get changed to XYZ.GIF when it's uploaded to the remote machine. This unexpected change in file names will often cause files to display improperly on the server even though they worked OK locally. A complete discussion of this can be found in Chapter 22, "Working with Public Web Pages."

To upload a file using Netscape, follow these steps:

1. Log into your account using authenticated FTP. (Remember, use a URL in the format ftp://[username]@[machine_name].)

2. From the File menu, select **Upload File**....

3. Locate and select the file you wish to upload.

4. Click **OK**.

VIRTUOSO

Or, you can use a Drag-and-Drop shortcut. After you've logged into your account, drag the icon for the file you wish to upload over the window for the browser. But be careful—in Netscape 2.0 and early releases of 3.0, you can only add files this way. If you attempt to drag an entire directory into the window, all the files will be uploaded, but the directory information will be lost—all the files in the directory will appear at the same level of your current directory on your host machine.

NOTE

Netscape Navigator Gold has more advanced file uploading capabilities than the regular browser. For more information on uploading files with Navigator Gold, see Chapter 22.

Disadvantages of Using Netscape to Upload Files

Netscape's serious limitation as an FTP client is that there's no provision for moving files from one location to another online, or for deleting files—if you want to move or copy files to another part of your directory structure, or remove them altogether, you're out of luck. If all you're doing is uploading a file or two to your personal Web site, then Netscape's uploading features may work just fine for you. But serious Webmasters who need to manage large collections of files will still need to use a dedicated FTP client like Fetch or WSFTP, and will probably even need to perform directory maintenance using a shell account.

About Gopher and Netscape

Gopher is a menu-driven hierarchical information system somewhat like anonymous FTP. As in anonymous FTP, you can change through directories to find information and download items to your own computer. However, gopher is different enough from FTP to be an important resource in its own right.

The most important difference between gopher and FTP is that gopher, like the World Wide Web, supports the inclusion of links in items. You can branch to other gopher sites anywhere in the world without having to launch another session. Gopher is also similar to the World Wide Web because it classifies documents according to type. Even though gopher can only display plain text documents, it can recognize and pass information to the browser about a variety of multimedia documents, including pictures, sounds, movies, and executable binary files.

Gophers are closely associated with campus-wide information systems and a variety of other information resources. They're widely used at universities across the world as a means of distributing information about departments, registration, contact information for faculty and staff, and a variety of computing resources that are interesting beyond the scope of the university. (For example, as we mentioned in Chapter 15, gophers often mirror Usenet newsgroups.) Gopher's unique geographical registration system makes it easy to locate any publicly registered gopher site in the world—nearly every main gopher menu contains a link for "All the Gopher Servers in the World," which lets you navigate through a hierarchical listing of the gopher servers on various continents.

Although there are dedicated graphical clients for gopher, such as TurboGopher for the Macintosh and WS Gopher for Windows, there's no reason not to use your Web browser to access gopher sites.

The URL to access the top level of a gopher site is constructed in the following way:

```
gopher://gopher_server_name
```

VIRTUOSO

If the first part of the machine name is gopher (for example, gopher.micro.umn.edu), you can just type the machine name without the type identifier gopher:// in front of it. Netscape is smart about determining what kind of protocol should be used to connect to a site; if the machine name begins with gopher, it assumes that the gopher protocol should be used.

A sample gopher screen viewed in Netscape is displayed in Figure 16.4.

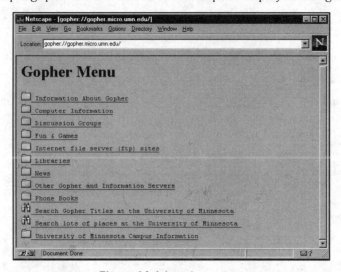

Figure 16.4 A gopher screen.

When you're looking at a gopher menu, every single item is a link to another item, whether it's a file, a folder, or a link to another gopher site. Every item in gopher has an associated address which identifies the document and its type in gopherspace. Gopher documents don't use MIME types; instead, a unique character or number is placed as part of the pathname for each document that identifies whether it's a directory, a text file, etc. When you start clicking links in a gopher site, you may notice that the URL displayed for each item contains a number as part of the directory pathname; this is the gopher type identifier.

As for FTP, Netscape has associated a series of unique icons with the most common kinds of items that you'll find in gopherspace, displayed in Table 16.2.

329

Table 16.2 Netscape Icons for Common Gopher Items

Description of gopher type	Gopher number	Icon in Netscape
Text file	0	
Directory	1	
Binhex Macintosh file	4	
DOS binary archive	5	
uuencoded file	6	
Searchable index	7	
Telnet session	8	
Binary file	9	
GIF image	g	
HTML file	h	
Image (other than GIF)	I	
MIME-encoded object	M	
Adobe Acrobat PDF file	P	
μlaw sound file	s	
TN3270 session	T	

Locating Information in Gopherspace

Because so many people use gopher to disseminate different kinds of information, there's no good way to determine what kinds of information might be stored at any given site. But there is a mechanism that lets you search through gopherspace to find information on a specific topic—Veronica.

As a keyword-oriented search engine, Veronica is to gopherspace roughly what Archie is to anonymous FTP file archives. You enter keywords describing the kind of information you're looking for, and Veronica returns a list of related gopher links.

Most gopher sites contain links to a variety of Veronica searches. Or, to locate a Veronica server near you, check out Yahoo's list of Veronica servers at http://www.yahoo.com/Computers_and_Internet/Internet/ Searching_the_Net/Veronica/.

About Telnet and TN3270

As we discussed in Chapter 8, telnet and TN3270 are terminal emulator tools that are launched by Netscape when they encounter a URL for that kind of session. These tools allow you to log into a remote computer in a fashion that's roughly equivalent to using a traditional dialup account with a terminal emulation package like ProComm or ZTerm, except that you're not paying for a long-distance call. Telnet and TN3270 are necessary to access certain kinds of text-only services, such as library catalogs or community freenets, which are traditionally not offered as Web-based services.

When you're finished with the terminal session, log out of the remote computer per the instructions provided at that site and quit the telnet or TN3270 application.

Wide Area Information Server (WAIS)

Wide Area Information Server, or WAIS (pronounced "wayz"), is a sophisticated database search mechanism linked to the Internet's client-server architecture. It allows the client searching software to run anywhere and access the information on the host servers' system (WAIS clients can search more than one database at a time).

A WAIS search looks at the content of the documents in the database instead of just the titles, and it assigns a score to each item that results from your search.

NOTE WAIS searches retrieve documents that contain any combination of the words that you enter in a query, even if they don't appear together. The numerical score between one and 1000—sometimes expressed as a decimal with three digits of precision—that is attached to the found item will give you an idea of how relevant the item actually is. Items are ranked according to their score, so the items near the top of the list are most likely to contain the information that you're looking for.

WAIS is an Internet protocol in itself, and there are dedicated WAIS client applications which communicate directly with WAIS servers. However, on the Web, it's likely that you'll encounter gateways to WAIS programs that invoke searches on the remote server. In fact, most popular Web search engines use WAIS technology to perform their index searching. (For more information about search engines, see Chapter 23.)

What You Learned

After reading this chapter, you should understand the following:

- How Netscape handles FTP and gopher.
- How to upload files using FTP.
- How to locate items at anonymous FTP sites and in gopherspace.
- Basic information about Internet services available through telnet and TN3270.
- Basic information about WAIS searches.

CHAPTER 17

FORMS, IMAGE MAPS, AND CGI

Up until this point, most of the documents that we've talked about have been *static documents*—HTML, text, or image files that reside on a Web server and which you retrieve and view in your browser. No matter who you are, no matter when you log in, you're always going to see the same document unless it's been updated by the person maintaining the site. But there's a totally different class of links on the Web that execute programs on remote servers to calculate, retrieve, or construct information on the fly and send it to your browser. This process is known as *serving dynamic documents*, because the content of each document is dynamically generated at the time that you issue your request. Examples of dynamic documents include the results of Internet search queries, image maps where you click on a section of the image to go to a URL, calculations that are performed on numbers that you enter, and more. Basically, any document that is created and/or displayed because of your unique user input (as opposed to simply clicking a regular link) falls into the class of dynamic documents.

As a virtuoso user, it's important to know some basic ideas about how your input is passed to and handled by the server so that you can better understand and use some of the Web's most interesting and interactive sites.

The Common Gateway Interface (CGI)

The Common Gateway Interface, commonly known as CGI, is the standard mechanism used on Web servers to allow the execution of programs which generate dynamic documents and send them back to your browser. Here's a general description of how it works:

1. Your click generates a unique URL (which may include the contents that you entered into a form).

2. Your browser sends the URL to the HTTP server.

3. The HTTP server recognizes that the URL is not a reference to a static document, and is instead meant to invoke a particular program that resides on the server.

4. The program called for by the URL is executed.

5. The results of the program are passed to the HTTP server and returned to your browser for display.

In short, by acting as an interface between the Web server and other programs that reside on the server, CGI provides the mechanism that allows your browser to execute programs on the remote server using your own input. Unlike static documents, which never change, the results that you see depend entirely on the actions that you take.

NOTE Netscape Communications has announced the development of NSAPI (Netscape Server Application Programming Interface), a new method of executing programs from an HTTP server. NSAPI is designed to address some of CGI's limitations, and may become powerful and interesting tool for Web developers and programmers.

Common Uses of CGI

Trying to describe what can be done with CGI is a lot like trying to describe what you can do with a computer. In the early days, when all you could do with computers was crunch scientific data, uses for computers were relatively easy to explain. But now, computers support a vast range of applications and interactions, from spreadsheets and data management to interactive multimedia, desktop publishing, and (of course) telecommunications. CGI's function is to provide a mechanism within a graphical user interface to take advantage of computational power and information on a widely distributed geographic scale. What can be done with CGI is really only limited by a developer's imagination. (We'll talk about a few simple examples later in this chapter, but a full discussion of interactive Web sites appears in Chapter 24.)

NOTE An important thing to note about CGI is that it doesn't work in a local environment—it can only work when you're connected to the network. Although you can save a document containing a form or an image map, you can't submit data or use the image for navigation without establishing a connection to the original site.

Clickable Image Maps

One of the earliest uses of CGI on the Web was clickable image maps that serve as navigational tools. While regular HTML supports the use of a single image as a clickable link, image maps let the developer define different regions of a single image as links to unique URLs.

The browser interprets the X and Y coordinates of your mouse click and sends them to the server; the CGI program determines where on the image you clicked and retrieves the appropriate file. (Because the server stores information about what file to send, these kinds of image maps are called *server-side image maps*; we'll talk about *client-side image maps* a little later in this section.) A single graphic can contain as many links as the developer wishes to define. The *hot regions* of an image map are usually implied by elements in the graphic, such as boxes, borders, icons, and 3-D effects, which give you a hint of the locations of the active areas.

For example, the map of the "Multimedia Gulch" area of San Francisco shown in Figure 17.1 is a clickable image map used to select a certain location that you want to know more information about.

Notice that the X and Y coordinates of the mouse location are displayed in the staus message area. Clicking the map at a location such as South Park will take you to more information about that area.

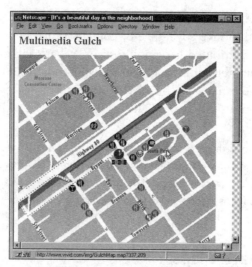

Figure 17.1 A clickable image map.

Image maps have become increasingly common as navigational tools. Besides being more attractive and engaging than text-based navigational systems, they can be used to create an immersive, exploratory environment. For example, at MCI's Gramercy Press site (http://www.mci.com/gramercy) you can navigate through the hallways and explore the contents of people's offices by clicking their computers, answering machines, and items on their desktop. This kind of navigation through a visual space has become a mainstay of computer games such as Myst and Seventh Guest; with the development of image maps, it's becoming an increasingly popular interface for accessing items on the Web.

If you're using a dialup IP connection to access the Web, you might find image maps to be more frustrating than fascinating as they can take a long time to load. Many sites that make extensive use of image maps also provide a text-only navigational system to access the information at the site; the best-designed sites will let you choose such an option instead of simply using the graphics-laden section with Auto Load Images turned off. However, you probably won't be able to enjoy the sites whose appeal is mainly based on the graphical interface without using the image maps.

N O T E   If you've disabled Auto Load Images and you see a graphic with a blue line around the border, it may be a clickable image map. To display the graphic, hold down the mouse button over the graphic (on Windows and UNIX, use the right mouse button) and select **Load this Image** from the pop-up menu.

As we mentioned at the beginning of this section, because CGI can't function in a local environment, image maps only work if you access them across the network. Though you can save a page containing an image and can view the image, you can't use it for navigation unless you're connected to the actual site.

To address this feature, Netscape 2.0 and later versions allow the use of *client-side image maps*, which store the active regions and associated URLs as part of the current HTML file. Instead of seeing coordinates in the status area as you move your mouse, a client-side image map actually displays the URLs that would be accessed if you clicked your mouse in that location. More and more Web pages are designed to use client-side image maps, so the days of not being able to view image maps while in local mode without an active Internet connection will soon be gone. Client-side image maps are also much faster to respond to mouse clicks, because the information about where to go is stored locally; network activity isn't required to find out the contents of the link.

About Forms

The most common use of the standard CGI gateway is the *form mechanism*, which passes user input from the browser to the server to the program being executed as a result. The specifications for HTML 2.0 include a number of features which support the use of forms within Web documents. (A form is any document on the Web that lets you enter unique information to be sent to the server. Basically, any time you type information, click a checkbox, or choose from a selection list, whether to enter a search query or register for permission to use a site, you're using the forms interface.)

Netscape is considered to be a *forms-capable browser* because it lets you enter and send information through forms correctly to take advantage of the Web's most interactive capabilities; some other browsers, unfortunately, are not. (On some interactive sites, you may see messages like "This requires a browser that supports the use of forms" as a warning that the site contains advanced interactive features that require a forms-capable browser.)

HTML forms and CGI work together to collect your input in the correct format, pass it to the remote server, and invoke the appropriate program to construct or calculate the response. The output is then transferred back to your browser for display. What kind of output you receive depends on what kind of program was invoked—on a search engine, it's likely to be a list of documents that meet your search parameters; on a survey form or contest entry, it's more likely to be a thank-you note for participating. Again, it depends entirely on the wishes of the program's developer.

Elements of a Form

The specifications for forms in HTML allow developers to accept input in a variety of ways—as text, as a selection from a pop-up menu, or from choosing checkboxes or radio buttons. Visually, most form elements consist of a white field that contrasts with the background of a Netscape window. Figure 17.2 is an example of a form containing many of the common ways that you may be asked for input.

- Text fields. Text fields are areas where you can type any alphanumeric information that you want. Text fields don't contain scroll bars to let you easily navigate through the information that you type; if you type more than the allotted space, you'll have to use the arrow keys on your keyboard to move back and forth. If desired, developers can choose to limit the number of characters that you can enter in a text field.

NOTE The size and font of text fields is determined by the settings you chose for your proportional font when you configured Netscape's preferences. Field sizes, which are specified in units of characters, will be automatically scaled in proportion to the font size you chose.

- Password fields. These are like regular text fields, but the characters that you type are echoed as asterisks or bullets on the screen. The information will be sent to the server as regular text, but people who glance over your shoulder will not be able to see your password as you type it on the screen.

- Text areas with scroll bars. Text areas let you type and view more than one line of information; use the scroll bars to review information that doesn't fit on the screen. Scrolling text areas are commonly used in forms requesting feedback or other information; consider them a prompt to write as much about the topic as you feel is necessary to express your thoughts.

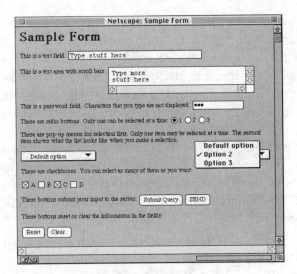

Figure 17.2 Sample form.

NOTE

Be sure to use a carriage return when you come to the right-hand side of the window so that all the text you type will be visible.

- Pop-up selection lists. Like the pop-up menus in applications and operating systems that you're used to using, these selection lists let you choose one option from a variety of listed options.

NOTE

If you hold down the mouse over a pop-up menu and see a diamond at the top or the bottom of the list, it means there are more items available to view in that location. Keeping the mouse button held down, move the mouse in the direction of the diamond to scroll the menu and display additional choices.

- Radio buttons. Like selection lists, you may only choose one of the options displayed in a list of radio buttons. Selecting a new radio button automatically deselects your previous choice. Developers use radio buttons to let you see all of your options at once.
- Checkboxes. Like radio buttons, checkboxes are all displayed directly on the page. However, they're not mutually exclusive—you can select as many checkboxes as you want.

339

- Buttons. Like buttons in any application or operating system, buttons are items that perform a specific action as soon as they're clicked. Common buttons on Web forms are **Submit** (which sends the information you entered to the server), **Clear** (which blanks out all the information in the fields), and **Reset** (which returns the fields to their default values).

When you click the **Submit** button or its equivalent on a form, all the input that you entered is collected and incorporated into a request that is sent to the server. The server then generates one or more screens of output based on the information that you sent, and redirects the output to your browser.

For example, if I want to do a Lycos search on "cats and dogs," I enter those terms in the form. When I click the **Submit** button, the search terms are sent to the server, which hands them off, along with several default values already in the form, as a request to the search engine. The resulting URLs and descriptions are sent back to my browser and displayed.

An important thing to keep in mind about dynamic documents like search results is that they do not exist as accessible files on the Web server—you are the only person who has a copy of the document that was generated. So you can't successfully bookmark a document's location on the server and return to it in another session (though you can save your results as a local HTML file).

Similarly, because the document only exists locally, if you try to return to a search page through your history list or the Back button during a session and the document is still in the cache, the page will be redisplayed. If the document is no longer in the cache, Netscape will repost the transaction to recreate the document. In some cases, Netscape may display a message like "Resubmit form data?" (The wording of the message may depend on your platform.) In this case, the browser is asking if you want to look at the old results of the earlier transaction, or if you want the CGI program to be re-executed using the same data. This is important if the information in the database is likely to have changed since you first submitted the request; for example, if you're checking stock quotes, it's crucial that you retrieve the most up-to-date information.

If you're on a page containing results generated by a query, you can force Netscape to resubmit your query and display the most recent information by clicking the **Reload** button.

URLs and CGI

The URLs that are used with CGI programs are different from the URLs of static documents. Instead of pointing to an HTML file or other stored item, the URL will actually name the program that should be executed. Often, the pathname to the program will contain a directory named cgi-bin, which is the usual name of the directory where common CGI programs reside. For example, in the URL

```
http://www.xyz.com/cgi-bin/imagemap
```

"imagemap" is the name of the CGI program on company XYZ's Web server that interprets clickable maps.

URLs for gateway programs that accept input from forms may contain unusual characters. In these cases, the URL sent to the server actually contains the input that you specified in the form. For example, the URL generated by clicking a normal or server-side image map might be

```
http://hostname/cgi-bin/imagemap?321,214
```

which tells the imagemap program that you clicked the mouse at X coordinate 321 and Y coordinate 214. In this kind of URL, the question mark denotes the boundary between the normal URL and the input data that you generated.

A more complicated but very common example is the URL generated by a query at a search engine such as Lycos. Not only do you enter words to search for, but you also specify parameters for what kind of search results you wish to view. For example, searching Lycos for "cats" and "dogs" in the same query using the default parameters for the number of hits to view, the number of terms to use, and the minimum relevance score generates this URL:

```
http://query.lycos.cs.cmu.edu/cgi-bin/
pursuit?query=cats+dogs&maxhits=15&minterms=1
&minscore=0.01
```

The name of the program executed was "pursuit," and all the information appearing after the question mark defines the parameters of my search.

NOTE Don't worry, we'll discuss the meaning of those parameters in complete detail in Chapter 23. Here we're just illustrating the way that CGI generates URLs.

However, it's not universally true that URLs for CGI will always contain a question mark followed by input variables. A newer method of transmitting your input to a CGI program has been developed called *posting*, in which the input parameters are not displayed in the URL, though the name of the program to be executed is. Form input is sent separately from the URL after the connection has been established. When the page containing the form is added to your history list, Netscape stores not only the URL but also the information that you entered. The WebCrawler search engine is an example of a commonly used CGI program that doesn't include your input in the URL submitted to the server.

More Examples of CGI

The following is a tiny list of some interesting uses of CGI on the Web so far. (Please keep in mind that with the number of sites being added or revised every day, this list is already out of date.)

- Blue Dog Counts. The famous subject of artist George Rodrigue's paintings will calculate and bark the answer to simple arithmetic problems at http://kao.ini.cmu.edu:5550/bdf.html.
- Australia's Telerobot on the Web, at http://telerobot.mech.uwa.edu.au, lets you control and view the motions of a robot in a laboratory at the University of Western Australia. (This is a sophisticated example of a common concept in Web sites—displaying an up-to-date picture

grabbed from a video camera. The Web contains a plethora of video cameras focused on coffee machines, fishbowls, telephones, and more. You can even retrieve a brand-new video clip of Niagara Falls. Yahoo maintains a list of Interesting Devices Connected to the Net at http://www.yahoo.com/Computers_and_Internet/Internet/Entertainm ent/Interesting_Devices_Connected_to_the_Net/.)

- Calculate the distance between any two points in the United States and view a map of the two locations at the How Far Is It? service at http://www.indo.com/distance/.

- Find out the status of your FedEx package by entering its airbill number at http://www.fedex.com/cgi-bin/track_it.

One of the most common usages of CGI on the Web is the use of forms for registration for information services. For example, the *New York Times* (http://www.nytimes.com) provides the full text of its paper online. The only requirement is that you provide your name and some other information—at this time, there's no charge involved to read the latest news from one of the best newspapers in the country.

Sites like this that require you to enter personal registration information lead us right into the topic that the rest of this section of the book will be about: data security and maintaining your privacy.

Who's Reading What I Enter in Forms?

Up until this point, security has been a matter of good judgment, not of protecting personal information—when you're looking at static documents, the information in the files is accessible to anyone in the world. For the most part, servers containing static documents don't care who accesses them.

But once you start sending data across the network to a server (instead of simply reading a file), you need to worry not only about who is receiving the information at the server but also about who might be intercepting your information along the way. If you're submitting a query to a search engine, providing feedback to a Web developer, or even registering to use a service like the *New York Times*, you really don't have much to worry about. Your search terms, comments, or email address simply aren't interesting enough to be considered compromising information, though you might be careful about any site that asks for your home telephone number or mailing address, simply because you may end up on a solicitation list.

However, if you want to purchase something advertised online and are asked to enter the number of your credit card or other confidential information, then you have to start worrying about the security of the data that you send.

Electronic commerce is one of the hottest business topics on the Web, and companies like Netscape are making extraordinary efforts to develop secure communications technology so that they can capitalize on the predicted explosion. Before online shopping becomes a commonplace occurrence, it's going to be necessary to inspire trust and confidence in the general public that the information exchanged between consumers and merchants through the Web is 100% protected from access by anyone other than authorized individuals.

In the next section, we'll talk more about electronic commerce, and explore Netscape Communications' efforts in that area. We'll also explain how to configure your browser to take advantage of the security technologies that are in place today.

What You Learned

After reading this chapter, you should be able to:

- Understand the difference between static and dynamic documents.
- Describe the function of CGI.
- Understand how forms and image maps work.
- Identify and understand URLs that are passed to CGI programs.
- Discuss basic issues of security on the Web.

CHAPTER 18

BUYING THINGS ON THE WEB

Since the repeal of the National Science Foundation's Acceptable Use Policy for the Internet, which prohibited the use of the network for commercial purposes, one of the hottest topics in the industry has been finding ways to use the Internet and the World Wide Web for electronic commerce. Although the policy banning such activity is no longer in place, a perfect scheme for managing the way that people purchase goods and services has not yet been developed. Nonetheless, online commerce is on the rise; International Data Corporation of Framingham, Massachusetts estimates that one out of three Internet users has already purchased something online, and companies like Sharper Image, a purveyor of high-quality, high-tech lifestyle enhancement gadgets, report that their income from online sales grew from $250,000 in 1995 to an annualized rate of $3 million in the first half of 1996.

In this chapter, we'll take a look at a few of the ways that it's currently possible to purchase items electronically. A complete discussion of the security issues involved with online purchases and information about configuring Netscape for use with secure transactions appears in the next chapter.

Purchasing Schemes on the Web

In the real, nonvirtual world, there are already several competing ways to pay for purchases; for example, you can pay for your groceries with cash, a personal check, a traveler's check, a credit card, or a bank debit or ATM card. We don't usually think about the many different transaction methods for spending money because they're all fairly commonplace—you choose your purchasing method because it's the most convenient.

Right now, things are no different on the Web. There are currently a variety of different ways that the Web is being used to promote the sales of goods and services, ranging from offline purchases to electronic cash equivalents to fully secure transactions. The difference in choices for Web commerce (as opposed to regular commerce) is less a matter of general convenience and more a matter of security: for the most part, you probably won't want to send your credit card number whizzing across the network unprotected. Although Netscape, Microsoft, Visa, Mastercard, and a number of other companies are working to create a standard format for online commerce, there are currently a number of online schemes available to let you spend your money without disconnecting your modem. In this section, we'll explore a few of the general ways that commerce is conducted online.

Conversion of Traditional Catalog Sales

One of the simplest methods of conducting commerce on the Web is to avoid the problem of transferring funds altogether. Several wonderful online storefronts exist that act as electronic catalogs—you can peruse the available products, and maybe have an expert answer your questions by email, but purchasing the product requires calling the company or sending in an order form. The advantage of this system is security—your credit card and personal information is protected from network theft. The disadvantage, in the eyes of the merchant, is the delayed gratification: the additional steps you must take to purchase the item may keep you from following through and actually placing the order. In general, large companies are much less likely to rely solely on this form of commerce than smaller shops; however, this method does provide a way to advertise and sell products online without a significant investment in software to manage electronic transactions.

One of our favorite online catalogs is the Archie McPhee store (Figure 18.1), at http://www.halcyon.com/mcphee/. The catalog from this wonderful, bizarre Seattle-based store has long been a staple in our house-hold; where else could you buy nun finger puppets, screaming cicada keyrings, voodoo dolls, build-it-yourself alarm clocks, and rubber chick-ens? Although their stock is basically that of a novelty store, the Archie McPhee catalog has long distinguished itself with its unusual catalog copy. Now you can peruse their catalog online, see color pictures, and in the case of the screaming cicada or squeaking Bibo, actually hear the noise instead of just reading a description.

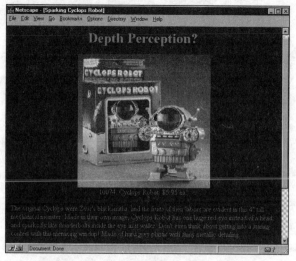

Figure 18.1 Archie McPhee's online catalog.

Many other standard retail companies with an electronic presence, such as Sharper Image (http://sharperimage.com), offer the ability to purchase offline via telephone or regular mail as part of the range of payment options.

Insecure Online Sales

You may encounter sites on the Web that do let you pay for products online...but which don't offer any methods of ensuring that your pur-chases are secure. For example, Excel's Internet Optical (http://www.direct.ca/excel/) provides an insecure form on their order page (Figure 18.2) to let you send your credit card information directly to them.

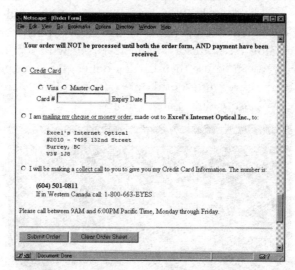

Figure 18.2 Insecure form for credit card payment.

In general, it's not a good idea to send your unprotected credit card number across the network. Chances are statistically fairly low that it'll actually be intercepted and used against you, but it's still not a safe practice.

WARNING

Most companies will provide some means of purchasing with a modicum of security; it's very rare that you'll encounter an online merchant whose only accepted method of payment is submitting an insecure credit card. For example, Fringeware, Inc.'s catalog (http://www.fringeware.com/HTML/shop.html) will also let you order by regular mail, or by electronic mail using PGP (Pretty Good Privacy, an example of the dual-key encryption technique described in the next chapter). There should always be an alternative to the security risk of sending your credit card number unprotected; if there isn't, you might think twice about purchasing from that vendor.

Electronic Cash and Digital Money

A significantly more secure method of letting people safely purchase goods and services online involves the use of an intermediary agency such as a bank, from whom you purchase electronic "money": digital tokens that you can exchange with vendors who have chosen to accept them as payment. This is a fairly complicated system which involves several parties: you must have an account at a participating bank which will let you use special software to transfer and convert "real" money from your account into digital money on your computer, and you must purchase items from companies who also have arrangements with a participating bank to honor such digital tokens as real money.

A leader in this technology is Digicash (http://www.digicash.com), a company that has been in the business of developing secure transaction technologies for banks and ATM networks since long before the Internet became a household word. In the past few years, Digicash has made efforts to address the secure online commerce problem with a product called ecash (short for electronic cash). In the ecash system, you prepurchase a certain number of dollars from a participating banking institution. The ecash software stores the digital money, which has been debited from your account, on your computer; the money can be spent anywhere that accepts ecash without having to open an account or send credit card numbers.

Despite its complexity, the ecash answer to online commerce is interesting for a number of reasons:

- No credit card information is ever exchanged, and the transactions with merchants are encrypted, so it's fundamentally a safe technology.

- Ecash transactions can be completely private matters; because you're exchanging cash and not credit card information, no validation is necessary: it's exactly the same as paying cash for a purchase.

- Ecash software allows anyone to receive digital money as well as spend it—if your friend owes you $10, he can transfer it from his computer to your computer without anyone else getting involved.

- Unlike credit cards, which provide access to a potentially limitless amount of funds, your maximum liability is limited to the amount of ecash that is stored on your computer.

Currently, the only participating bank in the United States is the Mark Twain Bank of St. Louis, Missouri; check out their Web site at http://www.marktwain.com for information about opening an account.

Protected Credit Card Payment Schemes

Another approach to online purchasing is systems that let you use your regular credit card but offer some kind of security in the way that the information is transmitted. The two companies we'll talk about here—Cybercash and First Virtual Holdings—handle this in rather different ways.

Cybercash

Cybercash's method of letting you purchase items without worrying about the safety of your credit card is to use special software, called the Cybercash Wallet, to store your credit card information. When you make a purchase, the Cybercash software initiates a secure connection with the merchant's server and sends an encrypted message containing your credit card information. The credit card information is then sent directly to the Cybercash server, which decodes the information and sends it to the merchant's bank. At this point, the process becomes exactly like a normal credit card transaction: the merchant's bank queries the institution that issued your credit card and then sends an authorization back to the merchant. The entire process reportedly takes less than 20 seconds.

An interesting thing to note about the Cybercash system is that it actually offers you more protection than a regular credit card purchase. In a restaurant or store, your credit card number is available to anyone who comes into contact with items in the register; with Cybercash, the vendor never sees your credit card number at all.

Like other proprietary systems, Cybercash can only be used with participating vendors. A list of merchants accepting Cybercash can be found at http://www.cybercash.com/cybercash/cool-places/.

First Virtual Holdings

First Virtual Holdings (http://www.fv.com) offers a different method of ensuring the privacy of your credit card that lets you shop without the use of additional software. Unfortunately, their methods require a somewhat Byzantine combination of online registration, offline verification, and email authorization for any purchase.

First you fill out an account application online, where you pick your VirtualPIN (which will identify you to merchants) without entering any credit card information. Then you receive an email message containing a telephone number and verification information; you must call First Virtual Holdings' toll-free number to confirm your account and provide your credit card number and expiration date. After receiving another verification by email, you're ready to shop. If you want to purchase something from a vendor who uses First Virtual's system, you identify the item and send your VirtualPIN. But you haven't purchased the item yet! You then check your email for a letter describing the purchase; you may choose to accept the charge, decline the charge, or identify the charge as fraudulent in case you believe your VirtualPIN has been compromised and you didn't place the order.

Like other proprietary systems, you can only purchase items with First Virtual Holdings at participating vendors. A list of merchants accepting First Virtual Holdings' payment method can be found at http://www.fv.com/infohaus/index.html.

Secure Transactions Managed by the Netscape Browser

The simplest method of purchasing something online would be to simply be sure you could send your credit card number without having it intercepted or tampered with along the way. Netscape, along with several other companies, has been working for a long time to develop technologies that let you safely send and receive confidential information.

The Netscape browser supports the use of a technology called the Secure Socket Layer, or SSL, which provides a safe link between your computer and the server you're communicating with. We'll discuss SSL in depth in the next chapter and provide information about configuring your browser for use with secure transactions.

What's interesting about the use of SSL instead of a proprietary scheme like ecash is its flexibility. The only requirement for its use is that both the browser and the server it's connecting to support SSL: no other protocols or software are involved. Because SSL is a general way to ensure private communication, instead of a specific way to send payment information, it can be used for a variety of purposes. For example, E*Trade (http://www.etrade.com) protects your confidential stock purchase orders with SSL, while some private corporations set up secure sites using SSL so that distant or traveling employees can view company information remotely. Of course, the most popular application of SSL so far is to protect your credit card number; because of the dominance of the Netscape browser, the number of online vendors using SSL-based transactions will likely continue to grow rapidly.

What You Learned

After reading this chapter, you should be able to:

- Understand the different ways of making purchases online.
- Evaluate the relative merits of different payment methods.

CHAPTER 19

ABOUT SECURE TRANSACTIONS

One of the most frequently discussed topics regarding the Internet and the World Wide Web is whether one can safely conduct commerce online; is the information that you send, such as credit card numbers and business correspondence, secure? In this chapter, we'll discuss different kinds of security threats, and we'll explore the ways that Netscape and other companies provide solutions to the most common security risks.

Security Threats and Electronic Commerce

On the Internet, there are basically three kinds of security threats to consider regarding electronic commerce:

- Is the data that you're looking at genuinely the product of the company or individual who claims ownership of the site?
- Can someone eavesdrop on or intercept your communications?
- Can someone tamper with the information that you send and receive?

All of these are valid concerns. The dark truth of the matter is that network transactions are, by their nature, not very secure. When data is sent from the browser to the server, its route typically passes through any number of intermediate machines which could, theoretically, have installed software to intercept data packets. The data packets could then be "snooped" to learn sensitive information like credit card numbers, user names, or passwords, or they could be modified, such as to change the shipping address of an order.

You not only have to worry about whether the information you send is safe, but also whether the information that you're retrieving is true. For example, if someone wants to manipulate stock prices, they could create a bogus Web site (possibly under the name of an established entity like a well-known brokerage firm) and provide false stock quote data. If enough people view and believe the data, the actual price of the stock may be affected by buy and sell decisions based on the falsified price.

A simple approach to this problem is to exercise caution and judgment. As with traditional media like newspapers, magazines, and books, you simply can't believe everything that you read. But if you're considering buying a product from an online source, you need to be absolutely certain that the people to whom you're giving your credit card number are the people they claim to be.

And, if you do trust the company to whom you're submitting an order, how can you be sure that the sensitive information you send them will remain private, free from interception or tampering?

Netscape has differentiated itself from the early, nonprofit Web software developers such as NCSA and CERN by staking out an interest in electronic commerce. Arguably, some of the most innovative features of the Netscape browser are its security functions, which were not part of any previous browser. Netscape's motive? To lend credibility to the idea of the Internet as a viable electronic marketplace by providing the ability to buy and sell goods and services safely and reliably. Netscape has worked to create a variety of mechanisms to protect you from security threats.

About Dual-Key Encryption

The underlying feature of all of Netscape's security functions is an already widely used technology called *dual-key encryption*. Netscape, in conjunction with other companies, is using dual-key encryption to ensure that servers are authenticated (the site is who they say they are) and that your personal information arrives confidential and intact. To understand how Netscape's security features work, you need to know a little bit about the fundamentals of encryption.

Before there was dual-key encryption, there was standard single-key encryption. In this case, there's one key, or code, that's applied to a *clear text* (unencrypted) message to encrypt it. The coded message is then delivered to the recipient, who must know the code used to encrypt the message in order to decrypt it. In this scenario, if a third party obtains the code, you're in trouble—not only can they read your messages but they can also send false ones using the same key.

Dual-key encryption takes care of that problem by generating matched pairs of encryption keys to be used with messages—a *public key*, which you give to people you want to communicate with, and a *private key*, which you keep to yourself and share with no one. Your public key can be used to decrypt any messages encoded with your private key, but—here's the great part—no one can encrypt messages with the public key and say that they came from you. The public key is only good for decrypting messages that were encoded with your private key. Likewise, a message sent to you that was encoded with your public key can only be decoded by your private key. No one but you can read that message.

The security of this kind of encryption is based on a mathematical principle called *uninvertability*. Encryption techniques possessing this quality can't be cracked by looking at several encoded messages and working backwards to decipher the message by identifying patterns. The only way to crack the codes generated by the public key or the private key without having both keys is by a technique called *exhaustive search*, in which every possible key combination is attempted. For example, if you forget the code to your combination lock, you could perform an exhaustive search to open the lock—if you sit there and methodically try every single possibility, eventually you'll crack the code. What makes combination locks a reasonable method to protect your possessions is that no one really has the time to sit for days, weeks, or years and attempt to enter every single numerical combination.

In computer-based encryption, the encoding and decoding keys are character strings of a fixed length. In an exhaustive search, you'd guess at the key, run the algorithm, and see if a clear text message showed up. The item that determines how long it'll take to complete an exhaustive search—and hence, how long it will take to decrypt an encoded message—is the number of bits in the key.

As you'll recall from previous chapters, bits (short for binary digits) have only two possible values: 1 or 0. If the encryption being used is 8-bit, then the key contains eight slots, each of which can be 0 or 1. The number of distinct combinations that would need to be attempted to find the key is 2^8 or 256. A computer program could find an 8-bit encryption key fairly easily, since it only needs to try 256 combinations, but when you use more bits in the keys, it gets exponentially more difficult to perform an exhaustive search in a timely manner. For example, 40-bit encryption, which is the default for the downloadable versions of Netscape (the version approved for export by the U.S. government), has 2^{40}, or 1.1 trillion, distinct possibilities. 40-bit encryption offers what is considered to be a moderate level of security, as it'll take a 64 MIPS computer (such as a top-of-the-line Pentium) one year to decode an encrypted message by exhaustive search.

NOTE Potential breaches of Netscape's security gained a great deal of press attention in 1995. First, a French graduate student commandeered 120 workstations and cracked a Netscape-encrypted message in eight days. This fact received a great deal of press, though it didn't prove anything that people who understand Netscape's encryption didn't already know. (Moreover, the student cracked the 40-bit version, not the 128-bit version, which is still considered uncrackable.) A somewhat more disturbing event occurred when two Berkeley graduate students proved that all the bits generated by Netscape's encryption algorithms were not random, making the code easy to crack quickly if you knew the pattern. Netscape Communications immediately admitted the error and made a security patch freely available on the Internet; the fix was then incorporated into Netscape 2.0 and later, so you no longer have to worry about this particular security problem.

If you're not a mathematician, it may be difficult to believe that encryption really works that well—but it does. In fact, it works so well that corporations like RSA Data Security, Inc. are closely monitored by the government to ensure that their best encryption technologies aren't made available outside the United States. And, people like Phil Zimmerman, inventor of Pretty Good Privacy (abbreviated PGP), freeware dual-key encryption software widely available on the Internet, have been placed under federal indictment. (The case against Zimmerman was dropped in 1996.) The government's concern about exporting encryption technology is so great that the only way to get a copy of Netscape with 128-bit encryption capabilities is to purchase the Netscape Navigator Personal Edition, which is only available in the United States (and currently only runs on Windows platforms). The 128-bit encryption in this product is so strong that all computers in existence working together couldn't crack the code within a human lifetime.

Netscape's Application of Dual-Key Encryption

Netscape has developed a line of security-related products and services for companies wishing to provide secure online transactions, ranging from proprietary servers and protocols to the proposal of SSL as a new open standard for the encryption of TCP/IP packets.

Netscape Secure Servers

Netscape's flagship products are their commercial secure servers—Web servers that are able to encrypt the exchange of information from browser to server and from server to browser to thwart eavesdroppers and tampering. Netscape's secure servers use a proprietary extension to the HTTP protocol called Secure HTTP. URLs that access a secure part of Netscape's server begin with the protocol identifier **https** instead of **http**.

Secure communication with Netscape's servers can only occur if the client is using the Netscape browser; while other browsers can view and exchange information on a Netscape secure server site, the exchanged information will not be secure. However, since more than 80% of people accessing the Web today use the Netscape browser, use of Netscape's servers is in no way a liability. In fact, if you're a merchant interested in conducting secure transactions across the Web, you don't have much of a choice except to use Netscape's servers, since research-oriented institutes like CERN and NCSA are not nearly as concerned about the commercial uses of the Web, and other companies' attempts at a security standard such as S-HTTP are not as dominant as Netscape's.

Netscape has seized the opportunity to develop commercial solutions to the problems of secure transactions and secure electronic communication, intending to capitalize on their lion's share of the browser marketplace by offering tools to commercial site developers. Currently, a complete line of commercial products is available that incorporates or builds upon Netscape's secure server and allows corporations to develop highly customized services on their Web sites with relative ease. These products include the Netscape SuiteSpot line of servers; Netscape's Commerce Extensions for building commercial Web sites, including the LivePayment product; and Netscape Commercial Applications, which help you develop a variety of Web sites, and whose products include the Netscape Publishing System, the Netscape Community System, and the Netscape Merchant System. For complete information about Netscape's line of products for commercial development, check out http://home.netscape.com/comprod/products/iapps/index.html.

The Secure Sockets Layer (SSL)

Cryptographic theory is one thing; getting it to work for real-time transactions across the Internet is another. To this end, Netscape introduced the first version of the Secure Sockets Layer (SSL) in 1994. SSL is a protocol for the encryption, authentication, and verification of data packets that can be used with any protocol that is based on TCP/IP (the Internet's basic transport protocol) including HTTP (the Web), gopher, FTP, telnet, and others.

SSL was originally developed for securing any transaction between Netscape's secure servers and its Web browser. It has three major functions:

- Encrypting the flow of data between the browser and a secure server.
- Verifying the identity of the server and, in some cases, the client.
- Protecting the data exchanged via the connection against tampering or unauthorized retransmission.

On a secure server, any information that's sent from the browser to the server (such as form input) or from the server to the browser (such as a confidential sales report) is encrypted. This ensures not only that your private information is safe, but also that the information you're viewing is genuine and has not been tampered with.

SSL uses two different encryption technologies. First, the connection is opened and the server is authenticated by an exchange of credentials, which are verified by the use of public/private key encryption. Then, the client application and the server invent a new encryption key to use as part of a bulk encryption algorithm. From then on, all data sent through the connection is encrypted with the second algorithm, which is more efficient than the original public/private key scheme, but is only good for the duration of the session. (Because it's only good for a brief period, there couldn't possibly be enough time for hostile third parties to crack the key with an exhaustive search.)

Netscape recognized the overall potential for this kind of secure communication across the Internet and uncoupled the SSL technology from their proprietary products. SSL is being promoted as an open standard, which means it's in the public domain—any developer of TCP/IP applications can incorporate this secure transaction technology into their products. The most recent version of SSL—version 3.0—was released in March, 1996. The SSL reference model is available free of charge for noncommercial use, and at a small price for commercial use; the specification itself is always available free of charge by any individual or organization.

The advantage to Netscape of developing an open standard is twofold. First, they get good press for placing their technology in the public domain for anyone to use. Second, by making the technology widely available, they increase the overall market for commercial use of the Internet, which can't hurt Netscape at all.

Meanwhile, Netscape has incorporated SSL into two of their other major commercial products: the Netscape News Server and the Netscape Proxy Server. (We'll talk about the Netscape News Server later in this section, and we'll discuss proxy servers in the next chapter.)

Certificates and Signatures

So far we've discussed the solutions to the problems of authenticating a server and a user, and ensuring that the exchanged information can't be intercepted or tampered with. But how can you be sure that the server you're communicating with is who they say that they are? And, for SSL to work, how do you get the public key of the company to begin the first step of authenticating the exchange? It may come as no surprise to find that Netscape has a solution for this as well.

When a company purchases a Netscape secure server, they must also obtain a *certificate* from a *certification authority*. A certificate is somewhat like a digital notary stamp—it's a method of guaranteeing that the site you're connecting to is really a service of the company it claims to be affiliated with. In this case, the "notary" is a company with an established reputation as a reliable authenticator of network sites. (Certification authorities also act as a registry of names to ensure that all certified names are unique—two legitimate businesses can't use the same name.) The certificates that Netscape supports conform to the ISO X.509 standard (ISO, or the International Standards Organization, is a worldwide consortium for the development of international standards in a variety of areas).

A certificate contains the name of the certification authority, the name of the company receiving the certificate, the public key of the company receiving the certificate, and some time stamps. The certificate is then *signed* with the private key of the certification authority.

The *digital signature* is a technique used with certificates and with other exchanges to ensure that the person who claims to have the private key actually has the private key. In a digital signature, the person with the private key sends a clear text message as well as a *digest* of the message. A digest is generated by running the clear text message through an algorithm to obtain a value that is significantly smaller than the original message. A digest is useful because it ensures that the person who generated it must have had the original clear text message, because it's nearly impossible to digest two different messages and get the same values.

The recipient of the clear text message and the digest performs the following steps. First, they compute a digest of the clear text message using the same algorithm as the sender. Then they use the public key to decrypt the encoded digest sent by the other person. If the two values match, then you can be sure that the person who sent the message actually has the private key to encrypt the message as well.

SSL handles these exchanges transparently. We've included this information so that you can understand the terminology if you encounter it in other discussions of encryption.

NOTE

Site Certificates and Personal Certificates

In Netscape 3.0, the browser has been extended with a mechanism for obtaining certificates from certification authorities (also known as CA certificates). Netscape comes preconfigured with a set of certificates from well-known certification authorities such as Netscape, RSA, and MCI, although you can add new CA certificates if desired. In order for any commercial server supporting SSL to run in secure mode, it must have a site certificate issued by one of these certification authorities.

Each CA certificate contains the *public* key of the certification authority. When you connect to a secure site using HTTPS, the browser checks the site's certificate. If it can decode the certificate, then the site is considered to be authentic since, theoretically, no one can forge the digital signature of the certification authority.

In some cases, you may encounter merchant sites whose certificates were issued by an authority for whom you don't have a CA certificate. In this case, you'll be asked if you want to accept a *site certificate* from that server. If you choose to accept that merchant's site certificate, you'll be presented with a series of screens in which you can examine the merchant's certificate; if you accept the certificate permanently, it will be saved on your disk as a site certificate along with the CA certificates. In this case, you're saying that you believe the site is authentic and are willing to engage in secure communications with it, even though the site doesn't have a certification from a certification authority that you already recognize. The risk in this case is that someone could present you with a fraudulent certificate, since you have no way of verifying that the site is who they say they are.

A third kind of certificate is the personal certificate, a new feature supported by SSL 3.0. A personal certificate is an extension by which both the client and the server exchange certificates during authentication. This allows a server to verify your identity in addition to letting you verify the server's identity. This scheme, which lets you positively identify yourself to others, can allow corporations to let remote employees view data on private servers by ensuring that no one without the appropriate certificate can get into the site. You can have multiple personal certificates, and you can obtain them from more than one certification authority. There are often fees associated with obtaining personal certificates, though they're usually nominal. If you have more than one personal certificate, you can choose which one to present by default to sites that request them.

Examples of Obtaining Personal and Site Certificates

Getting a Personal Certificate

In this section, we'll walk through an example of obtaining a personal certificate from Verisign (http://www.verisign.com), which has set up a "Digital ID" center for providing personal certificates. This example was obtained during a free trial period; by the time you read this, there may be a cost associated with obtaining the certificate. Keep in mind that the procedure for obtaining personal certificates from different authorities may be different; this is just an example of an existing procedure. For example, Verisign plans to offer a variety of levels of personal certificates, ranging from the simple one described below to certificates that will require you to have your application notarized so that they know you are who you represent yourself to be.

The first step in getting this personal certificate is to fill out your name and email address (Figure 19.1). You may choose whether to associate your email address with your personal certificate. Notice that the key in the lower-left corner and the blue line at the top of the window signify that you are at a secure site.

Then, you verify that the information is correct (Figure 19.2).

After going through a few more screens of licensing information, you'll be asked to submit the information. After submitting the information and waiting for the server to provide the new certificate information to the browser, you'll be asked to enter a nickname for the certificate which you'll use to identify it.

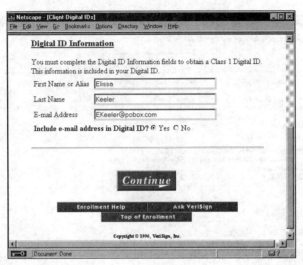

Figure 19.1 Entering name and email address for a personal certificate.

Figure 19.2 Certificate information verification.

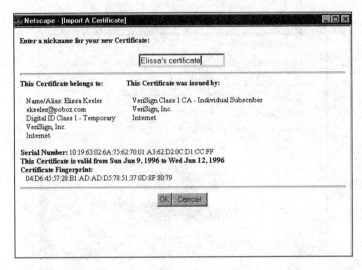

Figure 19.3 Nickname screen to identify a new certificate.

To see your personal certificate, follow these steps:

1. From the Options menu, select **Security Preferences**....
2. Click the **Personal Certificates** tab. A screen similar to Figure 19.4 will be displayed.

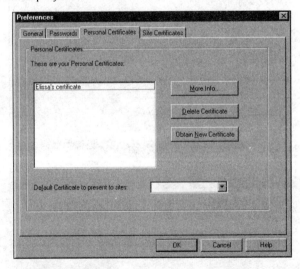

Figure 19.4 Personal Certificates information.

3. To see information about a specific certificate, select its name in the window and click **More Info....** A screen similar to Figure 19.5 will be displayed.

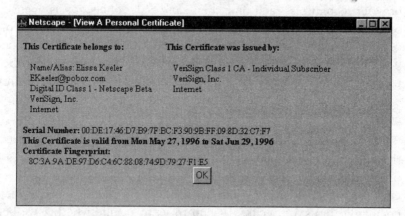

Figure 19.5 Information about a personal certificate.

If you attempt to access a site that requires a personal certificate but you don't have one, you may see a screen similar to Figure 19.6.

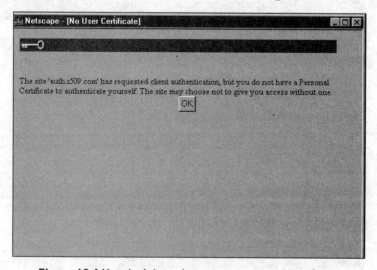

Figure 19.6 You don't have the necessary personal certificate.

Accepting a Site Certificate

Normally, your browser doesn't keep copies of site certificates for servers whose certificates were issued by the certification authorities that the browser recognizes; each time the secure SSL connection is opened, the server sends its certificate to you for verification against the list of CA certificates in the browser. However, if the browser doesn't recognize the CA who signed the server's certificate, you can choose to accept the certificate anyway. In this case, a new site certificate will be stored on your computer; you can choose whether to store it only for the length of the connection or to store it permanently until its expiration date.

In this section, we'll walk through an example of obtaining a site certificate from a company called Xcert (http://x.509.com). Xcert's own certificate was not issued by a company for which we have a CA certificate, but we may accept a site certificate from them to ensure that our communications are secure. (It's up to us to decide whether we believe they are who they say they are, but at least our exchanges will be private.) The steps in obtaining a site certificate are similar to the following.

When you first attempt to enter a secure site for which there is not a CA certificate, Netscape will provide a warning similar to Figure 19.7.

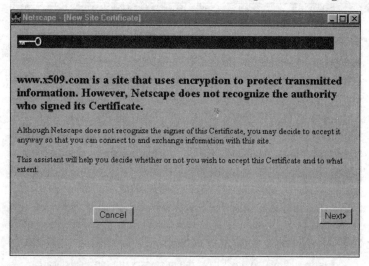

Figure 19.7 First screen for obtaining a new site certificate.

The next screen (Figure 19.8) shows information about the certificate, including the certification authority who issued it. In this case, the certification authority was Xcert, the company whose site we're connecting to.

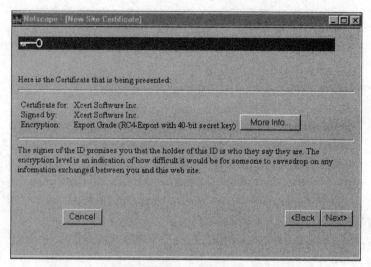

Figure 19.8 Information about the site certificate.

The next screen (Figure 19.9) lets you decide whether to accept the certificate and the duration of the acceptance. You may choose to not accept the certificate at all, to accept it only for the duration of the current session, or to permanently accept the certificate (until its expiration date).

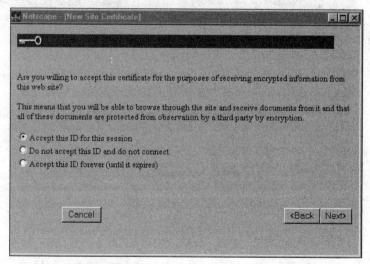

Figure 19.9 Your level of acceptance for the certificate.

You'll then be asked whether you want Netscape to warn you before submitting information to the site (Figure 19.10).

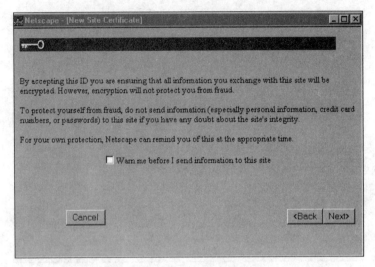

Figure 19.10 Warning options for a site certificate.

Finally, you'll be informed that the setup is complete; if you click **Finished**, you'll accept the certificate (Figure 19.11).

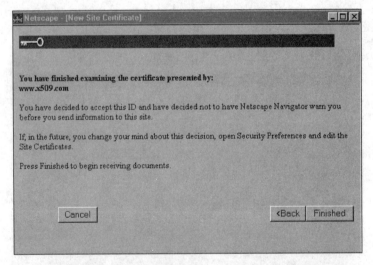

Figure 19.11 By clicking **Finished**, you accept the certificate.

If you accepted the certificate permanently, it will be visible in Security Preferences. To view a site certificate, follow these steps:

1. From the Options menu, select **Security Preferences**....

2. Click the **Site Certificates** tab. A screen similar to Figure 19.12 will be displayed. By default, all your CA certificates and site certificates will be displayed on the same screen.

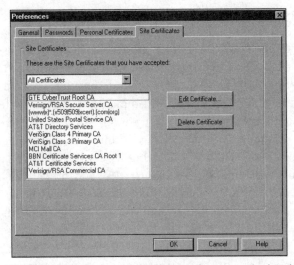

Figure 19.12 All your site and CA certificates are displayed.

3. To view only your site certificates, hold down the mouse over the pop-up menu and choose **Site Certificates**. Only your site certificates will now be displayed.

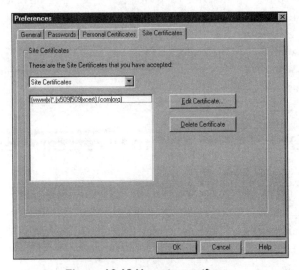

Figure 19.13 Your site certificates.

Information on modifying a site certificate appears at the end of this chapter.

The Netscape News Server

The Netscape News Server is a product that updates an older network service—NNTP (network news)—with several new features, including support for SSL. The major features of the Netscape News Server are security and support for MIME attachments. The security features make it possible for a corporation to set up internal bulletin boards that can be accessed remotely by authorized users and that can contain private company information while still ensuring its confidentiality. The MIME support means that pictures, sounds, movies, and other attachments can be included in an article; Netscape will either display the items directly or launch the appropriate helper application. It's Netscape's hope that these features will allow the Netscape News Server (coupled with the Netscape browser) to become a competitor with wide-area workgroup tools such as Lotus Notes. Like other Netscape products that provide security, the News Server can only operate in secure mode if the hosting company has purchased a certificate. URLs for connecting to a Netscape News Server operating in secure mode begin with the protocol identifier **snews**.

The News Server can also be used to provide access to regular Usenet News or to set up a series of proprietary but publicly accessible newsgroups, if desired. For example, Netscape hosts a variety of Netscape-related newsgroups on a Netscape News Server; although the newsgroups aren't available anywhere else in the world (as they would be if they were Usenet newsgroups), you navigate them with the same commands and buttons as you do in regular Usenet News.

Secure Documents and the Netscape Browser

The Netscape browser has a variety of features and functions for accessing secure servers, including:

- Visual cues to let you know you've accessed a secure site

- A variety of warnings notifying you upon entry and exit of a secure site
- A means of viewing a secure site's certificate

NOTE   An important thing to keep in mind is that many of Netscape's security features focus on ensuring that the information you're looking at is secure, as well as ensuring that any transactions you engage in are confidential and free from tampering. Although most of the media focus is on transactions, Netscape is also concerned with the general verification of a document's validity.

What a Secure Site Looks Like

When you're connected to a secure site, the appearance of the browser window will change in the following ways:

- A blue line appears at the top of the window.
- The key icon in the lower left appears solid, on top of a blue background (instead of broken, atop a gray background). If the key has one tooth, the document is of medium security (40-bit encryption); if the key has two teeth, the document is of high security (128-bit encryption).
- If the Location field is displayed, the URL displays a protocol identifier associated with a secure protocol (currently https:// or snews://).

Figure 19.14 shows the Netscape screen when connected to the secure Netscape General Store with medium-level security.

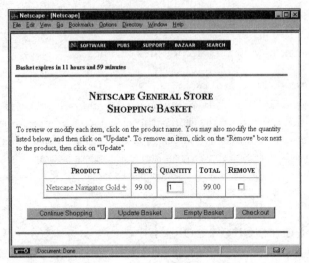

Figure 19.14 Connected to a medium-level secure site.

WARNING

You may notice that your performance at secure sites is poorer than usual; this is because by default, Netscape does not cache secure documents. Any time you revisit a secure site, the entire page will be reloaded from the server. If you wish to store secure documents in your cache, you can do so; we'll talk about the procedures toward the end of this chapter.

Viewing a Document's Security Information

Besides the browser's visual cues, you can find additional facts about the security level of a document on the Web, including its certification information.

To display information about a document's security, select **Document Info** from the View menu. A new HTML page will be displayed (Figure 19.15).

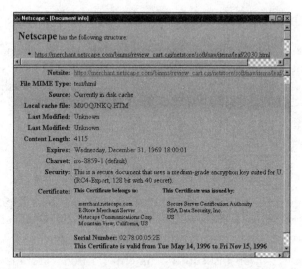

Figure 19.15 Document Information window for a secure document.

The Document Information window contains the following information:

- URL
- MIME type
- Location of the source Netscape is using to display the document
- Modification date
- Length of file
- Expiration date
- Type of character set encoding used
- Security information. If the document is not secure, you will be informed. If the document is secure, information about the level of encoding is displayed, as in the illustration.
- Information about the site's certificate, if it has one.

WARNING

To find out more about interpreting the information in a certificate, select **On Security** from Netscape's Help menu. Complete information about the items displayed is available under the heading **What does the Document Information dialog box tell me?**

Controlling the Security Notification Dialogs

Netscape has the ability to notify you when you enter and leave secure documents. To a certain extent, you can control when Netscape will display its warnings. But to do so, you need to understand how Netscape interprets a document's level of security.

Kinds of Documents

Netscape considers there to be three levels of security:

- Secure. In a secure document, all text and graphics displayed are considered to be authentic because of the site's certification, and any exchanges of information are considered secure.

- Insecure. In an insecure document, no items are guaranteed to be authentic, and no information that you submit is safe from interception or tampering.

- Mixed secure and insecure. In a document of mixed security, information that you exchange with the server is considered to be secure, and the text that you see is considered authentic, but the graphics in the document are stored on an insecure site and may have been tampered with.

WARNING

If you access a mixed-security document using a secure protocol identifier (such as **https**), the insecure items will not be displayed. A special security alert icon (Figure 19.16) will be displayed in their place.

Figure 19.16 Alert icon denoting that the items are not secure.

To display those items, reaccess the document using the nonsecure **http** protocol identifier. But, keep in mind that the information displayed and any exchanges you engage in will not be secure if you don't return to the secure screen (accessed with **https**) before proceeding.

When Netscape Provides Security Notification

There are six kinds of occasions when Netscape will provide notifications about security. (Netscape's intent is to raise awareness about security issues, but the constant warning may be considered overkill in an attempt to promote the use of its secure server products.) Four of the notifications can be suppressed with user-configurable settings, but two of them cannot. The six occasions are:

- When entering a secure document space, you're notified that the document you're receiving is encrypted, and that any information you send to the server will be encrypted. This notification is displayed in Figure 19.17. If desired, this notification may be suppressed.

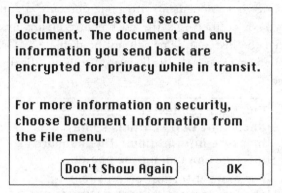

Figure 19.17 Requesting a secure document.

- When leaving a secure document space, you're notified that neither the document you're about to view nor any information you exchange with the server will be encrypted. This notification is displayed in Figure 19.18. If desired, this notification may be suppressed.

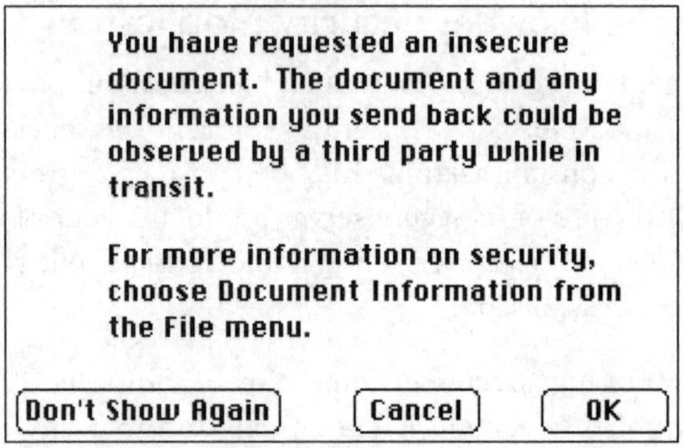

You have requested an insecure document. The document and any information you send back could be observed by a third party while in transit.

For more information on security, choose Document Information from the File menu.

[Don't Show Again]   [Cancel]   [OK]

Figure 19.18 Requesting an insecure document.

- When viewing a document with a mix of secure and insecure information, you're notified that the document contains mixed information and that the insecure items will not be displayed. This notification is displayed in Figure 19.19. If desired, this notification may be suppressed.

You have requested a secure document that contains some insecure information. The insecure information will not be shown.

For more information on security, choose Document Information from the File menu.

[Don't Show Again]   [OK]

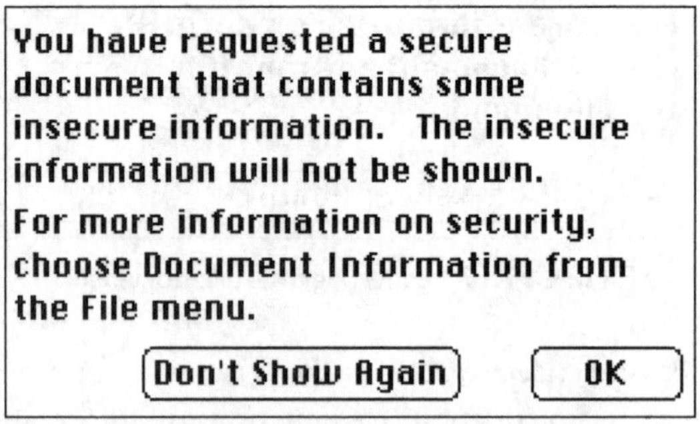

Figure 19.19 Requesting a document containing mixed-security information.

- When submitting any form using an insecure submission process, you're notified that the process is insecure and that the information can be intercepted or tampered with by a third party. This notification is displayed in Figure 19.20. If desired, this notification may be suppressed.

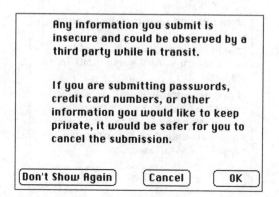

> Any information you submit is insecure and could be observed by a third party while in transit.
>
> If you are submitting passwords, credit card numbers, or other information you would like to keep private, it would be safer for you to cancel the submission.
>
> [Don't Show Again]   [Cancel]   [OK]

Figure 19.20 Submitting information insecurely.

- If Netscape expected a secure document but instead found an insecure document, you will always be notified. For example, if the page contains an image map which generates a URL to an insecure document, you'll be warned that the document is insecure, though it was expected to be secure. This notification, displayed in Figure 19.21, cannot be suppressed.

> Warning! You have requested an insecure document that was originally designated a secure document (the location has been redirected from a secure to an insecure document).
>
> The document and any information you send back could be observed by a third party while in transit.
>
> [Cancel]   [OK]

Figure 19.21 A secure document was expected but not found.

- If a form appears on a secure page but has an insecure submission process, you'll be warned that even though the document is secure, the submission is not. In this case, it is advisable to cancel the submission if it contains sensitive information such as passwords or credit card numbers. This notification, displayed in Figure 19.22, cannot be suppressed.

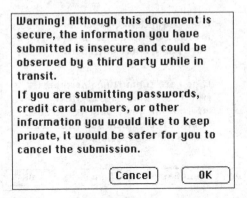

Figure 19.22 The submission process from this document is insecure.

Configuring the Browser to Show or Hide Notifications

The four notification dialog boxes that you can control may be configured in one of two ways. To turn each notification dialog box on or off, follow these steps:

1. In the Options menu, select **Security Preferences....**

2. Click the **General** tab. A screen similar to Figure 19.23 will be displayed.

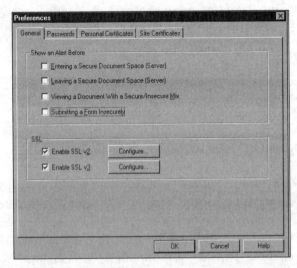

Figure 19.23 General security options.

3. Click the checkbox to the left of each item that you wish to be warned about. To suppress the notification, deselect the item.

SHORTCUT

If you haven't suppressed a notification alert, you can do so in the dialog box any time it appears. In Figures 19.17–19.20, notice the button **Don't Show Again**. When the dialog box is displayed, click **Don't Show Again** instead of **OK**. The dialog box will be suppressed until you change the settings in your Security preferences as described above. (On Windows, select the box next to the statement.)

Enabling Different Versions of SSL

Released in March, 1996, SSL 3.0 is a newer version of SSL that supersedes SSL 2.0. SSL 3.0 has the same functionality as SSL 2.0 but contains improved support for a wide array of protocols and encryption algorithms. It lets the client and server software negotiate on choices of the dual-key encryption and bulk cypher methods that will be used during the session, uses improved techniques to detect tampering, and contains allowances for future enhancements. SSL 3.0 also allows for *client authentication*, the process by which your personal certificate is analyzed by a site to make sure that you're who you say you are.

Despite SSL 3.0's advanced feature set, SSL 2.0 is still in use by commercial servers who adopted the standard when it was released in 1995 and have not yet upgraded to SSL 3.0. Netscape allows you to choose which versions of SSL should be enabled.

VIRTUOSO

By default, both SSL 2.0 and SSL 3.0 are enabled; for most people, there won't be any reason to change this.

To enable or disable different versions of SSL, follow these steps:

1. From the Options menu, select **Security Preferences**....
2. Click the **General** tab. A screen similar to Figure 19.23 will be displayed.
3. Select or deselect **SSL v2** or **SSL v3** as desired.

WARNING Unless you are an advanced user and understand cipher configuration options, or are expressly requested to change this information by your employer or another authority, we strongly recommend that you not change any of the configuration information for either implementation of SSL. If you are required to do so, click **Configure** and change information as instructed.

Working with Certification Authority Certificates

By default, Netscape provides a set of certificates from known certifying authorities. If you encounter a site whose certificate was provided by one of these authorities, you can be sure that they are who they say they are. Netscape lets you choose whether to allow connections to these sites and whether to be warned if you are connecting to a site that's certified by a specific certification authority. To do so, follow these steps:

1. From the Options menu, select **Security Preferences**....

2. Click the **Site Certificates** tab.

3. By default, all site certificates and CA certificates will be displayed. To display only the CA certificates, select **Certificate Authorities** from the pop-up menu. Only the CA certificates will be displayed in the window.

4. Select the certificate you wish to edit.

5. Click the **Edit Certificate** button. A screen similar to Figure 19.24 will be displayed.

6. If you wish to allow connections to sites certified by this authority, select **Allow connections to sites certified by this authority**. To disallow such connections, select **Do not allow connections to sites certified by this authority**.

7. If you wish to be warned before sending data to a site certified by the authority, select **Warn before sending data to sites certified by this authority**.

8. Click **OK** to save your changes and return to the Site Certificates options screen, or click **Cancel** to return without saving your changes.

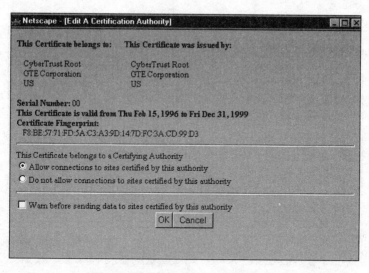

Figure 19.24 Editing a CA certificate.

Working with Site Certificates

If you have accepted any site certificates, you may modify the amount of information that you're willing to receive from those sites or delete the certificate altogether. To do so, follow these steps:

1. From the Options menu, select **Security Preferences**....

2. Click the **Site Certificates** tab.

3. By default, all site certificates and CA certificates will be displayed. To display only the site certificates, select **Site Certificates** from the pop-up menu. Only the site certificates will be displayed in the window.

4. Select the certificate you wish to edit.

5. Click the **Edit Certificate** button. A screen displaying information about the site certificate (Figure 19.25) will be displayed.

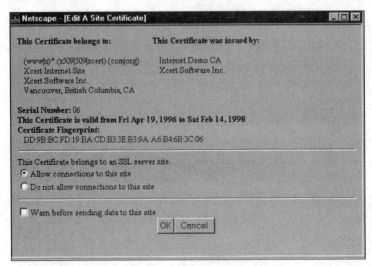

Figure 19.25 Editing a site certificate.

6. If you wish to allow connections to this site, select **Allow connections to this site**. If you wish to disallow connections to this site, select **Do not allow connections to this site**.

7. If you want to be warned when you are about to submit information to this site, select **Warn before sending data to this site**.

8. Click **OK** to save your changes and return to the Site Certificates screen; click **Cancel** to return without saving your changes.

Working with Personal Certificates

If you've accepted any personal certificates, Netscape provides you with a mechanism to delete individual certificates or to choose which of your certificates will be presented to sites who request them. To work with your personal certificates, follow these steps:

1. From the Options menu, select **Security Preferences...**.

2. Click the **Personal Certificates** tab. A screen similar to Figure 19.26 will be displayed.

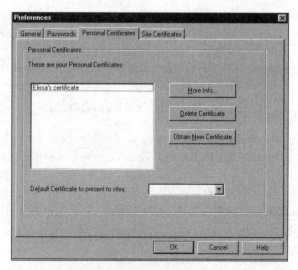

Figure 19.26 Personal Certificates information.

3. To view information about a certificate, select the certificate and click **More Info**....

4. To delete a certificate, select the certificate and click **Delete Certificate**.

5. To choose which certificate will be presented to sites requesting authentication, hold down the mouse over the **Default Certificate to present to sites** menu and select the nickname of the desired certificate.

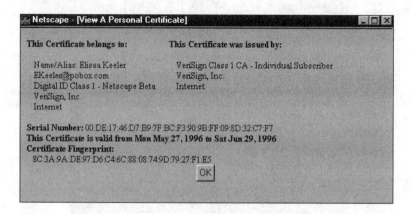

Figure 19.27 Information about a personal certificate.

VIRTUOSO

For detailed information about personal certificates, check out the FAQ and other documentation at Verisign's Digital ID Center (http://www.verisign.com).

Protecting Certificates with Passwords

If you use personal certificates and your computer can be used by other people, you may wish to protect your certificates with a password. This ensures that only you can use the personal certificates you've created, so no one but you can present themselves as you to a site that requires authentication.

To assign passwords to Netscape for the protection of personal certificates, follow these steps:

NOTE

The procedure on the Macintosh is conceptually similar to the one described below for Windows, but some of the screens are slightly different. Follow Netscape's prompts to successfully set a password on the Macintosh.

1. From the Options menu, select **Security Preferences**....
2. Click the **Passwords** tab. A screen similar to Figure 19.28 will be displayed.

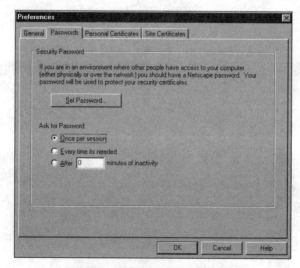

Figure 19.28 Password options.

3. Click the **Set Password** button. The Enable Your Password window will be displayed (Figure 19.29).

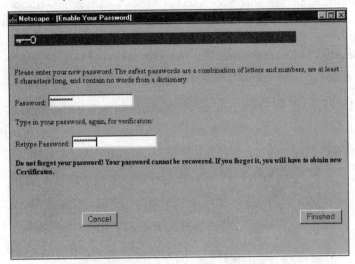

Figure 19.29 Setting up a password.

4. Enter your new password in the two fields that request it. You must enter the same password both times, or the password will not be changed.

5. Click **Finished**. You'll return to the Preferences screen.

6. Select whether you should be prompted to enter the password **Once per session, Every time it's needed,** or after a certain number of minutes of inactivity. (If you choose the last item, you'll need to enter a number of minutes.)

WARNING

Don't forget your password! If you do, Netscape won't let you use the site or personal certificates that you've obtained. If you forget your password, you'll have to delete the files containing your certificate information and obtain new site and personal certificates. (Your CA certificates are still embedded in the browser, so you won't have to recreate them.) To delete your certificates and password information if you lose your password, throw out the three *.db files in the Netscape directory on Windows; on the Macintosh, throw out the Security folder in the Netscape Preferences folder.

Controlling the Cache of SSL Documents

By default, secure pages will not be stored in your disk cache. This ensures that another person with access to your computer can not view secure pages that are stored in your cache. However, you may wish to cache documents from secure sites if the absence of caching is affecting your performance at secure sites or if you wish to view the information offline.

To allow caching of secure documents, follow these steps:

1. From the Options menu, select **Network Preferences**....

2. Click the **Cache** tab. A screen similar to Figure 19.30 will be displayed.

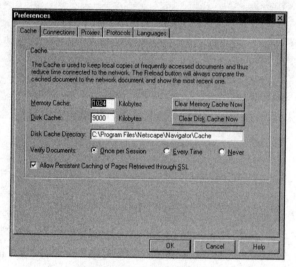

Figure 19.30 Cache options.

3. At the bottom of the window, select **Allow Persistent Caching of Pages Retrieved through SSL**.

Other Security Issues in Netscape

In this section, we'll talk about a number of security issues in Netscape that aren't related to matters of secure transactions.

Disabling Java and JavaScript

Because Java applets are downloaded and executed on your computer, there's a chance that a malicious programmer might use them to tamper with your system or retrieve information from your disk drive. Although Netscape has taken several precautions to ensure that Java applets can do no harm (see Chapter 13 for more information), researchers have found a variety of security holes that let applets bypass Netscape's security measures. (At the time of this writing, Princeton University researchers had just uncovered another security flaw regarding Java.)

Netscape has consistently made security patches available whenever a new potential security breach is found. However, if you're worried about Java applets causing trouble on your computer, you can disable Java and/or JavaScript by following these steps:

1. From the Options menu, select **Network Preferences**....

2. Click the **Languages** tab.

3. To disable Java or JavaScript, deselect **Enable Java** or **Enable JavaScript** so that no "X" is displayed. To enable them, select the items so that an "X" is displayed again.

NOTE If you're interested in finding out more about Java and security, check out Netscape's information at http://home.netscape.com/newsref/std/java_security.html.

Security Alerts for Cookies and Insecure Email Forms

In addition to the security alerts discussed earlier in this section, Netscape will warn you about two additional occurrences that might compromise the integrity of your computer or your information.

About Cookies

Cookies are a way that a server stores small amounts of information about your preferences for future use on your own computer. For example, Netscape's Personal Workspace (see Chapter 21) stores the layout and

URLs of your custom online home page in a file on your computer, which allows the Netscape server to display your personalized information every time you connect to the site. Theoretically, the information in a cookie can only be accessed by the site that put it there. But it's conceivable that a site could put an unwanted cookie on your machine or attempt to access a cookie it didn't place there itself.

You can set Netscape to warn you when a server is attempting to place a cookie on your system, and you can choose to decline the cookie at that time. To do so, follow these steps:

1. From the Options menu, select **Network Preferences**....

2. Click the **Protocols** tab. A screen similar to Figure 19.31 will be displayed.

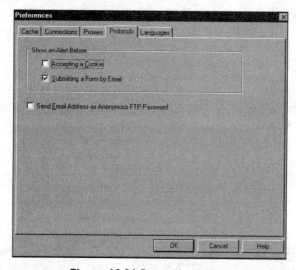

Figure 19.31 Protocols options.

3. In the Show an Alert Before panel, select **Accepting a Cookie**. (To turn this warning off, deselect the item.)

About Insecure Forms

Some forms that you fill out will send information to a recipient via email instead of "posting" the information to the server. (For more information on the use of forms, see Chapter 17.) Like other Internet email, the information that you're mailing is insecure and could conceivably be intercepted or tampered with in transit. For this reason, you shouldn't send credit card numbers or other sensitive materials in this way. To set Netscape to warn you when the information you typed in a form is being submitted by email, follow these steps:

1. From the Options menu, select **Network Preferences**....

2. Click the **Protocols** tab. A screen similar to Figure 19.31 will be displayed.

3. In the Show an Alert Before panel, select **Submitting a Form by Email**. (To turn this warning off, deselect the item.)

What You Learned

After reading this chapter, you should be able to:

- Understand basic issues related to secure transactions on the World Wide Web.

- Grasp the fundamental concepts of dual-key encryption, the Secure Sockets Layer, certification, and other technologies that underlie secure transactions.

- Identify some of the important players and products in the world of online commerce.

- Understand how the Netscape browser handles secure documents.

- Configure Netscape to display only the security warnings that you want to see.

CHAPTER 20

FIREWALLS AND PROXIES

In the previous chapter, we talked about Netscape's features for ensuring that information you exchange across the World Wide Web remains confidential and free from tampering. What we didn't delve into was protecting the information that actually resides on the disk storage of your computer itself—and for good reason. Basically, if you're using your computer at home, threats to the security of the information on your computer from the Internet aren't a realistic problem. You're not a good target for hostile crackers (people who break into computer systems for fun or profit), as home personal computers don't usually store information that can be used for someone else's gain. And, it's technically difficult to break into a personal computer since it's a client-only machine, especially if, like many users, your computer is only connected to the Internet through a telephone line a few times a day. You exchange information with the network, but since your computer isn't a server, it doesn't accept any kind of incoming connection requests from elsewhere in the world.

However, it's a different story in a corporate setting. Connection to the Internet is often through a local area network (LAN) that supports a large collection of client and server machines. Providing access to the Internet typically puts the servers on the LAN at risk, since most widely used server software has well-known weaknesses that can be exploited by crackers. If they know how to break into a server, and the server is unprotected, crackers anywhere in the world can break in, assume system privileges that allow them access to any information they can find, and compromise all the data that's available on the LAN.

About Firewalls

To protect against the threat of crackers and still provide Internet resources, corporations typically protect their LANs with *firewall* technology. In a firewall environment, one computer acts as a barrier between the inner network (the LAN) and the outer network (the Internet). Figure 20.1 shows a typical firewall arrangement.

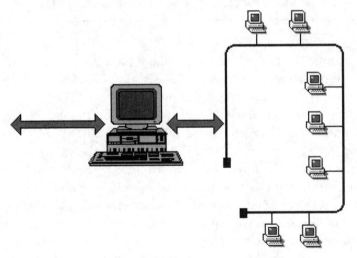

Figure 20.1 How firewalls work.

Without a firewall, requests from the client programs on the LAN (such as Netscape running on your office computer) go directly to the remote server, and vice versa—connection requests from the Internet for local servers go directly from the Internet to the local servers via the LAN. This means that a cracker could access every server that's part of the LAN, since all of them can be reached from the Internet. Firewall computers act as the single point of entry and exit for packet traffic between the LAN and the Internet, and they typically have much stronger security features than regular servers on a LAN that are only intended for local access.

A simple kind of firewall is called a *screening router*. Screening routers simply block all outside attempts to connect to addresses inside the corporate network except for the secured server, while allowing most or all outbound requests from the LAN to travel out to the network. This provides corporate users with access to Internet resources, but keeps outsiders from accessing any internal information. If you work at a company that uses a screening router, you won't use your client applications any differently than you would at home (except for a minor problem with FTP discussed below), since nothing is hindering your connection requests.

However, an equally common scenario is the use of a firewall host which has two separate network interfaces—one for the Internet and one for the LAN. The firewall host doesn't let requests flow freely in *or* out—both internal and external users can only access the firewall machine. This means that a company can place a Web server on the firewall machine and provide information and other services to outside users, while still maintaining the security of the information hosted on the internal LAN. Because this allows a company to provide Web and other network services to the outside world while protecting internal resources, this kind of firewall is quite common.

The problem with this kind of firewall is that not only does it not let outsiders into the LAN, but it also doesn't let internal users of the LAN issue outbound connection requests. Like external users, the internal users can only get as far as the information hosted on servers running on the firewall machine. If a company wants to provide information to the public while protecting its internal resources and allowing internal users to access the rest of the Internet, an additional technology is required—the use of a proxy server.

About Proxies

A proxy server, or simply *proxy*, is an agent program that resides on the firewall machine and acts on your behalf during a transaction. If you're using a computer that's behind a firewall and you want to connect to a site that's not on the LAN, the proxy issues the connection request, retrieves the information, and passes it back to you.

Proxies make it possible for companies to provide information to the public and to let internal users access the Internet, without compromising the security of the internal machines. For this reason, they're becoming increasingly popular with LAN-connected Internet users in the workplace. But because any connection request to the network requires the additional step of asking the proxy to issue the request, client applications such as Netscape need to know how to access the right proxy server.

Kinds of Proxy Servers

There are two kinds of proxy servers that are widely used with Netscape: SOCKS proxy servers and protocol-specific proxy servers.

SOCKS Proxies

SOCKS is a generic TCP/IP proxy mechanism that ferries data packets back and forth through the firewall. It can be configured to give local clients access to the Internet while keeping outsiders from getting to machines that are located within the firewall.

SOCKS can handle any kind of TCP/IP traffic as long as the client application that's requesting it knows how to send and receive packets through a SOCKS server—in other words, the client software must be *SOCKS-compliant*. SOCKS-compliant Internet applications use additional libraries of routines to handle the flow of information.

Netscape is a SOCKS-compliant application. If you configure Netscape to use a SOCKS proxy server, the SOCKS routines will be invoked with each connection request.

WARNING Using a SOCKS proxy server? You should get a SOCKS-compliant telnet application as well; otherwise, you won't be able to use telnet services. A SOCKS-compliant telnet client is available at ftp://ftp.nec.com. In general, you'll need special SOCKS-compliant versions of any helper applications that make their own Internet connections, such as TN3270.

Protocol-Specific Proxies

Protocol-specific proxies are designed to work with a single client application. For example, an HTTP proxy will only handle World Wide Web requests, and a gopher proxy will only handle gopher requests. Protocol-specific proxies are often used by corporations for reasons beyond security, as they offer the following additional benefits to system administrators:

- Caching. HTTP proxies can locally cache the items that it passes to clients within the LAN. If a site is accessed by more than one person in the company, the second person to access the site may be viewing information retrieved from the proxy cache and not from the network. This drastically reduces the amount of time spent retrieving the same items to local computers within the same LAN, since the speed of the LAN is typically many times faster than the speed of the connection to the Internet. In fact, some places in Europe provide publicly accessible HTTP proxies so that users in remote areas can share the cache and reduce the time and network resources spent in constantly retrieving the same items from the U.S. or other distant sites in the world.

- Logging and tracking. Because these kinds of proxies cache items, they necessarily track which Internet addresses are being used and how often they're accessed. This lets system administrators keep an eye on how the network is being used by employees.

- Outlawing access to specific sites. Protocol-specific proxies allow a system administrator to identify sites which users are not allowed to access. By telling the proxy server not to issue requests to specific addresses, system administrators can effectively keep you from accessing certain information.

 Some of the software designed to protect children from potentially controversial information on the Internet uses this capability of protocol-specific proxies to disallow sites which are considered inappropriate.

NOTE

Typically, Web server software packages have built-in protocol-specific proxies that site administrators can use as desired. The three most common protocols supported in server software are HTTP (the Web protocol), gopher, and FTP.

FTP, WAIS, and SSL Proxies

The FTP, WAIS, and SSL protocols behave somewhat differently from other protocols for network services and have special configuration requirements that must be met in order to work correctly. The information about FTP and SSL is specific to people working behind firewalls, while the information about WAIS is relevant to any user of Netscape.

About FTP and Proxies

Unlike sessions using other network protocols, FTP sessions, which occur when an FTP URL is encountered, require two different connections: one from the client to the server, and another from the server back to the client. In the absence of a firewall, this is handled invisibly and you'll never notice it. But if you're using FTP from behind a firewall, this can cause problems, since the firewall will often disallow the second kind of connection—the one between an external computer and a computer on the LAN.

There are ways to get around this. For example, if you're at a site that uses a screening router, you can configure Netscape to use an FTP proxy (provided by your network administrator) so that the inbound session can reach your desktop machine. (However, there may be another solution that your network administrator prefers, so be sure to ask.)

If you're at a site that uses a protocol-specific proxy, there's probably nothing to worry about. FTP protocol proxies are normally set up to handle this problem.

If you're at a site that uses a SOCKS proxy, using FTP will be more difficult. SOCKS has no way to know that your outbound packets are an FTP request, and will disallow the associated inbound FTP connection request. To use FTP with a SOCKS proxy you may have to use an FTP client application that supports a special "proxy mode" to access remote FTP sites. Contact your site administrator for the preferred solution.

About WAIS and Proxies

WAIS (Wide Area Information Server) is an Internet protocol used to support the searching of geographically distributed databases. When using Netscape, you'll usually access a WAIS search though a CGI gateway, though it's possible that you'll encounter a URL to directly access a WAIS database. (Such URLs are in the format wais://wais_server/database? search_terms. For more information about WAIS searches, see Chapter 23.)

Although the Mosaic Web browser allows you to access WAIS URLs directly, Netscape requires that you configure a WAIS proxy to handle requests to and information from WAIS servers. There are some publicly accessible WAIS proxy servers available on the Internet, such as www.w3.org port 8001, which is provided by the W3 consortium, a non-profit group headed by Tim Berners-Lee and devoted to the development and future of the Web. (To find other publicly accessible proxies, try a Lycos or WebCrawler search on the terms "public WAIS proxy".)

NOTE   Although WAIS searches are extremely common on the World Wide Web, they are nearly always gatewayed to be available through the HTTP protocol. It's unusual to find a WAIS URL that doesn't also have a Web-based front end to the search service. However, using a WAIS proxy allows you to access WAIS searches that are not otherwise mirrored onto the Web.

About SSL and Proxies

If you're using Netscape behind a firewall and want to engage in secure transactions using the SSL protocol (discussed in the previous chapter), you may need to configure the browser to use an SSL proxy. Otherwise, the proxy server may not know that your TCP/IP packets are secure, and it won't be able to handle them correctly.

An SSL proxy is currently only available if the proxy server at your site is a product of Netscape Communications. If your site is using a protocol-specific proxy server that doesn't support SSL, you can still view information on some secure sites, but the security of the information and of your transactions is not guaranteed. (Whether a secure site lets you submit information without a secure browser is up to the remote site administrator.) If your site is using a SOCKS proxy server, then you should be able to operate securely without specifying an SSL proxy.

Configuring Netscape to Work with Proxies

WARNING

This discussion of proxies and firewall architecture has been necessarily simplified; a complete discussion of the topic is beyond the scope of this book. Before attempting any kind of configuration, contact your network administrator for complete information, especially if you intend to run Web server software or any other kind of server software on your desktop machine.

Before you configure Netscape to work with the proxies on your LAN, you must obtain the following crucial information from your site administrator:

- Is your site using a firewall?
- Is the firewall based on a screening router or a firewall host with proxies for outbound requests? If the firewall uses a screening router, find out the name and port number of the FTP proxy (if one exists).
- If the firewall uses proxies, does it use a SOCKS proxy or protocol-specific proxies?

  If it uses SOCKS, ask for the machine name and port number of the SOCKS server.

  If it uses protocol-specific proxies, ask for the machine name and port number of each protocol that's supported.

- Is there a proxy configuration set up for you to use? (Netscape lets site administrators enter proxy information in a file that's accessible on the local network; in this case, all you need to do is enter the URL of the local proxy configuration file into the correct location in your Network Preferences file.)
- If you are behind a firewall and using proxies, ask for the names of the local servers at your site that you should access without the use of a proxy. (Accessing servers inside a firewall is different from accessing servers outside a firewall.) These may be all the servers at your site, in

which case all you need to know is the domain name of your site, or it may be specific machines, in which case you need to know the fully qualified host name of each machine that you should access without a proxy.

- If you're not operating behind a firewall and are only configuring Netscape to use a WAIS proxy, get the machine name and port number for the WAIS proxy you wish to use.

NOTE It's crucial that you identify a port number as well as a machine. Because proxy servers don't have fixed well-known port numbers, Netscape must know the exact Internet address and port number of the proxy so it can be invoked correctly.

Configuring Netscape for Proxies

To configure Netscape for proxies, follow these steps:

1. From the Options menu, select **Network Preferences**....
2. Click the **Proxies** tab. A screen similar to Figure 20.2 will be displayed.

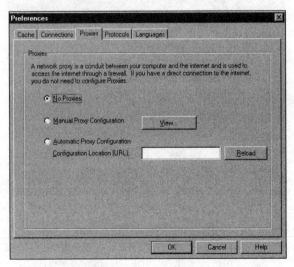

Figure 20.2 Proxies configuration screen.

3. If your site administrator has set up a proxy configuration file, follow these steps:

a. Select **Automatic Proxy Configuration**.

b. Type the exact URL of the proxy configuration file as provided by your site administrator in the **Configuration Location (URL)** field.

c. Click **OK** to save your changes and return to the browser.

If your site administrator has changed the information in the file designated by that URL, you'll need to click the **Reload** button to load the new information.

NOTE

4. If you need to configure the proxies manually, select **Manual Proxy Configuration**.

5. Click **View**.... The Manual Proxy Configuration screen (Figure 20.3) will be displayed.

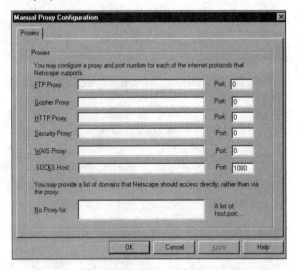

Figure 20.3 Manual proxy configuration screen.

6. If you're not behind a firewall and are simply entering the name of a WAIS proxy, enter the name of the proxy machine and the correct port number in the **WAIS Proxy** field.

7. If you're behind a firewall and are using protocol-specific proxies, enter the name of the proxy machine (FTP, gopher, HTTP, Security, WAIS) and the correct port number in the line provided for each proxy. (Enter SSL proxy information in the **Security Proxy** field.)

8. If you're behind a firewall and are using a SOCKS proxy, enter the name of the machine and the port number in the **SOCKS Host** field.

9. If you're behind a firewall and need to access local servers without going through the proxy, locate the **No Proxy On** field. Enter the fully qualified domain name (e.g., foobar.com) of your location or the fully qualified host names (e.g. xyz.foobar.com, abc.foobar.com) of each machine at the location that should be accessed without using a proxy. If you enter more than one name, separate the items with a comma.

10. Click **OK**.

What You Learned

After reading this chapter, you should be able to:

- Understand why firewalls and proxies are used.
- Identify the differences between screening routers, SOCKS proxies, and protocol-specific proxies.
- Understand why FTP, WAIS, and SSL are unique cases for proxies.
- Configure Netscape to work with available proxy servers.

CHAPTER 21

CREATING YOUR OWN HOME PAGE

There are plenty of good reasons for creating a personal home page that's stored locally—in other words, a home page that resides on your own computer instead of on a server, and that isn't accessible to anyone else through the Web. Using a local home page as a starting point is a powerful front end to using all features of your browser and the resources of the Web. The Bookmark menu is OK as far as it goes, but local home pages are a better way to keep track of the URLs that you like to visit most often. Local pages can include not only the links but also descriptive text, graphics, and other formatting features to make it easy to find the links you're looking for. And, local home pages can contain links to other materials on your disk drive, such as documentation files, in addition to links to the rest of the world. Think of a local home page as your custom directory to all the Internet-related resources that exist on the Web or on your own computer.

In this chapter, we'll talk about:

- What you can and can't do with local Web pages
- Ways to create a local Web page without learning HTML
- Ways to create a local Web page that do require learning HTML
- The very basics of creating an HTML document

In Chapter 22, we'll talk about how to create documents that consist of multiple pages and how to place your documents on a server so that they're accessible to others.

Features and Drawbacks of Local Web Pages

This section contains a brief description of the benefits of using Netscape's local mode of operation, as well as a discussion of some of the drawbacks you need to look out for. (The local mode of operation is important when you're creating your own Web pages since you're going to be creating pages locally on your own computer, regardless of what you plan to do with the pages you create.)

The Use of "Drag and Drop"

One great feature of the local mode of operation is that the "drag and drop" features of your operating system are in effect. You can open files simply by dragging the icon for a file over the icon for Netscape (so that the Netscape icon is highlighted), and then releasing the mouse. This launches Netscape and displays the file that you dragged.

The benefit of this feature isn't that evident when you work strictly with HTML files, which can easily be viewed and selected in the dialog box generated by the **Open File...** command, or with documents that are already associated with Netscape (double-clicking them will always launch the application). But text files such as README files for other applications can be opened with Netscape using this easy procedure.

The Limitations of Local Operation

It's important to remember that your browser's local mode of operation only lets you open and view the contents of files and follow links to visit other locations. Features requiring complex server interaction, such as the use of image maps or other forms of CGI (Common Gateway Interface), will not work on files that are stored on your local disk drive. For example, many buttons on Web pages are implemented as CGI image maps;

even if they look correct in local mode, they simply won't work. (For more information about the uses of CGI, see Chapter 17.)

NOTE This isn't a problem with client-side image maps, which were first supported in Netscape 2.0 and are now becoming widely used. In client-side image maps, navigation information is stored in the HTML file, so communication with the remote server isn't necessary and the image maps will work correctly in the local mode.

TCP/IP Requirements for Local Operation

Both Windows and Macintosh platforms require that you have some kind of TCP/IP software installed in order for Netscape to launch correctly.

Windows: Using a Null Socket Library

On Windows platforms, your interface to the Internet and the TCP/IP protocols are contained in a system extension—known as a socket library—called WINSOCK.DLL. The WINSOCK.DLL provides and manages your access to the outside world through your direct or dialup IP Internet connection. Most software applications designed to be used on the Internet will not launch if the WINSOCK.DLL isn't available.

If your computer is set up for Internet access, the Winsock library will already be installed on your computer. But it is possible for you to install a Web browser to look at local files on a Windows-based computer that doesn't have a connection to the Internet at all. However, in order for this to work, you must install a null or *dummy* socket library, which has an interface that looks like the WINSOCK.DLL but doesn't contain any of the algorithms. The null socket library makes it appear as if you have networking capabilities so that Netscape will launch correctly, but you don't actually have to have any kind of network connection.

At least two different null socket libraries are available for use with Netscape and other browsers. Netscape Communications provides the mozock.dll, available at ftp://ftp.mcom.com/pub/unsupported/windows/mozock.dll, and nullsock.dll, available at ftp://stargate.jpl.nasa.gov/pub/ddl/nullsock.dll. Be sure to check the associated documentation to ensure that you install these items correctly.

WARNING

Your browser may attempt to display the .dll files as text in the browser window, instead of downloading them to your disk drive. If this occurs, right-click the link and use the pop-up menu command to save the file to your disk drive.

Macintosh: TCP/IP is Required

On the Macintosh, your interface to the Internet and the TCP/IP protocols are contained in the MacTCP system extension or, if you're using a late-model PowerPC, the Open Transport system extension. MacTCP and Open Transport provide and manage your access to the outside world through your direct or dialup IP Internet connection. Most software applications designed to be used on the Internet can not launch if the system extension is not available.

If your computer is set up for Internet access, MacTCP or Open Transport are already installed on your computer. But it is possible for you to install a Web browser to look at local files on a Macintosh that isn't connected to the Internet at all. However, you must still install MacTCP or Open Transport, which will make it appear as if you have networking capabilities so that Netscape will launch correctly, even if it's not configured for use with dialup IP or direct Internet connection.

MacTCP is a standard component of the Macintosh operating system, though you may need to perform a custom install to ensure its availability. Open Transport is a standard component of the operating system for late-model PowerPCs, and it is frequently updated; you can always find the latest release by connecting to ftp.info.apple.com and following the path for the latest software updates (Open Transport will be in the directory for Networking and Communications).

About Creating Web Pages

As you probably already know, Web pages are created with a markup language called HTML (HyperText Markup Language). If you've ever viewed the source code of a Web document, you may have noticed that all the material in the file is plain text—there are no strange characters as there might be if you viewed a binary file. Instead, HTML uses *tags*—descriptive text set off in brackets, such as <BODY> and <H1>—to mark where different kinds of formatting begin and end. In this section, we'll talk about ways to create Web pages ranging from methods that require little or no knowledge of HTML to methods that require a great deal of HTML knowledge.

NOTE   For personal Web pages, especially ones that you plan to use locally, you should get by just fine with the methods that don't require much skill with HTML. However, as you become a more advanced Web author, you may find that you want to use advanced formatting features or that you simply wish to tweak your pages to make them look exactly as you want. At the end of this chapter, we'll provide a comprehensive list of resources that you can use to further your skills as an HTML virtuoso.

Creating Web Pages without Learning HTML

This section contains a brief list of ways to create your own Web pages without learning any HTML.

SHORTCUT   Any plain text document, such as those created by NotePad, SimpleText, TeachText, vi, or xedit, can always be viewed in your Web browser. If you have a daily to-do list, a README or other text-only file that you access regularly, you can open it with Netscape without any additional steps.

Exporting Your Bookmarks

As we discussed in Chapter 4, the Export feature of the Bookmark Manager is an ideal way to generate a fully formatted, custom home page containing the links you like the most, organized however you wish. You can include several layers of headings, descriptions of each link, and even separators to mark off unrelated items.

To export your bookmarks, follow these steps:

1. In the Bookmark Manager, organize your bookmarks as desired, including entering headings, descriptive text, and separators.

2. From the Bookmark Manager's File menu, select **Save as**.... A dialog box will be displayed.

3. Name and save the file. When you open it using the **Open File…** command, you'll see a formatted document containing your information.

Complete information about working with bookmarks can be found in Chapter 4.

Using Wizards

Wizards are programs that "interview" you about the desired contents of your Web pages by asking simple questions, and then create an HTML file for you based on your answers. Some wizards will also import your bookmarks into the file that they create.

A popular, easy-to-use wizard for the Windows platform is Web Wizard (aka The Duke of URL), available at http://www.halcyon.com/ artamedia/webwizard. Web Wizard (Figure 21.1) asks you to enter a title; choose a background pattern, color, or graphic; identify other graphics that you wish to include; and enter the names and URLs of links that you want on your home page. Web Wizard then creates an HTML file that contains all the information that you entered.

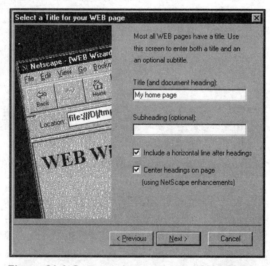

Figure 21.1 Creating a home page with Web Wizard.

Translators

A number of programs are available that turn existing documents into HTML files. The most popular of these is probably RTFtoHTML (information and program files are available at http://help.unc.edu/oit/share-ware/info/rtftohtml/rtftohtml_overview.html), which converts files saved in Microsoft's popular Rich Text Format into HTML documents. The advantage of this kind of program is that it preserves some of the formatting of the original document. You can create a document in Microsoft Word, save it as an RTF file, run it through RTFtoHTML, and have the same headings and styles as you did in the original.

A disadvantage of this kind of translator is that it isn't URL-aware; if you wish to include active links, you'll need to add them manually to the HTML file.

Text Editors Supporting HTML

Support for the HTML format is becoming increasingly popular in text and word processors for all platforms. For example, you can install Microsoft's Internet Assistant for Word for Windows (version 6.0 or later), which allows you to use a **Save as HTML** command so that your formatted Word document is immediately converted to HTML. As with translators, you'll still need to manually enter information about graphics and hyperlinks, but this is a simple way to create a nicely formatted document.

Customized Start Pages on Corporate Sites

Another option for customized pages that's recently become available is the ability to create a personal starting points page that's housed on a corporate site, such as at Netscape or the Microsoft Network. By letting users customize the information that's presented to them, the companies attempt to guarantee that you'll connect to their Web site each time you log on. Basically, these sites use wizards (as described above) to let you create a personal start page with custom links and up-to-the-minute information that's updated every time you connect to the site.

These custom start pages are not the same as having a "home page" on the World Wide Web; no one but you can view the information that you choose to place on your page. These pages take advantage of a technology called *cookies*, which store personal information (such as your favorite URLs) on your own computer. Each time you connect to a server that created a cookie, the server retrieves the cookie from your computer and presents you with your personalized information. (More information about cookies can be found in Chapter 19.)

Netscape's Personal Workspace

Netscape's contribution to the online customized page is the Personal Workspace, where you can create a page with any or all of the following features:

- The title, layout, and graphic of your choice, including a few nifty animated graphics.

- Your choice of colors for text, links, and background (as well as a selection of background patterns).

- A "Notepad" where you can type notes to yourself that will be there the next time you launch Netscape.

- The links of your choice. You can select from a variety of links provided by Netscape, or you can add as many of your own as you wish.

A completed Personal Workspace is shown in Figure 21.2.

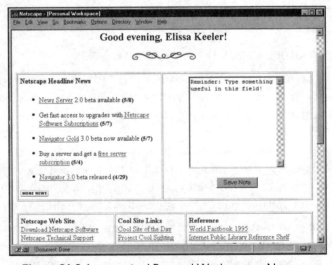

Figure 21.2 A customized Personal Workspace at Netscape.

To create a Personal Workspace, use the URL http://home.netscape.com/ custom/index.html (or follow the links for **My Page** at Netscape's home page; if you don't already have a Personal Workspace you'll be taken to the creation pages). Then, just follow the instructions in the frames. To visit your own Personal Workspace, add it to your bookmark list, or set it as your home page (for more information, see Chapter 2). Or, you can always just click the link for **My Page** at Netscape's home page. (The URL for your Personal Workspace will be http://home.netscape.com/custom/ show_page.html.)

Custom Start Page from MSN

The Microsoft Network also lets you customize your start page, and luckily, you don't have to subscribe to the Microsoft Network or use Microsoft's Internet Explorer browser to take advantage of this feature. As much as we hate to say it, MSN's customized start page is superior to Netscape's, at least at the time of this writing. While MSN doesn't let you change the layout of the page or choose a graphic, they do something more useful that Netscape doesn't: they provide links directly on your start page to the current information of your choice, such as stock quotes or sports scores. The bad news is, there are a few features such as background color and certain optional sounds that you can only use with the Microsoft browser, and there's a lot more advertising for Microsoft on their page than there is on a similar page at Netscape.

To create a custom start page at MSN, use the URL http://www.msn.com and click the link that says **Customize This Page**. After you enter the information, your custom start page will be displayed every time you go to the top level of the site.

WARNING

If you return to your custom start page at http://www.msn.com using the **Back** button, you may see a "Data Missing" error message. If this happens, just click the **Reload** button and your custom start page will reappear.

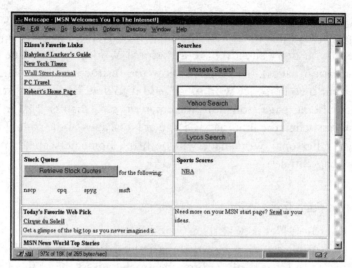

Figure 21.3 Custom start page at MSN.

Ways to Create Web Pages Using HTML

Creating Web pages by hand requires that you use some kind of text editor. The kinds of text editors that you can use to create HTML files fall into three categories: simple editors, tagged editors, and WYSIWYG editors.

Using Simple Text Editors

You can always use the text editors that shipped with your operating system—such as NotePad, WordPad, TeachText, SimpleText, xedit, or vi—to create HTML files. Using a simple text editor requires the greatest knowledge of HTML syntax, since you must type everything by hand. But using a simple text editor is a tried-and-true method guaranteed to work on any platform, and it gives you the greatest amount of control over the appearance of your files. Also, simple text editors won't require upgrading or updating when new HTML tags are adopted.

Using Tagged Editors

Tagged editors are essentially simple text editors that have additional built-in commands to create or modify HTML tags. Tagged editors still require knowledge of HTML syntax, but they automate the procedures to decrease the amount of time spent typing tags as well as the chance of typographical errors in the HTML codes.

Typically, tagged editors contain a menu heading for HTML items. When you reach a place in the document where you wish to include an HTML tag, you select the text in the document you wish to tag and issue the desired command from the HTML menu. The code for the tag is inserted into the document, and you enter the information that should appear within the tag. Some tagged editors will actually prompt you for information—such as providing a dialog box for you to locate a graphic you wish to include—but you still need some understanding of HTML to answer the questions you're being asked. Tagged editors often have viewing modes that let you see what your HTML file will look like in a browser.

NOTE Popular tagged HTML editors include BBEdit with HTML Extensions and HTML Writer; shareware versions of these products are commonly available online. The chapters on configuring helper applications (Chapters 9-11, depending on your platform) each contain information for downloading a common HTML editor for your platform. Or, see Chapter 23 for instructions on using Web search engines to find up-to-date locations for these files.

WYSIWYG Editors

WYSIWYG (pronounced wizzy-wig) is short for "what you see is what you get," a phrase commonly used to describe graphical applications such as word processors in which documents appear on the screen as they'll actually look on paper. When you use a WYSIWYG HTML editor, you'll never see the raw HTML tags as you do with simple or tagged editors. Instead, you'll type the information, select the text that should be formatted, and select the appropriate style for the text from the menu. The tag will be hidden from your view—instead, you'll see the text as it will appear in a browser. WYSIWYG editors are analogous to common word processors like Microsoft Word or WordPerfect for Windows; you never see the codes that describe the text format, you only see the formatted text as you wish it to appear.

For example, in a tagged editor, the codes to create a line of bold text in your file would look like this:

```
<B> This text is bold. </B>
```

But in a WYSIWYG editor, the text in the file would appear like this:

This text is bold.

NOTE

Don't worry about what those <B> and </B> tags mean yet; we'll talk about them in the next section. We're only using them here to illustrate the differences between the editors.

Like most word processors, WYSIWYG editors let you insert graphics either by pasting them directly into the document or by identifying a file to insert.

WYSIWYG editors have their advantages, as they're comparatively easy to use and don't require you to type occasionally complicated HTML codes. But, when you use a WYSIWYG editor, you're limited to the HTML codes that the editor already knows. You can't use new extensions without upgrading the editor, and depending on the editor, you might not be able to perform minor modifications on the code that you've created unless you reopen the file with a simple or tagged editor and make the changes there. This is an important point, since new HTML tags are created frequently.

A popular WYSIWYG editor for HTML on Windows and Sun OS platforms is HoTMetaL Free, available at http://www.sq.com/products/hotmetal/hm-ftp.htm. (A Macintosh version is in development and may be available by the time you read this.) Another popular WYSIWYG HTML editor is Hot Dog, available at http://www.sausage.com/dogindex.htm. Unfortunately, the downloadable versions expire after 30 days.

NOTE

If you're planning to do some serious HTML development, Adobe's Page Mill is considered to be one of the best products around. However, because it's a commercial product, you'll have to pay for it: at the time of this writing, the retail price was about $100.

VIRTUOSO

You may also want to try Netscape Navigator Gold, which incorporates a WYSIWYG HTML editor and an FTP uploading tool directly into the browser. We'll talk about using Gold, including its advantages and disadvantages, after the HTML primer.

A Basic HTML Primer

If you're going to create your Web page in any fashion besides automatic generation, you're going to need a basic understanding of common HTML tags and how they're used. This section contains an introduction to the most common HTML tags, such as tags for formatting text, placing graphics, and including URLs as links to other documents. All the examples will be created in a simple text editor so that you experience the entire HTML development process.

NOTE

We're only going to talk about basic HTML codes for creating personal home pages. We're not going to cover Netscape's advanced extensions to HTML for items such as frames, tables, and animation or the use of CGI for forms and image maps. As soon as you master the basic techniques of creating Web documents, you can consult the ample documentation available online for using these features. But, as with any other skill, it's crucial that you learn to walk before you learn to fly.

The Basics About Files and Tags

Here's a short list of the most basic information about using HTML that you need to know.

About Files

HTML files are always plain ASCII text. All the formatting information is included within tags that you create. In general, you should always save your HTML files with the **.html** extension to ensure that the browser will recognize them. (If you're using Windows 3.1 and are limited to the 8.3 file-naming convention, use the **.htm** extension.)

About Tags

Tags appear as angle brackets containing the HTML code. For example, the code to begin bold text is **<B>**.

Tags are either *matched* or *unmatched*. Unmatched tags require only a beginning tag. For example, the code to insert a horizontal rule on the page is **<HR>**. Such a tag can appear by itself, because it's obvious where the rule begins and ends.

A matched tag, on the other hand, requires a beginning code and an end code to mark the text that the code applies to. The tag that marks the end of the text contains the same code, preceded by a slash (/).

For example, using bold text requires a matched tag. The code to begin bold text is **<B>**. The code to end the bold text is **</B>**. To set off a phrase in bold text, the matched tags would be like this:

```
<B> This text is bold </B> but this text is not.
```

That text would appear as

This text is bold but this text is not.

About Text

For basic HTML, there are no codes to mark where lines of text should begin or end, as the length of lines will always vary depending on how the person looking at the document has configured their browser. (Check out Chapter 3, "Customizing Netscape's Look and Feel," for more information about how that works.) We'll discuss how to force a browser to display a document with line breaks and other items exactly how you want them at the end of the basic HTML primer.

Getting Started

As a concrete example, let's look at a basic HTML document.

```
<HTML>
<TITLE>Quick and Easy Recipes!</TITLE>
<BODY>
<H1>Quick and Easy Recipes for Anyone At All</H1>
<P>This document contains instructions for some very easy
recipes, as well as links to other sites on the Web where
you can find recipes and general information about cooking.
</BODY>
</HTML>
```

Here's a description of the tags used in that document:

- <HTML> and </HTML> are a required set of matched tags that mark the beginning and end of the file.

- <TITLE> and </TITLE> are an optional set of matched tags that mark the title of the document that you wish to appear in the banner of the window. If you don't include <TITLE> tags, then the URL of the document is displayed in the banner.

- <BODY> and </BODY> are a required set of matched tags that mark the beginning and end of the body of the document—that is, the part of the document that's visible in the browser.

- <H1> and </H1> are matched tags that denote the first heading level. Like an outline, an HTML document can contain multiple levels of headings.

- <P> marks the beginning of a paragraph. Although it's technically a matched tag, in simple cases like this the </P> is implied by the fact that another <P> paragraph has begun.

Figure 21.4 shows the current document as displayed in Netscape.

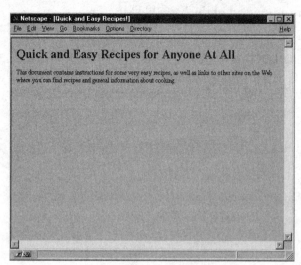

Figure 21.4 Our document so far.

Adding More Kinds of Text

Now that we've started our document, let's add an actual easy recipe for Quick Beer Bread. We're going to add the following elements:

- A horizontal rule to separate the recipe from the first paragraph.
- A second-level heading for the title of the recipe.
- Third-level headings for the ingredients and instructions.
- A bulleted list for the ingredients, since they can appear in any order.
- A numbered list for the instructions, since you must perform the steps in order.

Let's take a look at the code for the document with this additional information:

```
<HTML>

<TITLE>Quick and Easy Recipes!</TITLE>
```

```
<BODY>

<H1>Quick and Easy Recipes for Anyone At All</H1>

<P>This document contains instructions for some very easy
recipes, as well as links to other sites on the Web where
you can find recipes and general information about cooking.

<HR>

<H2>Quick Beer Bread</H2>

<P>This bread is just about foolproof, and contains
absolutely no cholesterol.

<H3>Ingredients</H3>

<P>You can use any kind of beer you want. Darker beers will
make the bread taste somewhat richer.

<UL>

<LI>One bottle (12 ounces) warm beer

<LI>3 cups self-rising flour

<LI>3 tablespoons of sugar

</UL>

<H3>Cooking Instructions</H3>

<OL>

<LI>Preheat the oven to 375 degrees.

<LI>Combine the flour and sugar in a large mixing bowl.

<LI>Add beer slowly and mix until all the flour is mixed
into the batter.

<LI>Pour the batter into a greased loaf pan.

<LI>Bake for 45 minutes, or until a toothpick inserted into
the middle of the loaf comes out clean. Cool 10 minutes
before slicing.

</OL>

</BODY>

</HTML>
```

Displayed in a browser, the most recent version of the document looks like Figure 21.5.

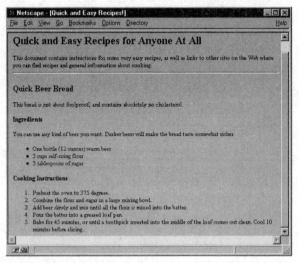

Figure 21.5 Our HTML document with the recipe included.

Here's a description of the new elements that we added:

- <HR> created the line that acts as a visual separator between the first paragraph of the document and the recipe.

- The matched <H2> and <H3> pairs created more levels of headings in the document.

- To create a bulleted list, we used the unordered list tag <UL>. This tag requires a matched </UL> to mark where the unnumbered list ends. Each item in the list was marked with an unmatched <LI>.

- To created a numbered list, we used the ordered list tag <OL>, which requires a matched </OL> to mark where the ordered list ends. As in the unordered list, each item was marked with an unmatched <LI>.

Including an Inline Image in a Document

Placing an inline image in a document requires the use of a special tag. To include an image called cook.gif in our document, the tag would look like:

```
<IMG SRC="cook.gif">
```

NOTE

If the image is in the same directory or folder as the document, you only need to include the simple file within the tag. If the image resides in a different directory or on a different Web site, other rules apply.

An extremely useful extension to HTML developed by Netscape is the ability to align images to the left, right, or center of text, allowing the words to flow around the image. For example, to place the graphic cook.gif in our document so that it appears to the left of the first paragraph, the code would look like this:

```
<IMG SRC="cook.gif" ALIGN=LEFT>This document contains
instructions for some very easy recipes, as well as links to
other sites on the Web where you can find recipes and gen-
eral information about cooking.
```

Our document with the added graphic looks like Figure 21.6.

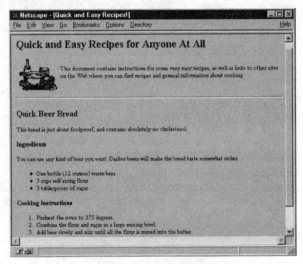

Figure 21.6 Document with graphic added.

If you want the text to start on the next line instead of next to the graphic, use the line break tag (<BR>) between the picture and the text.

Another feature of the IMG element allows you to add alternate text that will only be displayed to users who are not loading graphics. The ALT feature is used in the following way:

```
<IMG SRC="cook.gif" ALIGN=LEFT ALT="some cooking
utensils">This document contains instructions for some very
easy recipes, as well as links to other sites on the Web
where you can find recipes and general information about
cooking.
```

In Figure 21.7, the document is shown with Auto Load Images turned off, so that the alternate text is displayed.

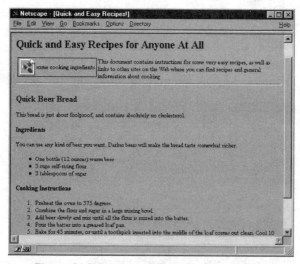

Figure 21.7 Document displaying alternate text.

Including URLs in a Document

Links to other documents on the Web use the following format:

```
<A HREF="url">descriptive text</A>
```

For example, to include a link to the Ragu Spaghetti Sauce Web site—which has lots of Italian recipes—and to a few other food locations on the Web, we might add the following to the end of our document:

```
<HR>

<H2>Other Sites with Recipes</H2>

<UL>

<LI>

<A HREF="http://www.eat.com">The Ragu site </A>contains sev-
eral good Italian recipes. (You can modify them as needed if
you don't want to use Ragu products.)

<LI>

<A
HREF="http://www.sar.usf.edu/~zazuetaa/recipe.html">Ridiculo
usly Easy Recipes</A> are exactly what they say they are.

<LI>You can always find whatever you want at <A
HREF="http://www.yahoo.com/Entertainment/Food_and_Eating/
Recipes/">Yahoo's cooking section</A>.
```

WARNING

If you're using a word processor instead of an HTML editor, it's absolutely critical that you turn off the "Smart Quotes" or "Curly Quotes" feature. These aren't standard ASCII characters and can cause severe problems for browsers.

Putting It All Together...

The code for the complete document we've created so far looks like this:

```
<HTML>

<TITLE>Quick and Easy Recipes!</TITLE>

<BODY>

<H1>Quick and Easy Recipes for Anyone At All</H1>
```

```
<IMG SRC="cook.gif" ALIGN=LEFT ALT="some cooking ingredi-
ents">This document contains instructions for some very easy
recipes, as well as links to other sites on the Web where
you can find recipes and general information about cooking.

<HR>

<H2>Quick Beer Bread</H2>

<P>This bread is just about foolproof, and contains
absolutely no cholesterol.

<H3>Ingredients</H3>

<P>You can use any kind of beer you want. Darker beers will
make the bread taste somewhat richer.

<UL>

<LI>One bottle (12 ounces) warm beer

<LI>3 cups self-rising flour

<LI>3 tablespoons of sugar

</UL>

<H3>Cooking Instructions</H3>

<OL>

<LI>Preheat the oven to 375 degrees.

<LI>Combine the flour and sugar in a large mixing bowl.

<LI>Add beer slowly and mix until all the flour is mixed
into the batter.

<LI>Pour the batter into a greased loaf pan.

<LI>Bake for 45 minutes, or until a toothpick inserted into
the middle of the loaf comes out clean. Cool 10 minutes
before slicing.

</OL>

<HR>

<H2>Other Sites with Recipes</H2>

<UL>
```

```
<LI>

<A HREF="http://www.eat.com">The Ragu site </A>contains sev-
eral good Italian recipes. (You can modify them as needed if
you don't want to use Ragu products.)

<LI>

<A HREF="http://www.sar.usf.edu/~zazuetaa/recipe.html">
Ridiculously Easy Recipes </A> are exactly what they say
they are.

<LI>You can always find whatever you want at <A
HREF="http://www.yahoo.com/Entertainment/Food_and_Eating/Rec
ipes/">Yahoo's cooking section</A>.

</UL>

</BODY>

</HTML>
```

And the complete page looks like Figure 21.8.

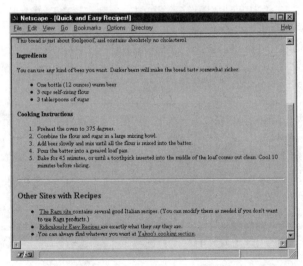

Figure 21.8 Completed page with links and graphics.

Emphasizing Text: Logical versus Absolute Markup

In the sample document above, we didn't apply any kind of style or emphasis to the text such as boldface, italics, or underlining. Before learning these commands, it's important to understand a distinction that markup languages such as HTML make between *logical* and *absolute* markup codes.

Strictly speaking, a markup language should never tell the viewer application how an item should look—it should only describe the style, and then let the application decide how that style should be displayed. Instead of saying "Make this text bold," a markup language would say "Make this text emphasized," and would leave it up to the application whether emphasized text is displayed in bold, italic, or in some other style such as colored text. This is referred to as logical markup because the language only describes the kind of style; it's up to the viewing application to decide what it actually looks like.

Absolute markup, on the other hand, always overrides the viewing application's settings to say "no matter what, display this text as bold" (or italic, or underline, etc.).

Although it's somewhat in violation of the principle of markup languages to use absolute references instead of logical references, the absolute codes for boldface (<B> and </B>), italics (<ITAL> and </ITAL>), and underlining (<U> and </U>) are used quite frequently in HTML documents on the Web, while logical markup codes such as "strong emphasis" (<STRONG> and </STRONG>) are used rather infrequently.

In all cases, these codes surround the text that you wish to be displayed in the coded style.

About Spaces in Documents

Browsers do not recognize the common methods of adding space to a document that you may be accustomed to using in word processors. For example, it doesn't matter how many spaces you place between words in an HTML file; a browser will only display a single space. Hard carriage returns that might be used to create additional space between lines are also treated only as spaces by the browser. In the next section, we'll talk about ways to increase the space between lines, which is known as *leading*.

Adding Leading to a Document

Two different unmatched tags are used to mark the ends of lines and to add space: <P>, which defines the beginning of a new paragraph, and <BR>, which defines a line break.

Though they may appear similar, the two commands are used in different ways. If you want to end a paragraph and begin a new one with a single line of white space between them, use the <P> command. If you want to end a paragraph and begin a new one with *no* white space between the lines, use the <BR> command.

To separate paragraphs in a regular document, the <P> command is the easiest to use. However, you can only use one <P> command at a time—browsers will ignore additional paragraph codes that don't contain any text. If you need more than one line of white space, you can use several <BR> codes, since HTML lets you "stack" those commands.

Modifying the Background Color

Netscape Communications has added an extension to HTML that allows you to specify the background color of a page. The color is specified as an addition to the <BODY> tag, using the following syntax:

```
<BODY BGCOLOR="#rrggbb">
```

where rr, gg, and bb are the hexadecimal codes identifying the red, green, and blue components of the color. A common example would look like:

```
<BODY BGCOLOR="#F0F0F0">
```

This is the standard light gray background color that Netscape displays by default.

Don't worry, you don't need to learn how to speak hexadecimal in order to use a pretty background color. Check out the color index at http://www.infi.net/wwwimages/colorindex.html, where you can see hundreds of different background colors and simply select the corresponding hexadecimal codes to copy into your document.

A Chart of Common HTML Commands

Table 21.1 is a reference guide for the HTML commands that you're most likely to need when creating documents. Items that appear in parentheses refer to the part of the document that appears between the tags.

Table 21.1 Common HTML Commands

Use	Tag	Matched Tag (if required)
define document	<HTML>	(entire document)</HTML>
document header	<HEAD>	(document header)</HEAD>
document body	<BODY>	(document body)</BODY>
document title	<TITLE>	(title line)</TITLE>
largest head	<H1>	(head line)</H1>
smaller head	<H2>	(head line)</H2>
smaller head	<H3>	(head line)</H3>
smaller head	<H4>	(head line)</H4>
smaller head	<H5>	(head line)</H5>
smallest head	<H6>	(head line)</H6>
new paragraph	<P>	(paragraph text)</P> Note: In practice, the closing tag isn't used.
line break	 	
horizontal rule	<HR SIZE=n>	
citation	<CITE>	(text)</CITE>
program code	<CODE>	(text)</CODE>
emphasis	<EM>	(text)</EM>

Table 21.1 Common HTML Commands (continued)

Use	Tag	Matched Tag (if required)
stronger emphasis	<STRONG>	(text)</STRONG>
bold	<B>	(text)</B>
italic	<I>	(text)</I>
typewriter	<TT>	(text)</TT>
underlined	<U>	(text)</U>
blink	<BLINK>	(text)</BLINK>
font size	<FONT SIZE=n>	(text)
font color	<FONT COLOR="rrggbb"	(text)</FONT>
centering	<CENTER>	(text)</CENTER>
address format	<ADDRESS>	(text)</ADDRESS>
block quote	<BLOCKQUOTE>	(text)</BLOCKQUOTE>
preformatted passage	<PRE>	(text)</PRE>
numbered list	<OL>	(list)</OL>
bulleted list	<UL>	(list)</UL>
list item	<LI>	(list item)
link to	<A HREF=file>	(link text)</A>
link to	<A HREF=url>	(link text)</A>
anchor	<A NAME=xx>	
inline image	<IMG SRC=url>	
inline image	<IMG SRC=file>	

Using Netscape to View Your Document

This section describes various ways that Netscape can be used to view your HTML documents.

Opening the Document with Netscape

To view your HTML file with Netscape, follow these steps:

1. Save the file with the .html or .htm extension. (If you're using a word processor instead of an HTML editor, be sure to save it as plain ASCII text.)

2. Use one of the following methods to display the file in Netscape:

   • Drag and drop the icon for the file onto Netscape. The browser will launch and display the file.

   • If Netscape is open, select the **Open File...** command in the File menu and locate the file you're working on.

If Netscape is open, you can also drag the icon for the file directly into the open browser window.

SHORTCUT

Viewing Your Changes in Netscape

You can keep Netscape open while you work on the file so you can see changes immediately. To ensure that you're always looking at the most recent version of the file, follow these steps (which assume that Netscape is already open and the file is already loaded):

VIRTUOSO

1. As you make changes to the file in the text editor, save the file so that the changes are stored on the disk drive.

2. Switch to the Netscape application. The old version of your document should still be displayed.

3. Click the **Reload** button or select **Reload** from the View menu. Netscape will reload the newer, saved version of the document from your disk drive.

WARNING

If you're looking at a local document in Netscape, be sure that you don't make the common mistake of using the **View Source** command in the View menu to look at the HTML code for a file, and then attempting to edit the HTML code displayed as a result! The View Source command is strictly for looking at the code of a document; it actually creates a temporary version of the HTML document that lasts only as long as you view the document. If you attempt to edit a file displayed in this way, your changes simply won't be available to the browser. If you intend to modify the HTML of a remote document, use the **Save as...** command to save the source code as a separate file before you begin. If you're working locally, you should always be sure to go back to the editor and work with the actual named HTML file that you created.

Using Netscape Navigator Gold

Netscape Navigator Gold is a version of the Netscape Navigator browser that includes a reasonably robust WYSIWYG HTML editor. Some of the advantages of Navigator Gold include the following:

- As with Netscape's other tools, a free version of Navigator Gold 3.0 can be downloaded from Netscape Communications' FTP sites.

- The editor is built right into the browser, so you can not only view the results of your own documents but you can also easily modify documents that come across on the Web.

- Navigator Gold 3.0 has a table editor, which easily lets you create and insert tables into your own documents.

- Gold has a built-in method of uploading all the files associated with a page, so if you're creating public pages, you can move all the files for your pages in a single step. (We'll talk about this more in the next chapter.)

However, Gold has some disadvantages as well:

- If you want to edit the HTML directly to tweak it into shape or create a certain effect, you have to use another program that lets you manipulate the code directly. However, Navigator Gold does let you set a default text editor to use for working directly with the source code.

- The built-in help for Navigator Gold explains each command individually, but it is difficult to use if you need a conceptual overview of the software or guidance about which procedure to use.

- In some cases, the WYSIWYG concept doesn't hold true. For example, some kinds of changes to the way that text wraps around graphics or to the display of numbers in a numbered list will only be visible when you look at the document in a browser window; what you see in the text editor is not always what you get in the browser, despite claims otherwise.

Despite these limitations, Navigator Gold is a handy way to create HTML if you don't need a professional-level development tool.

NOTE A complete treatment of Navigator Gold's functionality is beyond the scope of this chapter. However, after working through this section, you should be reasonably adept at using Gold to create simple, elegant HTML documents.

About Navigator Gold

Changes in the Browser Window

If you use Navigator Gold after using the regular Netscape browser, you'll notice that certain items are different. First of all, the toolbar in the browser window will contain a new item: the **Edit** button, which downloads the current document to your disk drive and opens it in the HTML editor. Second, you'll find the following additional commands in the File menu:

- **New Document**. Lets you create a new document from scratch.
- **Edit Document**. The same as the Edit button in the toolbar—lets you edit the document currently displayed.
- **Open File in Browser**.... The same as Open File... in regular Netscape. Opens the file that you select in the browser window.
- **Open File in Editor**.... Lets you open the selected file in Gold's HTML editor.

WARNING

In the supported commercial release of Netscape Navigator Gold 2.01, the dialog box displayed by the Open File in Editor... command had only two options for the **Files of Type:** pop-up menu: **HTML files** and **Netscape Default Plugin (*.*)**. Although selecting **Netscape Default Plugin (*.*)** lets you see all the files in your directories, Gold will not let you open any file for editing that doesn't end with the .htm or .html extension. So, if you plan to work with an existing file on your disk drive, make sure that its name ends with .htm or .html—even if it's really only a text file. (The dialog box in the beta release of Netscape Navigator Gold 3.0 showed **HTML Files** and all the file extensions associated with the default plug-in as well as a *.* extension at the bottom of the list; however, you can't open the various sound and VRML files with the editor, and selecting *.* doesn't work: you'll still only see the text files that have the correct HTML extension.)

WARNING

Another problem associated with opening text files in Gold has to do with the way that different kinds of computers handle line breaks and carriage returns. (We discussed this problem in Chapter 4, when we talked about problems importing bookmarks.) If you attempt to edit a text file that was created on another kind of computer, you may open it in the editor to find that all the line breaks have disappeared. If this occurs, you'll need to add them manually.

Another change is in the Go menu, which contains a command called **Default Publishing Location**. This takes you to the default publishing location for your files that you specify in the Editor Preferences.

Additional Options in Preferences

In the Options menu, you'll notice a new item: **Editor Preferences**. This lets you configure some basic properties for the HTML editor. The Editor Preferences window contains the following sections:

- General. This window lets you enter your name as the author of the document; configure external applications for directly editing images or HTML tags; and set up a new default location for templates. (This is only important if you use templates to create your documents and don't want to use Netscape's.)

- Appearance. This window lets you customize color schemes and background patterns to use as the default for your documents. If you change settings in this window, keep in mind that the new settings will apply to new documents, not to any documents that are currently open in the editor.

- Publish. This window lets you set the options to be used when uploading files to a Web site. We'll talk more about using Navigator Gold to place Web pages on a public server in Chapter 22.

About the Editor Window

The editor window can be opened in several ways. To edit the document that's currently displayed in the browser, click the **Edit** button on the toolbar or select **Edit Document** from the File menu. To create a new, blank document, select one of the **New Document** options in the File menu. (We'll talk about these options in the next section.)

The editor window is shown in Figure 21.9.

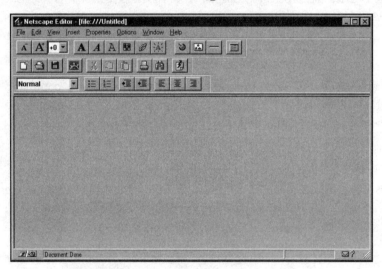

Figure 21.9 The Navigator Gold Editor window.

The editor window contains the following elements:

- Menu bar. These drop-down menus contain all the commands that you can use in the Gold editor. Most of these commands are also available on the toolbars or the pop-up menu.

- Toolbars. The toolbars contain buttons for the most common commands you'll use in creating HTML documents, such as changing the size and color of fonts and adding links, anchors, graphics, rules, and more. More information about the toolbars can be found in the next section.

VIRTUOSO

To find out what each item does, hold the mouse over the item. A label will appear beneath the pointer and an explanation will be explained in the status area.

- The editing window is where you'll actually create or edit the HTML document.

About the Toolbars

There are three toolbars in Navigator Gold: the Character Format toolbar, the File/Edit toolbar; and the Paragraph Format toolbar.

NOTE

The toolbars in the Navigator Gold editor will always be displayed in pictures, even if you set Netscape's general preferences to display the browser's toolbar as text, or as pictures and text. To turn on or off the display of individual toolbars, select the name of the toolbar from the Options menu in the editor window.

The Character Format toolbar (Figure 21.10) lets you easily apply and remove character formatting such as bold, italic, and colors to text. It also contains tools to insert links to other documents, named targets, graphics, and horizontal rules.

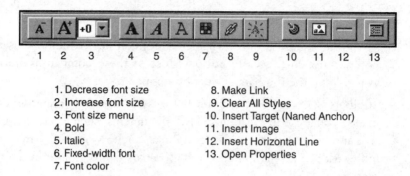

1. Decrease font size
2. Increase font size
3. Font size menu
4. Bold
5. Italic
6. Fixed-width font
7. Font color

8. Make Link
9. Clear All Styles
10. Insert Target (Naned Anchor)
11. Insert Image
12. Insert Horizontal Line
13. Open Properties

Figure 21.10 Character Format toolbar.

The File/Edit toolbar (Figure 21.11) lets you edit text, view the file in the Netscape browser, and upload files to Web or FTP sites.

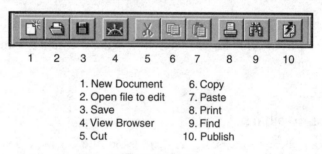

1. New Document
2. Open file to edit
3. Save
4. View Browser
5. Cut

6. Copy
7. Paste
8. Print
9. Find
10. Publish

Figure 21.11 File/Edit toolbar.

The Paragraph Format toolbar (Figure 21.12) lets you apply styles to selected paragraphs, such as headings or list items, and control the indentation and alignment of text.

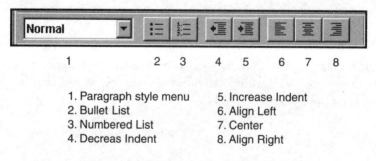

1. Paragraph style menu
2. Bullet List
3. Numbered List
4. Decreas Indent

5. Increase Indent
6. Align Left
7. Center
8. Align Right

Figure 21.12 Paragraph Format toolbar.

Creating a Document with Gold

Three options are available for creating a new document with Navigator Gold: creating a blank document, creating a document using a predefined template, and creating a document using a wizard at Netscape. To create a document, follow these steps:

1. In the browser or in the editor window, drag the mouse to the **New Document** item in the File menu.
2. Select **Blank**, **From Template**, or **From Wizard...** as desired.

NOTE

The **From Template** and **From Wizard...** options will attempt to establish a connection to Netscape's Web site.

About Templates

As a service to the users of Navigator Gold, Netscape has provided an online site that contains predesigned templates that you can customize; you'll find templates for resumes, family pages, sales announcements, departmental information, special interest groups, and more. To use them, just follow the steps provided by Netscape.

VIRTUOSO

Even if you don't want to use Netscape's templates, you can get good ideas for layout and design from these samples. You'll find lots of good getting-started pointers at http://home.netscape.com/assist/net_sites/starter/samples/index.html, and some interesting animated graphics that you can use in your own pages at http://home.netscape.com/assist/net_sites/starter/samples/animate.html.

About Wizards

If you select **From Wizard...** to create a new document, you'll be taken to an online wizard at Netscape that's very similar to the one used to create a Personal Workspace (discussed earlier in this chapter), but without the personal features. The wizard will step you through the general procedure for building a home page, including creating a title, writing an introduction, adding links and an email address, and choosing colors, bullets, and rules.

NOTE When you use the wizard to create a home page, you're actually creating it online at Netscape's site—if you want to keep the page you create, you have to follow their special instructions to save it to your disk drive.

Saving Documents in Navigator Gold

As with any computer application program, save your work early and save your work often. To save a document, follow these steps:

1. From the File menu, select **Save**.
2. Choose a location and enter a name for the document. (If this document will be placed on a public site, follow the rules for naming documents described in Chapter 22.)

NOTE If you don't use the .htm or .html file extension, Navigator Gold will automatically assign the .html extension.

3. Click **Save**.

Certain operations will cause Gold to prompt you to save your file, such as viewing it in the browser, adding graphics, or attempting to upload it to an online server.

Entering Text in the Window

You can enter text in the Gold editing window just like you would in a regular word processor. For this document, we'll use the same information we used in the sample at the beginning of the chapter.

Let's start by entering the first parts of the "Quick and Easy Recipes" file. We're just going to type the text—we'll apply styles such as headings, bullets, and numbered lists in the next section.

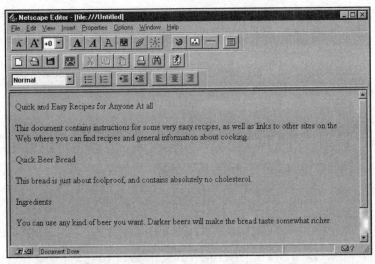

Figure 21.13 Unformatted text in the Navigator Gold window.

Applying Styles and Formats to Text

Applying styles and formats to text in Navigator Gold is just like formatting text in a word processor like Microsoft Word: type your text, select it, and choose the desired style. In this section, we'll work with the text from our original sample.

Adding and Removing Heading Styles

Adding Heading Styles

First, we'll apply the Heading 1 style to the first line of text. To do so, follow these steps:

1. Select the first line of text.

2. Perform one of the following actions:

   • From the Styles menu in the Paragraph Format toolbar, select **Heading 1**.

- In the Properties menu, drag the mouse to the **Paragraph** option. A list of styles will be displayed at the right; select **Heading 1**.

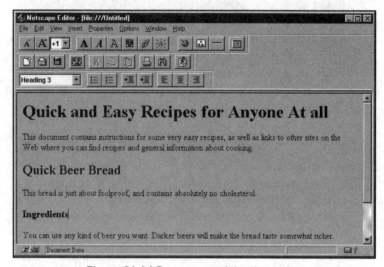

Figure 21.14 Document with heading styles.

We'll use the same steps to add the Heading 2 style to "Quick Beer Bread" and the Heading 3 style to "Ingredients."

Removing a Heading Style

To remove a heading style, follow these steps:

1. Select the text.
2. Perform one of the following actions:

- From the Styles menu in the Paragraph Format toolbar, select **Normal**.
- In the Properties menu, drag the mouse to the **Paragraph** option and select **Normal**.

Working with Bulleted and Numbered Lists

Adding a Bulleted List

To make the list of ingredients a bulleted list, follow these steps:

1. Select the three lines of ingredients.

2. Click the **Bullet List** button. (It's the one directly to the right of the Styles menu in the Paragraph Format toolbar; in Figure 21.15, the pointer shows the location.)

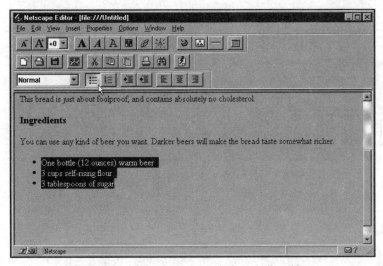

Figure 21.15 Applying the style for a bulleted list.

By default, applying a list style will indent the text one level. If you want the list to be displayed with no indentation, select it and click the **Decrease Indent** button on the Paragraph Format toolbar.

NOTE

Adding a Numbered List

To make the cooking procedures a numbered list, follow these steps:

1. Select the five paragraphs of procedures.

2. Click the **Numbered List** button. (It's the one directly to the right of the Bullet List button in the Paragraph Format toolbar; in Figure 21.16, the pointer shows the location.) The button will appear depressed, and the style will be applied.

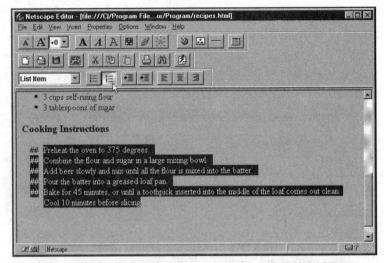

Figure 21.16 Applying the style for a numbered list.

You won't actually see numbers for the numbered list; placeholders are displayed instead. When you view the document in the browser, the correct numbers will be shown. (As we said, it's not exactly 100% WYSIWYG.)

NOTE

Removing List Formatting

To remove list formatting, select the text that's been formatted and click the appropriate button. (For a bulleted list, click the **Bullet List** button; for a numbered list, click the **Numbered List** button.) The button will no longer appear depressed, and the formatting will be removed.

In theory, you should be able to simply select the **Normal** style from the Styles menu to remove the formatting, but in practice, Gold has a minor bug. If you remove the list formatting by selecting the Normal style, the bullets or numbering are removed, but the text remains indented—it doesn't completely return to the Normal style. Use the **Decrease Indent** button on the Paragraph Format toolbar to return the text to its unindented state.

WARNING

Adding a Horizontal Rule

To add a horizontal rule, follow these steps:

1. Place the cursor in the desired location.

2. Click the **Horizontal Rule** button (the next-to-last item on the Character Format toolbar.) A rule will be inserted at the location of the cursor (Figure 21.17).

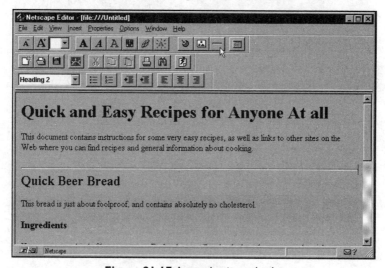

Figure 21.17 A new horizontal rule.

Want to change the height, width, or alignment of the rule? Just double-click it. The Horizontal Line Properties window will be displayed, where you can change a number of options.

VIRTUOSO

Adding a Graphic

Now, let's add the graphic called cook.gif. To add a graphic, follow these steps:

443

1. Place the mouse before the text that starts with "This document contains..." at the top of the page.

2. Click the **Insert Image** button on the Character Format toolbar (it's the third item from the end of the first row; it looks like a graphics placeholder), or select **Image...** from the Insert menu. The Properties window will be displayed, showing the options for an image (Figure 21.18).

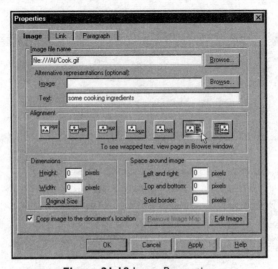

Figure 21.18 Image Properties.

3. In the Image file name field, click **Browse...** and locate the image.

4. In the Alternative Representations area, type the desired alternate text in the **Text** field.

5. In the Alignment area, click the button for aligning on the left (the next-to-last button in the field).

WARNING

Notice the warning that you won't see the text wrapped correctly unless you view it in the browser window! Otherwise, you may be very confused about why the text in the editor is in the wrong place.

6. Click **OK**. When you return to the editor, it'll look like Figure 21.19; select **Browse Document** from the File menu or click the **View in Browser** button (the anchor icon in the second row of the toolbar) to see it in the browser (Figure 21.20), where the text will be wrapped correctly.

Figure 21.19 Text does not wrap around a graphic in the editor window.

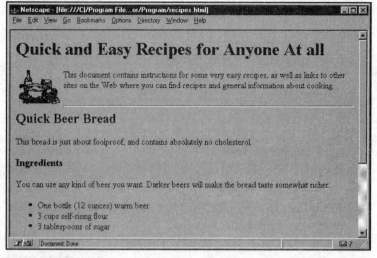

Figure 21.20 Our document in the browser with the text wrapped correctly.

To return to the editor, click the **Edit** button on the browser's toolbar.

Changing an Image's Properties

To change the image's properties (such as to replace it with another image, change the alternate text, or modify the alignment), display the Image Properties window in one of the following ways:

- Double-click the image.
- Left-click the image and select **Image Properties** from the pop-up menu.
- Select the image and choose **Image**... from the Properties menu or click the button on the toolbar.

Working with Links

Creating Links

To create the links to other sites, follow these steps:

1. Select the text that you want to appear to the user.
2. Click the **Make Link** button on the Character Format toolbar (it's on the top row and looks like a link in a chain) or select **Link**... from the Insert menu. The Link Properties window will be displayed.

SHORTCUT

Or, right-click the text and select **Create Link using selected...**.

3. In the **Link to a page location or local file** field, type the URL of the document you want to link to.
4. Click **OK**.

When you return to the document, the text will be highlighted in the color you chose for links.

To edit a URL, select the text and follow the steps above to display the Link Properties window.

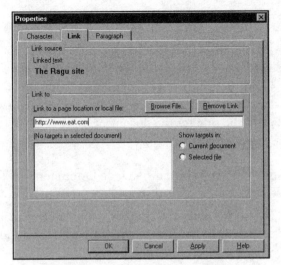

Figure 21.21 Link Properties window.

SHORTCUT

Or, left-click the text and select **Link properties...** from the pop-up menu.

VIRTUOSO

You can also embed a link in a graphic. Just select the graphic, click the **Make Link** button, and enter the link information as described above.

Removing Links

To remove a link, display the Link Properties window and delete the information.

SHORTCUT

Or, right-click the link and select **Remove Link**.

Adding the Title

When you create an HTML document from scratch, the title is usually one of the first things that you enter. But with a WYSIWYG editor like Navigator Gold, you don't create the initial <HTML>, <BODY>, and <TITLE> tags like you do in a text editor, so you might well forget that you need to add the title for the document.

To add a title, follow these steps:

1. From the Properties menu, select **Document...** The Document Properties window will be displayed.

2. In the **Title** field, enter the title for the document that should be displayed at the top of the browser window when the document is open.

3. Click **OK** to return to the editor.

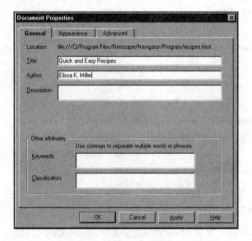

Figure 21.22 Document Properties window.

Navigator Gold Hints and Tips

As we said at the beginning, Navigator Gold is a reasonably sophisticated product that can't be fully covered in one chapter. However, this section contains some hints and tips for exploring Navigator Gold's features and for learning more about it on your own.

Many commands are available simultaneously in the toolbar, the pop-up menu, and the pull-down menus at the top of the screen. In this section, we've used the method that requires the fewest steps.

- In most dialog boxes, the **Help** button is active. Use it to find out the effects of the options in the window.

- The pop-up menu displayed by right-clicking an item is always different for different kinds of items. Try right-clicking normal text, links, graphics, and rules to see what options are available.

- To remove links that are embedded in text while keeping the text itself, select the area with the link and then select **Remove Links** from the Properties menu or **Remove all links in selection** from the pop-up menu.

- To change the style of characters, such as to use bold, italic, or superscript text or to change the color, highlight the text and use the appropriate button in the top row of the toolbar. To remove properties, select the text and click the appropriate button again; to remove multiple styles, click the **Clear All Styles** button (next to the button to create a link).

- When you type text directly into the editor, pressing the Return key will insert a paragraph break (a new <P> tag). If you want to use a regular line break (the <BR> tag), don't press Return; instead, select **New Line Break** from the Insert menu.

- To create targets within a document, click the **Insert Target** tag at the desired location and enter a name for the target. The next time you create a link, the name of the target will be visible in the Link Properties window. Selecting the name of the target creates a link that takes you to that target.

- If you're familiar with HTML and want to use a tag that isn't supported by the Gold editor, you can select **HTML Tag...** from the Insert menu to enter the desired tag.

- To create a table, use the **Table...** command from the Insert menu. The Table Properties window will let you create a table to your specifications.

Learning More About HTML

The following is a short list of online resources to help you get started learning more about HTML:

- You can find a comprehensive, up-to-date list of online reference material and tutorials at Yahoo (http://www.yahoo.com/Computers_and_Internet/Software/Data_Formats/HTML/). Keep in mind that Yahoo's structure changes frequently; if this URL doesn't work, you can search for the locations of their HTML categories at the first page.

- "A Beginner's Guide to HTML," at http://www.ncsa.uiuc.edu/General/Internet/WWW/HTMLPrimer.html. This basic primer, developed at NCSA, is one of the best general introductions to how HTML works.

- "A Beginner's Guide to URLs," at http://www.ncsa.uiuc.edu/demoweb/url-primer.html. Like "The Beginner's Guide to HTML," this provides basic information about how URLs are constructed and used.

- Netscape maintains a page of links to useful information about creating Web documents at http://home.netscape.com/home/how-to-create-web-services.html.

You can reach this page by selecting **How to Create Web Services** from the Help menu.

SHORTCUT

Additionally, your local bookstore will have dozens of books about online publishing and HTML design.

What You Learned

After reading this chapter, you should be able to:

- Identify various methods of creating Web documents.
- Evaluate HTML editors.
- Create a simple HTML document containing graphics, lists, rules, and links to other sites on the Web.
- Understand the basics of using the Netscape Navigator Gold editor.
- Find other resources to learn more about HTML.

CHAPTER 22

WORKING WITH PUBLIC WEB PAGES

In Chapter 21, we talked about how to develop a single Web page for local, private use. In this chapter, we're going to discuss various methods of electronic publishing, including making materials available for others to access, mining the Web for resources you can use in your own projects, and creating local copies of useful information.

Now that you understand the basics of working with HTML documents, we can explore some more advanced topics, including:

- Creating and working with multiple HTML documents
- Uploading your pages to a publicly accessible server
- Building local replicas of other Web sites to use for demonstrations or reference
- Extracting items from the Web for your own use
- Creating local Web sites on a LAN for sharing by workgroups

Working with Multiple Documents

In the last chapter, we created a single Web page to be accessed with a local URL. The inline image was stored in the same directory as the HTML document, and we only created one new page. There weren't links to other HTML documents that we created, only links to known documents elsewhere on the Web. If you plan to make your Web pages accessible to the public, or if your project requires that you create more than one document, the situation is a little bit more complicated. You must construct the links and anchors in your document in a way that they'll still be correct when the documents are placed on a server.

NOTE

In this chapter, we'll be using *link* to mean a clickable item that takes you to another location, and *anchor* to mean a location within a document where you arrive as a result of clicking a link.

Working Locally

If you're creating a multipage document for local use, you can avoid a multitude of problems by following these two simple rules:

- Store every single item required by your pages—including HTML files and associated graphics—in the same directory or folder.

- When you construct anchors or links, only use the simple file name within the brackets. For example, a link to another document in the directory would be **<A HREF="document.html">** and a link for a GIF image would be **<IMG SRC="image.gif">**. By only specifying the names of the files, the browser will automatically look in the same directory as the current HTML file, whether the directory is on your disk drive or on a server.

WARNING

If you're using an HTML editor, you might find that it creates full pathnames in your links and anchors for items which appear in the same directory. If you don't plan on moving your directory or placing the files online, this isn't much of a problem. But if you do move the files, rename the directory, or upload the files to a server, the information in those tags will be entirely wrong. We'll discuss this problem more when we talk about document portability issues later in this chapter.

If you need to include links in your document that refer to items that reside elsewhere on the Web, use the full URL of the item you're including. For example, to link to a document at another Web site, use the construction <A HREF="http://host_name/path_name/file.html">. To include a graphic that's located at another site, use the same construction—e.g., <IMG SRC="http://host_name/path_name/image.gif">.

You can also construct links to multimedia objects like sounds or movies. For example, a link to a sound file would be <A HREF="http://host_name/ path_name/sound.au"> a sound</A> and a link to a movie would be <A HREF="http://host_name/path_name/movie.mpg">a video</A>.

VIRTUOSO

There are a number of other schemes that utilize what are known as *relative URLs*, which allow you to organize projects containing so many files that you can't keep them all in the same directory. Unfortunately, the issues involved in the construction of relative URLs are fairly complicated and beyond the scope of this book. You can find introductory information on this topic at http://www.ncsa.uiuc.edu/ demoweb/url-primer.html.

Links Within a Single Document

You may have noticed that some Web documents, such as FAQs and other long documents (including some of Netscape's own online manuals), have a "table of contents" at the top that appears as a series of clickable links. Instead of going to another file, these links take you to a designated location within the same document. The HTML construction that allows this is a powerful way to organize and provide access to large amounts of information without requiring several smaller, separate files. It's advantageous to the person reading the document, since as soon as the original document is loaded, they can navigate without waiting for another file to be accessed and without going back to the original document to select another item. Most importantly, this construction is highly portable; the single file can be copied anywhere and will still work, because it contains all the necessary links and information.

There are two steps involved in using this construction. First, you must identify the location in the file that you wish to link to by placing an anchor tag <A NAME="unique_name"> at the beginning of the line.

453

(Each location identified in this way must have a unique name.) Then, to create the link that takes you to this destination, use the tag **<A HREF="#unique_name">some text</A>**. When the reader clicks the link for **some text**, they'll jump to the location in the file that you identified in the anchor.

VIRTUOSO

You can even use links to named anchors in other people's documents, if the original creator included them. To link to a named location in a document elsewhere on the Web, use the construction **<A HREF="http://host_name/path_name/ file.html#unique_name">**, where the URL is the URL of the document you're accessing and the unique name is the one assigned to it by the creator. (To see the unique names, if any, in the document you're linking to, display the document and use the **View Source** command.) If you're jumping to an anchor located in a document in the same directory, you can use the simple construction **<A HREF="file.html#unique_name">**.

Creating Anchors with Netscape Navigator Gold

The HTML editor in Netscape Navigator Gold has a simple method for creating anchors. To create an anchor, follow these steps:

1. Place the cursor in the location where you want to put the anchor, or select a chunk of text.

2. Click the **Insert Target** (**Named Anchor**) button on the Character Format toolbar. The Target Properties window will be displayed.

3. In the Target Properties window, enter a name for the target. (If you selected text, then the words you selected will be displayed in the window by default.)

4. Click **OK**.

5. At the location where you wish the link to the target to appear, select the item you wish to link to the target and click the **Make Link** button. The Link Properties window will be displayed.

6. In the **Select a named target in the current document** field, select the name of the target you created.

7. Click **OK**. When you return to the editor window, the text will be a link to the target you selected.

To create links from one document to an anchor in another, follow these steps:

1. Follow steps 1–4, above, to create the target.

2. Save your changes to the document containing the target. (If you don't save the changes, then Gold won't be able to see the target that you created.)

3. Open the document that should contain the link to the target.

4. At the location where you wish the link to the target to appear, select the item you wish to link to the target and click the **Make Link** button. The Link Properties window will be displayed.

5. In the **Link to** area, click **Browse File**....

6. Locate and select the file containing the desired target. The name of the file will be displayed in the **Link to a page location or local file** field; the **Show targets in Selected file** radio button will be selected; and all named targets in that file will be displayed.

NOTE

To redisplay the targets in the current file, select the **Show targets in Current document** radio button.

7. Select the name of the desired target.

8. Click **OK**. When you return to the editor window, the text will be a link to the target you selected.

Placing Web Pages on a Public Server

Remember, your Web pages aren't available to the public until they're placed on a publicly accessible Web server. For most individuals, the Web server will be managed by their Internet service provider. The process of transferring files from your desktop computer to a publicly accessible Web server is generally called *uploading*.

In this section, we'll talk about what it takes to actually turn your HTML creations into part of the World Wide Web. First we'll talk about some of the very real portability problems that you might encounter when you place a document that you created locally onto a publicly accessible server. Then we'll talk about the actual methods of placing your pages on a server, and we'll discuss the critical information that you need to get from your service provider before you start.

Portability Issues

As we touched on in the section about local documents, you can get into real problems if your documents refer to other items that you created by absolute pathnames. (That is, if your links contain the full name of a file, such as C:\MY_DIR\FILE.HTM.) These documents are not *portable*—that is, you can't upload them to a server and have these kinds of links still work. After all, if the document is on a Web server at your service provider's location, it certainly won't be able to find your C drive! Anyone who clicks these links will get the "Error 404 URL Not Found" error message.

Portability is the nemesis of beginning Web developers. If you plan to create documents on your desktop machine that will be placed on a server, following these tips can help you avoid a lot of aggravation:

- If possible, keep all your files in a single directory and use links and anchors that only contain the simple file name (such as <A HREF="other_file.html">). As long as all the files are in the same directory, a referenced file can always be found by its simple name.

- If you must make reference to files that will be stored in other directories, use fully qualified URLs to describe the other files, even if they're located on the same host machine. For example, a link to a document in another directory would be written as <A HREF="http://my_host/other_directory/other_file.html">. If you use this construction, you'll need to test all your links after they're uploaded to make sure that they function correctly. (You can modify the links either before or after uploading them to the server. The disadvantage of modifying links before you upload them is that the modified links will no longer work locally; the disadvantage of the second choice is that modifying the files when they're on the server will probably require that you use some kind of UNIX text editor, such as vi—pronounced vee-eye—or emacs.)

- Be sure to use a naming convention for your files that's compatible with the intended server. You'll be really frustrated if you find that you have to rename all your files after you've created them, since you'll probably also have to modify your links to other files in your HTML documents. Read on for a thorough discussion of these issues.

More About File Naming Conventions

Here are some important tips for ensuring that your files adhere to standard naming conventions:

- Don't use file names that contain blank spaces or unusual punctuation. If you absolutely must have some kind of separator between words, use the underscore character (shift-hyphen on most keyboards). Using anything other than letters and numbers in file names will almost always violate the conventions of some file system that might retrieve those items. Even though you can use spaces in Macintosh file names, for example, they're guaranteed to mess up a UNIX system.

- In general, it's safest to only use lowercase letters in file names. Some servers are case-sensitive—in other words, they think there's a difference between ABC.TXT, abc.txt, and Abc.Txt. Even if your desktop computer treats these files as the same, it's quite possible that your Web server will not.

- Use the standard file extensions—.html, .gif, .jpeg, .jpg, and so on.

NOTE
If your operating system requires the 8.3 naming standard, you can name your local files with the .htm extension, but you may need to modify their names to *.html on the server if it doesn't recognize them as HTML files. Chances are good that it will, but you should check with your service provider.

- Be conservative about the length of your file names. Although servers tend to have less restrictive policies about length than most desktop machines (you're always safe if you use the old DOS-based 8.3 con-

457

vention), keep in mind that people may need to manually type your URL. Try to keep the names brief but meaningful.

NOTE

These are only general tips. Your service provider may have different requirements, which we'll discuss in the next section.

About Uploading Files

The only way that you can make your Web documents available to others around the world is to place them on a publicly accessible Web server. If your service provider allows you to create public Web pages, you'll usually have a shell account that lets you perform file management operations on the server in addition to your dialup IP account so that you can put files from your desktop onto the server.

Here's a short list of the information that you need to get from your service provider so that you can upload your files with ease and be sure that they'll work without additional modification to the file names or the links included in the document:

- How should URLs to your public pages be constructed? One established convention for URLs on servers that contain hundreds of individual home pages is the construction **http://host_name/~username/file.html**. (The ~ character, called a tilde, is usually created by pressing shift-back-quote—or accent grave, if you're continental—located in the upper-left corner of your keyboard.) This URL tells the browser to connect to the host machine and find the Web-accessible directory associated with your unique user name. Then it displays the designated file within the directory.

- What are the naming requirements for the files themselves?

- Are there any limitations to the total amount of space that your files can use? Many service providers limit you to a few megabytes.

- What is the accepted method for placing files online? Most service providers will let you create HTML files locally and upload them to the server using FTP (which we'll describe later in this section), but others may require that you construct your files online using a wizard or a regular text editor like vi, or that you email them to the Web administrator, or some other scheme.

SHORTCUT

If, like Prodigy, your service provider requires that you create your files online with an editor, you can decrease the amount of time that you're actually connected by creating and testing the documents on your desktop computer, connecting to the site, opening the online text editor, and copying and pasting the contents of the entire HTML document into the text editor.

- Where, exactly, should you put files that you upload? Typically, you'll have a special subdirectory for Web pages in your home directory, but this varies from service provider to service provider.

Uploading Files with FTP

By and large, the most common scheme of Internet service providers to let users place their pages online is to put them on the server using the file transfer protocol FTP. Until recently, Netscape (like other browsers) didn't allow you to upload files—it only let you view and download files, which won't help you in this case. For this reason, Web developers have come to rely on other Internet tools called *graphical FTP clients*.

Because you must have an IP connection to use Netscape, you can use a graphical FTP client to put your files on the server, which is much easier and more intuitive than mastering the typed commands of a text-only terminal emulator program. Common graphical FTP clients include WS-FTP for Windows, available at several locations including ftp://maui.net/pub/windows/wsftp.exe, and Fetch for the Macintosh, available at several locations including http://mirror.apple.com/mirrors/Info-Mac.Archive/comm/tcp/fetch-301.hqx.

Here are the basic procedures for putting files on a server with a graphical FTP client. Your actual steps may vary, depending on the client package you use and your service provider's requirements:

1. Log into your home account on your service provider's Web server. (Because this isn't anonymous FTP, you'll need to enter the user name and password to access your account on the Web server.)

2. Change to the directory on the server where your files should be located. With most graphical clients, you usually double-click the name of the directory you wish to open.

3. Your FTP client will contain a configuration option that lets you choose whether the file being uploaded is binary or ASCII. (On the Macintosh, there may be additional choices of file types.) If you're moving an HTML file, you can select **ASCII**. If you're moving an image or other binary file, select **Binary**.

VIRTUOSO

Most FTP clients allow you to move several files at once. If you're sure that you won't need to edit your HTML files online, you can upload all your graphic and HTML files at once, using the **Binary** setting. However, while the HTML files will still be readable if you upload them as binaries, you may not be able to edit them directly when they're online.

4. Issue the **put** command according to the FTP client's documentation to put your local files on the Web server.

WARNING

Many graphical FTP clients have the potential to rename files on the fly. (For example, Fetch has a setting which appends .txt to the end of your text files, which will make it impossible for a browser to interpret your files as HTML.) After carefully choosing your file names and ensuring that they adhere to conventions, make sure that this feature is not enabled.

Uploading Files with Netscape Navigator

Netscape Navigator 2.0 and later versions have a built-in FTP client that can be used to upload files to an FTP site. To upload a file, follow these steps:

1. Connect to the site where you wish to upload a file. You'll usually upload files using authenticated FTP, which we discussed in Chapter 16. (As a refresher, the URL for using authenticated FTP will look like ftp://username@foo.bar.com; after you enter your password, you'll be logged in to the top-level directory for the account.)

2. If you wish to upload the files to a specific directory, navigate to the directory so that its contents are displayed in the browser window.

3. From the File menu, select **Upload File**.... The File Upload dialog box will be displayed.

4. Locate and select the file you wish to upload.

5. Click **Open**. A progress gauge will be displayed, showing the status of your upload.

WARNING

To upload more than one file at a time, or as a shortcut that avoids using the menu command, you can upload files by using "drag and drop." Select the file or files you wish to upload, hold down the mouse button, and drag the files over the open browser window. You'll be asked if you want to upload those files; when you confirm the action, the files will be uploaded.

WARNING

Unfortunately, the FTP client in the browser-only version of Netscape is somewhat limited. Although you can drag multiple files into the window at a time, you can't drag a folder representing a directory and have the directory automatically created for you. This means that you may need to log in to your shell account and create the appropriate directory structure before you start uploading your files with Netscape.

Uploading Files with Navigator Gold

Navigator Gold has a more robust built-in FTP client than the regular Netscape browser. The Gold FTP client lets you publish (i.e., upload) files directly from the editor and choose whether to automatically upload associated items such as other files in the folder or the images that are called for within the document.

To upload a file or files from the Navigator Gold editor, follow these steps:

1. From the File menu, select **Publish**... or click the **Publish** button on the File/Edit toolbar. The Publish Files dialog box (Figure 22.1) will be displayed.

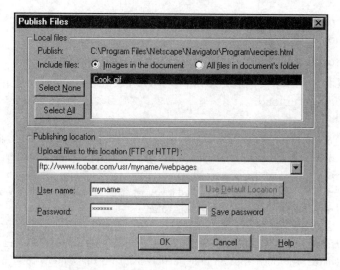

Figure 22.1 The Publish Files dialog box.

2. If you wish to upload additional files in the same directory, such as graphics, sound files, or other HTML documents, click **All Files in document's folder**. All the files in the folder will be displayed. Select or deselect the items you wish to upload.

3. If you *only* wish to upload images associated with the document, click **Images in the document** and make sure that all the images you wish to upload are selected. (You can select or deselect them individually or use the **Select None** or **Select All** buttons.)

4. In the Publishing location section, follow these steps to identify the site where the files will be placed:

   • If you're uploading the file with FTP, type the **ftp://** type specifier followed by the complete pathname to the location where you plan to upload the files in the **Upload files to this location (FTP or HTTP)** field.

NOTE

The FTP pathname is not always the same as the URL that other people will use to reach your pages. Be sure to check with your service provider to find the correct path for uploading files.

NOTE

The ability to upload files using the HTTP protocol is currently a proprietary feature of Netscape's server software. Be sure to check with your service provider before using this feature; if in doubt, try FTP, which will probably work in any case.

- In the **User name** field, type your user name for the system where you're placing the files.

- In the **Password** field, type the password for the account. (If you want Netscape to remember the password the next time you publish files, click **Save password**.)

5. When you're ready to upload the files, click **OK**. The selected files will be uploaded.

SHORTCUT

Want to skip the part where you identify the publishing location when you get ready to upload more files? You can set a default publishing location by following the steps in the next section.

Working With the Default Publishing Location

As a time-saving feature, Netscape Navigator Gold lets you set default locations for uploading files and for browsing files. (Setting a default location for browsing files is similar to using a bookmark; after you enter a URL to use as the default, you can go directly to the site by selecting **Default Publishing Location** from the Go menu.)

To set default locations, follow these steps:

1. From the Options menu, select **Editor Preferences**....

2. Click the **Publish** tab. A screen similar to Figure 22.2 will be displayed.

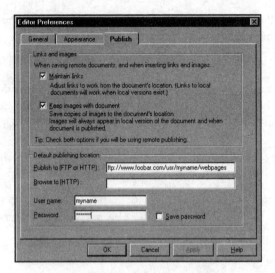

Figure 22.2 Publish options.

3. In the **Publish to (FTP or HTTP)** field, type the URL of the location where you want files to be uploaded by default from the editor.

NOTE

The ability to upload files using the HTTP protocol is currently a proprietary feature of Netscape's server software. Be sure to check with your service provider before using this feature.

4. In the **Browse to (HTTP)** field, type the URL of the location where your files will be stored. You can then view your uploaded files by simply selecting **Default Publishing Location** from the Go menu.

5. In the **User name** field, type your user name for the system where you're placing the files.

6. In the **Password** field, type the password for the account. (If you want Netscape to remember the password the next time you publish files, click **Save password**.)

7. When you're finished, click **OK**.

Mining Cyberspace

As you travel around the world of the Web, you may find that you want to download your own copies of items you find for personal use. For example, you might want to download a collection of pages, along with associated links and images, and reassemble it on your own machine for reference purposes. Or you might want to retrieve graphical elements for a variety of purposes. Items such as buttons, bullets, rules, icons, graphics, and patterns can be reused in your own documents, while high-quality digital images may be desired for uses other than Web documents.

Creating Replicas of Other Sites

If your goal is to replicate a set of linked Web pages (such as an online manual) on your local machine, you need a mechanism for copying a potentially large number of HTML files and images to your desktop machine. To make matters more complicated, you need to make sure that the links and anchors from the original site will function as local URLs. (It's the reverse of the portability problem we discussed when you place files created locally onto a public Web server.) Typically, when you transfer other people's Web files to your local machine, the linkages will not be portable, and you'll need to manually modify all the URLs in the file.

There are two possible ways to handle this problem, one of which requires the use of software other than Netscape:

- Use a commercial site replicator package like Web Whacker, MilkTruck, Freeloader, or Surfbot. These applications download HTML pages and their associated images, and automatically modify the URLs so that you can successfully browse offline without manually editing the links. In general, if you need to download and navigate the contents of a large site, this might be your best approach. Trial versions of Web Whacker for Macintosh, Windows 3.1, and Windows 95 are available at http://www.ffg.com/whacker.html. MilkTruck for Windows 95 and NT can be found at http://www.milktruck.com/download/index.htm (versions for the Macintosh and Windows 3.1 were announced but not available at the time of this writing). Freeloader for Windows 95 and Windows 3.1 can be found

465

at http://www.freeloader.net/dlfl.htm. Surfbot for Windows 95 and NT is available at http://www.surflogic.com/sb20install.html.

- Use Netscape's powerful disk caching features to invisibly capture all the HTML and graphics files at a remote site to your local drive simply by visiting each page of the site you wish to replicate.

Using the Netscape Disk Cache

Each time you visit a site, the contents that you view are saved to your disk cache. (Caching is covered in detail in Chapter 5.) Depending on your settings, when you revisit a page, it can be recalled directly from your disk cache even though you used a remote URL. Because the files stored in the disk cache are accessed as if they were networked documents, the links and anchors of the files will not need to be changed. And, because all the files are in your disk cache, you won't need to connect to the network to access them.

WARNING

This trick only works with static documents. Your copies of the site will fail if you try to cache and use documents that contain server-side image maps or other applications of CGI. (However, there shouldn't be a problem with downloading client-side image maps, which don't rely on CGI.)

To create a local replica of a Web site in your disk cache, follow these steps:

1. Set your disk cache to be large enough to contain all the HTML, GIF, and JPEG files that are part of the site you wish to replicate.
2. Turn Auto Load Images on.
3. Visit the site you wish to replicate and explore every page. You need to perform an *exhaustive search*—that is, deliberately view every item on every page that's part of the site. If you're replicating a large site, this will require not only time but also organizational skills to make sure that you load every single page.

WARNING

While you don't need to actually use the scroll bars to look at each item on a page, it's crucial that you let the entire page load before clicking another link. Web documents are not cached until the full page is loaded; this is denoted by the "Done" message in the status area and the disappearance of the red line from the progress gauge. If you leave a page before it's completely loaded, it won't be in the cache and your attempt to use the replicated site will fail.

4. Bookmark the starting point or points of the replicated site. (You can now disconnect from the network, if you wish.)

5. To use the replicated site, set Netscape's "check documents" option in the Cache section of Network Preferences to **Never**. This ensures that Netscape will not attempt to create a network connection to check for newer versions of the remote files. Since all the files in the replicated site should be available locally in your disk cache, you can use the cached site even when you're disconnected from the network.

6. Use the Bookmark menu to go to the top level of the replicated site and explore as desired. If at any time Netscape attempts to establish a network connection, that indicates that you failed to let all the documents load into the cache or that you attempted to cache a file that used a clickable image map or other application of CGI.

Now you can do a "live" demonstration of the Web using a portable computer and "real" URLs that haven't been modified for local use...and you don't even need a network connection or a telephone line. Pre-caching the items you wish to demonstrate is highly recommended even if you will be connecting to the Internet, since Murphy's Law often strikes at the worst time, and you might not be able to access remote servers.

VIRTUOSO

Want to use Netscape to explore the Web but still keep your copy of the replicated site intact? After you've replicated the site, change the name of the cache directory that stores it. Then, when you want to use the site, change Netscape's cache directory to look at the directory containing the files, instead of the default cache directory you use when you're browsing.

Repurposing Materials on the Web

Sometimes you don't want to create a full replica of a Web site—you just want to copy a page or two of HTML source code or a graphic element that you want to use in your own documents. In this case, the easiest method is to simply download the individual items that you wish to use.

Copying HTML Documents

Netscape has two simple ways to make a local copy of HTML pages:

- If the page you want to copy is displayed, choose **Save as...** from the File menu and save the document as **Source**.
- If you're on a page that contains a link to a document you wish to copy, drag the link to your desktop or to the folder where you want the copy of the file. This automatically saves a copy of the file referred to in the link as an HTML document. Or, hold down the **Alt** key (**Option** on the Macintosh) while you click the link to display a standard dialog box to save the file.

SHORTCUT

This second method is especially useful if you're copying several files that are linked to a single document. Instead of visiting each link, waiting for it to load, and issuing the menu command, you save time and mouse clicks by just dragging the link from the referring page. However, you'll still have to wait for the document to be saved to the disk.

There are two things you need to keep in mind when you save documents this way. First, these methods only save the HTML file, not any associated graphics such as inline images or background patterns. And, even if you download the images, the tags in the HTML files will probably require that you modify them to use the local copies of the files.

If you're using Navigator Gold, there's a third way to save individual files or small collections of files without any problem; Gold provides settings to let you download images and keep links intact. To use this feature, follow these steps:

1. When you're viewing a page you wish to store locally, *don't* use the Save command; instead, click the **Edit** button on the Toolbar or select **Edit Document** from the File menu. The Save Remote Document dialog box will be displayed.

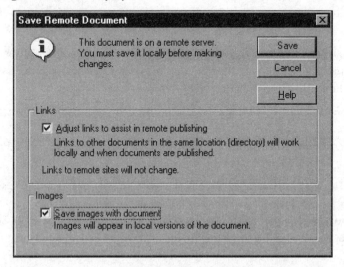

Figure 22.3 The Save Remote Document dialog box.

2. Make sure that the Adjust links to assist in remote publishing and Save images with document items are selected.

3. Click Save.

4. If this is the first time that you've downloaded documents this way, you may see a dialog box warning you about using copyrighted images or documents. If the dialog box is displayed, dismiss it. Eventually, a regular dialog box to save the file will be displayed.

5. Choose a name and a location for the file. (By default, the item will have the same name as the file on the server.)

6. Click **Save**. The HTML and graphics associated with the document will all be downloaded to the location you specified.

This feature works whether you have Auto Load Images selected in the Options menu or not. If you just want to save the HTML without the associated images, use the **Save as...** command in the File menu.

NOTE

Saving Inline Images

The best way to save an individual inline image to your desktop is to use the pop-up menu. To save a graphic, follow these steps:

1. Place the mouse pointer over the image you wish to save to your desktop.

2. Display the pop-up menu. (On Windows and UNIX, click the right mouse button; on the Macintosh, hold down the mouse button until the pop-up menu is displayed.)

3. Select **Save this Image as**... and enter the requested information.

(For complete information about using the pop-up menu, see Chapter 7.)

NOTE Tiny graphics like small buttons and icons or very thin separator bars (that are graphic images, not generated by HTML) can be retrieved in this way, but you have to be very precise about where you place the mouse pointer. If you're off the image by even a pixel, the **Save this Image as**... option will be grayed out.

Saving Background Patterns

Saving the background patterns used by online documents presents a special challenge, since you can't use the pop-up menu on the background. But, Netscape 3.0's Document Info feature makes it easy to locate and download the graphics file used for a background. To do so, follow these steps:

1. Display the document whose background image you wish to use.

2. From the View menu, select **Document Info**.... Information about the structure of the current document will be displayed.

3. Locate the item that describes the location of the background image and click the link. Information about that image will be displayed in the lower frame.

4. Click the URL of the item in the lower frame. The graphic will be loaded into the window.

5. Use the pop-up menu to save the image to your computer.

Interested in finding other background images to use in your documents? Check out Netscape's Background Sample page at http://home.netscape.com/ assist/net_sites/bg/backgrounds.html. They have several different backgrounds available for you to use, as well as instructions and tips for using them in your documents.

VIRTUOSO

Portability Problems

This section is only relevant if you didn't use a site replicator like Web Whacker or the features of Navigator Gold that ensure links remain correct.

NOTE

If you wish to display any pages that you've saved using the methods described above, you'll probably find that the graphics won't display and the links to other pages won't work, even if you've downloaded those graphics or the linked pages. For example, if the anchors for graphics used a pathname on the server instead of a simple file name, the browser won't know to look for the local copy of the graphic. To make sure that the links and graphics in these documents display correctly, you'll need to change all the <A HREF>, <IMG SRC>, and <BODY BACKGROUND> tags in the HTML files so that they point to the correct local image files.

If you've followed our advice and placed all of your pictures and HTML files in the same directory, this task will be easy. You can simply delete the pathnames from the links and image references so that only the simple file names remain. For example, an <HREF> tag of the form <A HREF="http://abc.com/rxrel/icons/ball.gif"> could be shortened to <A HREF="ball.gif">.

Transparent Images

As you start retrieving items from the Web, you might notice that many Web sites contain images that have transparent backgrounds and that appear to "float" on the screen of the browser, no matter what the background color or pattern is.

VIRTUOSO

If you've tried creating your own graphics for use in your Web page, you might wonder how that transparent effect is created, since most image editing programs require that each part of the image be assigned a color. The answer is to use a utility that supports the GIF89a format, which allows transparencies. On Windows, LView Pro 1.8 or later supports this feature; on the Macintosh, your best bet is a shareware utility called Transparency, available at several locations including ftp://mirror.apple.com/mirrors/Info-Mac.Archive/gst/grf/transparency-10.hqx. These utilities let you select and change a single color in a GIF image to transparent so that the background color of the browser screen shows through the image to create the floating effect. (Be sure to select the color that surrounds the graphic instead of one of the colors that defines the lines of the graphic itself!)

Placing Local Web Files on a LAN

Even without a network connection, Netscape is a great front end for viewing hypertext information. If you have a large collection of static HTML documents (such as procedures manuals), you can share them with your coworkers and employees on a corporate LAN without requiring any kind of connection to the Internet.

Netscape's local mode of operation (using the file:/// construction) can almost always be extended to work across a LAN. For example, on a Windows-based server, instead of accessing files with the URL construction file:///Cl/path_name/file.htm, you could just as easily access them on a network drive with file:///Hl/path_name/file.htm, replacing "H" with the correct name of the network drive.

SHORTCUT

Once you've placed the files on the local server, it's easy to email the URL for the top file in the directory to others. They can simply copy and paste it into the Location field, and then bookmark the page.

If you decide to use Netscape as a local browser for documents on a LAN, there are two important issues to keep in mind:

- The portability problem that we've discussed several times in this chapter may once again be an issue. If you place all the items in a single directory and use simple file names as links to graphics and other documents, there won't be a problem—as long as everyone starts at a page in the directory, all the items referred to can be found. However, if you wish to use a more complicated scheme where objects are stored in multiple directories, then you need to use a special kind of relative URL which is an advanced topic beyond the scope of this chapter.

• If Netscape is installed at your site for the sole purpose of viewing local files, without any kind of TCP/IP connectivity, a null socket library (on Windows) or MacTCP (on a Macintosh) will need to be installed to ensure that Netscape will launch. (For more information, see the discussion of this topic in Chapter 21.)

What You Learned

After reading this chapter, you should be able to:

• Construct a series of portable Web pages that can be placed on other servers without requiring modification.

• Understand the basic issues of uploading your Web pages to a server, including asking crucial questions of your service provider.

• Create a complete replica of another Web site on your desktop computer.

• Extract graphics and HTML source code from files on the Web.

• Understand the issues involved in using Netscape to browse local collections of documents on a LAN.

CHAPTER 23

STRATEGIES FOR SEARCHING THE WEB

Often, it's fun to cruise around the Web without much of a purpose in mind, exploring whatever interesting links present themselves. But at other times, like when you're trying to research a topic or find information fast, the inherently chaotic nature of the Web can be your worst enemy.

The Web is very much like one of Borges' labyrinthine, unending libraries, where all the information you could ever want is available, except there's no organization system and therefore no way to find anything. Unlike regular libraries, there is no Dewey Decimal System or Library of Congress cataloging standards to ensure that you can find the URLs you're looking for in the system. Luckily, through the efforts of several individuals and organizations, tools for locating resources such as search engines and subject indices are publicly available to help you find the information most relevant to your needs. And, if you're just getting started, "Starting Points" pages contain good ideas about areas of the Web that you might want to explore first.

NOTE Because there is no standard cataloging and search mechanism for the World Wide Web, the information provided by each resource listed below will vary, sometimes slightly and sometimes wildly. Most people find the one or two search engines and subject indices that they like the best and use them almost exclusively. You'll have to figure out the strategy for locating information that works best for you.

Web and Internet Search Engines

The quickest and most powerful way to find information on the Internet is to use a *search engine*. With a search engine, you search a comprehensive database for the terms that you want to find information about (much like the computerized card catalog at the library). The result is a list of links containing the terms you entered, usually in descending order of likelihood that the document contains the kind of information you were looking for.

VIRTUOSO

In this section, we've focused on the concepts involved in using search engines, instead of on specific procedural documentation. The appearance and interface of a search engine can change considerably over the course of even a few months. (In fact, we found out while writing the section on Lycos that they're planning to change the format of the displayed results, so some of the information below may already be out of date.) But the general ideas behind effective use of a search engine—structuring your queries, choosing what kind of results you want, identifying strengths and weaknesses, etc.—will always be true, no matter what kind of search engine you use. So don't worry if the screens you see don't exactly match the ones below; the concepts should always be the same.

About Search Engine Results

It's possible that you'll encounter some problems working with search engines. The most common ones are outlined below:

- Results that don't fit what you're looking for. If you enter too broad a query, the search engine may return several documents which contain the terms you entered but not in the context that you're interested in.

- Not enough results. If you narrow your search too much, the search engine may not find any matches at all.

- Results containing links that you can't access. This is an unfortunate by-product of large databases that can't be updated frequently. It's entirely possible that a link will have been moved or deleted from the address in the database. And, some sites that are accessible to search engines aren't always accessible to users. For example, FTP sites often limit access to outsiders during business hours so that networking resources aren't tied up, while other sites may only be available to users in certain regions (determined by the IP number of the site you're connecting from).

To sum up, you'll need to be flexible in your search strategies and in your expectations in order to find useful information with a minimum of frustration on the Web.

Protocol-Specific Searches: Archie, Veronica, Jughead, and WAIS

Despite the immense popularity of the Web as an information medium, protocol-specific searches that only locate materials in FTP space or gopherspace are still an important search tool. These protocol-specific searches are often the best tools for locating certain information. For example, if you want to retrieve a software package, Archie is the best and fastest way to find it, as FTP sites remain the most common way to distribute software. Since Archie only searches FTP space, it won't retrieve endless URLs pointing to discussions about the use of the package. And if you know you want to find information that's on a gopher server (for example, most directory services of universities are only available in gopherspace), you're a lot more likely to find what you want by performing a narrow Veronica or Jughead search than by searching all the Web sites in the world as well.

Archie and FTP

In Chapter 16 we discussed Archie, the tool for searching FTP archives. In short, Archie searches through an index of files available at FTP sites to find the location of the software package that you're looking for. Interfaces to a variety of Archie servers are available on the Web, including NCSA's, displayed in Figure 23.1. (NCSA's Archie search form is located at http://hoohoo.ncsa.uiuc.edu/archie.html.)

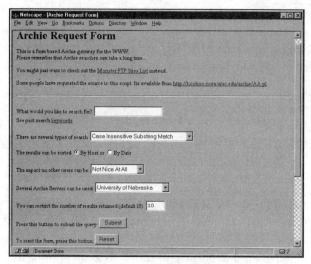

Figure 23.1 NCSA's Archie search form.

The elements of this form are common to nearly every Archie search that you'll encounter:

- **Search term**. Always enter the name of the file that you're looking for (which may not always be the name of the software package itself). Be as specific as you can; the more information you can give Archie, the better. For example, if you can enter the complete name and file extension of the archived software package that you're looking for, you're more likely to get a useful result from your search.

WARNING

Archie only searches the names of files, not their descriptions. So if you don't know the name that a file is stored under, Archie can't help. For example, the Trumpet Winsock package is stored under the name twskb20.zip. If you did an Archie search for Trumpet Winsock, you wouldn't get any results.

- **Type of search**. The item that you should select here depends on how specific you were able to be about the name of the file that you entered.
- **Case Insensitive Substring Match** will return all the files that contain the search term that you entered, regardless of capitalization and

placement in the name of the file. For example, a case-insensitive substring match on **tex** would retrieve **Texas**, **textile**, **TeX**, and **LaTeX**.

- **Exact Match** will return only the items that exactly match the search term that you enter. For example, an exact match search on **tex** would only return files called **tex**.

- **Case Sensitive Substring Match** will return all files that contain the search term that you enter, as long as the capitalization is the same. For example, a case-sensitive substring match search on **TeX** would return **TeX** and **LaTeX**, but not **tex** or **Texas**.

- **Regular Expression Match** allows you to use special characters to narrow your search even more. (A good explanation of the use of regular expressions can be found in "A Gentle Introduction to Regular Expressions," by T. Joseph W. Lazio, at http://astrosun.tn.cornell.edu/lcarus/regex.html.)

- **Method of sorting results**. Sorting by date displays the files matching your query that were most recently added to FTP sites at the top of the list. Sorting by host displays all the files that match your query organized by the name of the archive containing them.

- **Impact on other users** ("**niceness**"). Each Archie query that you submit causes a strain on the Archie server, since it must search through thousands of items to find the ones that match your request. If other people are using the same Archie server at the same time, everyone's search may slow to a crawl. To help address this issue, Archie servers have a "niceness" setting, ranging from "Not Nice At All" to "Nicest," which allows you to judge the relative importance of your results and to set Archie accordingly. You'll always get your results, but choosing a nicer setting whenever you can ensures that other people performing critical searches aren't impacted by queries for game software.

- **Which Archie server to use**. Each Archie server contains slightly different information. For example, servers in Italy will have a preference to store information about FTP archives in Italy and nearby countries, while American Archie servers will tend to list more North American sites. You should always choose a server which is geographically near you to preserve network resources both for your search and for retrieving the software that you locate.

- **Number of results**. This is the number of matches to your query that will be displayed at the end of the search. The displayed items will be the ones that best match the query that you entered. The default for this particular site is ten, which is generally a good choice, as it displays enough results that you'll have a variety to select from but not so many that it'll take a long time to review. Other sites may have different defaults.

NOTE

A quick Web-based way to search for freeware and shareware is to use Shareware.com (http://www.shareware.com). The site is a vast archive and catalog of publicly available software for a variety of computer platforms.

Veronica, Jughead, and Gopher

Veronica and Jughead are two different methods of searching for items stored on gopher servers. Veronica (short for Very Easy Rodent-Oriented Net-wide Index to Computerized Archives) can search for items in the titles of directories and the titles of gopher objects themselves in all of gopherspace, while Jughead only searches the titles of directories and is usually configured to only search the site on which it's housed. While Veronica and Jughead searches appear on most gopher servers in the world (look for a top-level directory called "Search Gopherspace" or "Other Internet Starting Points"), you can always find a Veronica search and a Jughead search at gopher://gopher.utah.edu. For Veronica, click **Search titles in Gopherspace using veronica**, and for Jughead, click **Search menu titles using jughead**.

Wide Area Information Server (WAIS)

WAIS is an extremely sophisticated protocol for searching the full text of databases that are connected to the Internet. It is a significant improvement over other database search technologies which only let you search for titles or keywords of documents. A WAIS query, by comparison, searches the complete text of documents in its database, determines which of the located documents are the most relevant to you, and displays the results with a numerical ranking. This "intelligent" search mechanism represents huge leaps in the field of information science because it doesn't rely solely on titles and keywords assigned to the document—it actually searches the document itself.

The two ways that regular WAIS databases appear on the Web are through a gateway, where you submit your query to the WAIS server through a regular form on an HTTP page, and through directly connecting to a WAIS server using the special WAIS URL. (As we discussed in Chapters 16 and 20, accessing WAIS directly through Netscape requires that you enter the name of a WAIS proxy in the Proxies section of your preferences. If your service provider doesn't have a WAIS proxy, try the publicly accessible proxy at www.w3.org, port 8001.) The first method—searching through a form on a regular Web page—is easily the one that you're most likely to use.

Figure 23.2 shows the results of a WAIS search of the National Performance Review database for the words "space station."

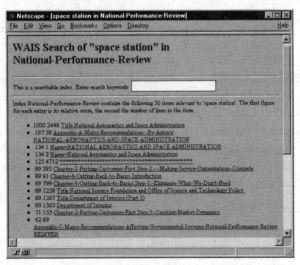

Figure 23.2 Results of a WAIS search.

For detailed information about structuring a WAIS query, check out http://town.hall.org/util/wais_help.html.

NOTE

But WAIS searching isn't limited to large, full-text databases on special WAIS sites. The algorithms and searching patterns that WAIS uses to match search terms to documents is the foundation of all Web search engines, which we'll discuss in the next section. Any time you enter a search term and retrieve a list of documents that are ranked numerically, you can bet that you performed a search based on WAIS technology.

Web Searches

Unlike the FTP, gopher, and WAIS searches described above, Web search engines construct and retrieve information from databases of links to all kinds of information on the Internet. The returned links may be to HTTP, gopher, or FTP sites (or to sites for any other kind of supported protocol). If a site is accessible through a World Wide Web browser, then it can be indexed for use by a general Web search engine.

N O T E Because most search engines are supported by the sale of advertising, a trend at sites that host search engines is to provide a variety of "value-added" information as well so that you'll frequently use their site. So, don't be surprised to find that search engine sites also offer services like index-style directories of reviewed Web sites, random links for spontaneous surfing, news services, and more. For example, WebCrawler also hosts a list of GNN's "Best of the Web" sites, as well as some interesting special features, such as WebRoulette, which pulls ten URLs at random from its database, and a "backwards search" capability so that you can check to see how many people in the world have links to your home page from their own Web sites. Lycos and other search engines offer similar services.

Where the Information Comes from: Robots, Wanderers, Worms, and Spiders

The databases that are used by search engines are all created in roughly the same way. Automatic programs called *robots*, *wanderers*, *worms*, or *spiders* continually explore all the links that they can find, indexing the URLs (and often an excerpt of the content) into a searchable database. The search strategies used by the robots and how often the new information is added to the public database will impact the kind of information that you find as well as its timeliness.

Robots are a controversial topic on the Web since they require a lot of network resources. Not only do they use up Internet traffic capacity to connect to remote sites, but they can also place a strain on individual servers. However, since robots are currently the only way to create near-comprehensive indices of Web sites, they are necessary for creating data-bases that you can search. A *robot exclusion standard* has been developed so that sites which are sensitive to robot searches can keep unwanted robots out; the best search engines willingly comply with this exclusion standard.

NOTE You might be wondering if it's possible to use search engines to locate sites that exclude robots. The answer is yes—nearly all search engines have a method to add URLs manually to the database. So site administrators who don't want robots to use up their resources but do want people to locate them can enter their information for inclusion in the database.

NOTE nterested in finding out more about robots? Check out Martijn Koster's World Wide Web Robots, Wanderers, and Spiders page at http://info.webcrawler.com/mak/ projects/robots/robots.html.

About Queries

As you'll undoubtedly notice as you skim through this section, most search engine interfaces are comprised of very similar components, which vary slightly in name and functionality from site to site. In general, the components of a search engine query will be some combination of the fol-lowing:

- **Search terms**. These are the words that you're searching for. Try to be as specific as possible—for example, if you're searching for Wells Fargo bank information, don't enter **bank**; enter **Wells Fargo bank** instead.

NOTE Nearly all search engines provide a way to make your queries even more specific; always look for a link to something like "Advanced search tips" to learn how to make your queries more specific. It's definitely worth the trouble.

- **Relevance**. Results of search engines are usually given a numeric score that lets you gauge the relative *relevance* of each document—that is, how likely it is that the document is actually what you're looking for. Relevance will show up in two places: first, when you structure your query, some search engines will ask you to describe how "loose" or "strong" a match you want; second, when you receive the results of the query, nearly all search engines will provide a relevance score for each retrieved document. Each search engine handles relevance differently, but most of them assume that words found in the URL, title, or the first few paragraphs of a document mean that the document is more likely to meet your needs. If you search for more than one word, preference will be given to the documents that have those words close to each other. Most searches are based on a WAIS-type retrieval system, so the most relevant document found will have a score of 1000, while the least relevant will have a much lower score. (Some engines, like Lycos, use a decimalized version of this rating system, where the highest rating is 1.000.)

- **Boolean operators**. All major search engines have some form of Boolean operators, which use the concepts of AND, OR, and NOT to let you enter complex queries. For example, an AND query for ham and eggs would retrieve only documents containing both words; a query for ham OR eggs would retrieve all documents with ham and all documents with eggs, regardless of whether both words appeared in the document; and a search for ham AND eggs NOT seuss would return all documents containing both ham and eggs but would exclude the ones with any reference to Dr. Seuss (beloved author of *Green Eggs and Ham*). Each search engine has a different way of handling search operators—some require you to enter the actual word AND or OR; others let you select from a somewhat more explanatory list.

- **Which databases to search**. Some search engines, such as Infoseek, contain different searchable databases of information. For example, if you're only looking for information in a Usenet article, it's much more practical to limit your search strictly to Usenet—you'll get better, faster results.

- **Number of results to return**. Generally, search engines will retrieve all the documents in the database that match your request; however, it would be very time- and resource-consuming to put thousands of entries on a single Web page! You can usually choose the number of results to display on a page; the most relevant documents will be on the first page of results. You can then choose to display as many more pages of results as were returned.

- **Format of results**. You can usually choose the amount of additional information about the results to be displayed. The least information you can choose is usually to simply see the title of the site (which is a link); more verbose results include relevance scores, an abstract or summary of the document, or the first several lines of text on the page.

WebCrawler

The WebCrawler search engine (Figure 23.3), originally developed by Brian Pinkerton at the University of Washington, was the first full-text search engine available on the Web. WebCrawler is now owned by America Online (who also owns the Global Network Navigator service) and is provided free of charge as a service to the Web-using public. WebCrawler is located at http://www.webcrawler.com.

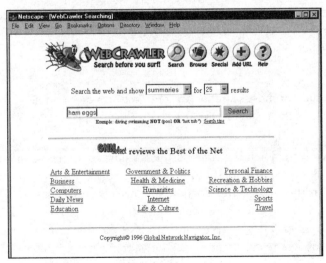

Figure 23.3 The WebCrawler search engine.

- **Titles/Summaries** pop-up menu. If you want the search results just to display the title of the page, select **titles** (the default); if you want to see a description of each result, a relevance score, and a link to find other pages similar to an item that appears on the results page, select **summaries**. The downside to selecting **summaries** is that the results page can take slightly longer to load.

NOTE

If you decide that you wanted to see the summaries after all, you can choose to do so on the results page.

- **Number of results to return**. This item lets you select how many of the results of your query will be displayed. The default will display the 25 responses that best match your query; your other choices are 10 responses or 100 responses.

- **Search entry field**. Enter the words that you want to search for. As an example, to search for items containing **ham** and **eggs** but not containing **Seuss**, enter **ham eggs NOT seuss**; to search just for ham and eggs, we'll enter **ham eggs**.

VIRTUOSO

For complete details on structuring complex queries, including the use of adjacency and relevance, see the Advanced Search Tips at http://www.webcrawler.com/WebCrawler/Help/Advanced.html.

The results of most searches are returned to you in a few seconds. Figure 23.4 shows the results of the search displayed in Figure 23.3.

The first line tells you how many documents were located and how many are displayed. Then the titles of the documents are listed in order of relevance. A score close to 100% means that all the words in the search were found in the title of the document; lower scores mean that both words appeared in the document, but not near the top, or not near each other. (The capsule-shaped graphic at the left of the title is also a relevance indicator; the less relevant the document, the fewer lines in the capsule. This visual relevance indicator is also visible if you only display the titles instead of the summaries.)

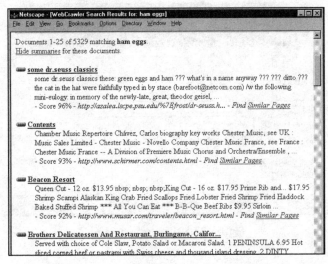

Figure 23.4 Results of a WebCrawler search.

Lycos

Originally developed at Carnegie Mellon University, the Lycos search engine, available at http://www.lycos.com, is named after a predatory wolf spider of the family *Lycosidae*.

Lycos lets you construct somewhat more sophisticated queries than WebCrawler, allowing you to choose the desired amount of relevance as well as the format of the output. (For more information about structuring Lycos queries, check out Lycos' FAQ at http://www.lycos.com/info/ faq.html.)

When you first access Lycos, a very simple search form appears at the top level of the site. However, to construct a sophisticated query, click the **Enhance your search** link to display a more complex search form (Figure 23.5).

We're going to search on the same terms as we did on the WebCrawler search engine and compare the results.

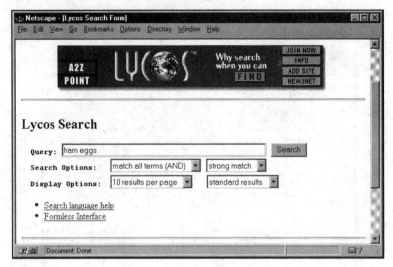

Figure 23.5 Lycos search form.

- **Query**. Enter the word or words you want to search for in this field.
- **Search options: match term** pop-up menu. Lets you select the number of words in the query that you want to match. For example, selecting **match any term (OR)** means that Lycos will return all items that contain one of the search terms you enter; selecting **match all items (AND)** means that only items containing both search terms will be retrieved. The remainder of the choices let you choose how many of your search terms will be matched.
- **Search options: match strength** pop-up menu. This menu lets you select the strength (relevance) of the match. Choices range from **loose match** to **strong match**.
- **Display options: results page size** menu. This menu lets you select the number of results that will be displayed on each page.
- **Display options: results detail** menu. This menu lets you select the amount of information displayed about each result. The choices range from summary (the least information) to standard (the default) to detailed (the most information).

Figure 23.6 shows the results of our search.

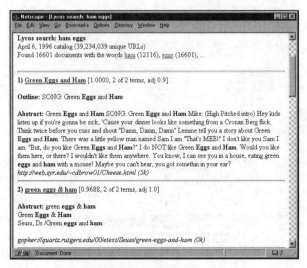

Figure 23.6 Results of a Lycos search.

The first item shows the last date that the catalog was updated and the number of URLs contained in the database. For standard Lycos results, each entry begins with the title of the result (which is a link to the page); the relevance score; the number of terms matched; and the adjacency of the terms in the document. Then, an outline (when available) and an abstract are provided, followed by the URL of the site and the size, in kilobytes, of the document.

Lycos also provides access to the A2Z index of Web sites (a relatively recent directory service) and to Point Communications' Web site reviews.

Infoseek

Infoseek, at http://www.infoseek.com, provides a free search engine to a database of Web pages, Usenet news archives, FTP and Gopher sites, and more. For a fee, you can join Infoseek Professional, which lets you access a variety of commercial databases as well.

Figure 23.7 shows Infoseek's search page. Although you can't choose the number of results, you can exert limited control over the search by using Infoseek's query parameters (click **Search Tips** at the top page to find out more).

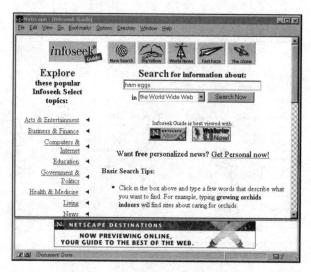

Figure 23.7 Infoseek's search page.

- **Query** field. Enter the words you're looking for.
- **Database selection** menu. You can choose the Web, FAQs (Frequently Asked Questions lists), Usenet newsgroups, email addresses, and more.

Figure 23.8 shows the results of our search.

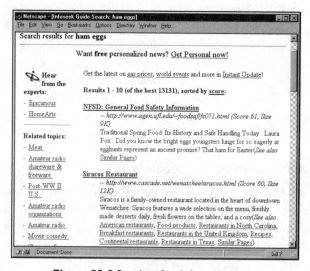

Figure 23.8 Results of an Infoseek search.

The results show the total number of returned documents that matched your query. Each individual record shows the title, the URL, the size of the document, an abstract of the document, and links to other categories at the Infoseek site that may contain information related to your query.

Alta Vista

Alta Vista (http://altavista.digital.com) is a search engine developed and maintained by Digital Equipment Corporation. Alta Vista allows you to perform either a simple or a complex search; our example (Figure 23.9) shows a simple one originated on the top page of the site. For complete information on structuring queries for Alta Vista, follow the links for "Help" and for "Advanced Search."

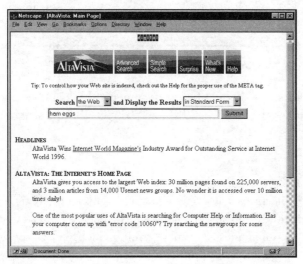

Figure 23.9 Search form at Alta Vista.

- **Search**. This menu lets you select whether to search items retrieved from the Web or those stored in archives of Usenet News.
- **Results**. This menu lets you select the level of detail of the results: standard, compact, or detailed.
- **Query** field. Enter the words you're looking for in this field.

Figure 23.10 shows the results of our search.

Figure 23.10 Results of an Alta Vista search.

The results show the number of documents that matched the words; each record shows the title, the URL, an abstract, the file size, and the date of creation.

Open Text

Open Text, at http://www.opentext.com, is a search engine which searches the complete text of the documents in its database, instead of just keywords, abstracts, or summaries. You may specify which part of the document you want to search—URL, title, description, etc. Open Text's "power search" form, at http://www.opentext.com/omw/xpowrsrch_c.html, is shown in Figure 23.11.

- **Search for** fields. Enter the individual terms or phrases that you're looking for in each field.
- **Within** pop-up menu. Select the part of the document in which the search term should appear; the choices are **anywhere**, **summary**, **title**, **heading**, and **Web location (URL)**.

- **Operators** pop-up menu. Select **AND**, **OR**, **BUT NOT**, **NEAR**, or **FOLLOWED BY** to create the precise query for the item you're looking for. The results of this search are shown in Figure 23.12.

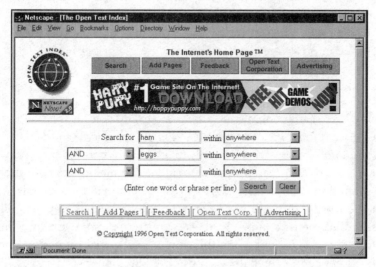

Figure 23.11 Search form at Open Text.

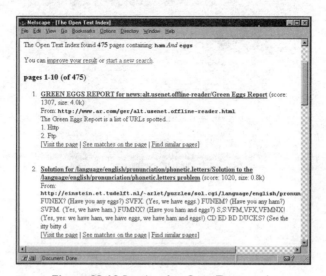

Figure 23.12 Results of an Open Text search.

The returned information includes the title of the site, the relevance score, the size of the document, and a few words of descriptive text. You may choose to visit the document, to see the words on the page that matched your query (which can help you choose whether you want to visit the document), or to find other pages in the index considered similar to the one described in the record. (You may also choose to start a new search or improve the result of the search you just performed.)

Excite

The Excite search engine, at http://www.excite.com, is unusual because it uses "fuzzy" logic instead of Boolean logic. Documents in the database are indexed not only by the keywords they contain, but also by synonyms for the keyword, so a search can be broadened to include items that are relevant but don't contain the exact words you entered. For example, a search for the words "software piracy" at a traditional search engine would only return documents containing those words; a search at Excite would also return documents containing the words "intellectual property," since it's a related concept. (For help with using Excite's query language, click the link for **Advanced Search Tips** or follow the links to the handbook.) Figure 23.13 shows the Excite search form.

Figure 23.13 Excite search form.

- **Query** field. Enter the word or words you're looking for.

- **Search location** menu. You can choose to search the Web, reviews of Web sites, Usenet news, or a large set of online classified ads.

- **Type of search** menu. Choose **by concept** to let Excite's engine find concepts related to your query, as described above; choose **by keyword** to search only for items that contain the specific words you entered.

Figure 23.14 shows the results of the search.

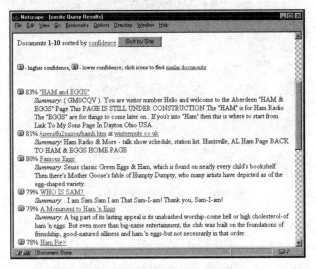

Figure 23.14 Results of a search at Excite.

Excite's results provide a confidence rating of how much the Excite engine thinks each result matches your request; you can choose to see results with higher or lower ratings or to resubmit your search.

Inktomi

Inktomi is a search engine originally developed at the University of California at Berkeley as part of a project to create scalable computer systems (that is, systems that can be expanded as the need for additional resources grows). At the time of this writing, Inktomi was about to become commercial partners with *Wired* Magazine's online *HotWired* publication, so the URL and interface may likely be different by the time you read this. Inktomi is named after a mythological spider of the Plains Indians who brought culture to the people and who represents the underdog. The Inktomi search engine (http://inktomi.berkeley.edu) is shown in Figure 23.15.

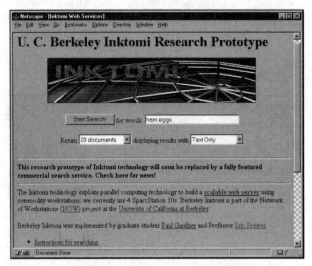

Figure 23.15 Inktomi search engine.

- **Query** field. Type the word or phrase you're looking for here.
- **Return** menu. Choose the number of results to be displayed.
- **Displaying results with** menu. Choose whether to show full graphics, text only, or terse results. (If you're using a dialup connection, we strongly suggest that you not retrieve full graphics.)

The results of the search are shown in Figure 23.16.

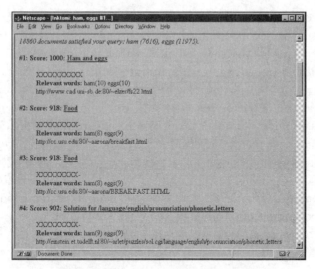

Figure 23.16 Results of an Inktomi search.

Finding Other Search Engines

The search engines listed above aren't the only ones available; they're just considered the most popular. You might find that other search engines suit your needs better. A huge list of search engines can be found on Yahoo at http://www.yahoo.com/Computers_and_Internet/Internet/World_Wide_Web/Searching_the_Web.

SHORTCUT

Netscape also maintains a short list of search engines at http://home.netscape.com/home/internet-search.html. To get there quickly, just click **Net Search** on the directory button bar or select **Internet Search** from the Directory menu.

Meta-searches

As more and more search engines become available, all with different strengths and weaknesses, it's become increasingly difficult to choose the search engine that will guarantee the best results. The next logical tool would be a search engine that searches all the other search engines on the Web—a *meta-search engine*, as it were.

497

Several of these meta-search engines have appeared recently. They are all similar in concept: they take your query, submit it in the appropriate format to all the search engines that you choose, and collate the results into a single page with a uniform format. The advantage of such a system is obvious—you can be confident that you've exhaustively searched the Web for relevant information. Also, some meta-search engines provide verification options to ensure that a document exists, which ordinary search indices don't provide. The disadvantage, however, is that meta-searches can operate extremely slowly, as they must submit your query to several search engines, all of which may be extremely busy, and then collate the results for display. Often, you can find approximately the same amount of information just as fast if you only use a single search engine but structure your query with care.

MetaCrawler

One of the most popular meta-search engines is MetaCrawler, developed by Erik Selberg and Oren Etzioni. MetaCrawler, located at http://metacrawler.cs.washington.edu/, submits your query to: Open Text, Lycos, WebCrawler, Infoseek, Excite, Inktomi, Alta Vista, Yahoo, and Galaxy. (The University of Washington, which hosts this site, is also the original site of the ever-popular WebCrawler search engine.)

Figure 23.17 shows the MetaCrawler query screen.

Figure 23.17 MetaCrawler query screen.

- **Search for:** field. Enter the terms you're searching for here. To search for the text you entered as a phrase, select **as a Phrase;** to search for documents that contain all of the words, select **All of these words;** and to search for documents containing any of the words (same as an OR operator), select **Any of these words.**

- **Fast Search/Comprehensive Search. Fast Search** returns results quickly. **Comprehensive Search** takes longer to perform, but will return more results.

- **Search Region.** This option lets you limit the results of your search to servers in your continent, your country, or your top-level domain (.com, .edu, etc.). The default is to search the world, but you should consider limiting your searches at least to your continent.

- **Search Sites.** This option lets you specify a top-level domain to search. It differs from choosing a domain for the Region option as it lets you select the domain instead of defaulting to the same top-level domain that you're connecting from.

- **Max wait.** This lets you specify how long MetaCrawler should try to submit its query to a busy search engine before giving up. (If you've ever tried to connect to Lycos during peak hours, you can understand why this is an important option.) The default is one minute, which allows MetaCrawler to attempt a few connections before moving on to another search engine.

- **Match type.** Strong, medium, loose, any...relevance rating without numbers.

Figure 23.18 shows the results of our search.

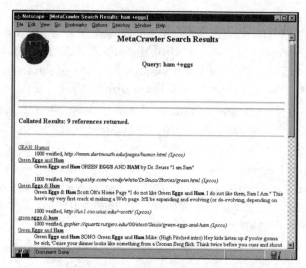

Figure 23.18 Results of a MetaCrawler search.

The displayed information is the title of the document, an excerpt of the document's text, the URL, and the search engine from which the information was retrieved.

SavvySearch

SavvySearch (http://rampal.cs.colostate.edu:2000/) was developed by Daniel Dreilinger at Colorado State University. SavvySearch offers fewer search parameters (which may come as a relief) but has an innovative way of limiting the databases which are searched. In addition to the standard big Internet search services, SavvySearch will also search sites like the Internet Movie Database, Time Warner's Pathfinder service, several name-and-address lookup services, and more. Figure 23.19 shows the SavvySearch query screen.

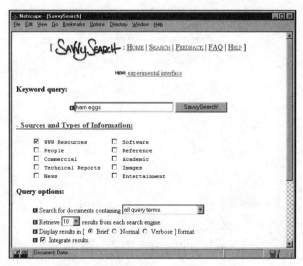

Figure 23.19 SavvySearch query screen.

- **Keyword Query**. Enter the word or words you're searching for. If you enter two words, the search will give preference to the items containing both words (SavvySearch "ands" them together).

- **Sources and Types of Information**. If you're not just looking for a general Web resource, select the desired items to help SavvySearch get a better idea of what to look for.

- **Query Options**. Select how many of the terms should be matched and how; the number of results from each search engine; the format of results; and whether results should be integrated (when selected, results are not separated by search engine and duplicates are removed).

The results of our search are displayed in Figure 23.20.

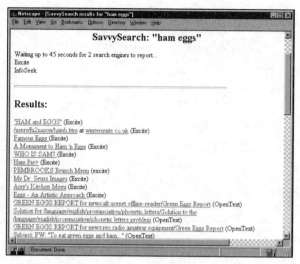

Figure 23.20 Results of a SavvySearch query.

The engines that were searched are listed at the top of the page. The title of each item is displayed, as well as a URL to the document itself. To the right of each returned item, SavvySearch displays which search engine or engines gave that document as a result.

Unified Search Pages

Another trend on the Web is to provide pages where you can actually submit queries to individual search engines. Unlike meta-searches (described in the previous section), these sites only let you search one engine at a time, but you can issue your queries to different search engines from a single page, regardless of which site you wish to use. A popular unified search location is Search.com, at http://www.search.com.

Just pick your engine, enter your query, choose any parameters specific to the engine, and click **Search**. Search.com will take you to the actual results page for the search engine you chose; use the **Back** function or the Go menu to return to Search.com, if desired.

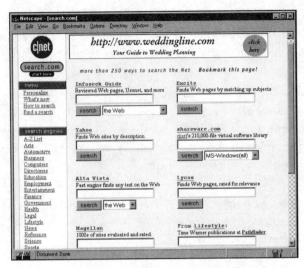

Figure 23.21 Unified search form at Search.com.

Although it's convenient to have an interface to all the search engines in one place, it still may be a good idea to use the search engine directly at its local site if you want to take advantage of the engine's additional features, such as choosing databases, the format of results, the use of special syntax to focus your query, etc.

WARNING

Search.com's best feature is probably their access to very specialized search engines, listed on the left side of each screen. If you know you only want information about employment, entertainment, or any of the categories on the list, you're likely to get the very specific results you're looking for.

NOTE

Subject Indices

Search engines are great if you have a pretty good idea of what you're looking for, as they let you locate specific information quickly. But if you're looking for general information on a topic, a search engine might not always be the right tool. Since entering a good query requires that you be as specific as possible, you might not see sites that contain information on related topics or that are simply indexed under a synonym for your search terms. If you're looking for a broader range of information than a search engine provides, check out one of the subject indices listed below.

A subject index works just like an index in the offline world. Several top-level categories are displayed, such as Commerce, Education, Entertainment, etc. Clicking a top-level category displays subcategories, which you can navigate through until you reach a page of links to sites that fall into the same classification.

NOTE Besides being a good way to find information on a general topic, subject indices can be a great place to start exploring the Web by clicking whatever category strikes your interest.

Yahoo

Yahoo, at http://www.yahoo.com, is one of the most popular subject indices available today. Originally developed in April, 1994 by David Filo and Jerry Yang, doctoral students in Electrical Engineering at Stanford University, Yahoo (Figure 23.22) quickly grew to be one of the most popular sites on the Web.

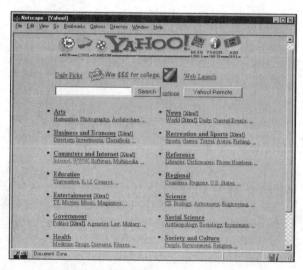

Figure 23.22 The top level of Yahoo.

The *San Jose Mercury News* says "Yahoo is closest in spirit to the work of Linnaeus, the 18th century botanist whose classification system organized the natural world." True, Yahoo's categories are comprehensive enough to include almost anything you can think of. Many categories are cross-referenced so you can reach the same information from different paths. For example, while a listing of sites for books about the Internet can be reached at http://www.yahoo.com/Business_and_Economy/Companies /Books/Computer_Books/Internet_Books/, you can also get to the same information by following a different path to http://www.yahoo.com/ Computers_and_Internet/Internet/World_Wide_Web/ and clicking the link for **Books**.

Yahoo also provides a mechanism to search the titles that are cataloged at the site, as well as their own "What's New" and "What's Cool" pages and a button to take you to a URL randomly selected from their huge catalog.

A financial arrangement with software giant SoftBank and a public offering in 1996 gave Yahoo the capital to create a slew of additional services, including an interactive map (type a street address anywhere in the United States and see it on a map; you can then pan or zoom around it); Yahooligans, a subject index of sites for kids; an index of images, where you can look for pictures instead of text; articles directly from the Reuters news wire; and more.

SHORTCUT
Yahoo has a built-in search engine that lets you search the entire site or specific categories. Best of all, if you don't find the site you're looking for in their catalog, Yahoo lets you submit your query immediately to one of several other search engines (many of which are described in this chapter.)

The Whole Internet Catalog

The Whole Internet Catalog is a much-expanded electronic version of Ed Krol's eponymous book, published by O'Reilly and Associates. This site was originally developed and maintained by O'Reilly, but is now managed by a joint venture between O'Reilly and America Online.

The Whole Internet Catalog (Figure 23.23) is located at http://www-e1c.gnn.com/gnn/wic/wics/index.html.

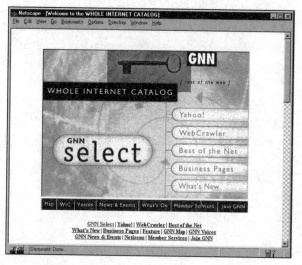

Figure 23.23 The Whole Internet Catalog.

The Whole Internet Catalog only has one level of categories, displayed on the first page; clicking any heading takes you to a list of links in that category. Clicking a heading there doesn't take you directly to the site—instead, a page of editorial information and comments about the information that you'll find at that site is displayed. This can be invaluable in determining if the site is really going to meet your needs before wasting the bandwidth to visit it.

The Whole Internet Catalog isn't as large as Yahoo, since all the sites listed must pass editorial inspection before being added. While this doesn't provide as many links, it does ensure that the links that are available are of a uniformly high quality.

TradeWave Galaxy

Formerly known as EINet Galaxy, the Austin-based company sponsoring this index recently changed the corporate name and the name of their Web sites and products. However, at the time of this writing, the URL for

Galaxy had not been changed; it could still be reached at http://www.einet.net.

The Galaxy subject index (Figure 23.24) is a nice trade-off between the comprehensiveness of Yahoo and the smaller-but-verified Whole Internet Catalog. (One nice feature is that each page of links lists recent additions to the catalog at the top of the page.) There are multiple layers of categories, but not so many entries that you find yourself clicking through a maze before you arrive at a page of useful information. Galaxy also has a search engine to find information in its own databases as well as Hytelnet (a database of telnet-accessible resources) and Gopher.

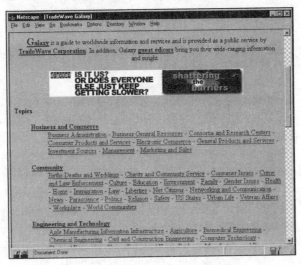

Figure 23.24 TradeWave Galaxy.

Magellan

Magellan (http://www.mckinley.com) is another example of a directory service combined with a search engine; it allows you to see information about and links to more than 50,000 reviewed and rated sites. You can explore the site as an index, or you can choose to search its own database of reviewed documents or of all Web documents.

Figure 23.25 Magellan.

Point Communications

Point Communications (http://www.pointcom.com), which is owned by
Lycos, Inc., provides descriptions and ratings of the sites that they consider
to be the top 5% of all Web sites in the world. (Chosen sites frequently display a logo stating that they've been honored as such.) Point also provides
original content in the form of general news and feature articles.

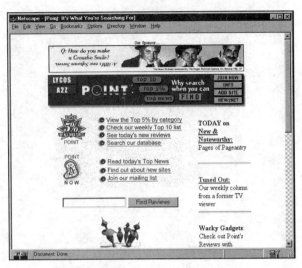

Figure 23.26 Point Communications.

The Virtual Library

The Virtual Library (Figure 23.27), at http://www.w3.org/hypertext/
DataSources/bySubject/Overview.html, is managed by the World Wide
Web Consortium (W3C), a joint effort of MIT, CERN (where the Web
began), and INRIA, the European W3C center in France. This subject
index is a distributed database—the information within the top-level
headings (which are organized alphabetically and are surprisingly comprehensive) is maintained by people at other locations around the world.
This somewhat alleviates the Herculean task of managing an index of the
exponentially growing number of URLs.

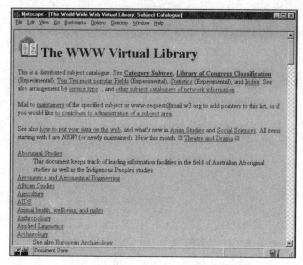

Figure 23.27 The Virtual Library.

Starting Points

If you're just getting started with the Web or are simply looking for a good place to begin your surfing, consider the use of "Starting Points," "What's New," and "What's Cool" pages as jumping-off points to the rest of the Web.

Official "Starting Points" Pages

Several sites exist for the purpose of helping people understand the Internet and the World Wide Web as well as to provide jumping-off points for further exploration.

- Netscape's "Destinations" section at http://home.netscape.com/escapes /index.html (though links to individual categories are currently available on the home page) provides a short, manageable list of some of the best sites in a variety of categories.

- NCSA, the pioneering developers of Mosaic, have consistently provided some of the most useful (though somewhat utilitarian) pages available. Their "Starting Points for Internet Exploration" page, located at http://www.ncsa.uiuc.edu/SDG/Software/Mosaic/ StartingPoints/NetworkStartingPoints.html, contains several links to information about general Internet and World Wide Web services, as well as a small but interesting selection of Web pages.

"What's New" Pages

Many sites provide a "What's New" listing of interesting URLs that recently appeared on the Net. Because so many new sites are created daily and the information expires rapidly, it might be difficult to find something specific that you're looking for. Also, the democratic nature of some "What's New" lists, which present every single new URL regardless of its content, can make it difficult to find information that's interesting to you. Nonetheless, "What's New" pages are where you'll always find the latest information. The following is a list of some popular "What's New" pages:

- NCSA maintains one of the granddaddies of all the "What's New" pages on the Web, available at http://www.ncsa.uiuc.edu/SDG/ Software/Mosaic/Docs/whats-new.html. NCSA updates the list daily, provides an alphabetical list of all new or changed URLs, and names a "Pick of the Week."

- Netscape Communications' "What's New" page is available at http://home.netscape.com/home/whats-new.html. The page is edited by staff members and only includes information that is both new to the Web and uses or advances the technology in some way. This lofty goal isn't necessarily always met—although many of the listings may be considered interesting, it's a bit of a stretch to say that the offerings only represent truly innovative sites.

- Yahoo maintains a list of new URLs added to their database each day at http://www.yahoo.com/new.

NOTE

This "What's New" list is notable as the only one to organize the links by topic, making it possible to quickly locate new links in categories of interest.

"What's Cool" Pages

Some locations are dedicated to listing the locations that they find cool, interesting, innovative, amusing, or just plain weird. Generally reflecting the personality of the developer, the following sites are always good starting points for diving into some of the more eclectic parts of the Web. Some popular "What's Cool" pages include:

- "Spider's Pick of the Day" at http://gagme.wwa.com/~boba/pick.html, maintained by Bob Allison.

- "Cool Site of the Day" at http://www.infi.net/cool.html, maintained by Glenn Davis. Winning Davis' "Cool Site of the Year" contest is considered such a feather in a developer's cap that one year a nominee vandalized his own site for publicity.

- Netscape Communications' "What's Cool" page, at http://home .netscape.com/home/whats-cool.html.

SHORTCUT

To get there, just click the **What's Cool?** button or select **What's Cool?** from the Directory menu.

- Yahoo's "Cool Links" category at http://www.yahoo.com/Entertain ment/COOL_links.

Also of Note...

The following items are also great resources for finding new Web sites and for searching repositories of existing information.

NetSurfer Digest

NetSurfer Digest is a free biweekly newsletter distributed by email that contains descriptions of and links to a variety of interesting sites. You can receive the file either as a regular text message or as an HTML file that you can save to your disk drive and open with Netscape.

The latest edition of *NetSurfer Digest* and subscription information can be found at http://www.netsurf.com.

Usenet News FAQs

As we discussed in Chapter 15, Usenet News is a system of worldwide discussion groups containing an immense amount of disparate information. Most newsgroups maintain a Frequently Asked Questions list, or FAQ, which contains concise answers to the questions most commonly asked about the topic. If you're looking for technical information or are interested in less weighty topics like a television show or home brewing beer, you can almost always find a FAQ that will answer your questions.

The complete text of every Usenet FAQ is maintained at http://www.cis.ohio-state.edu/hypertext/faq/usenet/FAQ-List.html. This site has a mini-search engine that looks through the titles of newsgroups and articles, as well as an alphabetical locator to go directly to a topic in its alphabetical listing.

Usenet News Archives at DejaNews

Occasionally, the answer that you're looking for doesn't appear on a Web page or in a Usenet FAQ—you might be looking for something arcane or related to a topic for which there is no FAQ, like a specific problem with a piece of software. If this is the case, your new best friend may be DejaNews, at http://dejanews.com, which houses a searchable archive of more than a year's worth of articles posted to Usenet News.

What You Learned

After reading this chapter, you should be able to:

- Use and evaluate search engines and subject indices to find the information you're looking for on the World Wide Web.
- Choose when to search the Web and when to limit your search to gopher, FTP, and WAIS sites.
- Locate other search engines and subject indices.
- Use "Starting Points" pages to begin Web exploration.
- Easily locate archives of Usenet FAQs and articles.

CHAPTER 24

EMERGING TRENDS AND TECHNOLOGIES

When the scientists at CERN first envisioned the Web as a means of sharing hypertext information, they certainly couldn't have envisioned that it would turn into the all-purpose multimedia publishing forum that it's become today. Instead of being a relatively sedate repository of research and administrative materials, today's Web is a manic free-for-all jumble of solid news, personal expression, and commercial entities competing for your attention.

In this chapter, we'll look at some Web sites that are pushing the limits of traditional electronic communications. Some of them introduce new technologies, while others modify existing Internet services such as live chat and discussion forums to take advantage of the unique features of the Web for promoting community. Other sites simply provide content that is either inherently engaging (such as the ongoing soap opera at The Spot) or simply very useful (like stock quote service or travel information and booking).

Please keep in mind that this chapter is by no means comprehensive. There are more cool, interactive sites than you can point a mouse at, and the numbers are growing every day. And, cool sites come and go—in a few months' time, there will be another batch of amazing sites, and the ones listed here may be obsolete or even nonexistent. (Later in the chapter, we'll take a look at some new technologies which might soon make even these sites obsolete.) However, the categories that these sites fall into will remain more or less the same, including:

- Computer-mediated communication, which encompasses any kind of online activity that lets you communicate or share information with others, whether singly or in a group that shares a common interest.

- Graphical environments, where you can browse intensely visual online information, ranging from live weather maps to fully immersive games.

- Distribution of real-time data, including materials as diverse as live video, real-time audio, and up-to-date stock quotes and airline ticket prices.

- HTML generators, which let you create new Web documents "on the fly" while you're connected to a site.

- Multimedia delivery, either in conjunction with or instead of more traditional technologies such as CD-ROM.

NOTE As this book went to press, Web sites were only beginning to fully use the newer innovations that we've talked about in this book, such as Java, plug-ins, cookies, and personal certificates. A tremendous amount of innovation is occurring, but it's a safe bet that the sites that will be most successful in the future are the ones that will utilize these new technologies.

Computer-Mediated Communication

Some of the most interesting sites on the Web allow you to communicate immediately with others, whether by faxing your opinions to governmental organizations or participating in live, real-time forums such as round-table discussions with public figures. In addition to these highbrow activities, there are also plenty of places where you can pull up a virtual chair and chat directly with others from all over the world.

Live Faxing

It's relatively simple for a site developer to include a CGI gateway program that allows you to send a fax directly from your browser to a regular fax machine anywhere in the world. One site that uses this technology is The Rainforest Action Network at http://www.ran.org/ran/, which lets you compose and send a fax online to companies and consulates of countries currently responsible for damage to the environment.

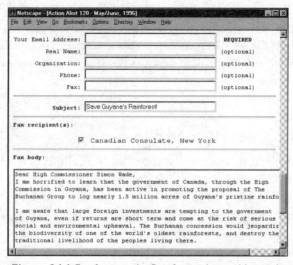

Figure 24.1 Fax form at the Rainforest Action Network.

A number of other sites are also experimenting with fax delivery through the Web. If you're interested, try a keyword search for the terms "fax delivery."

Live Chat

Live chat, where you converse in real-time with other people, has been an Internet staple for years. Until the rise of graphical Internet applications, chatting online required that you learn a series of arcane commands that you typed into your terminal emulator program. But now, talking to other people is as easy as typing your message and pressing a button.

A great deal of the online chat on the Web is based on IRC (Internet Relay Chat), a standard for multi-user real-time communication that's been in use for years. At first IRC was simply gatewayed onto the Web, but now many companies have developed IRC client programs that work as helper applications with your Web browser. (Netscape Chat for Windows can be retrieved from http://home.netscape.com/comprod/chat_install.html. The Global Village Chat client for all platforms is available at http://www.quarterdeck.com/chat/realdownload.html.)

NOTE A popular Web attraction is to schedule celebrities to appear in interactive forums where they answer the questions of their online fans. Schedules change, so check Global Village Chat's most up-to-date list at http://www.quarterdeck.com/chat/schedule.html.

Chat Directly Through Your Browser

No matter what your interests, there are several topics of chat gatewayed directly into the browser that don't require special clients. Some general chats include: InfiNet's Talker at http://www.infi.net/talker/, where you get to pick an icon or other graphic to represent you in addition to choosing a name (or "handle"); and L'Hotel Chat, at http://chat.magmacom.com/lhotel/hotel.html, where the metaphor of a luxury hotel in Monaco is used to let you pick what kind of chat you want to engage in (for example, singles congregate at the bar, while lively general conversation can be found in the restaurant).

An example of a good thematic chat area is ParentsPlace at http://www.parentsplace.com/talking.html, where you discuss the joys and occasional heartbreaks of being a parent with others who have similar experiences.

NOTE As this book went to press, HotWired announced the beta version of a Java-based chat service at their site which simulates the kinds of chat you'll find in services like America Online. You'll be able to join thematic chat areas, start your own area, and chat privately with others or publicly for everyone to view. You can check it out at http://talk.hotwired.com/.

Interactive and Serial Fiction

Several experiments in interactive and serial fiction are available on the Web. The first successful (and commercial) soap opera was The Spot, at http://www.thespot.com. Based on the lives of the fictional residents of a California beach house, The Spot contains new installments about the characters every day, as well as several weeks of archived information, discussion groups where you can talk about the latest happenings with other fans, the ability to send email directly to the characters, and even a chance to explore the reminiscences of the house pet, Spotnik the dog.

A recent newcomer to the online soap world is East Village (http://www.eastvillage.com/), which, despite its funding by Time Warner, has a lot more of an edge to it. East Village's features are pretty much the same as The Spot's, though you can join "cliques" to get special information about characters that's not otherwise available.

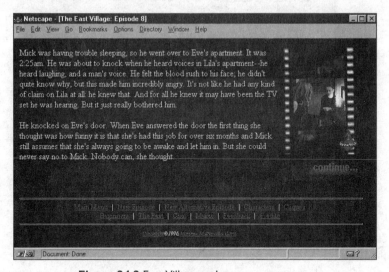

Figure 24.2 East Village, an Internet soap opera.

Posting Your Own Comments

Another online trend that encourages a sense of electronic community is letting users post their own comments about the topics covered at a site.

Unlike chat, where your comments are usually directed at a few other people and are gone as soon as you type them, these forums allow you to read other people's comments and post your own follow-ups for others to view. (It's conceptually similar to Usenet News, except that the discussion remains on the host site instead of being mirrored to thousands of computers around the world.) Sites with their own discussion groups abound; two good examples are the discussion sections at HotWired (http://www.hotwired.com) and Time Warner's Pathfinder service at http://www.pathfinder.com (Figure 24.3), which also operates a chat server.

Figure 24.3 A discussion group at Pathfinder.

Graphical Environments

For some time, graphical environments and information systems have allowed people to use GUI software on dedicated computers for non-textual exploration of data. However, it's only recently that such graphical exploration could be used for worldwide databases through the World Wide Web.

Immersive Environments

One early example of a highly graphical site that allows you to fully explore a physical environment is MCI's Gramercy Press (http://www.mci.com/gramercy), which lets you navigate through the hallways and offices of a Manhattan publishing company, reading the staff's email, listening to their answering machines, and exploring items on their walls and desktops. Although MCI has abandoned the Gramercy Press ad campaign on television, the Web site is still available; it serves as a very good example of an immersive multimedia environment that's still accessible to people using low-bandwidth dialup connections.

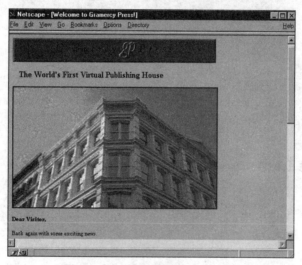

Figure 24.4 MCI's Gramercy Press.

The next generation of fully immersive, three-dimensional environments—similar to those in CD-ROM games—is beginning to take shape on the Web using Virtual Reality Modeling Language, or VRML, whose standards were recently adopted by the World Wide Web Consortium. Netscape 3.0 supports VRML through the Live3D plug-in, opening a world of possibility for delivering eye-popping, 3-D real-time simulations through the Internet. Figure 24.5 shows a clip from Intel's "Inside the System" game at http://www.intel.com; you can't really get an idea from this 2-D picture what it's like to zoom around and rotate your views of the objects, but trust us, it's way cool, and we don't use that phrase lightly.

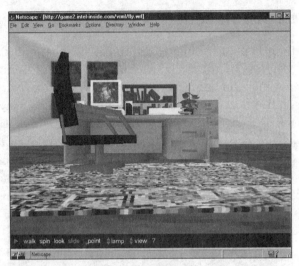

Figure 24.5 "Inside the System" with VRML.

As connection speeds and processor power increase, expect to see more and more fully immersive worlds developed in VRML.

Navigable Maps

A navigation feature that's becoming increasingly common is allowing users to navigate through a site based on graphical information. For example, to choose a destination on City.Net (http://www.city.net), you start by clicking a continent on a globe. A map of the continent is then displayed; you select a country, region, and finally a city on successive maps. This method of locating information is a far cry from typing complicated pathnames.

Instead of using maps as navigation aids, other services exist to actually help you find a specific usable map. For example, Mapquest (http://www.mapquest.com) lets you view maps of highways and major cities, and even provides a TripQuest service to help you plan the best route for your road trip. (You can even use a Java-based "mapplet," which has more customizable features than the CGI-based version.) Yahoo's mapping program (http://maps.yahoo.com/yahoo) lets you view a map for any street address in the United States; you can then explore surrounding areas or zoom in and out to become better oriented. And Subway Navigator, a France-based service at http://metro.jussieu.fr:10001/bin/cities/english, lets you find subway route information for several major cities around the globe.

Figure 24.6 Map of Europe at City.Net.

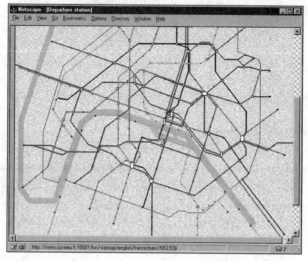

Figure 24.7 The Paris subway at Subway Navigator.

Weather Information

Weather World (http://www.atmos.uiuc.edu/wxworld/html/top.html), at the University of Illinois at Urbana-Champaign, hosts all kinds of weather satellite images from GOES-7 and GOES-8 that are updated by computers every 30 minutes. (One satellite is centered over the East coast, and the other is near the Pacific Basin.) You can see still images as well as short animations of the last 24 hours of satellite radar activity; these animations are the same as you see on the Weather Channel or your local news!

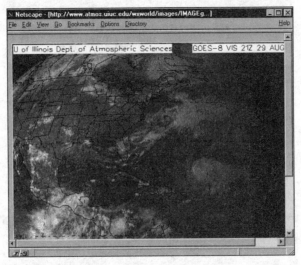

Figure 24.8 Live satellite images at Weather World.

Real-Time Data

The kind of information you can retrieve from the Web isn't limited to just static text, sound, graphics, and movies anymore. The following sites have developed new technologies or modified existing ones to greatly boost the level of real-time interaction available on the Web.

Immediate Audio with RealAudio

RealAudio, a product of Progressive Networks, Inc., uses a new MIME type and associated helper application to let you hear sound files in "real time." Instead of waiting for the entire sound file to download, RealAudio uses *streaming* to let you begin playback of the sound while it's still downloading. This makes it easier to cope with large sound files on the Web; if you want to listen to a half-hour program, you don't need to wait for the huge file to download before starting.

RealAudio is available as a helper application or plug-in from http://www.prognet.com. Programs available at Progressive Networks in the RealAudio format include National Public Radio's "All Things Considered," "Morning Edition," and "Talk of the Nation"; several selections from ABC News; Internet Hourly News, a 15-minute news feature updated every hour; and a slew of other news, business, technology, entertainment, and comedy offerings. Many other sites on the Web also offer news and entertainment in the RealAudio format; a major source for all kinds of audio is AudioNet at http://www.audionet.com/.

Customized News

The personalized, cookie-based Web pages we discussed in Chapter 21 were really just the tip of the customized information iceberg; in the past year, several companies have entered into the "pointcasting" (as opposed to "broadcasting") information delivery market. The theory behind pointcasting is simple: instead of receiving and viewing the same information as everyone else, like watching television, you only see the information that you've asked for, and it's delivered to you personally.

The first, and so far the best, entry into the marketplace is PointCast, Inc. (http://www.pointcast.com), whose information can be viewed either in a screen saver or through your browser. After you tell the service what kind of information you're looking for and how often you want it updated, the news you want will be delivered in the time and format you requested. (If you're using a dialup connection, PointCast will retrieve the news while you're connected and display it while you're not.) PointCast's information sources include Pathfinder (Time Warner's huge Web site), the *Los*

Angeles Times, Hambrecht & Quist, the *Boston Globe*, the Weather Channel, and more. PointCast is also being used by corporate intranets to deliver locally created information directly to their internal users.

Airline Tickets and Travel

Lots of airlines have some kind of Web site, but Southwest (http://www.iflyswa.com) was one of the first to let you display flight information and fares simply by choosing the cities you're flying between and the dates of travel. (If you've ever tried to find a flight in the Official Airlines Guide, you know how difficult it can be to find what you're looking for in pages and pages of text!) The site also provides a wealth of other travel resources, such as material about the 46 airports Southwest serves, including directions to the airports.

However, the online travel ante has been upped recently by several services that not only let you search for flight information on more than one airline, but even let you book your own trips from your desktop. For example, Travelocity (http://www.travelocity.com) lets you search for and book flights on all major airlines, in addition to hosting a slew of travel-related material, merchandise, chat areas, and forums.

Stock Quotes and Financial Information

Want to find out how your investments are doing, even if you can't watch CNBC at work? Just enter the ticker symbol at the Investor's Edge Web Site at http://www.irnet.com/pages/stock.stm to see the recent prices. You can even create a portfolio of up to 15 stocks and regularly track their performance. (Stock quotes are delayed by 15 minutes.)

A number of other companies provide the same kind of free delayed stock quote service, including PC Quote Server (http://www.pcquote.com), the Security APL Quote Server (http://www.secapl.com/cgi-bin/qs), and the Data Broadcasting Corporation (http://www.dbc.com/quote.html).

If you're serious about managing your own investments, then an online brokerage may well be the right place for you. Services such as E*Trade (http://www.etrade.com) will let you trade shares at a discount price, directly through your Web browser.

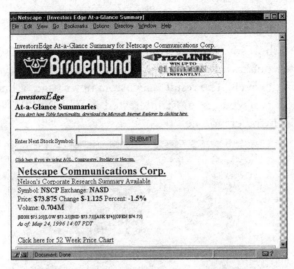

Figure 24.9 Stock quotes at Investor's Edge.

Real-time Video

As we briefly discussed in Chapter 17, a vast range of video equipment is hooked up to the Web, allowing you to see up-to-the-minute images from all over the world. For a comprehensive list of live video sites, check out the Peeping Tom home page at http://www.ts.umu.se/~spaceman/camera.html.

HTML Generators

A fairly recent trend on the Web is sites that let you create HTML documents on the fly, while you're connected. Some, like Prodigy's ScratchPad (which is only for Prodigy subscribers), let you develop custom home pages. Others harness the power of network information systems to generate HTML documents which are graphically rich or dynamically updated, for your own use or for viewing by others.

CRAYON

CRAYON, short for "CReAte Your Own Newspaper," is a service that lets you create your own HTML pages containing links to a variety of news sources on the Web. The result is a custom news page of links to the daily information that you are most interested in. CRAYON (Figure 24.10) is available at http://crayon.net/.

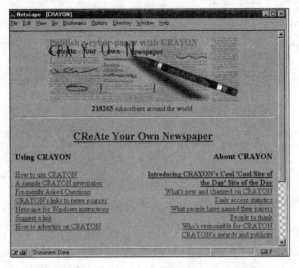

Figure 24.10 The CReAte Your Own Newspaper home page.

The first step in creating your own newspaper is to give it a name. Then you choose the news sources that you want to include as links in your newspaper. Available categories include United States and world news, local and world weather, sports, editorials, arts and entertainment—in other words, all the sections of a regular newspaper. You can even rearrange the order of the categories for your own newspaper; for example, if you like to read the comics and the weather first, place these links near the top of your paper.

The last step is to generate the HTML document (Figure 24.11), which you should save as HTML source to your disk drive. You can then bookmark the file or set it to be your home page.

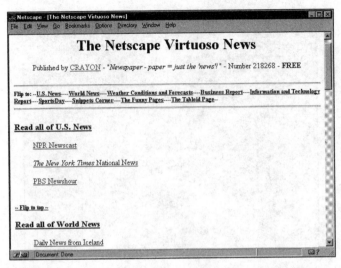

Figure 24.11 A personal newspaper created with CRAYON.

If you click the link for a specific news source, you go to the site for that news source. But, if you click the heading of a section of the newspaper, you automatically connect to the CRAYON site, where all the information from the various sites in the section is combined into a single page as a "personal newspaper."

NOTE

CRAYON is a simple idea, but a sure sign of things to come. Newspaper publishers are already looking for new ways to add value to their content on the Web; it's likely that you'll soon see such customizable services offered by conglomerates.

Greeting Cards

Several sites let you create an HTML greeting card from a variety of templates. Some let you send them directly to the recipient; others let you post them online and inform the receiver of the URL.

The following greeting card (Figure 24.12) was created at Build-A-Card, located at http://buildacard.com.

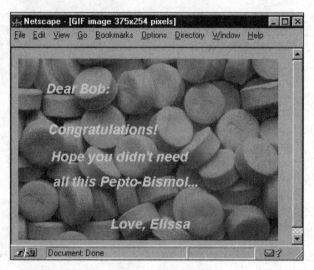

Figure 24.12 A custom card for author Robert Miller.

Build-A-Card lets you choose a card and add as much text or as many additional pictures as you desire. You can even choose the font, style, and alignment features. And, if you don't like what you've created so far, you can delete or edit items until you do.

When the card is complete, it's assigned a custom URL that you can mail to others so they can see the card. The card will be available for viewing for about one week. Or, you can save the card as a GIF image to your disk drive.

For a complete list of sites that let you create greeting cards, check out http://www.yahoo.com/text/Entertainment/Humor__Jokes__and_ Fun/Greeting_Cards_on_WWW.

Multimedia

Another kind of emerging technology is the use of the Web to deliver multimedia information and entertainment, instead of or in conjunction with more traditional delivery media such as CD-ROMs.

Games

Cretins, Inc., at http://www.nembley.com/, takes advantage of the Shockwave and RealAudio plug-ins to create a satirical look at workplace life. You've just gone to work for BilgeCorp, a company that makes, among other things, industrial-strength flea spray, candy-flavored cigarettes, and canned lunch meat. You want to get a promotion, which requires you perform a series of items on your to-do list, but you need the help of your coworkers…and everyone you work with is a cretin—incompetent at best and just plain mean at worst. You can navigate through the working week as either a diligent employee or a back-stabbing cutthroat like everyone else. Like most other sites with immersive games, Cretins, Inc. is in support of a CD-ROM.

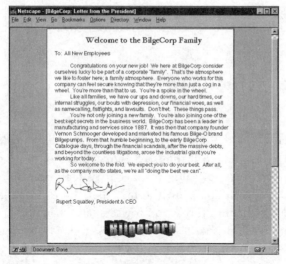

Figure 24.13 Cretins, Inc.

Another interactive site is a promotion for the Burn:Cycle CD-ROM game (http://www.burncycle.com). In addition to letting you download movies and sound clips from the game, several portions of the CD-ROM have been modified to allow exploration of the virtual land called Trip World, where your character must navigate through the seedy underworld of cyberspace to complete a dangerous mission.

CDLink

The Voyager Company's CDLink software, conceptualized by Todd Fahrner, merges two kinds of multimedia technologies: the up-to-the-minute publishing capabilities of the Web and the high-quality digital audio of consumer audio CDs. CDLink is the equivalent of "digital liner notes." You can read descriptions and explications of music online, then click a link to make your CD-ROM drive play the passage that the author is talking about. Existing applications of CDLink include Ray Manzarek (formerly of The Doors) describing why he loves X; Tufts University music professor and jazz pianist Michael Ullman explaining a Thelonius Monk album; and *Spin* Magazine's review of the twenty best alternative albums.

Software is available at http://www.voyagerco.com/cdlink. (You'll also need a CD-ROM drive as well as the audio CD that you're reading about.)

The Web of Tomorrow

If you've made it all the way through the book so far, you've learned almost everything there is to know about using Netscape Navigator, from basic tips about hidden features to explanations of more complex topics like Java, MIME types, plug-ins, security features, and understanding URLs. But you can count on the fact that the technologies behind the Web, and thus behind the Web browsers, are changing at an astonishing pace. Don't be surprised if, in a few years, today's cutting edge interfaces will be as out-of-date as black and white, VHF-only television sets with rabbit-ear antennas.

In the rest of this chapter, we're going to talk a little bit about the emerging trends and technologies that are already beginning to change the way we view and interact through the Web.

New Connectivity Options

For some time, a debate has raged about the best method of high-speed data delivery that can be easily used by homes and small businesses.

While corporations and other large organizations can take advantage of ISDN, T1, and other extremely fast connectivity options, most home and small business users are limited to the speed of their modems, currently 28.8 Kbps.

You can hardly avoid hearing about the current crop of telecommunications mergers between cable television companies, telephone service providers, and content providers such as movie production firms, television networks, and publishing houses. One result of these alliances will undoubtedly be a high-speed integrated method of providing content-on-demand, which might range from videos and TV shows to browsing the Web or its descendants.

Some parts of the country already have experimental delivery of Internet services through their cable television system, while others can take advantage of residential ISDN (at speeds of 64 and 128 kilobits per second) for as little as the price of premium cable channels. There's even an apartment building in New York that offers full T1 access to its residents (at an additional monthly cost of about $80).

Though it may take a few years before an affordable and widespread standard for such high-speed access emerges on a national and worldwide scale, rest assured that in the future, those at home won't be limited to 14.4 or 28.8 Kbps of data.

Changes in Web Commerce and Content

In the next few years, you can almost certainly expect to see more and more vendors selling products on the Web, relying on security schemes like SSL and other protocols, as well as on electronic cash schemes like First Virtual Holdings and DigiCash's ecash. It seems probable that we'll eventually get used to the idea of buying things through the Web; at least, hundreds of companies are banking millions of dollars on it.

If you haven't purchased anything online yet, you might consider trying it once. If you're using Netscape (especially the Personal Edition, with the fundamentally uncrackable 128-bit dual-key encryption) and purchasing from a site that has a secure Netscape server, you're probably much safer than you are using a credit card at a shopping mall or restaurant, where any number of people might come across your card number on the credit slip or the carbons. Then, you can make your own judgments about whether or not you like the experience. Some people enjoy being able to purchase things 24 hours a day without ever talking to another person (to say nothing of the control over the spelling of your name and address!), while others miss the personal touch of talking to the sales representative and the immediate feedback about whether or not an item is in stock. Anyway, if you try online shopping, you'll have more of a basis to analyze its pros and cons than if you just read other people's descriptions of the experience.

You can also expect to see even more advertising on all kinds of sites. You've probably already noticed that some of the best free search engines, subject indices, and information sources prominently display clickable "billboards" for sponsoring companies on various pages. Though you may find this rather annoying, keep in mind that such large-scale corporate sponsorship makes it possible to provide these useful services free of charge.

That leads right into another trend you can expect to become more widespread: services available through your browser which require registration and/or fees for their use. Registration without fees is already in place at several sites, often to provide a validated ID for people to post items in local discussion groups, or, as in the case of the *News and Observer*, to satisfy requirements for redistributing certain kinds of information. *The Wall Street Journal* was one of the first online publishing ventures to charge a fee for access—currently, the price is $29 if you subscribe to the regular paper ($169/year), and $49 if you're only subscribing to view the electronic version.

You can expect to find more and more services with associated fees as comprehensive commercial databases become available online. (Except at a public library, the best information is rarely free.)

Another emerging trend on the Web that has immense social and legal ramifications is online gambling. The technology of the Web makes it possible for people in states that don't allow gambling to easily place secure bets on out-of-state casinos or on offshore servers in countries that do.

A lot of people are betting that online gambling will be a cash cow, taking advantage of people's predilection toward wagering in the same way as expanded state lotteries, casinos, and gambling cruises have in recent years in the United States. At the moment, the future of online gambling is clouded by federal restrictions that prohibit private enterprises from establishing gaming operations in most states. However, this hasn't prevented people from establishing prototypical Internet gambling casinos at offshore locations. If you're interested in seeing an example, check out the Casino Strip's Web site at http//www.casino.org, a graphics-intensive, well-designed site in the Turks and Caicos Islands.

NOTE While it's interesting to look at these sites, don't get your credit card out just yet. Even though you can access these sites with your browser, federal restrictions make it illegal for American citizens to gamble online, even if the casino is outside the United States.

Another area that's expected to become very, very hot over the next few years is online gaming. As Skye Dayton, executive officer of EarthLink (a large Internet service provider) said in *Interactive Age Daily*, "It is clear to us that there are still significant barriers (including consumer comfort) to commerce becoming that killer application, whereas with gaming we have the technology today and the infrastructure in place to have ubiquitous interactivity." This statement was in reference to an announcement that EarthLink subscribers would be able to play a variety of online games similar to those that are currently only offered on CD-ROM. As more and more CD-ROM publishing begins to include "hybrid" links to obtain data from Web sites, you can probably expect to see more and more online games that are based on or linked to CD-ROM games, allowing online updates and multiple players. (As an example, Activision's "Spycraft" CD-ROM game already comes with Web links for daily updates.)

Changes in Computing Technology

Computers are getting faster and faster, but they're still basically either Macintosh or Windows-based. But if Oracle chairman and CEO Larry Ellison has his way, more and more people and businesses will use a less expensive alternative: instead of the PC, or personal computer, people will use the NC, or "network computer." Such a device would have minimal storage capacity but would be able to connect to a network (such as, say, the Internet) and display text and graphics. Ellison expects to be able to sell such a device for under $500, which could drastically lower the entry barriers to the Internet for the huge population of the public who don't own personal computers.

Unfortunately, the ability for home users to support such devices depends on how the various players in the telecommunications industry deliver connectivity in the future. Though NCs are being developed to allow Web and Internet access, the immediate plan for the NC is to be used in businesses as a terminal for viewing and entering information such as purchase orders or airline reservations.

Meanwhile, many computer and electronics manufacturers are retooling their product lines so that computers look more like televisions, and televisions look more like computers (some new TVs even come equipped with a modem port). When and how these devices will become part of the mainstream remains to be seen) but the convergence of televison and personal computers is happening faster than anyone expected.

Broadcasting

Because the Internet can deliver large quantities of data on a worldwide scale for no more than the cost of access to your local service provider, many researchers and developers are experimenting with Internet-based communication technologies that allow live delivery of audio or video, either as broadcast or point-to-point communications. At this time, the best examples are the use of RealAudio and similar technologies for the delivery of news and entertainment.

Telephony

Broadcasting focuses on sending a message from a single source to a wide number of receivers, without concern for how many people are listening or who they are, and without providing any means for response—in other words, it's one-way transmission just like TV or radio. Point-to-point communication, on the other hand, is connection-oriented communication, where each connection has a sender and a recipient. For example, telephone calls and electronic mail are point-to-point communications, as they are only directed at one or a few other people. The Internet has the potential to be used for both kinds of communications.

An area of great interest is using the Internet to transmit real-time voice communications so that you can essentially make free long distance calls through your computer for no more than the cost of your local Internet connection.

Netscape's CoolTalk application, which is shipped with Netscape 3.0 but is not currently integrated into the browser, is Netscape's first entry into the telephony market. Like other Internet telephone software—such as VocalTec's Internet Phone (http://www.vocaltec.com) and Voxware's Televox (http://www.voxware.com)—CoolTalk doesn't let you call up another person directly; instead, you connect to a CoolTalk server, where you select the name of the person you want to talk to from a list. You can also use CoolTalk to set up conference calls with two or more other people who are similarly connected; a "white board" feature is included so that participants can share written information as well as conversation, as in a business conference.

Unlike CoolTalk and Internet Phone, NetSpeak's commercial WebPhone software (http://www.netspeak.com) lets you call other online users directly without logging into a server first.

NOTE

The quality of the audio tends to vary, and without special equipment you may feel like you're on an old-fashioned speaker phone, but these products represent some of the first viable attempts for teleconferencing and workgroup collaboration. The most recent Internet telephone products offer the same features that you can get with a regular telephone, such as voice mail and Caller ID, and also provide new functions not available with telephones, such as private, encrypted communications.

In addition to its use for personal communications, you might see some customer service activities being handled with Internet telephony; for example, if you couldn't find a solution to your problem in an online help section, you'd eventually reach a live representative at the end of the line. Eventually, it's expected that you'll be able to call regular telephone numbers and have regular conversations using your computer and Internet connection.

NOTE

Another technology that should improve software customer support as well as project collaboration is similar to Farallon's Look@Me plug-in, based on their award-winning Timbuktu software. Look@Me lets you view and control another person's computer remotely; you can probably expect to see these products support voice communications as well.

Videoconferencing

Another area of great interest is the use of the Internet for videoconferencing. While some commercial products are available today, the first attempt at a viable live video product for the Internet was CU See Me, originally developed by Cornell University, and now a product of White Pine Software (http://www.wpine.com). CU See Me displays live video on computers participating in a "video telephone call." CU See Me is used for point-to-point communications, but it's possible—with the use of a *reflector*—to use it for broadcasting. (However, as we'll discuss in the next section, it's not an ideal technology for that use.)

Another video conferencing product comes from Connectix, makers of the affordable QuickCam digital video camera, who now sell their VideoPhone software bundled with the Color QuickCam; you can purchase the software separately if you already own an earlier model. If you and another person both have QuickCams and VideoPhone software, you can see *and* hear each other in a conversation that only costs as much as your service provider's rates.

Unlike some of the telephone products we discussed earlier, CU See Me and VideoPhone let you connect directly to an IP number without requiring an additional server connection. At the time this was written, VideoPhone for Windows could work with a 28.8 Kbps connection to the Internet, but the Macintosh software required a connection of ISDN speed or greater.

Multicasting

While applications like CU See Me and RealAudio can be used for broadcasting purposes, they're best used for point-to-point communications. These technologies use connection-oriented protocols that require a connection between each sender and each receiver. While this is fine for sending information between a few users, these protocols place a huge strain on the Internet when they're used for simultaneous transmissions to large numbers of people.

A more efficient broadcasting technique sends out a single packet to all points on the network; any computer interested in receiving the broadcast can "tune in" to receive the packet. The technical word for this technique is *multicasting*, and it's in use today on the Internet with the Multicast Backbone, or MBone.

Developed in 1992, MBone has been used for a variety of audio and video broadcasting purposes, including a Rolling Stones concert and a musical tribute to Martin Luther King, Jr. at the House of Blues. (For more information about online musical events, check out the Internet Underground Music Archive at http://www.iuma.com.) Other uses include broadcasts of supercomputing conferences and the very popular NASA Select, NASA's in-house cable channel. And, in the Jason/Medea project, managed by the Woods Hole Oceanographic Institute, K–12 students around the world were able to track the progress of the research ship Laney Chouest. Another extremely popular ongoing use of the MBone is Internet Talk Radio, a weekly talk show.

NOTE

As great as CU See Me and MBone may sound, they're not yet useful in a home or small business setting where you're connected through dialup IP. MBone, for instance, has a minimum requirement of an Ethernet or T1 connection to your site, and is typically only available at universities, corporations, and research institutions. However, with ISDN and cable delivery of Internet service potentially on the horizon, these may be viable in the future.

Summary

In this chapter we discussed some emerging technologies that will have an impact on the way we browse the Web, and we explored a few non-Web technologies that may also change the way that we communicate. As you explore online worlds, keep an eye out for information about new kinds of graphical Internet applications, from Netscape, from other vendors, and even from research institutions like CERN, NCSA, and MIT. After all, the Web wasn't invented in Silicon Valley; it was invented by a physicist at a European physics laboratory, and the graphical Web browser that started it all was developed at the NCSA—two not-for-profit research organizations.

NOTE The World Wide Web as we know it today is not the final frontier of the telecommunications revolution, and Netscape Navigator may not be the all-time "killer app" of the Internet. The best advice we can give you is to stay abreast of new developments and to stay flexible in the way that you think about using your Internet connection. Don't limit your explorations of cyberspace to "the world as seen through Netscape." In other words, don't just be a Netscape virtuoso ... be an Internet virtuoso!

APPENDIX A

NETSCAPE NAVIGATOR
QUICK REFERENCE

This appendix is a quick guide to the parts of a page and the meaning of menu commands in Netscape Navigator. For more information about any item, consult the index or table of contents.

Parts of a Page

Figure A.1 shows a typical Web document displayed in Netscape Navigator. (For information about documents that use frames, see Chapter 6, "Frames and Tables.")

Toolbar
Link Icon
Directory buttons
Location field

Netscape
Logo

Clickable
image

Scrollbars

Link

Security indicator

Status message area

Mail
icon

Image placeholder

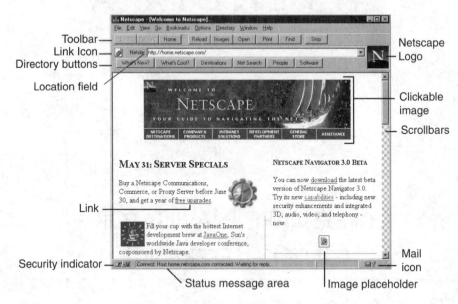

Figure A.1 Typical Web document.

Toolbar	Useful buttons for navigation and image management.
Link icon (Windows 95 only)	Used for creating Internet shortcuts (drag to desktop) or bookmarks (drag to Bookmark window).
Location field	Shows current URL. You can type a URL directly into the field and press **Enter** to go to that location.
Directory buttons	Quick links to Netscape sites.
Netscape logo	Animates to show that the browser is actively engaged in retrieving or displaying a document. Clicking the logo will display Netscape's home page.
Clickable image map	Clicking different items on the map will take you to locations designated by the site's developers.
Image placeholder	If **Auto Load Images** is not selected, the presence of graphics will be indicated by this image.

Links	Clickable links to other documents. If you point the mouse at a link, its URL appears in the status message area.
Security indicator	Indicates a document's level of security. A broken key indicates that the document is not secure. Click the icon to display detailed information about the security of the current document.
Status message area	Displays text messages related to the current action of the browser. For example, if a file is being retrieved, this area describes the progress; if the mouse pointer is over a link in a document, this area shows the URL associated with that link.
Progress gauge	Visual indicator of a document's progress in loading.
Mail icon	Indicates whether you have received new mail. Click the envelope to check for mail at any time.
Scroll bar	Lets you view parts of the document that don't fit on the screen.

Menu Command Reference

This section contains a quick reference to Netscape's menu commands, as well as alternate methods to perform the same action using the items that appear directly on the screen.

NOTE Nearly all menu commands have keyboard shortcuts associated with them. To find the keyboard shortcut for a menu command, display the menu containing the item and look to the right. The characters there represent the combinations you can press on your keyboard to invoke the command.

The File Menu

Item	Action	Alternate
New Web Browser	Opens a new browser window.	
New Mail Message	Creates a new blank mail message.	
Mail Document... or Mail Frame...	Creates a mail message containing the current document or frame.	
Open Location...	Displays dialog box for entering a new URL.	Type the URL directly into Location field.
Open File...	Displays standard file dialog box to locate and open a local file.	
Save As... or Save Frame As...	Saves the current document or frame as plain text or as HTML source code.	
Upload File...	Uses FTP to upload a file or files.	Drag the file over the window and release. (You must be logged into a site where you can use authenticated FTP.)
Page Setup...	Displays options for printing characteristics of the current page.	
Print... or Print Frame...	Sends the current document to the printer. If the document contains frames, prints the contents of the current frame.	
Print Preview (Windows)	Shows you what current page will look like when printed.	
Close	Closes the current Netscape window.	
Exit	Quits the Netscape application.	

The Edit Menu

Item	Action	Alternate
Undo	Reverses the last editing action you performed.	
Cut	Deletes current selection and copies it to the Clipboard.	
Copy	Copies current selection to the Clipboard.	
Paste	Pastes contents of Clipboard at insertion point.	
Clear (Macintosh)	Clears current selection.	
Select All	Selects entire contents of screen.	
Find...	Displays a dialog box to enter text you want to locate in current document.	
Find Again	Searches for next occurrence of text specified in Find command.	

The View Menu

Item	Action	Alternate
Reload	Displays a fresh copy of the current document, either from cache or network (if document has changes).	Click **Reload** button on toolbar.
Reload Frame	Reloads the contents of the currently selected frame.	
Load Images	Displays all images in current document.	Click **Images** button on Toolbar. To display a single image, right-click the image placeholder and select **Load Image**. (On the Macintosh, hold down mouse button.)

The View Menu (continued)

Item	Action	Alternate
Refresh (Windows)	Displays fresh copy of document from memory cache (does not check network time stamps).	
Document Source	Displays the current document's HTML source code in the viewer that you specified or the default for your operating system.	
Document Info	Displays information about the current document, including structure, security features, creation date, and more.	
Frame Source	Displays the selected frame's HTML source code in the viewer that you specified or the default for your operating system.	
Frame Info	Displays information about the selected frame, including structure, security features, creation date, and more.	

The Go Menu

Item	Action	Alternate
Back	Displays previous page in history list.	Click the **Back** button on toolbar.
Forward	Displays next page in history list (only available if you've gone back in list).	Click the **Forward** button on toolbar.
Home	Displays the home page specified in your preferences.	Click the **Home** button on toolbar.
Stop Loading	Stops the current transfer of a document to your screen.	Click the **Stop** button on toolbar.

The Go Menu (continued)

Item	Action	Alternate
Item #1, Item #2, etc.	Each item is the title of a page you visited. Selecting a title displays that page.	

The Bookmarks Menu

Item	Action	Alternate
Add Bookmark	Creates a bookmark for the current page and adds it to the list.	Use the pop-up menu.
Items in Bookmark list	Each item is the title of a page that you created a bookmark for. Selecting an item displays that page.	

The Options Menu

Item	Action	Alternate
General Preferences...	Displays Preferences window containing configurable options for appearance, helper applications, languages, and more.	
Mail and News Preferences...	Displays Preferences window containing configurable options for mail and news servers, message composition, appearance, and more.	
Network Preferences...	Displays Preferences window containing configurable options for cache, connections, proxies, protocols, and more.	
Security Preferences	Displays Preferences window containing configurable options for security alerts, password protection, and digital certificates.	
Show Toolbar	Hides or displays the toolbar.	
Show Location	Hides or displays the Location field.	

The Options Menu (continued)

Item	Action	Alternate**S**
how Directory Buttons	Hides or displays Directory buttons.	
Show Java Console	Hides or displays Java Console, which may contain information from some Java programs.	
Auto Load Images	Hides or displays inline images when loading a new document.	
Document Encoding	Lets you select which character set encoding is used when document encoding is either not specified or unavailable.	
Save Options (Macintosh)	Causes any changes you made to the items in this menu or to the size of the window to be saved and used in later sessions.	

The Directory Menu

Item	Action	Alternate
Netscape's Home	Displays Netscape Communications' home page.	Click the **N** logo on the upper-right corner of the screen.
What's New?	Displays Netscape's list of new sites on the Web.	Click the **What's New?** directory button.
What's Cool?	Displays a list of sites considered "cool" by Netscape.	Click the **What's Cool?** directory button.
Netscape Galleria	Displays a list of sites and services that use Netscape's server products.	

The Directory Menu (continued)

Item	Action	Alternate
Internet Destinations	Displays a comprehensive list of Internet sites and directories.	Click the **Destination**sdirectory button.
Internet Search	Displays a list of Web search engines.	Click the **Net Search** directory button.
People	Displays a list of services to help you locate other Internet users.	Click the **People** directory button.
About the Internet	Displays general information and background about the Internet.	

The Window Menu

Item	Action	Alternate
Netscape Mail	Displays the Netscape Mail window.	Click envelope icon at lower-right of screen.
Netscape News	Displays the Netscape News window.	
Address Book	Displays your Address Book for review and editing.	
Bookmarks	Displays your bookmarks for review and editing.	
History	Displays a window with the title and URL of items in your history list, with additional navigation options.	
Item #1, Item #2, etc.	Brings selected Netscape window to front.	

The Help Menu

Item	Action	Alternate
About Netscape (In the Apple menu on the Macintosh)	Displays copyright, license and version information.	
About Plug-ins (In the Apple menu on the Macintosh)	Displays information about the plug-ins that are installed.	
Registration Information	Displays registration information and instructions.	
Software	Displays information about additional software products that work with Netscape.	Click the **Software** directory button.
Handbook	Displays online manual.	
Release Notes	Displays information about new features and other items for different releases of the product.	
Frequently Asked Questions	Displays the answers to commonly asked questions about Netscape, the Internet, and the Web.	
On Security	Explains Netscape's security features.	
How to Give Feedback	Displays a form for you to send feedback to Netscape.	
How to Get Support	Explains Netscape's various support programs.	
How to Create Web Services	Explains the basics of developing for the Web and contains links to more information.	

APPENDIX B

CONNECTIVITY OPTIONS FOR INTERNET ACCESS

Unlike the telephone system or cable television, it's a little more difficult to access the Internet than simply calling a single public utility and saying "hey, hook me up!" To get connected to the Internet, you'll have to research and evaluate the options available in your area to determine what best meets your needs. This appendix contains information about the two most common ways to connect to the Internet: through a local area network (LAN) at your business or university, or through dialup IP, in which you use a modem and telephone line each time you wish to use the Internet to establish a temporary connection supplied by an Internet service provider in your area.

Some Basic Internet Terminology

To understand your options for getting connected to the Internet, you'll need to know a little bit about how the Internet works in the first place. In this section, we'll talk about the following terms and how they affect the way that you access the Internet.

- Packet-switching networks
- Transmission Control Protocol/Internet Protocol (TCP/IP)

- IP numbers and addresses

The network that we're most familiar with is the North American telephone system, where a direct link, or point-to-point connection, is established between the two parties involved in the conversation. If anything happens to that single link between the two telephones, the connection is dead. By contrast, the Internet is a *packet-switching network*, where information can take several different routes as it attempts to get to its final destination. The advantage of this system is that if any point along the way isn't working, the information can reroute itself indefinitely until it reaches its target. Packet switching makes it possible to send and receive information from remote locations quickly and efficiently. If you think of packet switching as working like the post office, then each letter you send to a remote site is parceled up into small packets, like postcards, each of which is delivered by the post office using whatever paths are available at any instant in time. The postcards, or packets, may take several different routes, but they eventually arrive at the same destination. Once the postcards or packets arrive, they're reassembled into the correct order and the complete message is available to the reader.

Transmission Control Protocol/Internet Protocol (TCP/IP) is the communications standard that governs how dissimilar machines on the Internet talk to and exchange data packets with each other. TCP/IP makes it possible for applications on a PC running Windows 95, a DEC mainframe running VMS, and a Silicon Graphics workstation running UNIX to communicate with each other using a common language.

IP addresses are the unique identifiers assigned to each computer on the Internet so that all the packets of information being switched and sent around the world can identify their final destination. As you retrieve data from sites around the world, the site containing the data knows to send the information directly to your computer because it knows your IP address. Whenever you use Netscape, you'll have an IP address all your own for the duration of the session. (Depending on how your Internet connection is set up, you might even have a dedicated IP address assigned to you for permanent use!)

Connecting to the Internet through a LAN

If you're lucky enough to work at a university or a company that provides direct Internet access through a local network, then using Netscape to explore the World Wide Web will be relatively simple—once your computer is connected to the network and equipped with TCP/IP support (the "language" that all computers on the Internet use to talk to each other), using Netscape will be as easy as just launching the program.

SHORTCUT

Although it's easy to use the Internet when you're connected to a LAN, it's a little bit harder to set up your computer to use the Internet over a LAN in the first place. In fact, it can be a daunting task to the novice user, since you must understand not only how to set up your computer for Internet access but also how your LAN connects or gateways to the Internet. Chances are very good that there's a system or network administrator who can give you exact instructions on how to get connected, or who can even install and configure the software for you! If there's an MIS or technical support group at your location, you can save yourself a lot of pain and trouble by starting there before attempting a connection on your own.

Connecting to the Internet through SLIP and PPP

By far the most common way for individual users to connect to the Internet is through a fairly recent technological innovation known as dialup IP. In dialup IP, a regular telephone line is used to establish an IP connection that allows you to exchange data packets directly across the Internet, using either the SLIP (Serial Line Internet Protocol) or PPP (Point to Point Protocol) communications standards. Unlike direct or dedicated Internet connections which can require expensive hardware, software, and telecommunications lines to maintain, a SLIP or PPP connection can be established with only the following items:

- A computer with TCP/IP and dialup IP software
- A high-speed modem and high-speed modem cable
- A telephone line with an RJ-11 jack
- A SLIP or PPP account with an Internet service provider

NOTE

It's beyond the scope of this book to explain how to set up your computer to use dialup IP. This information is only provided to help you get started collecting the pieces that you need. For complete information about establishing dialup IP for the Macintosh, Windows 95, and Windows 3.1 operating systems, check out *Internet Direct: Connecting Through SLIP and PPP*, also published by MIS:Press.

Computer Requirements for Dialup IP

The memory and disk space requirements for TCP/IP and dialup IP software are minimal. The amount of available RAM, hard drive space, and processor speed are more important to the efficiency and performance of applications such as Netscape than of the SLIP or PPP connection itself. In general, the following minimum requirements are sufficient for getting started.

For the Macintosh platform:

- 68030 or better processor
- System 7
- 8 MB RAM (4 MB is the absolute minimum to run TCP/IP and dialup IP software, but your performance will suffer if you try to have multiple applications open at the same time or to play movies and display graphics while Netscape is open.)
- Several MB of free disk space to install helper applications and plug-ins to handle movies, graphics, and sound.

For the Windows platform:

- 386 or better processor
- Window 3.1, Windows for Workgroups, Windows NT, or Windows 95
- 8 MB RAM (4 MB is the absolute minimum to run TCP/IP and dialup IP software, but you won't be able to have multiple applications open at the same time or to play movies and display graphics while Netscape is open.)
- Several MB of free disk space to install helper applications and plug-ins to handle movies, graphics, and sound

Finding TCP/IP and Dialup IP Software

To establish a dialup IP connection, you'll need both TCP/IP software and some kind of SLIP or PPP software for your computer. Some SLIP packages also support a protocol called CSLIP, or Compressed SLIP, which is preferable to use if it is supported by your service provider. In general, PPP is preferable to both SLIP and CSLIP.

For the Macintosh...

Prior to the release of System 7.5.3, the Macintosh platform almost always used MacTCP as the TCP/IP package, although some of the most powerful PowerPC computers were originally released with a product called Open Transport. In the future, Apple Computer plans to migrate all TCP/IP support to Open Transport, leaving MacTCP as the protocol stack for certain older 68000-based Macintoshes.

The most recent version of MacTCP 2.x is considered commercial software and is bundled with the latest releases of the Macintosh operating system, as well as with some packaged dialup IP software products. Open Transport is a standard component of the operating system for late-model PowerPCs and is frequently updated; you can always find the latest release by connecting to ftp.info.apple.com and following the path for the latest software updates (Open Transport will be in the directory for Networking and Communications).

Popular Macintosh dialup IP packages are summarized in Table B.1. (Remember, you'll always use MacTCP or Open Transport as the TCP/IP package.)

Table B.1 Macintosh Dialup IP Packages

Dialup IP Package	Supported Protocols	Availability of Dialup IP Package
InterSLIP	SLIP, CSLIP	Freeware, FTP from ftp://mirror.apple.com/mirrors/Info-Mac.Archive/comm/inet/conn/
MacSLIP	SLIP, CSLIP	Commercial, from TriSoft (512-472-0744)
MacPPP (FreePPP for Open Transport)	PPP	Freeware, FTP from ftp://mirror.apple.com/mirrors/Info-Mac.Archive/comm/inet/conn/

For Windows…

TCP/IP and dialup IP support for the PC is available from a variety of shareware and commercial packages. And, the Windows 95 operating system includes built-in TCP/IP and PPP support.

If you don't plan to use Windows 95 built-in support, the packages listed in Table B.2 provide both TCP/IP and dialup IP support.

Table B.2 TCP/IP and Dialup IP Packages for Windows

TCP/IP Package	Dialup IP Package	Supported Protocols	Availability
Trumpet Winsock	Trumpet Winsock	SLIP, CSLIP, PPP	Shareware, FTP from ftp.trumpet.com.au
Netmanage Chameleon	Netmanage Chameleon	SLIP, CSLIP, PPP	Commercial, available in many books about the Internet
Windows 95	Included in OS	SLIP, CSLIP, PPP	Commercial, part of the Windows 95 operating system

WARNING Configuring TCP/IP and dialup IP for any platform will take a little bit of work, and generally requires that you write a short computer program called a connection script. To save yourself a lot of frustration, you should definitely familiarize yourself with the requirements of the packages before you commit to a decision.

About High-Speed Modems

A modem is a device that allows your computer to exchange data with other computers through a telephone line. The most critical factor in choosing a modem is its speed, generally measured in bits per second (bps); the faster the modem, the more seamless your communications will be. At this writing, the fastest modems available for consumers are 28,800 bps, costing around $200; 14,400 and 9600 bps modems can be found for under $100. In general, you want to buy the fastest modem that your service provider can support and that your budget allows.

Another important consideration in purchasing a modem is whether it conforms to the CCITT/ITU-TSS v-dot standards for speed, data compression, and error correction. These international standards, developed by a French plenary body, are used worldwide to ensure that modems can communicate with each other no matter who manufactured them. The v-dot standards, so called because they all begin with "v." followed by a number, are listed in Table B.3. In general, you want a modem with the correct v.number for the speed, and with v.42 error correction and v.42bis data compression.

Table B.3 The V-Dot Standards

Name of standard	Purpose
v.32	Defines communications at 9600 and 4800 bps
v.32bis	Defines communications at 14,400 bps, with the ability to adapt to lower rates if conditions require
v.34	Defines communications at 28,800 bps
v.42	Defines error correction, regardless of the speed of the modem
v.42bis	Defines data compression, regardless of the speed of the modem

About High-Speed Modem Cables

If you're using an external modem, it's critical that you use a high-speed, hardware handshaking modem cable to attach it to your computer. If you don't use the right kind of modem cable, the performance of your dialup IP connection will be drastically reduced.

Unfortunately, high-speed hardware handshaking modem cables look exactly like other modem cables. Worse, the only indication of an incorrect modem cable is poor performance and reliability, which can often be attributed to other items in your dialup IP configuration. However, a high-speed hardware handshaking modem cable only costs about $10, so if you have any doubts as to whether you have the right kind of modem cable, it's easy to either purchase a new cable or to have your existing cable tested.

About Telephone Lines

A telephone line is definitely needed for dialup IP, since it's the medium that will transmit the Internet data packets that you send and receive. Although Touch-Tone telephone lines are the most common, the old-fashioned pulse telephone lines will work just as well. The only critical feature of the telephone line is that it must have a modular RJ-11 jack (the kind you simply plug the cord into). If you have an older pronged connector, you can purchase an adapter at Radio Shack that allows you to plug in an RJ-11 device.

WARNING Please be aware that you must have an ordinary telephone line (sometimes called POTS, for Plain Old Telephone Service), and not a specialized telephone system like a PBX. If you're setting up your computer at home, it's unlikely that you'll have anything but a POTS line, but if you're in a school or business setting, you might have a problem. You can damage a PBX by using telecommunications equipment, so check to be sure that it's OK to plug in a modem before you start.

About Dialup IP Accounts and Service Providers

Be sure that you have a dialup IP account instead of a "shell" or text-only account; these accounts don't let you use a unique IP number, and you won't be able to run graphical Internet applications like Netscape. Depending on where you live, you can probably choose from a wide range of local, regional, and national service providers in your area. And if you're affiliated with a university that provides Internet access to faculty, staff, and students, you can probably get a dialup IP account for free.

WARNING The business of providing Internet access to individual customers is an area of rapidly changing options and vendors. It's far beyond the scope of this appendix to discuss different kinds of service classes and methods of evaluating your available choices. However, please be sure to investigate a variety of local, regional, and national service providers who supply Internet access in your area, and carefully compare the costs and the structures of the different pricing schemes. A complete treatment of this subject can be found in Chapter 5 of *Internet Direct*.

APPENDIX C

OBTAINING AND INSTALLING NETSCAPE

A version of the Netscape Navigator browser for Windows, Macintosh, and UNIX workstations is available free of charge to individuals and educational institutions via anonymous FTP. Companies wishing to use Netscape may download a free copy for evaluation but are required to pay a licensing fee for use beyond evaluation purposes.

NOTE Various commercial versions of Netscape Navigator and Netscape Navigator Gold are available in retail stores and in Netscape's online General Store (http://merchant.netscape.com/netstore/soft/nav/items/leaf/product0.html). These products, currently available only for Windows, have stronger security features (see Chapter 19 for more information) and are often bundled with a number of other software products and printed documentation. You can also purchase a subscription to upgrade your existing licensed, paid-for Netscape browser as new versions become available.

Obtaining Netscape via Anonymous FTP

To obtain Netscape via anonymous FTP, you must have some kind of access to the Internet. If you already have a network or dialup IP connection, you may use a graphical FTP client application to obtain the program, which is significantly easier than using a traditional shell account.

Because of Netscape's popularity, there are a number of sites that *mirror* the contents of Netscape's own FTP archive. This means that more people can download files at the same time because the software is available in a variety of places. To obtain Netscape, issue an FTP connection request to the site that's geographically nearest you. Table C.1 contains a list of some North American sites that carry Netscape software.

N O T E If you are already using a version of Netscape or any other forms-capable browser, use Netscape's forms-based interface at http://home.netscape.com/comprod/mirror/client_download.html to find the right FTP sites for your platform and geographical location.

Table C.1 Sites Carrying Netscape Software

Location	Machine	Pathname
Netscape Communications Corp., Mountain View, California	ftp2.netscape.com through ftp20.netscape.com	/pub
University of Nebraska at Omaha	unicron.unomaha.edu	/pub/NETSCAPE/
University of North Carolina at Chapel Hill	SunSITE.unc.edu	/pub/packages/ infosystems/WWW/ clients/Netscape/
University of Texas at Dallas	mirror1.utdallas.edu	/pub/web/netscape/
Washington University, St. Louis, Missouri	wuarchive.wustl.edu	/packages/ www/Netscape/

N O T E Each of these locations constructs its archive sites differently. To find the most recent version of Netscape for your platform, you'll have to navigate through the directories at each archive.

N O T E Mirror sites are changed and added frequently. To get an up-to-date list, try logging on to one of Netscape's sites. If the site is full, a current list of mirror sites will be displayed.

Obtaining Netscape via a Shell Account

If you don't have a graphical FTP client for your dialup IP or network connection, you can obtain Netscape using a traditional text-only shell account. To do so, you'll need a shell account that supports the use of anonymous FTP, and terminal emulator software such as Kermit or ZTerm.

If you obtain the software this way, you'll have to go through the extra step of downloading the software from your shell account to your desktop machine. And remember, you won't be able to use Netscape without a dialup IP or direct network connection, even though you can download and install it.

Here are the basic steps for retrieving a file with anonymous FTP. These steps assume that you're already logged into your shell account.

1. At your shell prompt, enter **ftp sitename**, where sitename is the name of the FTP archive site that you wish to access.

2. When a login prompt is displayed, enter **anonymous**.

3. At the password prompt, enter your electronic mail address.

4. When you're logged into the site, locate and change to the directory containing the file that you wish to retrieve.

   • To see a listing of file directories, type **ls**.

   • To change to a directory, type **cd directoryname**, where directoryname is the name of the directory you wish to access.

5. Determine whether the file you wish to download is binary or ASCII text. Binary files end with the extensions .exe, .zip, .Z, and .bin. Text files end with the extensions .hqx and .txt.

6. If the file is binary, enter **bin**. If the file is text, enter **ASCII**.

7. To transfer the file, type **get filename**, where filename is the name of the file you wish to retrieve.

8. When a message is displayed that the transfer is complete, end the FTP session by entering **bye** at the FTP prompt.

9. At your login shell prompt, issue the command to download the file to your local disk drive. If you're using Kermit, enter **kermit -s**

filename; if you're using ZTerm, enter **sz filename**. For other packages, consult the documentation for the correct command.

10. In the communications software package, issue the command to receive the file. This is generally a menu item called something like **Receive File**.

The file will be downloaded to your hard drive. Follow the instructions in the section for your platform to decompress and install the files.

Installing Netscape for Windows

System Requirements

The general system requirements for using Netscape on a Windows platform are:

- A 386 or better processor
- Windows 95, Windows NT, Windows for Workgroups, or Windows 3.1 (See note below regarding which version of Netscape to use with each version of Windows.)
- 8 MB of available RAM
- Sufficient disk space (probably 10 MB or more) for Netscape and associated helper applications and plug-ins

NOTE There are two versions of Netscape for Windows platforms—a 16-bit version and a 32-bit version. If you are using Windows 3.1 or Windows for Workgroups, you must use the 16-bit version of Netscape, even if you have win32s installed. If you are using Windows 95 or Windows NT, you should use the 32-bit version of Netscape; you should also make sure that you're using a 32-bit Winsock protocol stack.

At the time this book was written, Netscape 3.0 had only been released as beta software. The final system requirements may be different.

NOTE

Installing the Software

The file that you retrieve for your Windows platform will be an executable file with the extension .exe. To extract and install the software, follow these steps:

1. Launch the executable file by issuing the **Run** command or by double-clicking its icon. A built-in utility will extract all the files in the archive, including an installer program called Setup.exe.

2. Locate and review the README file for any additional installation instructions specific to your platform.

3. Locate and launch the Setup.exe program and follow the prompts on the screen to choose the destination of Netscape and its associated files.

NOTE Recently, Netscape has begun using installers that don't require the additional step of extracting the archive before running the setup program. So, you may find that the prompts to identify an installation location for Netscape are immediately displayed after you launch the executable file that you downloaded.

Installing Netscape for the Macintosh

System Requirements

The general system requirements for using Netscape on a Macintosh platform are:

- A 68020 or better processor (preferably 68030 or better)
- System 7, 7.1, or 7.5
- 8 MB of available RAM
- Sufficient disk space for Netscape and associated helper applications and plug-ins

At the time this book was written, Netscape 3.0 had only been released as beta software. The final system requirements may be different.

NOTE

Installing the Software

Extracting the files for the Macintosh requires the use of an additional utility to decode the binhexed files. (A complete discussion of binhex appears in Chapter 8.) A good freeware package for this purpose is Aladdin Systems' StuffIt Expander, available via anonymous FTP from ftp.aladdinsys.com with the pathname pub/stuffit_exp_40_installer.hqx.

It's important that you retrieve the file with the MacBinary .bin extension, since you do not yet have a utility that handles .hqx files. However, most Macintosh file transfer programs can handle MacBinary files correctly.

NOTE

To extract and install Netscape for the Macintosh, follow these steps:

1. Drag the icon for the binhexed Netscape file over the icon for StuffIt Expander until that icon is highlighted, then drop the icon for Netscape by releasing the mouse. StuffIt Expander will launch automatically to decode the Netscape archive file.

   The result of this operation will be a Netscape installer application.

2. Double-click the installer application and follow the online instructions for installing the regular, Power Macintosh, or "fat" binary versions of Netscape. (If you don't know what this means, use the **Easy Install** option.)

   The installer will place all the files related to Netscape in their correct locations.

Installing Netscape for UNIX

System Requirements

The Netscape browser is available for the following UNIX platforms:

- Digital Equipment Corporation Alpha (OSF/1 2.0. 3.2)
- Hewlett-Packard 700-series (HP-UX 9.03, 9.05, 10.x)
- IBM RS/6000 AIX 3.25
- Silicon Graphics (IRIX 5.2, 5.3)
- Sun SPARC (Solaris 2.3, 2.4, 2.5, SunOS 4.1.3)
- 386/486/Pentium (BSDI)
- Linux

Installing the Software

Once you've retrieved the software to your storage drive, uncompress the archive and expand its contents.

NOTE The remainder of the installation instructions for UNIX workstations vary from platform to platform. It's crucial that you review the README file and other associated documentation for your platform before attempting to complete the installation of the software.

Unpacking Compressed Tar Files

To unpack a compressed tar file into the current directory, use some variation of this command:

```
zcat file_name.tar.Z | tar -vxf -
```

Special Note for SunOS 4.1

Because Sun workstations may use one of two different methods to resolve host names (DNS or Sun Microsystems' NIS), the package for this platform contains two different executables. Be sure to install the correct one for your system.

Special Note for SunOS 4.1, Linux, and BSDI

For these systems, Netscape has been linked against the /nls directory, which is a standard part of the MIT X11R5 distribution. If you do not have the /nls directory, attempting to cut and paste to or from a text field in Netscape will cause a core dump.

Default pathnames for the /nls directory are encoded in the Netscape executable. For SunOS 4.1, Netscape will look for the /nls directory in /usr/lin/X11/nls/. For Linux, Netscape will look for the /nls directory in /usr/X386/lib/X11/nls/. For BSDI, Netscape will look for the /nls directory in /usr/X11/lib/X11/nls/.

If you do not have the /nls directory on your system, you must create it. If you create it in a location other than the one listed above, set the $XNLSPATH environment variable.

Getting Started

To get started using Netscape, follow these steps:

1. If you're using dialup IP, establish a connection to your service provider. If you're directly connected to a network, contact your site administrator for information about installing and configuring TCP/IP connectivity on your desktop computer.

2. Launch the Netscape application. You'll connect directly to Netscape Communications' own home page. That's all there is to it! For an introductory quick reference to using Netscape, see Appendix A, "Netscape Navigator Quick Reference." For intermediate and advanced configuration and navigation options, see the main body of this book

INDEX